MW01194506

THE SOUL IN ANGUISH

Psychotherapeutic Approaches to Suffering

LIONEL CORBETT

 CHIRON PUBLICATIONS • ASHEVILLE, NORTH CAROLINA

© 2015 by Chiron Publications. All rights reserved. No part of this publication may be reproduced, stored in a retrieval system, or transmitted, in any form by any means, electronic, mechanical, photocopying, recording, or otherwise, without the prior written permission of the publisher, Chiron Publications, 932 Hendersonville Road, Suite 104, Asheville, North Carolina 28803.

www.ChironPublicatons.com

Book and cover design by Nelly Murariu
Printed in the United States of America.

Library of Congress Cataloging-in-Publication Data

Corbett, Lionel.
  The soul in anguish : psychotherapeutic approaches to suffering / Lionel Corbett.
     pages cm
  Includes bibliographical references and index.
   ISBN 978-1-63051-235-4 (pbk. : alk. paper) -- ISBN 978-1-63051-236-1 (hardcover : alk. paper) -- ISBN 978-1-63051-237-8 (ebook)
   1. Psychology, Pathological. 2. Distress (Psychology) 3. Suffering--Religious aspects. 4. Psychotherapy--Religious aspects. I. Title.

  RC454.C653 2015
  616.89'14--dc23

                        2015019996

Cover image used with permission from The J. Paul Getty Museum, Los Angeles
Dorothea Lange, Print by Arthur Rothstein; Migrant Mother, Nipomo, California; Negative March 1936; print about 1960; Gelatin silver print, 9 1/2 x 7 5/8 inches

Sine afflictione nulla salus:
Without suffering, there is no well-being.

CONTENTS

PREFACE

Suffering is the central issue which brings people to psychotherapy. This book addresses the subjective experience of suffering, describes some of its many causes and qualities, and offers approaches to suffering based on depth psychology. I suggest that the psychotherapist's primary focus should be on the specificity of the individual's suffering. The mental health profession is currently much concerned with diagnosis, but diagnosis is often of limited help to the psychotherapist dealing with suffering. People with the same diagnosis may suffer in radically different ways, so that a focus on diagnosis is often too distant from the suffering person's actual experience, especially in situations which are not covered by the textbooks. The psychotherapist frequently comes across situations which demand the deepest possible human response, sometimes outstripping anything we could explain using our theoretical models of psychotherapy. All suffering is unique to the individual; there is no objective way of viewing human suffering. We make sense of the world in a way that takes our suffering into account, and when we suffer intensely we may view the world through the lens of our suffering. This book tries to widen the range of available frameworks through which the psychotherapist and the suffering individual may approach the adversity with which they are working.

Our current research-based models of psychotherapy may be of limited help in a given situation, because any approach to research in psychotherapy constrains our understanding of the person based on the assumptions underlying the research. In particular, the drive to quantify human experience cannot capture the richness of our subjectivity or do justice to the complexity and depth of human suffering. Attempts at such measurement tend to focus on narrow aspects of the situation which are of interest to the researcher, while often ignoring what matters to the suffering person. Many critics of contemporary psychotherapy point out that empirical, "evidence-based," medical and natural science models of psychology and psychotherapy do not take into account some important elements of human existence (eg, Slife, 1995, 2005). This type of research is not the only valid approach for the psychotherapist, because many aspects of our lives do not lend themselves to this kind of validation.

There have been many trenchant critiques of the tendency of modern psychological theories to present themselves as if they were objective and value-neutral, while in fact they conceal an ideology and surreptitiously advocate for particular cultural and moral values (Richardson, 2005). Many writers stress that psychotherapy is not only about behavior and mental operations or even the alleviation of suffering; it is also about the discovery of the meaning of our experience and the full development of the personality. For me and for many psychotherapists, the stress on meaning as revealed in human experience is far more useful than approaches to psychotherapy based on positivistic scientific methods. These approaches are often not applicable to the unique context of the individual.

In psychotherapeutic practice we encounter patients who take us beyond our theories and everything we have learned. That is why many psychotherapists reject the approach of the *Diagnostic and Statistical Manual* (hereafter the DSM), whose very thin descriptions try to fit people into conceptual or abstract categories which reduce the complexity of human suffering. In some circles, suffering is reduced to brain mechanisms or to mechanical, learned processes or to cognitive errors, using fixed formulations (Horwitz, 2002; Carlat, 2010). These approaches ignore the mystery of the person, and they cannot help us to understand him or her because the person is always more than our theories will allow us to say. Diagnostic manuals, like manualized theories of psychotherapy, risk limiting our ability to understand a person's suffering by overly narrowing our focus.

My interest in writing this book has been stimulated by various sources. The first has been teaching Jungian and psychoanalytic psychotherapy to graduate students and analytic candidates. Many students work in settings in which they are required to make DSM diagnoses, in spite of the fact that once the patient's specific life circumstances and human problems appear in the therapy, and a complex psychotherapeutic relationship is established, the patient's diagnosis fades into the background. The psychotherapist then has to work with suffering at its own level, not at the level of an experience-distant, abstract classification.

A further source of my interest in the problem of suffering lies in its spiritual significance. This is important to the psychotherapist because increasing numbers of people are alienated from traditional religion, which used to provide answers and meaning to life's difficulties but often no longer does so. Nevertheless, many people have a personal form of spirituality, and they seek meaning in their own ways. Sometimes therefore the psychotherapist becomes a *de facto* spiritual advisor in this quest (Corbett, 2011). Fortunately, there is no longer a taboo about talking about spirituality in psychotherapy. Another motivating factor determining my interest in suffering has been my father's experience in the Buchenwald concentration camp during the Second World War, which radically affected the emotional atmosphere in my childhood home.

Yet another source of my attention to the problem of suffering is my experience of a severe illness. In 2008 I developed acute myeloid leukemia, which eventually led to a successful bone marrow transplant. I was in two hospitals for a total of several months, during which time I encountered many different types of health care professionals. I was fortunate to receive a great deal of emotional and physical support from my wife, my family, friends, and the generosity of my colleagues at Pacifica Graduate Institute where I teach. Fortunately too, earlier in my career I had practiced consultation-liason psychiatry and I had worked psychotherapeutically with many cancer patients. I was familiar with the literature on the use of imagery and meditation in the treatment of cancer, and my background as a Jungian analyst was invaluable. Needless to say I worked with my own dreams and imagery around the illness as much as I was able to.

What was striking during the illness was the lack of any attempts at emotional or spiritual support or consolation on the part of my hospital caregivers. I am grateful for the fact that the physicians and the nursing staff in both hospitals were very competent technically, which I'm sure is why I survived a potentially fatal illness. However our conversations were invariably about medication, blood counts, pain, and other physical issues, which did not exhaust the causes of my suffering. At no time did any of these caregivers ask me ordinary human questions, such as whether I was afraid of dying, what effect the illness was having on my family, how the illness was affecting my spirituality, what the illness meant to me, its effect on my work life and personality, and so on. It was as if the meaning of the suffering, rather than the symptoms causing the suffering, was either too difficult to discuss or it never occurred to anyone to ask about it. Although it was obvious that these caregivers took care to perform their professional tasks as well as possible, only a minority of them actually expressed a quality of caring that I could feel at an emotional level. Indeed a few of them were quite mechanical, emotionally unavailable, and remote in the way they approached my treatment, obviously unwilling to attach emotionally to someone who might die. I often felt I needed to support their need for distance by not making any demands beyond the ordinary. Others however were present with an open heart and radiated a healing presence.

The problem of the alienation of patients from their physicians and from the de-humanizing effects of medical technology is well-known and long-standing (Odegaard, 1986). The medical preoccupation with disease down to the molecular and genetic level threatens to exclude the psyche and the patient's personality from the physician's purview, which leads to an incomplete approach to the patient's suffering. Even when physicians would like to be able to integrate the psychological aspects of care into their practice, the administrative structures in which they work may not allow them to do so.

Human suffering is of major importance not only to psychotherapists but also to medicine, philosophy, religion, and society as a whole, not least because suffering calls into question our sense that life is meaningful. With notable exceptions, such as the hospice movement, our society can be insensitive when dealing with suffering; many suffering people are marginalized and feel isolated, and the "pursuit of happiness" enshrined in the Declaration of Independence is beyond their reach. We may even ask whether attention to suffering is somehow antithetical to national values such as optimism and self-sufficiency, which are part of our cultural mythology. The question of the meaning of suffering seems to have been relegated to the cultural unconscious, which may account for our surprise when suffering strikes. It would be of value to our society if we were to embrace the importance of suffering rather than maintain the illusion that it can either be indefinitely warded off if we live properly, or dealt with using the appropriate medicines, political system, or technology. As Jung (CW 11, para. 291) pointed out: "the suffering that necessarily attaches to life cannot be evaded," and human advances and creativity arise from suffering (ibid, para. 497). Or: "There is no birth of consciousness without pain" (CW 17, p. 193).

I wish to join the chorus of voices which would like to stop seeing suffering as invariably due to pathology. Instead we might start to normalize certain types of suffering, viewing the capacity to embrace suffering as an aspect of human wholeness, even developmentally necessary at times (Davies, 2012). At times, suffering may be transformative and even redemptive. In Jung's (CW16, p. 81) words: "The principle aim of psychotherapy is not to transport the patient to an impossible state of happiness, but to help him acquire steadfastness and philosophic patience in the face of suffering." The psychotherapeutic problem is how to accomplish that end, especially when the person's suffering is intractable or irreversible—I hope this book will contribute to that goal.

Throughout the book I have referred to the work of Emmanuel Levinas, for whom the alleviation of others' suffering is an absolute ethical obligation. For him, meaning in life is not solely dependent on our everyday experiences in the world (what philosophers call our ontology); in fact he believes that our responsibility to the other is even more fundamental (Manning, 1993). However, the relevance of Levinas for psychotherapy is not without controversy. He was hostile to psychological theories because of his fear that they may do violence to the self—for example, when a DSM diagnosis reduces the complexity of human suffering. He believed that the experience of another person comes before the imposition of any such category which might limit our ability to understand that person. Levinas felt there is much more to human relationships than our theories and diagnoses can accommodate. His work has been criticized on the grounds that it did not offer much practical help for human suffering (Hutchens, 2007). However, Levinas offers an attitude and a philosophical background for the practice of psychotherapy, and some relational psychotherapists are now engaging with his work because it addresses the structures of human subjectivity and intersubjectivity (Orange, 2011). For him, to be human is to exist in obligation to others. To insist that this assertion requires some kind of empirical validation hardly seems necessary.

In this book I have used the term "patient" to refer to the person in psychotherapy, rather than the popular term "client," not because the medical model is of any value in psychotherapy but because the Latin etymology of the word "patient" implies one who suffers patiently. In contrast, the word "client" suggests a purely commercial relationship with a customer and is etymologically related to Latin words suggesting a follower, or one who leans on another.

Many disciplines beside psychotherapy attempt to deal with human suffering; I need only mention economics, religion, and the social sciences. Their contributions are important, but I mainly address myself to psychotherapists, especially to students in the field, because that is my professional interest. I have used the term "depth psychotherapy" to distinguish between cognitive-behavioral approaches and those which take into account the unconscious. This phrase is grammatically awkward because the word "depth" is not an adjective, but the term is a useful shorthand in common use.

As much as possible I have tried to apply a principle of Simone Weil: "Method of investigation: as soon as we have thought something, try to see in what way the contrary is true" (2002, p. 102).

*I wish to acknowledge the help
given to me by the reference librarians
at Pacifica Graduate Institute.*

*Thanks are also due to Dr. Tiffany Baugher
for her helpful comments on an early
version of this work.*

1

INTRODUCTION

Suffering and psychotherapy

The problem of suffering lies at the heart of psychotherapy. Psychotherapists see many people who would agree with Thoreau that they are living "lives of quiet desperation," and that "an unconscious despair is concealed under what are called the games and amusements of mankind" (2004, p. 6). All schools of psychotherapy claim to explain the psychological sources of suffering and try to alleviate it. Some approaches even make something of a virtue of suffering by pointing out that suffering increases the person's motivation to be in psychotherapy (Strupp, 1978)[1]. In our psychotherapy training programs we emphasize dealing with specific disorders and symptomatology (Roth et al, 2005). However, these are only our professional perspective—from the patient's point of view, the overarching problem is suffering, sorrow, crisis, anguish, helplessness, alienation, despair, and other complex human problems which make it difficult for people to cope with their lives. Many forms of suffering cut across all diagnostic considerations and encompass situations which have no particular name and do not fit into the *Diagnostic and Statistical Manual* (hereafter, the DSM). There are many forms of emotional distress or mental pain which are suffered silently, which cannot even be put into words. Many painful emotions, such as envy, hatred, and loneliness

---

1   In his 1895 *Studies on Hysteria*, Freud famously said that the goal of psychoanalysis is to convert hysterical forms of suffering into everyday unhappiness, which he viewed as inevitable. He believed that neurotic suffering is a way of avoiding the harsher realities of life that must be faced. Although people go into psychotherapy because they are suffering, Freud rejects happiness as a goal of psychotherapy; for him, the most the psychotherapist can do is strengthen the person so that he or she can bear suffering. Jung had a very similar attitude. Another reason people undergo psychotherapy is to find the truth about themselves, which may be hard to bear without the emotional containment provided by the psychotherapy. This process may lead to reconciliation with the person's suffering, which is a form of healing.

cause enormous suffering but are not necessarily part of any recognizable syndrome. These situations cannot always be addressed using the empirical approaches of the natural sciences because these are based on norms that are true for large populations, but the individual has a unique personality, a specific life story, and a multitude of specific personal factors to take into account. Every time we meet a suffering person we are presented with an unpredictable experience.

Behind the application of a system of diagnosis such as the DSM lies an implicit standard of normal mental health and socially acceptable behavior, but many individuals who deviate from such standards would not consider themselves to be suffering from a disorder, while many people who behave normally and have no DSM diagnosis are extremely unhappy—this is one reason the popular term "behavioral health" is so misleading. Suffering is not always the result of a disorder; suffering is *normal* under certain circumstances which may present themselves to the psychotherapist.

Suffering is an inevitable aspect of human life, and not necessarily the result of psychopathology. For example, rather than seeing depression as a disorder, it can be seen from a spiritual point of view as a dark night of the soul or from an existential viewpoint as an intrinsic aspect of the human condition, perfectly appropriate in certain situations. The worker who suffers because he is in a job he hates, the person who feels unloved, or those who suffer from political violence or forced migration, do not necessarily suffer from a disorder that can be found in the DSM. It is reductive and limiting to see these kinds of suffering as disorders instead of a much broader aspect of human life. A DSM diagnosis is an abstraction, but suffering is desperately real, and may occur for societal reasons that have nothing to do with the developmental history or the psychodynamics of the individual who appears in psychotherapy. Many of us suffer because we feel trapped in a social system that puts too much stress on power, vested interest, economic competition, and self-interest, which sometimes combine to violate people. We sense that there is something deeply wrong with this system but we are resigned to living in it, following its rules, with no idea what to do to change it. Much of this kind of human suffering is invisible, partly because our culture either denies it or fosters a stoic attitude towards it.

In this text, I suggest a variety of approaches that may be of help to the psychotherapist when working with a suffering individual. Needless to say, clinical experience, skill, and tact are necessary in deciding which approach may be useful for any given person. While it is true that certain diagnoses carry specific therapeutic implications, depth psychologists often find that the initial diagnosis is not much help, because of the complexities of the individual's life and mind. Over time the diagnosis becomes much less important than the relational process within the psychotherapy.

It can be argued that disorders are the root cause of suffering and so should be the prime target of psychotherapy; but we do not treat disorders, we treat suffering people who are vastly more complex than their diagnosis. The subjective experience of suffering cannot be reduced to the presence of a disorder; suffering is much more complex and presents an individual level of difficulty. Suffering produced by widely different life situations may result in clinical pictures that look alike from a descriptive (DSM) point of view, but the nature of each person's suffering is unique, even when they have the same diagnosis. A syndrome approach to problems of living is narrow, and often leads to interventions at the wrong level; existential distress due to loneliness or alienation is not a brain disease that can be repaired with medication.[2] Problems of living permeate many areas of a person's life, and they do not fit into precise categories. Part of the fallacy of a descriptive approach to emotional distress lies in the fact that even if people have the same group of symptoms (such as "major depression") their suffering always has unique developmental, interpersonal or social origins, and the sufferer is embedded in a specific social context. People with the same disorder will attribute different meanings to the problem, they will have different associations or ideas about it, different feelings about it, different reactions from their families, and their suffering will have different implications for their lives. As Dorothee Söelle (1975) points out, suffering is a global experience, a total state of one's being, with physical, psychological, and social components. Suffering affects every dimension of life, including freedom of movement, opportunity for development, association with others, food, health, and living space. Suffering has social dimensions such as isolation and failure to be understood by others. The psychotherapist needs a psychologically informed exploration of all these contextual factors. We need a response to the individual's suffering *from the subjective perspective of the one who suffers*, irrespective of how the clinician conceptualizes the underlying disorder. The person's suffering and

---

2   Unfortunately, much clinical psychology is biased towards a medical model of approach to emotional distress, using the language of disorder instead of focusing on subjectivity, societal, and relationship issues. Psychological problems such as depression are often described as illnesses, as if they are internal to a passive sufferer, a random misfortune rather than related to our life circumstances and difficulties in self-actualization. This approach is now firmly entrenched and supported by economic factors.

17

the clinical (DSM) diagnosis are not synonymous; knowing the diagnosis does not tell us enough about how the patient is suffering. If we insist on viewing a suffering person's subjective experience through the lens of our own categories, such as those of the DSM, we may enhance the person's suffering by ignoring what the patient himself is concerned about. The use of the DSM may become a way of telling the person how he (and his society) *should* think about his difficulties. If a woman is depressed because she is in an abusive relationship, she is not mentally ill; she is reacting normally to a painful life situation, but she could potentially be given a DSM diagnosis as if there is something wrong with her for being unhappy. Critics of the DSM point out that it pathologizes normal human troubles and life's vicissitudes. It also tries to homogenize suffering by gathering it into constructs with arbitrary boundaries. Whether these categories are valid is still open for debate; some of them have minimal empirical justification and may be nothing more than value judgments about how we should behave. It is well known that the classification of mental disorders is fraught with political, economic, personal, and professional pressures, all hammered out by a majority vote in committees—hardly a scientific approach. The diagnosis of mental disorder is subject to subjective and social influences that do not apply to the diagnosis of most medical illness. In brief, it is a mistake to see a suffering patient in terms of a diagnostic category and then apply a method that is related to the diagnosis rather than to the specific aspects of a person's suffering.

The situation in the field of mental health has a parallel in medicine. Cassell (2004) has shown how high-tech medicine often focuses exclusively on symptoms of illness and pays minimal attention to the person who is ill, which may have a kind of de-humanizing effect. He notes that bodies do not suffer, persons do.[3] Cassell also points out that, for several reasons, suffering is not the same as physical pain. Whether pain causes suffering depends on one's perspective on the pain and its meaning to the person. The degree of a person's suffering may not be related to the intensity of his or her pain; the same kind of pain may make some people suffer while others do not, and sometimes patients who complain of severe pain are not completely helped by analgesic medications, suggesting that although they are in pain their suffering has additional causes. A mild pain that is known to have a serious

---

3 Cassell makes the important historical point that medicine adopted Cartesian mind-body dualism in the 17th century, and this unfortunately led to the false assumption that questions about the meaning of suffering were not within the purview of medical science, which is only about the body.

cause may produce intense suffering, and suffering may occur even in the absence of pain if one fears its return. Or one may suffer watching the pain of a loved one without being in pain oneself. However, the situations in medicine and in mental health are not exactly analogous, because, unlike physical pain, emotional distress is a form of suffering by its very nature; one cannot have anxiety or depression without suffering. Furthermore, it is possible to have a pain in one part of the body without the totality of the personality being affected, but emotional distress affects the whole of the personality.

Suffering is an experience of the whole person, who has a unique history and emotional life, a future, hopes and fears, occupational and family concerns. Suffering therefore has ramifications beyond its immediate causes; for example, it may be an intimation of death, with all that that means to the person. Levinas (1969) points out that suffering is made worse because it is inescapable. "The whole acuity of suffering lies in the impossibility of fleeing it, of being protected in oneself from oneself; it lies in being cut off from every living spring." (p. 238). Suffering is a "supreme ordeal" of our will (ibid).

Unfortunately, some contemporary approaches to psychotherapy have adopted a quasi-medical approach to suffering, which is inadequate for several reasons. Most importantly, in medicine itself, suffering is seen as a symptom of an underlying illness, not as primary in its own right. Because medicine always tries to treat diseases, not just symptoms, the diagnosis is critically important to the physician. With this kind of model in mind, the psychotherapist oriented to a DSM approach may pay less attention to the patient's subjective suffering than to its putative underlying cause, as if the cause were a discreet entity that could be rooted out. However, many types of suffering that psychotherapists see do not fit into a specific syndrome with a particular cause; a syndrome has definable limits, but suffering extends into many areas of a person's life. Therefore, for the psychotherapist, instead of focusing on an underlying diagnosis it is often preferable to see the person's suffering itself as the primary problem, at least from the person's subjective viewpoint. The spectrum of human suffering is too broad to fit into the DSM; there are innumerable sources of suffering and innumerable qualities of suffering.

A further important difference between medicine and psychotherapy is that, whereas the physician's philosophical commitments do not make much difference to the treatment of most diseases, the psychotherapist's approach to suffering is radically affected by his or her view of human nature. Similarly, whereas the theory underlying the physician's treatment would have broad general agreement among her or his colleagues, the psychotherapist's theoretical commitments may be quite controversial within the field of psychotherapy.

Suffering eludes specific definition. Suffering has been defined as the sense that one cannot maintain one's cohesiveness, or it is understood to be a state in which there is a threat to the integrity or sense of intactness of the personality (Cassell, 2004). However, this definition would not satisfy psychoanalytic self-psychologists because it does not take into account the nature of the self that is suffering. That is, one may have a fragile sense of self, prone to anxiety, depression, affective instability or low self-esteem, which makes one vulnerable to suffering under minimal conditions of threat because the self fragments easily. In contrast, a person whose sense of self is strong enough to contain painful affects without fragmentation may suffer from emotional or physical distress with no threat to the cohesion of the personality, without the ominous sense that he is about to fall apart at any moment. A person with a firm sense of self that is not in itself threatened may nevertheless suffer intensely because of loss or grief, or because of empathic connection with the suffering of a loved one. Another view of suffering is suggested by James Davies (2012), who uses a relational perspective; for him, we suffer when relationships with either the external or internal world impede the realization of our human potential and the satisfaction of human needs. Suffering then arises as a signal that all is not well, or as a protest against our conditions. In a moving paper about his own illness, Arthur Frank (2001) points out that suffering is a lived reality that resists articulation. "Suffering involves experiencing yourself on the other side of life as it should be.... Suffering is the unspeakable....dread, beyond what is tangible" (p. 355).

Emotional suffering is typically produced by grief, loss, deprivation, the sense that one's sense of self is slipping away, or a feeling that one has lost control of one's life—but there are a range of other possible causes. We suffer from feeling unloved, from alienation, abandonment, emptiness, lack of fulfillment, an inability to express our talents and abilities, loss of intimacy, or just a diffuse unhappiness with no exact focus. In addition, any such form of suffering may lead to social withdrawal which intensifies the person's suffering—suffering can make one very lonely. The suffering person feels cut off from his or her past as well as from other people. Sometimes intense suffering makes one feel different from those who have not suffered. To try to force all these situations into a diagnostic (DSM) category may discount some aspects of the individual's experience and may narrow the psychotherapist's focus. The psychotherapist may then ignore the effects of the suffering on aspects of the person's life that seem peripheral to the diagnosis, such as the person's hopes and dreams.

A crisis or loss may cause considerable secondary suffering. In addition to the suffering caused by the primary problem, the individual suffers because his or her world no longer exists as he or she thought it did—the self may feel intact but the world has become unfamiliar, insecure, and unpredictable. We suddenly become aware of our vulnerability in a way that we had been able to deny. Radical disillusionment may set in; one's fantasy of the future may be destroyed. If the sufferer is a religious person, his deepest beliefs may be challenged. He may feel betrayed by the God he once worshiped, and he may wonder if he is being punished for some sin. Like Job, the religiously-oriented sufferer may ask what she has done to deserve what has happened, and why less worthy people seem to be quite happy. Although some people find that suffering deepens their spiritual commitment, others cannot sustain any form of spirituality when they suffer. The sufferer who is an atheist may be confirmed in his view that the universe is uncaring, cold, and arbitrary in meting out suffering. After a life-changing crisis, the sufferer may question whether she can live with what has happened and whether life will ever seem meaningful again. Existential questions may have long been at the back of the sufferer's mind, but they rush to foreground when her world is shaken by serious suffering. It is as if the sufferer must discover a new personal myth that allows her to find a place in the world. Needless to say, these kinds of questions are also stirred up in the psychotherapist when working with a person in a major life crisis.

Whatever form of suffering we are talking about, it is useful to remember what Levinas (1998b) says about the burden of the suffering self: "the ground of suffering consists of the impossibility of interrupting it, and of an acute feeling of being held fast" (p. 52). When suffering becomes sufficiently intense, it overwhelms us and makes us passive; we can only submit to something beyond the grasp of our will. There are levels of affliction that take us beyond our ability to hope. Suffering can rupture meaning and destroy our capacity for dealing with the world and making our life our own. Unlike writers such as Jung and Frankl who seek meaning in suffering, Levinas thinks that suffering is absurd, meaningless, and incomprehensible; it overwhelms our freedom, it cannot be justified by rational argument, and all suffering is therefore evil. In fact, for him evil is about whatever causes suffering

(1998a). The psychotherapist practicing with a Levinasian sensibility has an ethical responsibility to suffer with and even sometimes suffer for the other person, and this sharing of suffering is an important aspect of the practice of psychotherapy; theoretical aspects of psychotherapy are important but secondary (Gantt, 2000).

It is useful for the psychotherapist to remember that Levinas reminds us that we can never fully understand the other person, because the reality of the other always overflows our categories. The other person is always a mystery, a radical otherness that cannot be contained in a diagnosis. "The other remains infinitely transcendent, infinitely foreign" (Levinas, 1969, p. 194). A contemporary psychotherapist might protest at Levinas's suggestion that there is such a great distance between oneself and the other, because we can close the gap by means of affective attunement and other relational approaches. Nevertheless, we can view the situation through both these lenses simultaneously; we can remain related and empathically connected to the patient at the human level and at the same time realize we are in the presence of the infinite.

Mental Pain

Some psychoanalysts (Fleming, 2005, 2006; Akhtar, 2000) distinguish mental pain from psychological suffering. In a broad sense, mental pain means any kind of emotional distress. In a narrower sense, mental pain means a diffuse, painful emotional state that seems to make no sense, which cannot be put into words or symbolized, and so cannot be communicated to another person. That is, we cannot think about it, name it, give it an image or find a metaphor to express it. We may feel mental pain in the form of vague discomfort in the abdomen or chest, which we know does not result from a bodily problem—we know it is emotional pain, or something on the border of the mental and physical. Mental pain is an inchoate form of longing, helplessness or despair that cannot be elaborated, in contrast to suffering which can be described, talked about, and elaborated by the work of mourning. Suffering due to bereavement or the loss of a vital selfobject is somewhat relieved when it is talked about and grieved normally. However, mental pain occurs because the person cannot put into words how he feels, and can only talk about distress that has no name—it is not a clearly defined emotion. The psychotherapist feels this in the countertransference as intense distress which is difficult to articulate, sometimes felt in the therapist's body.

In Bion's language, mental pain is the result of toxic beta elements (raw, un-metabolized affective experiences) derived from traumatic experiences that cannot be symbolized or imagined or given meaning (Bion, 1970). In contrast to mental pain, true suffering is the result of a negative experiences which can be symbolized by the "alpha function" of the mental apparatus, becoming thoughts and images that can be talked about. Bion (1963) emphasizes the need for psychotherapy to increase the patient's capacity for suffering at the same time as patient and psychotherapist hope to decrease the suffering itself.

Mental pain is so unbearable it often leads to a variety of defensive maneuvers. Psychic retreat or withdrawal from painful reality may occur, in which the patient seems out of reach, sometimes reflected in dreams of being in a deserted place. At times the patient hopelessly gives up. Denial or psychic numbing may supervene, or manic defense may occur with feverish over-activity such as multiple sexual encounters used to avoid feeling the pain of loss. Salman Ahktar (2000) points out that manic defense, such as intensified effort at work while facing a loss of love, can allow the pain-ridden part of the personality to carry out its work of mourning at the same time. Alternatively, mental pain can be induced in others, perhaps by projective identification, or it can be acted out physically by self-mutilation. The use of a creative outlet is an important way of managing mental pain; there is a well-known relationship between loss and creativity. Ahktar believes that poetry is a particularly effective way of processing emotional pain because it achieves all the defenses mentioned above. Reading or writing allows withdrawal of attention from one's surroundings, and is a form of psychic retreat. Such mental work acts as a defense; the traumatic event is changed into a creative product, and the writer's pain is shared with an imaginary audience with whom the poet is in dialog. For him, poetry has direct access to the deepest levels of the psyche, which is where mental pain resides—poetry speaks to the unconscious directly, informs one of the internal state of affairs, and facilitates both mourning and mentalization[4] of non-verbal levels of the psyche.

---

4   Mentalization here means the ability to think about and understand one's thoughts and feelings and their relationship to one's behavior.

Suffering and the training of psychotherapists

A student often wants to become a psychotherapist because of his or her personal emotional difficulties combined with a genuine desire to help others. However, the student is often disappointed to discover that much of the academic content in programs that teach "scientific" or "empirically based" psychotherapy is never used once he or she graduates. A great deal of this material is irrelevant to the kind of suffering that is the daily fare of the psychotherapist. Many of the problems we see in psychotherapy require a response which emerges from the fundamental humanity of the therapeutic couple, from their life experience, and from an understanding of the complexities of relationships combined with an appreciation for the depths of the soul. The patient's unique situation may not lend itself to the application of a specific law of learning or some other empirically derived approach that is said to apply to everyone.

Empirically derived cognitive-behavioral approaches sometimes imply that psychotherapy can be carried out independently of the vagaries of the relationship in which it takes place, or without taking into account the patient's transference to the therapist—yet these factors are never standard. Human relationships are much too complex to be fully contained in the net of empirical research. Measurement is not an appropriate approach to the unconscious, which is too slippery for quantitative methods. Empirical approaches obviously have their place, but there is a middle ground between rigid adherence to a scientific approach and a human response to suffering based on the psychotherapist's own intuition, feelings, and life experience. Furthermore, there is a big difference between psychotherapy geared towards symptom relief and psychotherapy geared towards personal growth, individuation, and self-understanding. However, a caveat is in order in the context of therapies promising personal growth; the opposite extreme to a rigidly scientific approach is a flash-in-the-pan self-help approach based on a charismatic individual. These become popular because they promise the moon, but eventually they either find a modest place in the psychotherapeutic repertoire or they die a natural death as they increasingly disappoint people.

Many training programs in psychotherapy teach students in a way that is directed to passing standardized exams, but I find little or no correlation between being a good psychotherapist and the ability to pass exams and write academic papers. Many training programs ignore the wisdom traditions, literature, and the humanities, in the service of dogmatic, almost cultist scientism, the notion that the scientific outlook is the only valid one. With this attitude, the student is not encouraged to inquire deeply into the human condition, or to value mystery, or to develop self-awareness, imagination, and compassion (Mahoney, 2005)—these are very important but difficult or impossible to measure.

Accrediting agencies impose a series of mandated courses for licensure, but with little emphasis on the personal development of the student and little attention to the way the student actually implements the course material in practice. As a result, some training programs turn out practitioners who have a good deal of theoretical knowledge about behavior but who are not equipped at the human level to deal with their patients. It is quite difficult to measure a student's capacity for compassion and empathy, and these are not always stressed in academic psychology departments which primarily offer experimentally validated approaches to emotional distress. In practice these approaches may fall short of helping with suffering when they are deployed by fallible human beings with limited empathic capacity and inadequate relationship to their own psychological difficulties. One cannot do psychotherapy using a paint-by-numbers approach. Some students are well-meaning but they have never suffered serious hardships in their personal lives, so that they simply cannot empathize with the level of pain and suffering that their patients are experiencing. The kinds of experimental research carried out by graduate students in psychology may also be irrelevant to the problem of helping a suffering person. As a result, some students appear in their clinical training sites to be ineffective or even harmful because their academic training has paid insufficient attention to their relational ability, their emotional maturity, their self-awareness, and their overall self-development. Licensing exams and the type of degree one has are not indicators of psychotherapeutic aptitude or one's natural therapeutic intelligence, and there are wide variations in individual ability among psychotherapists with the same academic training. The psychotherapist's motivation to alleviate suffering, which is integral to the process of psychotherapy, seems to be one of its covert but active ingredients. Perhaps it is a *sine qua non*. But with the best will in the world, in psychotherapeutic practice, while there are times when theory is helpful at other times we are on our own with no adequate theory in sight. We must then improvise and feel our way along, using our humanity, our experience, intuition, tacit knowledge, and our subjective judgment about what to say, and we have to live with uncertainty—or become narcissistically insistent on a specific school of thought. The uncertainty inherent to psychotherapy can produce considerable anxiety, which seems to be one of the reasons that students gravitate to approaches that purport to be scientific, only to learn that theoretical responses are often inadequate.

The moral dimension of psychotherapy

Ronald Miller (2004, p. x) pointed out that "psychology has lost sight of suffering itself...we have forgotten that our primary *raison d'être*...is to try to alleviate the pain and suffering of human existence." Miller (ibid.) stresses the importance of the moral characteristics of psychotherapy, because many of the practical problems of life brought to the psychotherapist are about difficult choices, dilemmas, and life decisions that involve moral problems: "what to do, how to act, how to treat others, or how one is being treated by others" (p. 18). For example, Miller points out that if we make a diagnosis of Post-Traumatic Stress Disorder, we shift the focus to what is wrong with the person rather than what is morally wrong with what happened to him. That is, the psychotherapist may obscure the moral context of a person's suffering by giving a diagnosis.

Miller points out that although training programs often stress the moral neutrality of psychotherapeutic practice, there are times when the moral dimension of psychotherapy is central, for example when a person has been abandoned, manipulated, or abused. At these times the psychotherapist must acknowledge that what happened to the person was wrong and should not have happened. Psychotherapists make moral judgments when they decide how to respond to a person's guilt or shame, and this requires not just emotional but also a moral sensitivity.

The psychotherapist's world view and view of human nature

The psychotherapist's theory of human nature, his or her view of the world and the philosophy of life underlying it, may radically affect his or her approach to suffering. These beliefs and their associated attitudes may or may not be conscious, but they affect the practitioner's choice of a theoretical orientation and style of practice. They are also important because the psychotherapist and the patient may hold incompatible world views— different assumptions about humanity and the nature of reality. They may have different views about whether our behavior is determined or freely chosen, about whether behavior is rationally chosen or largely influenced by unconscious material, about whether character is essentially immutable or changeable, and about spiritual questions (Koltko-Revira, 2004). Jung (CW 16) believed that a world view is inevitable, largely unconscious, transmitted by culture, and of great importance in guiding the individual's perceptions and choices. These attitudes, our values and our sense that life is or is not meaningful, are part of what Victor Frankl (1969, p. 15) calls the "metaclinical" aspects of psychotherapy.

For example, Roy Schafer (1976) suggested four different visions of the world or of human nature, and showed that these are implicit in different forms of psychotherapy and are communicated in the therapist's interventions. Importantly, if the preferred vision of therapist and patient are not compatible, they may be radically mis-attuned. The comic vision emphasizes optimism, hope, progress, and the overcoming of difficulties; here, no suffering is too intense to be relieved. The romantic vision sees life as an adventure or quest, and psychotherapy as a heroic journey of discovery in the face of suffering; descent into one's inner world and authenticity in the face of difficulties are greatly valued. The tragic vision stresses deep involvement in life's dilemmas and ambiguities; it requires knowing and confronting oneself, and growth occurs by dealing with adversity and pain. The ironic vision is more detached than the tragic, more interested in accepting the paradoxes and contradictions of life; it tries to keep them in perspective, challenges received wisdom, and stresses the arbitrary nature of absolutes.

Because different types of psychotherapy imply different views of humanity and have different treatment priorities, they are difficult to compare. Classical psychoanalysis sees human beings as biologically driven, while Kleinian theorists believe we are in a constant struggle between our loving and our destructive impulses. Object relations and attachment theorists see our primary task as connection to others and the establishment and maintenance of relationships, while other writers see human beings as essentially meaning-seeking. Some approaches to psychotherapy are rather mechanical; witness the stimulus-response psychology of the early behaviorists. Psychotherapists with a humanistic and existentialist orientation believe that one of our most important characteristics is our capacity for free choice. They emphasize our uniqueness and insist that our reality is constituted by our private, subjective experience, which is more important than our outward behavior. Freudians have always valued self-knowledge, self-determination, and understanding human passions. Jungian psychologists value awareness of the shadow, relationship to the unconscious and to the contrasexual aspects of the personality, connection to the transpersonal Self, and spiritual development. By and large, supporters of empirically supported treatments value symptomatic improvement, while depth psychologists of all kinds are more interested in subjectivity, self-understanding, finding meaning in life, understanding the complexities of our relationships, and dealing with existential difficulties with some equanimity.

Many students of psychotherapy do not realize that their approach to the patient has a long intellectual history, because what we now refer to as psychology was for a long time an integral component of philosophy. With the development of psychology as a scientific discipline in the 19th century, the field became estranged from its philosophical origins, but a new dialog between these disciplines has emerged, such as the philosophical implications of discoveries in neuroscience (Bennett, Dennett, Hacker & Searle, 2007). All theories of psychotherapy rest on philosophical or metaphysical assumptions about human nature, but because the philosophical underpinnings of our theories are rarely discussed in our training programs they may never be consciously articulated even when they have a major effect on the way we understand the people with whom we work.[5]

Many training programs teach students reductive, cognitive-behavioral or purely biological views of the person because these are considered to be scientific—the unspoken philosophical commitment here is that science is the best approach to reality. In the process, these programs gloss over intractable philosophical problems and often ignore the limitations of cognitive-behavioral psychology (discussed further in chapter 7). For example, as Robertson (2007) points out, by using the term "cognitive neuroscience" the long-standing problem of the relationship of mind and brain *appears* to have been solved merely by joining two words together. When such terminology is the unchallenged language of his or her training program, the unsuspecting student is led to believe that mind and brain are synonymous, without being

---

5   For example, how is human subjectivity constituted? Does our subjectivity precede relationships with others, so that it is a pre-condition of our intersubjectivity, or is our subjectivity entirely constructed by relationships with other people and by language and society? Can the self only be understood in relationship to others or is there an essential self? Hersch (2000) has suggested a hierarchical approach to compare the philosophical basis of psychological theories. He begins with fundamental questions such as whether there is such a thing as Reality independent or partially independent of us, and whether there is absolute Truth. Then, what is our relation to that reality? How do we validate knowledge in psychology, what are the best methods to do so, and what are the limits of the field?

told that this is a controversial (metaphysical, physicalist) opinion and the question is by no means settled. The student is not told that the conceptual problems involved, such as the *nature* of the mind (rather than the question of whether and how neurons *produce* the mind) cannot be solved by empirical means. The student may not be told about the philosophical view that consciousness is an irreducible property of the universe and not reducible to brain functioning. The student may not be aware of eastern traditions which see consciousness as the ground of being.

None of this means the brain is not important; it means that an account of behavior, thoughts, and feelings only in terms of the brain leaves out the person who has the brain. For many of us, it is more useful to understand a person empathically, at the human level, than it is to have an explanation at the level of neurophysiology or scientifically-derived laws of behavior, which are distant from direct experience and too abstract to be helpful with the details of an individual life. The student of psychotherapy may not realize that there are alternatives to the view of human nature that underpins his or her training program. But surely these philosophical positions should be articulated during training, or the student might be unwittingly signing on to a set of beliefs that are incompatible with the student's personal values.

Brain, mind, and suffering

The ancient question of the relationship between mind and brain has not been solved. Currently we have no idea how the brain could produce consciousness, and indeed many philosophers believe there is something about consciousness that cannot be explained by the brain *alone*. Nevertheless, the doctrine of physicalism—that the mind can be fully explained by scientific descriptions of the brain—is dominant in academic circles.

A brain-based explanation for a psychological issue seems to carry more weight than a hundred years of accumulated psychotherapeutic wisdom. However, much of the enormous knowledge accumulated about the brain over the last 20 years has only confirmed pre-existing psychotherapeutic insights. For example, psychotherapists (and philosophers) have been aware of the importance of empathy and affective attunement for much longer than we have known about mirror neurons and the importance of the right hemisphere.[6] Brain-based theories of psychopathology seem to promise clear treatment strategies, which policy-makers and third-party payers prefer. These economic and social influences, combined with a lack of articulation of the underlying mind-brain question, have important consequences for treatment. Thus, in most training programs today, difficulties such as bipolar disorder are automatically assumed to be the result of biochemical changes in the brain. Convincing alternative—*psychological*—theories are ignored. For example, Brandchaft (1993, p. 225) explains how mania may arise as the result of release from "an enslaving tie to a self-annihilating selfobject." Brandchaft explains how this process begins with a parent who commandeers the child's development, such that the child cannot rely on his own spontaneous, authentic experience but instead becomes hostage to the responses of another person for defining who he is. The child is not allowed to own himself, but is imprisoned by a feeling of responsibility for the parent's state of mind. Later in life, mania occurs when the person is able to transiently free himself from this oppression, and depression supervenes when such a tie is re-established, with the loss of a vital part of himself. Of course there must be brain mechanisms going on which correspond to this psychological situation, but to assume that the biology is primarily at fault is to ignore the psychological source of the problem.

Various approaches to psychotherapy unconsciously assume a materialistic and reductionist philosophy; they assume that human behavior is nothing but the result of evolution, genetic endowment, brain processes, family, and culture. These approaches ignore what Frankl calls the noetic dimensions of the person—the realm of meaning, values, the domains of spiritual, intellectual, and artistic concerns, and self-awareness. My contention is that the meaning of suffering to the individual cannot be fully understood using approaches to psychotherapy based on scientific physicalism—the doctrine that reality is entirely based on the physical properties of objects—and naturalism, the doctrine that science must confine itself to the study of natural causes, excluding anything that might be deemed spiritual. (The issue of meaning is discussed further in chapter 8.) Painful life dilemmas such as whether to leave a marriage or a job often

---

6   The philosopher Theodor Lipps used the German term Einfülung (feeling into) in the 19th century to explain how we know that others have a sense of self (Pigman, 1995). Edward Titchener introduced the term empathy into American psychology in 1909, but the idea was already well known to philosophers because of empathy's importance to the aesthetic appreciation of art. Freud realized that empathy was central to the development of clinical rapport, and Carl Rogers in the 1930's and Heinz Kohut in the 1960's stressed its importance in psychotherapy. In Winnicott's work, the "good enough mother" is able to resonate empathically with the baby's wants and needs.

produce intense suffering, but the psychotherapist cannot be helpful by using neurological or positivist⁷ approaches to them, because even if we knew all the brain mechanisms involved, these could not give us an answer to such questions. When these kinds of issues arise in psychotherapy they demand the entire person of the psychotherapist. There is often an analogous gap between what we can demonstrate scientifically and what we actually must do in the psychotherapy room in the absence of empirical data about what would be helpful. The attempt to squeeze the practice of psychotherapy into a scientific model seems to be a defense against the difficulty of working with severe emotional pain for which there is no obvious remediation. Perhaps this is one reason that many psychotherapists do not read research journals— the kinds of questions that arise when dealing with suffering people are not always dealt with by researchers who are interested in generalizations and large-scale theoretical questions. The psychotherapist is only interested in the specific details of the individual in the room.

Values and assumptions in psychotherapy

All theories of treatment are laden with (often unspoken) assumptions about what is good, desirable, important, and beneficial for human life; these are the values which guide our behavior. For many post-modern writers, the search for binding human values (or guiding principles) is obsolete, but in practice the psychotherapist cannot avoid the issue of values. Values are inherently part of the way we treat people; they bias our attitudes and they are reflected in our goals of treatment, our method of treatment, and even our definition of mental health. For example, the values of pharmaceutical and insurance companies are financial, so it is in their interest to support the assumption that quicker treatments are preferable. When a psychiatrist uses medication

---

7   Positivism is a philosophy of science that asserts that only empirical information derived from systematic observation and experimentation provides valid knowledge. Positivism rejects intuitive or introspectively obtained knowledge. Many people find positivism too restrictive, because empiricism is only one way to study psychology; it is clear that the humanities teach us a great deal about the psyche, and it is also clear that our intuitions are often correct even if unprovable. Our moral and ethical intuitions, for instance about right and wrong, may be hard to prove empirically but we could not live without them. Personal meaning is important to us, but impossible to validate empirically. Some important experiences cannot be rigorously tested even though they are useful. Positivists cannot prove that there are no principles beyond what we can observe, so they cannot prove their own assertion. Bertrand Russell pointed out that if the positivists are correct, there is no end to the verification process, since we would keep having to verify the method we use to verify each proposition, then verify that method, ad infinitum. There is no authoritative ground for insisting that empirical verification is the only valid criterion of psychological truth. Today, post-positivists believe we need several different types of observation to understand reality, and that all observations are laden with theory and the experimenter's biases and ideology. We need multiple perspectives, even if each is fallible.

on the assumption that an abnormality of brain metabolism is the origin of a person's emotional difficulty or is the best way of alleviating it, the psychiatrist is then consciously or unconsciously aligned with the notion that the brain is more fundamental than the psyche. Not only is the psychiatrist adopting this philosophical (metaphysical) position, he or she is also aligned with the values of pharmaceutical and insurance companies which have a vested interest in a biological approach because it seems to be quicker and less expensive than psychotherapy. Using biologically-oriented treatment as the primary modality implies that to treat the brain is more important than to address the existential, relational or spiritual dimensions of the person's suffering—these factors take a different set of values into account. Like it or not, the attitude that quicker is better and brain is more important than mind expresses a set of values which makes the financial aspects of treatment primary, but this implication is rarely articulated in practice and it is easily disguised as an empirically validated approach to treatment.

Strictly behavioral therapies are also value-laden, since to treat a distressed individual by focusing on external behavior is to imply that introspection or subjectivity is less important than overt behavior. But the person is more than his or her observable behavior, and from a depth psychological perspective the same behavior can arise from very different sources, which are important to understand. Cognitive-behavioral approaches to psychological suffering are often able to alleviate symptoms, but they ignore what depth psychologists of all schools stress; the overt symptom is not the real problem—it is the manifestation of a deeper problem. The symptom is the attempt of the personality to deal with an underlying problem. Symptoms are signals that something within the personality or in the individual's life needs attention; to remove the symptom without attending to its origin is like taking the bulb out of a warning light.

A further value-laden problem is that both biological and cognitive-behavioral approaches to suffering tend to assume that social norms of behavior are universally applicable. What applies to most people is then applied to the individual. This implies a kind of mass psychology, which unknowingly turns these therapists into agents of social conformity, or at least promoters of acquiescence to social standards, again justified by reliance on empirically validated science. However, what is statistically true for a large group of people may not be true or important for a given individual. Needless to say, all schools of psychotherapy are similarly subject to a scrutiny of their implicit values, which have an important if latent influence on the goals of this work. (For a fuller discussion of values in psychotherapy see Corbett, 2011).

Suffering in the practice of psychotherapy

The experience of suffering is so complex and mysterious that it requires that we take into account all the sources of wisdom that are part of our human heritage; in particular, we must borrow from our spiritual traditions, our philosophers, poets, writers, historians, and artists, as well as from psychologists. This situation is particularly important in our day, since increasing numbers of people are now taking their spiritual and existential problems to psychotherapist rather than to clergy, so that many contemporary psychotherapist have become *de facto* spiritual directors, providing a latter-day form of care of the soul (Corbett, 2011).

It is often assumed that the goal of psychotherapy is whatever version of normality one's theory dictates, but as Jung (1939) pointed out, normality is only a helpful goal for people who have not been able to cope with life. For those who are successful in the world but nevertheless feel a painful sense that life has become sterile and meaningless, "normality" in the sense of social adaptation may become a Procrustean bed. More than normality is then needed. For a person in this predicament, a biological or cognitive-behavioral approach to an existential crisis may not be adequate to discover new sources of meaning. Sometimes the most we can do in psychotherapy is to make the full ramifications of a person's situation as conscious as possible, perhaps trying to find its possible meaning and purpose in the life of the individual.

We can never finally answer the problem of suffering. This realization leads to what the Spanish intellectual Miguel de Unamuno termed the tragic sense of life, meaning that although we constantly strive to understand life rationally, we finally recognize life's ultimately irrational nature. Unamuno believed that "suffering is the substance of life and the root of personality, for it is only suffering that makes us persons...it is the universal or divine blood that flows through us all" (1912, p. 205). One might acknowledge here that suffering can be over-idealized, as it has been in some religious traditions. This tendency may have been the result of the fact that earlier generations have been unable to cope with it, given their limited technological ability.

There seems to be natural human need to make sense of suffering and to understand its effects on people and on the world at large. Nowhere is this more evident than in the practice of psychotherapy, where we daily see the effects of suffering on the personality. However, to suggest an approach to suffering that does not correspond to a person's psychological structures can be irritating and damaging to the therapeutic relationship. Psychotherapists who have themselves suffered are particularly concerned not to offer clichés which they know are unhelpful. There are many occasions during psychotherapy when silence, presence, and the sense that one can only be a witness, are the only possible responses to a person's suffering. We may have to help someone bear the unbearable. We often do not know what to say, but we have to sit with the person who is in an agony of soul, and all we can provide is a containing space in which the suffering can be expressed. This practice requires endurance and a kind of spiritual fortitude. These are the times when we realize how unhelpful rigidly manualized approaches to psychotherapy are. These are the occasions when science, therapeutic technique, and the textbooks fail us and we have to fall back on our own humanity. In these situations of mutual helplessness, any therapeutic narcissism, any need to be admired, any difficulty tolerating criticism, or any tendency to blame the patient, will reveal themselves.

The confrontation with another person's suffering places a constant demand on the psychotherapist. When we work therapeutically with suffering people we have to be prepared to consciously participate in their suffering, and see their suffering and our own suffering as part of the common suffering of humanity. Doing so is part of the spiritual practice of psychotherapy; to be effective, the psychotherapist must not ward off or defend against the distress he or she feels when hearing stories of severe emotional pain. To allow oneself to feel the other's pain is a conscious sacrifice made by the psychotherapist, and may be essential for healing to occur.

Depression and the use of antidepressants: a test case for our approach to suffering

All psychotherapists and psychiatrists see depressed people who either do not do well in treatment or who relapse. We may then wonder how our treatment was inadequate, and many possible reasons come to mind. Perhaps we made a technical error in the therapy or the choice of medication, or our model of psychotherapy was not suitable for that particular individual, or the patient was not sufficiently committed to the treatment, or an unrecognized transference or countertransference problem interfered with the work. Perhaps another clinician would have been a better choice. However, as well as these technical and personal factors, we must also recognize that some painful states of mind are due to insoluble difficulties in the person's life; there are forms of human unhappiness that are not necessarily the result of psychopathology. As discussed above, many trainees in psychotherapy have been taught to think of human suffering purely in terms of the model typified by the DSM and fostered by an emphasis on neuroscience, as if our problems of relationship, abandonment, loss, and life dissatisfaction were primary *brain* disorders. In the case of depression, this approach seems an offense to common sense, because although these existential problems may affect the brain's chemistry, producing neurotransmitter changes that are associated with depression, these brain changes are secondary to our appraisal of our life situation. A life crisis is not a primary brain disorder. Just because there are brain correlates of depression does not mean the brain changes are causal. Depression is a normal response to certain types of psychological stress such as loss; life can be very depressing at times. It is however rare to see the suggestion that a low brain serotonin level might be the *result* of depression rather than the cause. Very often, biological-ly-oriented psychiatrists pay insufficient attention to the psychological and existential level of a patient's suffering, and focus almost exclusively on the neurochemical level. They feel that serious depression, for example, is a final common path, and even if it results from a painful life situation, the end result is a neurotransmitter abnormality that must become the focus of treatment regardless of its origin. In other words, the problem becomes the patient's disordered brain chemistry or behavior rather than his or her life situation; brain has then replaced mind, and certainly soul. Unfortunately however, effective antidepressant treatment only allows the person to remain in a difficult life situation without too much distress. Then, nothing needs to change, and the psychological function of depression—a call to evaluate one's situation and address a problem in living—can be ignored.

A common defense of the biological view of depression is that antidepressants help in about two thirds of cases, whereas only about a third of depressed patients respond to placebos.[8] The logic is that if depression responds to a chemical treatment, depression must be a chemical disorder.

---

8   The placebo effect is a demonstration of the importance of the psyche in the healing process. Even some of the people who appear to respond to active medication are probably having a placebo response.

This is of course a specious argument; aspirin relieves a headache, but headache is not due to aspirin deficiency. Only a pre-existing philosophical bias in favor of the primacy of the brain makes clinicians assume that the neurotransmitter changes in depression are primary rather than secondary to psychological changes. Furthermore, even among people who appear to respond to antidepressants, it is not always clear whether the person is responding to the psychiatrist's care and attention, or perhaps to an idealizing transference, rather than to the medication itself. It is noteworthy that in William Styron's (1992) moving account of his depression he points out that he felt better after only a few days in hospital because he felt safe, stabilized in a sanctuary. I have seen patients in whom the antidepressant effect of a medication seems to fade at the same time as the idealization of their psychiatrist also fades. I have also seen depressed patients who fail to get better on medication because of an intense dislike of their psychiatrist— sometimes due to a negative transference, and sometimes because of the psychiatrist's attitude. Further complicating the issue is that we occasionally see sudden, inexplicable improvement in the severity of depression in the absence of treatment of any kind.

As a result of the mainstream emphasis on medication to treat depression, opposing minority voices have arisen. Peter Breggin (1991) has insisted that antidepressants make people less able to find more effective ways of living, pointing out the ancient theme that suffering is an opportunity for growth and is a signal that something needs attention. There is widespread concern that psychiatric diagnoses are expanding to match the evolving scope of medications, thanks to the influence of the pharmaceutical industry on both the psychiatric profession and our cultural approach to unhappiness. We see this particularly with respect to people who have "subsyndromal" or mild depression that may or may not need antidepressants, depending on whether the psychiatrist thinks the patient's mental state is appropriate to his life situation. This is a problematic approach to such individuals, especially because of the possibility that long-term antidepressant use may cause emotional blunting, reduced motivation or indifference—so-called antidepressant apathy syndrome (Barnhart et al, 2004; Price et al., 2009), which can be quite difficult to distinguish from depression itself. Some research suggests that antidepressants may worsen the chronicity of depression (El-Mallakh et al., 2011). People taking antidepressants may say that they do feel emotions but they are somehow detached from their feelings, or that positive emotions such as enjoyment, enthusiasm, and excitement are dampened down. These individuals have told me that they can still feel their depression in the background of their minds, even though the depression is no longer painful. On balance therefore, while antidepressants clearly have a place in alleviating intolerable suffering and preventing suicide, they also have drawbacks in terms of subduing the voice of the soul, preventing the emergence of the new consciousness that depression demands, and sometimes allowing the suffering person to avoid necessary life changes. It seems clear that they are best used in combination with psychotherapy. They might reasonably be thought of as analogous to pain medication used while an illness is being treated with a specific remedy.

The transformative effects of suffering

Our culture tends to see suffering as of no value, often the result of pathology, and to be avoided as much as possible. An alternative view sees suffering as essential for the transformation and growth of the personality. Personality development in childhood inevitably requires experiences involving frustration and loss, but we accept that these are necessary for the child to learn to cope with the challenges he or she will later face. In adulthood, once the personality is relatively consolidated, intense suffering may lead to further transformation, although the psychotherapist cannot betray the present by borrowing from the future. Working with a suffering person, we do not know what will happen. Accordingly, even if we believe a person's suffering will eventually be beneficial for his development, we cannot take an attitude of "it's good for you" towards suffering, because in the therapeutic setting this would be patronizing and radically unempathic. Another risk is that such an attitude would suggest that the psychotherapists is advocating nothing more than stoicism.

In spite of these caveats, there are ways in which suffering can be spiritually and developmentally important. Although the mechanism of psychological change is often mysterious, we can sometimes see the mechanism by which suffering produces its effects.

Suffering turns both our outer and our inner life upside down; it forces a reorganization of the personality and of our beliefs and values. Suffering both leads to defensive operations such as denial and also penetrates defenses when it is severe enough. When we suffer, it is as if the rules by which we live have been changed. We might feel betrayed or forsaken by whatever we have relied on—everything from religious faith and the sense that life is just, to our own sense that we are in control of our lives. In all these ways, suffering can expand awareness of reality and "relativize" the ego, which means the ego consciously realizes it is related to the transpersonal dimension. Like the biblical Job, a new God-image may be forced upon the sufferer. The new awareness produced by suffering produces humility, a sense of the ego's limitations. Suffering deflates narcissism, but new psychological structures form, and with them a new sense of identity. Suffering demands courage; the suffering person may have to decide between giving up and going on living in spite of major losses such as mobility and comfort. He or she has to try to see into the future in spite of uncertainty, maintain self-esteem, and develop the patience to live with infirmity. The suffering person may allow the necessary transformation or may refuse it.

Our personal suffering is often a reflection of a cultural problem such as racism or homophobia. Nevertheless it remains important to find an individual response, which may add to the possibility of social transformation at the same time. Like the biblical Job, this means we must maintain our own stance and resist settling for existing collective attitudes.

Radical acceptance of one's situation (discussed further in chapter 10) fosters positive transformation. Extreme situations offer a good example of this potential; during the Second World War, von Durckheim (1992) noticed spiritual transformation among soldiers, concentration camp inmates, and refugees who were able to accept the fact that they would probably die soon. He points out that the prospect of immanent death, for example during an air raid or a severe illness, may lead to the collapse of internal resistance to the situation so that we can accept it fully: "....we are then suddenly calm, our fears are instantly forgotten, and we have the certainty that there is something in us that death and destruction cannot touch...We do not know its source or purpose—we only know that we are standing in it, that it encloses us utterly" (p. 16).

Suffering of some kind or other is inevitable in all lives; perhaps the most important aspect of suffering is our response to it. Painful existential dilemmas, emotional wounds, and life situations arise which may never fully heal. The changes produced by such suffering may be either positive or negative. For example, a sense that injustice is taking place may lead to nothing more than smoldering resentment or to a civil rights movement. That is, suffering may act as a fertilizer or a poison. Suffering may be a stimulus to the imagination and may be essential to producing an important creative product, or it may become a source of achievement and fulfillment. Without the challenge of suffering we may never strive. Many great works of art take a long time to produce and involve great suffering.

It is sometimes suggested that suffering may have stimulated the ability of human beings to think, and certainly suffering influenced the development of religion. The biblical *Book of Job*, and much later Freud, both point out that, given the evidence, it is simplistic to believe in a benevolent divine power who rewards and punishes people according to their behavior. But Freud and Job reach diametrically opposite conclusions, each of which are prototypical types of response to the problem of suffering; Freud dismisses religion as illusory, based on an infantile wish for a heavenly protector, while for Job suffering is the beginning of a new understanding of the divine. His suffering meant that he had to develop a new image of God and challenge the traditional idea that suffering is a punishment for sin. The psychotherapist is constantly faced with people in situations analogous to Job; they do not know why they are suffering, or their suffering seems disproportionate to the lives they lead, and none of the traditional religious explanations for their suffering are helpful. In spite of that they may retain a sense of a larger purpose or meaning. Many people are helped by this kind of broadly spiritual approach, which allows one to develop an attitude to one's suffering that makes it tolerable. However, the attempt to find meaning has its pitfalls. If the psychotherapists attempts to force the discovery of meaning before the suffering person has any clarity about his or her situation, the psychotherapist may inadvertently silence the person altogether. Until the time is right for a discussion of meaning, suffering provides an opportunity for the psychotherapist to practice attention, compassion, and care.

Psychotherapists and patients who are committed to a particular religious tradition may be helped by the tradition's attitude to suffering. For others, now probably in the majority, one's attitude to suffering has to be individual, and traditional religious approaches are unhelpful; they invoke a meaningless God-image or their explanations for suffering do not ring true. It is common today for the psychotherapist to be working with people who have no allegiance to any traditional religious institution. Some of these are avowed atheists who would prefer no reference to spirituality in psychotherapy, while others have a personal spirituality but distrust traditional doctrine and dogma. A similar spectrum of attitudes is found among psychotherapists. Whatever the psychotherapist's personal attitude to spirituality may be, because of the importance of religion and spirituality in helping to deal with suffering for many people, it is useful for the therapist to understand the ways in which various religions and spiritual teachers have approached the problem. These are discussed in chapter 6.

2

FORMS OF SUFFERING

Suffering due to painful emotions

This chapter discusses a variety of painful emotions, which cause considerable suffering but which do not belong to any specific disorder.

Suffering due to envy

Envy is one of the most malignant and destructive states of mind. The word "envy" is derived from the Latin *invidere*, meaning to look into, with the connotation of doing so with hostility and hatred.

The envious person wishes to spoil in another person what he feels he cannot have himself, even if doing so results in self-harm. Envy therefore wants to destroy goodness because it is good, in contrast to other forms of aggression. Envy causes enormous ill-will towards others and spoils the envious person's capacity for creativity and pleasure. Envy is seen in all walks of life, including the workplace, politics, and in academia, where we see it in the form of mean-spirited criticism of the envied person. Even criticism that sounds reasonable often disguises underlying envy. Envy may take the form of distress at the thought of another's success, or pleasure at the failure of the envied person, captured by the German word *schadenfreude*, which means malicious joy. We are embarrassed by envy, both individually and culturally, so that envy may be repressed, and even if conscious, we may be reluctant to admit it.

Serious envy is associated with depression, self-pity, and poor overall mental health (Smith et al., 1999). An envious person is unable to feel gratitude and is unable to form trusting, warm relationships, so his inner world becomes insecure, which increases his hatred of others whom he perceives to be happier.

41

Feelings of inadequacy, humiliation, and unfairness compared to others worsen his envy, leading to a vicious circle. The envious person feels ashamed, inferior, and impotent compared to the one he envies, whose happiness or goodness must therefore be destroyed, so that envious people are hostile to anyone they see as more successful than themselves. Envy spoils relationships, so that the envious person tends to experience the world as hostile, and may become paranoid. Envy believes there is not enough goodness for everyone, so if one of us has it, the other cannot. Especially under stress, one's trust in the goodness of others can be spoiled by envy of them.

In the extreme, malignant envy can lead to murderous rage. Gilligan (2000) suggests that Hitler persecuted the Jews of Europe partly because of envy. He also felt great shame at his own early environment and about the treatment of Germans after the First World War, so for Gilligan there is close connection between envy and shame, because to feel envious of someone is to feel shamefully inferior in comparison to that person.

Creativity in another person, or even in oneself, is a potent trigger of envy. Critics are often those who create nothing themselves. Creative blocks may be the result of the internalization of an envious parent or sibling, because internalized envy makes the person feel that everything he creates is worthless. When the creative person sits down to write or paint, internal envy attacks begin, devaluing what she has produced. Internalized envy may also make the individual self-destructive, since there is something in the personality which will not allow success. It is as if part of the personality envies and depreciates another part.

Envy is frequently mentioned in the Bible, and it is one of the seven deadly sins of the Christian tradition. (Ulanov [1983] has a comprehensive discussion of the theological dimensions of envy). The superstitious idea of the "evil eye," the folk belief that the gaze of an envious person may cause harm, is found in many traditions all over the world (Berger, 2012). Envy also has a long history in psychotherapeutic thought. Karl Abraham (1927) described patients who could not tolerate what he offered them; they tried to surpass him and depreciate his achievements because of envy. In those early years of psychoanalysis, envy was seen as a resistance and was considered to be one of the main factors which prevented good results in psychotherapy. Later, envy became central to the theories of Melanie Klein, and many contemporary discussions of envy build on or argue with her ideas. For Klein, envy is a kind of original sin, the opposite of love, gratitude, and relatedness.

She believes that envy can stifle feelings of love and intensify hatred, leading to the appearance of indifference to people or withdrawal from them (Klein, 1957). She suggests that envy begins early in life; the baby feels envious of its parents because they gratify each other. According to Klein, envy is an inevitable aspect of the baby-mother relationship because the baby believes that the breast is hoarding all the goodness for itself, thereby asserting its power over the infant. It is as if mother withholds the goodness of the breast for her own enjoyment, making the baby frustrated and humiliated, leading to envious attacks on the breast; destroying its goodness would remove the source of envy. Envy therefore spoils the goodness of the baby's early objects and prevents enjoyment of them. If the baby is able to work through this primary envy, normal development goes on; ideally, gratitude and trust eventually soften envy—it is hard to be envious and grateful at the same time. But if envy is excessive, personality development is damaged. If the goodness of the mother is no longer certain, greed results, so that one wants more than one can use. However, in contrast to envy's wish to destroy goodness, the greedy person sees what he wants as valuable and wants to fill himself up with it rather than destroy it. Excessive greed can exhaust the goodness of the mother or breast, so that mother seems to be withholding, leading to envy. Modern Kleinians are inclined to see envy as a reaction to and a flight from dependency and the anxiety it produces—how can I depend on what is not mine, or on a mother who does not want me?

Klein (1957/1975) believes that envy is largely constitutional, an inborn expression of the death instinct which is evoked by the environment (Spillius, 1993). However, I should note here that Klein's critics believe that envy is too complex a mental state to be found in babies, who do not have the cognitive abilities or enough awareness of social comparisons to be envious. As discussed below, it also seems likely that failure of maternal attunement or inadequate containment of a child's distress may provoke envy, which therefore cannot be attributed to something in the baby alone. Klein's work has always been subject to the criticism that she draws too many conclusions about the life of the baby from the material of adults.

Because Klein felt that envy was so primary, she believed treatment could have limited effect. However, rather than seeing envy as constitutional, one can see it as secondary to psychological factors such as narcissistic injury leading to narcissistic rage, so that envy is defensive, an attempt to restore a painfully wounded, fragmenting sense of self, albeit in a pathological manner. Narcissistic people may suffer intensely from envy when they see qualities in another which they feel they lack. To cope with their feelings, these individuals may either devalue those they envy or inflate themselves. By focusing on the one whom one envies, one does not need to look at one's own feelings of inadequacy. Narcissistic people often compare themselves to others, and feel shame or inadequacy compared to another person. Envy is then secondary to their shame, a painful feeling of disgrace or defectiveness, often the result of being frequently publicly humiliated or demeaned in childhood. Such shame may be unconscious, or shameful material may be consciously suppressed, making it difficult to access psychotherapeutically.

Envy typically arises when one realizes that someone has something good that one wants, but one feels that one can never have it; the gap between oneself and the envied person seems to be too great ever to be bridged. Then, the problem is the disparity between oneself and the envied person; we see the one we envy as impossibly greater than oneself. Compensatory feelings of personal pride or contempt for the other are other defensive outcomes of such comparison. It is not clear at what age envy begins, but it is likely to occur when children learn to compare themselves with others. It also seems that witnessing chronically envious parents predisposes to the development of envy in childhood. It is also true that some parents envy their children because they have a future which the parents do not have, or for the child's health and beauty. Not surprisingly, we see envy of the young among the aged.

Envy reminds us of what is undeveloped in us, so that if we can become conscious enough, envy has the potential to stimulate us to develop new skills and capacities instead of separating us from others. This approach is typical of a rather benign approach to envy which has recently emerged, which affirms its adaptive importance when it motivates people to greater achievement by raising their own ability to the level of the envied one, instead of trying to bring others down (van de Ven, 2009). However, this kind of benign envy is a form of praise, and since it is not destructive it does not meet a strict definition of envy. It is possible to simply admire another person without feeling that one is inferior and without envy, so that person becomes a stimulus for our own development.

Some writers see envy as the result of terror of the "unfathomable other" (Anderson, 1997, p. 370), because the experience of otherness may evoke either the terror of abandonment or of predation. In such a situation, envy's rage helps to hold together the fragile ego, protecting it from fragmentation. Murry Stein (1990) suggested that children are often envied because the child represents the transpersonal Self, the highest value in the personality, so that envy indicates the ego's envy of the Self, because the ego lacks an inner connection to the Self. We then envy another in whom we perceive the Self which we cannot connect to in ourselves. Barry Proner (1986) has described "envy of the Self," meaning that the patient reports anxiety when good things happen and when he experiences good parts of himself.

Envy is often distinguished from jealousy, and being jealous is often seen as more socially acceptable and less shameful than envy. Jealousy is a triangular, three-person problem of rivalry for affection, often due to frustrated love or the sense that someone else is loved more than oneself, or that there is a danger one will lose a loved person to a rival. Psychoanalysts attribute jealousy to the original Oedipal triangle between child and parents, but this does not need to be understood in its classical form in which the child is rivalrous with the opposite sex parent. One can imagine that the child feels rivalry because he is afraid of the loss of the love of a parent to whom the child is very attached and dependent, which is a terrifying prospect. Such unconscious anxiety, rooted in childhood, may account for the way in which the jealous person is often irrationally possessive. Whereas the envious person feels he lacks something the other has, the jealous person is afraid to lose what he possesses. This dynamic would account for the fear that one will lose the love of an important selfobject to a rival, but might not account for the jealousy of a person who knows that the object of his jealousy is attached to someone else and does not love him. This jealousy might arise if one adversely compares oneself to one's rival, leading to feelings of inferiority or shame. One feels a blow to one's grandiosity or feelings of specialness if the object of one's affection choses someone else. Interestingly, jealousy in heterosexual men is said to be primarily related to fear of their partner's sexual infidelity, while jealousy in heterosexual women is thought to be due to a fear of loss of love and abandonment—the difference may be the result of our evolutionary biology (Buss, 2000). Jealousy is more tolerable than envy, and often more understandable. However, these states may coincide and intertwine with each other; one may be envious of the attributes of a person of whom one is a jealous rival.

Helmut Schoeck's (1966) classic study of the sociology and politics of envy has been neglected. He believes that envy is at the core of our lives as social beings. For him, envy is an important determinant of social behavior, and envy is not necessarily the result of inequality because it is innate in human beings. He shows how societies have tried to soften the effects of envy by belief in luck or fate, by belief in God and an afterlife, and by religious endorsement of high achievement. He suggests that some political and economic theories of social equality and the redistribution of wealth are often disguises for envy—a view that distresses people with a liberal orientation. Schoeck sees envy as a phenomenon necessary to the coherence of social groups because envy helps to regulate relationships between people in society, where we go to some lengths to avoid envy. According to Schoeck, fear of the envy of others and of one's own envy keeps excessive individualism in check, and thus stabilizes the life of a society. It may be that in our society envy at times leads to healthy competition and technological innovation. Schoeck's work is relevant to our current debate about the discrepancy between the poor and the very rich in our society.

On being envied

Being envied feels like an unpleasant attack, which may occur for no reason that one can understand. The fear of being envied may make people act in a helpful way towards others, in an attempt to ward off the destructive effects of their envy (van de Ven, 2010). The fear of envy can lead to excessive modesty in order to avoid standing out too much, and can make it difficult to know whom we can trust. The experience of being the subject of envy may be pleasurable if one has no fear of success, but fear of envy may make one fear success. Fear of envy may make one hide one's abilities or possessions, or one might devalue one's assets to avoid envy. At the same time as the importance of the envied one is exaggerated in the mind of the envier, envy can make the envied one feel helpless, totally discounted, as if his or her subjectivity does not exist. When there is a great fear of envy, perhaps due to the presence of an envious parent or sibling in childhood, it is helpful to be in relationships with people who can admire the individual without confirming the expectation that she will be envied.

Envy destroys the possibility of being empathic with the envied one. Even if the envied one would like to maintain a connection to the envier, this may not be not allowed; efforts by the envied one to make a connection with the envier are often rebuffed or seen as patronizing. The envied one may then either assume some unwarranted responsibility and guilt for the disruption in the relationship, or the envied one may withdraw, discount the goodness for which she is being envied, or she may retaliate angrily; in all these cases the situation becomes toxic for both parties. It is important to note that envy can be projected onto another person, in which case the projector feels he is the object of another's envy which is actually his own.

Psychotherapeutic Treatment of envy

To become conscious of one's envy is to take an important step towards dealing with it. It also helps if one can minimize the habit of comparing oneself with others. All this can be addressed in psychotherapy, but envy can sabotage therapy, either because the patient is envious of some attribute of the therapist, such as the therapist's capacity for empathy, or because the patient's envy will not allow him to give the therapist the satisfaction of being helpful. This envy might be unconscious, acted out in the form of resistance, constant complaints about the therapy, or withdrawal. The patient may not be able to acknowledge how much he needs the therapist, for fear that this would stir up the patient's envy. However, direct interpretation of a person's envy is often counterproductive because it feels like an attack, or it is too shaming. Narcissistically vulnerable people are easily shamed, and shame is a potent source of defensiveness in psychotherapy. Because of shame, it is quite difficult to admit that one is envious. Therefore, given the close relationship between envy and shame, it is important for the psychotherapist to first be sensitive to the feelings of shame and inferiority which are driving the envy. The therapist has to be very tactful in approaching hidden shame; one might begin by looking at the patient's tendency to see himself in a negative light compared to others and with the underlying self-esteem problem. To be conscious of one's own value is helpful in dealing with one's envy of others. When envy is clearly present, as long as the self-selfobject connection is firm enough, the therapist can tactfully suggest the possibility and expect to work with denial. The therapist can try to help the envious patient develop what he feels he lacks, or help him find the goodness and value in himself which he cannot claim. When the patient wishes to attain something truly impossible for him, he can be helped to come to terms with his limitations, grief, and resentment.

Psychotherapy with envious people is made difficult because giving to an envious person worsens his envy, which makes gratitude impossible. Giving worsens envy because the envious person feels that the giver has so much goodness that he or she can afford to give it away, as if giving demonstrates the giver's superiority. This may make the envious person refuse the psychotherapist's attempts to be helpful, or the therapist's good intentions may be undermined. Envy may make the patient try to take over the therapist's suggestions as if they originated in the patient, so that the patient does not need to feel that the therapist is giving him anything valuable of which he might feel envious. When a person begins to improve in psychotherapy, internal envy tries to interfere with the process. Very envious people cannot enjoy what comes from others even in everyday relationships, not only in psychotherapy. The envious patient resents the therapist's apparent control over goodness, such as the ability to be soothing and nurturing, which seem to be doled out by the therapist according to her own whims. Sometimes any goodness given to the patient has to be destroyed by envy because it may stimulate hope, which risks painful disappointment. When the envious patient begrudges the therapist's success in treating him and so wants to spoil the therapy, envy may make it impossible for the patient to really use the therapy constructively. However, envy can be mitigated by love and gratitude, and when envy is eventually metabolized the result is a deepened capacity for gratitude for what one has, and for the enjoyment of others' success. Genuine admiration of others is an important counter to envy. In the end, personal happiness is the best solution to envy, but unfortunately envy makes happiness difficult to attain.

Some psychotherapists believe that the negative therapeutic reaction— the patient's negative response to what the therapist believes is a helpful intervention—is often due to envy, although others believe such a response is more likely to be due to the patient's experience of the intervention as hurtful. Occasionally, envious attacks on the therapist are misunderstood as the result of a transference to an earlier object, while they are actually a here-and-now, competitive phenomenon in which the patient cannot tolerate the therapist's apparent superiority in some area. From an intersubjective perspective, the therapist may be stimulating the patient's envy in some way, for example because of a paternalistic attitude, or by failing a necessary selfobject function so that the patient senses the therapist's emotional distance. Finally, it is important to note that a psychotherapist may suffer from envy of a patient, perhaps because of the patient's talents or financial situation, or because of the nurturance the patient is receiving, or even because the patient is receiving better therapy than the therapist has had (Whitman, 1990). This situation may lead to a countertransference difficulty.

There are a variety of defenses against envy, so that the therapist sometimes sees a mixture of unalloyed envy and defenses against it. The simplest defense is to avoid all situations and people that might stimulate envy. Another defense is one of "sour grapes"; by being contemptuous or by devaluing what one envies, one no longer needs to feel one's envy. Alternatively one might idealize the person one envies as a defense against feeling envy. When the therapist feels idealized, she has to decide if she is experiencing an authentic idealization based on an early selfobject need which is being expressed in the transference, or whether the idealization is defensive. The therapist's countertransference is helpful here. If the patient makes an idealizing remark but the therapist feels an edge of hostility or competition, rather than the satisfaction of being sincerely admired, the therapist is probably experiencing a defensive idealization. Sometimes the countertransference response to a defensive idealization is felt as slight nausea in the therapist, because the patient's unconscious hostility is registered somatically. Self-depreciation, which also widens the gap between patient and therapist, is another strategy to avoid feeling envy. When envy is acknowledged, it can be used as an incentive for personal development. However, envy can be unmanageably intense, at times enough to ruin the therapy.

Suffering produced by holding unpopular opinions:[9] Socrates and Semmelweis

Suffering may result from holding opinions which are socially unpopular; Socrates is an important historical example. He was executed by the Athenians for encouraging people to examine and question received beliefs and social conventions, and for bursting narcissistic bubbles. It may be painful to be part of a small minority, convinced nevertheless that one is right. In such a situation, it can be some consolation to remember that many important thinkers have been pilloried by their contemporaries but subsequently shown to be correct. Another poignant example is the story of Ignaz Semmelweis, a Hungarian obstetrician who discovered a way to prevent infection during childbirth. In the middle of the 19th century, many women died soon after childbirth. Their deaths were attributed to "poisonous vapors" at a time when no one knew that this problem was due to infection and unsanitary conditions. Semmelweis realized that the obstetricians themselves were making mothers ill by examining women

---

9   I am indebted to De Botton's *The Consolations of Philosophy* for pointing out this form of suffering.

in labor with dirty hands. By encouraging proper hygiene, the mortality rate among his patients was reduced to almost zero. For this discovery, he was ridiculed, attacked, persecuted by his colleagues, and dismissed from his position. It took a further 20 years for his work to receive the acknowledgment it deserved, as a result of Lister's confirmation of the germ theory of disease. In the meantime Semmelweis's mental health was overwhelmed by the controversy. Whereas Socrates was able to accept his death sentence with remarkable equanimity, as a result of Semmelweis's rejection by the medical community he became severely depressed, alcoholic, and erratic in his behavior. He died in an asylum at a young age. This story gave rise to a term for behavior which rejects new knowledge that contradicts received beliefs and punishes its proponents—the Semmelweis reflex.

Semmelweis fragmented in the face of very bitter opposition. In contrast, Socrates was able to maintain his composure partly because of his commitment to his philosophical beliefs and partly because he did not need the approval of others to maintain his sense of self. At his trial, he noted in his defense that he had no interest in things that concern most people, such as money and power—evidently a function of his high self-esteem. He was a sufficiently good thinker to know that reasoning can be more reliable than popular opinion. He recognized that his opponents were in a majority and had power over him, but he had the emotional strength to maintain his position without collapsing, even in the face of death. He knew that an unpopular opinion was not necessarily wrong. Another good example is the poet William Blake, whose work was regarded as eccentric or nonsensical by many of his contemporaries. However, Blake never doubted that he was right and his critics were wrong, and he is now considered to be a major literary and artistic figure.

It is often fairly easy to see the vulnerabilities of another person and direct an attack to the person's weaknesses—such attacks are often motivated by envy. Hurtful criticism, emotional withdrawal, and other forms of psychological attacks may inflict intense suffering on their target. In today's world of social media, nasty comments about others have become all too common, as Stephanie Rosenbloom pointed out in a recent article in the New York Times (Aug. 24, 2014). The attacker's conscious or unconscious motive is to hurt, and the effect may indeed produce some kind of fragmentation of the target's sense of self. Depending on the nature of one's shadow or one's particular vulnerability, the resulting fragmentation may take a variety of forms; it may feel as if one is falling apart, or as if one does not exist, or it may produce feelings such as inadequacy, worthlessness, isolation, or self-loathing. Such attacks are particularly painful when they repeat similar childhood experiences. Attacks may be the result of the projection of a trait which belongs to the attacker, because we tend to attack in others what we cannot tolerate in ourselves. Such an attack may nevertheless sting if it corresponds to an actual trait in one's personality—what the Jungians call a "hook" for the projection, or somewhere within us where the projection finds a place to land. At the same time therefore, a critical attack can increase self-awareness in important ways which may be discussed in psychotherapy. The psychotherapist can help the individual to understand the criticism and prevent or soften an irrational or exaggerated response. The therapist can help the individual look at whether the criticism is really justified and proportionate, the degree to which it is accurate, and whether the individual can learn from it. Sometimes making fun of a manifestly distorted attack is helpful. If the attack is reviving a childhood scenario, the attack is an opportunity to re-work it. The therapist can point out aspects of the patient, which directly contradict what the attacker accused him of, in order to avoid excessive attention to the negative aspects of the attack. It may also be helpful to point out that the attacker is envious or bitter or projecting his own difficulty. Strategies of response may be discussed. The therapist can help restore damaged self-esteem by emphasizing and validating the sufferer's positive attributes, and where necessary soften a harsh internal critic and encourage self-forgiveness.

The suffering of alienation

The word "alienation" has a long history, and has been given different meanings in different contexts and time periods. Alienation usually refers to some combination of social isolation, estrangement, loneliness, loss of interest in the world, and the feeling that one's existence is meaningless. Alienation can also refer to a feeling of powerlessness, as if one is unable to control one's own life because one is at the mercy of unknown forces. One might feel alienated from the values of the society in which one lives. One can be alienated from oneself, in the sense that one feels removed from one's real nature, or one does not like the person one has become. Sometimes without realizing it, one can become distant from one's own feelings and wishes, perhaps because one feels not good enough to be true to oneself, so one tries to live up to an artificial, ideal sense of self. Such an alienated individual may feel as if he is in a fog, may behave mechanically, and may show a lack of expression in the face and eyes. He might talk about himself as if he is talking about someone else. This kind of self-alienation is usually associated with alienation from the world. Culturally marginalized individuals such as the aged, the handicapped, and mentally ill are frequently alienated from the larger society in which they live. Many workers have difficulty adapting to our changing economy, and some are concerned that they will no longer be necessary as technology advances. Alienation of workers from productive work and society may lead to boredom, frustration, and a feeling of powerlessness, a combination which often leads to problems with alcohol or drugs in an attempt to deaden emotional pain.

The problem of alienation lies on a spectrum of severity; some people who feel subjectively alienated can function well socially and there is nothing unusual about their outward behavior. A more severe form of alienation is found in the schizoid person who is overly self-absorbed, withdrawn, idiosyncratic, and preoccupied with his inner world. Schizoid people lack an alive sense of connection to others. In Guntrip's words: "The vital heart of the self is lost, and an inner 'deadness' is experienced" (1969, p. 97). Guntrip saw the schizoid problem as the hidden but fundamental core of much emotional illness. Even if alienated people are not frankly schizoid, they feel profoundly lonely, often lacking intimacy or feeling as if they do not belong. Another group of alienated people are those suffering from an intense need for twinship (Kohut, 1984), the need to feel that one is like other human beings and that one belongs. When this need was not adequately met in childhood, the individual feels different, an alien, a lonely or marginalized misfit, often to the extent that he feels he cannot be understood by others and so cannot be included in relationships with them. Social scientists think of alienation in terms of problems with the individual's social network. In this view, alienation results from lack of opportunity, racial bias, poor education, and similar factors. The notion of alienation was particularly popular in the 18th and 19th centuries. For example, Karl Marx believed that productive work makes us feel meaningfully connected to others and to ourselves, but capitalism alienates workers from what they produce and forces them to make meaningless things, leading to alienation from themselves and from others. Today, technology is said to have an alienating effect because it removes us from an authentic connection to nature, makes us feel more isolated, produces artificial environments, and is in danger of treating us like objects. Even though the Internet seems to connect us, at the same time it may encapsulate us in virtual images.

For some time in the literature of sociology, alienation was used to explain social phenomena such as racial prejudice. Alienation was often considered to be the result of economic and social inequality and the increasing bureaucratization of society. However, in the last decades of the 20th century the idea of alienation fell out of fashion because it was thought to imply a rather naive notion of an originally ideal state of harmony and naturalness. Nevertheless, the idea that we feel alienated from ourselves or from others cannot be easily dismissed, even though this concept has vague conceptual boundaries. The importance of alienation has been again recognized by organizations such as the New Thinking on Alienation project at the University of Liverpool in the UK, which in 2009 began to study interdisciplinary aspects of alienation in psychology, sociology, the environment, politics, and other fields.

Loneliness

Loneliness is a good example of a state of mind[10] or an existential condition which causes great suffering but which is not unique to any particular disorder. Loneliness is one of the eternal preoccupations of poets, artists, and writers, because it is a ubiquitous human experience and a major human problem. It has even been suggested that the fear of loneliness is the central motive of human behavior (Mijuskovic, 1979). Although loneliness has always been a feature of human life, some authors believe that loneliness has become a modern epidemic that may be related to the organization of our society; we may be in an Age of Loneliness because of the loosening of social bonds and community (Stivers, 2004). Few people escape loneliness at some time in life. One estimate is that 20% of the people of the USA are lonely (Cacioppo, 2008). Given the social factors in our society which foster social isolation, such as the number of people living alone, in poverty and poor health, it is not surprising that loneliness has become an important topic in recent decades. (For a multi-author review of loneliness from a psychological viewpoint, see Willock, 2011).

When severe, loneliness produces painful feelings of hopelessness and futility, often accompanied by the sense that the pain will never end and one will always be in this state. Loneliness is often destructive; it is associated with

---

10   It is not clear whether loneliness is an emotion in itself, a mixture of emotions, or if it is only a correlate of other negatively toned emotions such as sadness.

a variety of health problems such as heart disease, hypertension, depression, suicidal ideation, and an increase in overall mortality (Tilvis et al, 2004), yet few physicians think of loneliness and lack of intimacy when considering the etiology of an illness. Partly because of the social stigma attached to mental illness (Ritsher et al., 2004), people with a variety of emotional difficulties are additionally burdened by loneliness.

There are several theories about the psychological sources of loneliness. Presumably it has evolutionary roots, since early hominids needed to remain in close groups in order to survive, suggesting an attachment theory of loneliness—needing others would increase the individual's chances of survival. The need to belong is a fundamental human need, and the threat of social exclusion has negative behavioral, cognitive, and emotional effects (Baumeister et al., 2002). For psychoanalytic self-psychologists, loneliness is due to the absence of a necessary selfobject someone who acts to hold the self together and support its vitality. For classical psychoanalysts, loneliness might result from a yearning for the pre-Oedipal mother. In her essay on loneliness, Melanie Klein (1959) suggested that there is a universal need for a perfect but unattainable internal state of mind which corresponds to a longing for the earliest relationship with mother. This longing is combined with the realization that this loss is irreparable, so she believes that loneliness can never be fully eliminated, but it encourages the development of object relationships.

As well as such developmental factors, there may also be a more primary form of loneliness, which has been attributed to an inborn sense that we are alone and helpless in the world (von Witzleben, 1958). The theme of primary aloneness is the thesis of a study which suggests that the primordial state of human beings is essentially to be alienated and alone (Mijuskovic 1979). Rather than see relatedness as primary, this author sees relatedness, love, and companionship as futile attempts to escape the fundamental solitude which is our human condition. He believes that the ultimate origin of loneliness is the unity of the ego, or the feeling of having a separate identity—the recognition that there is a "me" that is separate from everything that is not me. The ego knows it is alone; the most it can do to remain master of its identity is to achieve fame, wealth, power, or love in order to force others to recognize the ego's desires. For Mijuskovic therefore, loneliness is constituted by the structures of human consciousness, so it is unavoidable.

Sometimes the cause of loneliness is obvious, for example when we lose a loved one, or after a divorce, immigration, retirement, or a move to a new area of the country with few contacts. Loneliness is a common accompaniment of separation, grief, and loss, especially if one feels that the resulting void will never be filled. Another form of loneliness occurs when the individual does not have the capacity for connection to others and may not even be aware that this is missing.

Loneliness is so painful we take great pains to avoid it, using every possible form of escape, including entertainment, fantasy, over-eating, excess alcohol, or compulsive social life or sexuality. Some people are more afraid of loneliness than any other existential difficulty or deprivation. Our attachment to texting, social media, and email may be ways of avoiding loneliness. Participation in a religious congregation or other associations may have more to do with avoiding loneliness than with the ideology of the group. Even as part of a group it is possible to feel lonely if one does not feel the necessary level of intimacy and if there is no one to whom one is particularly important. Some individuals appear to be self-sufficient but their lack of real relatedness makes them subjectively lonely. Loneliness often adds to the burden of people suffering from physical illness. One can be lonely while ill in a busy hospital, in spite of a great deal of medical and nursing attention, just as one can be lonely in the middle of a big city surrounded by people. The quality of one's relationships is more important than their number.

Introverted people may tolerate being alone more than extraverts, although introverts may also be lonely if they are unhappy with the quality of their relationships. Some research suggests that very anxious and emotionally reactive people tend to be prone to loneliness; they have difficulty with relationships because others find them hard to tolerate (Saklofske et al, 1986). Socially competent people tend to report less loneliness, whereas excessive shyness and social clumsiness reduce the individual's social attractiveness, leading to a negative feedback cycle of anxiety, loneliness, and low self-esteem. The inability to trust others makes loneliness more likely. Mendelson (1990) makes the point that there is a relationship between loneliness and boredom, which consists of feelings of emptiness and longing but with more anger and protest than is felt in the passivity and resignation of loneliness. He suggests that boredom may defend against loneliness. Frieda Fromm-Reichmann (1990) believes that loneliness occurs when our need for intimacy cannot be met. She describes loneliness as a state of mind in which one not only forgets that there have been people available earlier in one's life, one also cannot imagine the possibility of relationships in the future. She uses Binswanger's terms "naked horror" or "mere existence" to describe this state. She notes that the experience of severe loneliness (rather than temporary loneliness during a creative project or an illness) is often not readily communicable to others. Because loneliness induces anxiety when we try to talk to others about it, it is difficult to share empathically. There is sometimes a "blame the victim" attitude towards lonely people, as if it were mostly a problem of personality, although its origin may be environmental. Therefore, lonely people are often secretive about their feelings and may believe that nobody else has ever felt what they are going through. Even when they emerge from loneliness they may be unable to talk about it.

Fromm-Reichmann notes that there is a wide range of variation in the way people respond to being alone. Some people are deeply afraid of being alone, while others find solitude peaceful, so that loneliness must be distinguished from aloneness, which may be necessary for creative work, self-discovery or spiritual enrichment. Winnicott (1958) suggests that one can develop the capacity to be comfortably alone if one has had the childhood experience of being absorbed in play while in the presence of a mother who provides a sense of security; it is then as if her support is built into the developing sense of self, so that she becomes a life-long intra-psychic presence which allows one to be alone contentedly. The ability to tolerate solitude is often a sign of emotional maturity, and such individuals sometimes seek solitude, whereas the lonely person is unhappy about her solitude. For Fromm-Reichmann, the degree of one's dependency on others accounts for one's ability to tolerate being alone. She believes that separation anxiety is a form of loneliness, but separation anxiety produces apprehension and protest, while one can be lonely in a passive way without separation anxiety. Loneliness may produce shame at needing others, so loneliness may be repressed and transformed into a pretense of needing others for some important purpose.

Fromm-Reichmann notes experimental studies of isolation, and situations such as polar exploration and solitary confinement, which show the potential for loneliness to produce disintegration of the personality and psychotic symptoms. She was particularly interested in loneliness in relation to psychosis; she believed that severe loneliness itself could lead to psychosis, and in turn psychosis produces severe loneliness. Delusions of world catastrophe, for example, are expressions of profound loneliness.

One of the common emotional difficulties seen in psychotherapy is the unsatisfied need for connection to others, and much neurotic behavior is the result of a desperate attempt to connect with others. However, loneliness is such a private experience it sometimes goes unrecognized even during a long psychotherapeutic process, so the therapist may need to specifically ask about it. This reticence happens because people may feel ashamed of being lonely, as if being emotionally strong means that one is never lonely. Accordingly, rather than use the word loneliness, the patient may describe it in terms of depression or unhappiness, and partly because loneliness is difficult to recognize and acknowledge, clinicians may also misinterpret it as anxiety or depression.

Therapeutic approaches to loneliness

The treatment of loneliness partly involves the therapist offering his or her presence. It may also be helpful to find connections between the person's present life situation and childhood periods of loneliness, because the person may be unconsciously longing for someone who is now unavailable. At times, working through buried or frozen grief from the past may be helpful in ameliorating present-day loneliness. We may remember an early attachment figure and long for a re-connection with her, but these early objects may also be forgotten, or any hope of re-connection may be lost—the resulting resignation and sadness may be experienced as emptiness rather than loneliness (Greene et al, 1978). When one is lonely due to a loss, one may still have the capacity for connection even if one has given up hope that it will ever happen again, but there are states of emptiness where this capacity feels completely absent. Some complaints of loneliness indicate what the individual needs to work on relationally; for example, the lonely person may need to re-evaluate his insistence that others be absolutely trustworthy before he can relate to them, or he must accept that a degree of uncertainty and the potential for pain exists in all relationships, or that past losses cannot be recovered. Resignation, excessive dependency, indifference to one's own welfare, or apathy must be worked with therapeutically, because these traits all foster loneliness.

The lonely person may be hanging onto substitute gratifications by means of fantasy, which may have been necessary in childhood—this may account for some overuse of video games. Very lonely children may have difficulty separating fantasy from reality and may remain socially isolated throughout life. Loneliness may be the result of psychological structures which alienate the individual from others—such as excessive narcissism, aggression, or extreme competitiveness—in which case the treatment is the treatment of the characterological problem. Social rejection causes loneliness, and lonely people are very sensitive to social cues indicating rejection or acceptance. In the end, because the best remedy for loneliness is the development of satisfying relationships, the therapy has to focus on that dimension. Needless to say this work involves increasing social skills, self-acceptance, self-esteem, and the avoidance of strategies of withdrawal. Animal-assisted therapy may be helpful; the presence of companion animals clearly helps lonely people.

It is important to note that not all loneliness is due to psychological factors. Loneliness may result from a life situation that cannot be changed, such as an incapacitating physical problem that puts others out of reach. In such situations it may be necessary for the person to develop skills that can be used in solitude.

Practicing as a psychotherapist invariably involves a degree of loneliness, because it requires a degree of deprivation of the therapist's own needs combined with the tension produced by the therapeutic frame, especially when the therapist does not feel he or she can respond in an ordinary human way to the patient's demands. Sometimes the patient in a classical psychoanalytic therapy feels alone as a result of the analyst's behavior. However, contemporary relational psychotherapists are more willing to share their own feelings than their classically trained colleagues, who were much more withholding of themselves. To treat a lonely person, the therapist must be able to cope with or at least be very conscious of his or her personal loneliness and fear of loneliness. The loneliness of the therapist may sometimes account for sexual acting out with patients.

Hatred as a cause of suffering

Hatred is an important motivator of evil and of acts of inhumanity towards others. Hatred can be conceptualized in a variety of ways. One approach is to see hatred as a form of rage which has become chronic or hardened, so that it is a stable feature within the personality. Such rage wants to "destroy a bad object, to make it suffer, and to control it" (Kernberg, 1995, p. 64). Hatred can be distinguished from a transient episode of rage in response to frustration or conflict. Although one can experience brief periods of hatred which dissipate, typically rage wants immediate discharge while hatred is a more complex and long lasting affective state which can tolerate delay in the service of revenge. Unlike pure rage, hatred may contain an element of hope that one can make the hated object suffer in the future. Hatred is especially generated if one perceives that one (or someone one loves) is being maltreated sadistically. Frustrated or unrequited love notoriously turns to hatred—which may then coexist with love. When hatred is prolonged, it eventually becomes part of the individual's identity, a phenomenon we see in members of hate groups.

Hatred is sometimes said to be "nursed," usually with obsessive, recurrent memories of the injustice which provoked it, combined with fantasies of taking revenge on the perpetrator. Because of this preoccupation, hatred keeps us tied to the one we hate. Alford (2005, p. 236) suggests that in this way, hatred produces an intrapsychic merger with the hated person which reassures the one who hates that he is not alone, as it produces a temporary loss of self-other boundaries. Alford therefore believes that hatred is a grotesque distortion or imitation of love, but hatred ultimately "corrodes the ego," leaving one empty and depleted. Whereas rage wants to free us from the source of the rage, hatred actually ties the hater to it and sometimes traps the hater. Hatred simplifies the complexity of the hater's relationship with the hated object, by annihilating the object's subjectivity.

Thomas Merton (2007, p. 72) suggests that there is "in every weak, lost and isolated member of the human race an agony of hatred born of his own helplessness, his own isolation." Furthermore: "It is the rankling, tormenting sense of unworthiness that lies at the root of all hate" (p. 74). Merton is concerned that such self-hatred is dangerous because it if it is too deep and powerful to be consciously faced, it makes us project our own evil onto others and unable to see it in our selves.

Intense shame can induce an individual to feel hatred towards the person who has shamed him. Possessed by narcissistic rage and the need for vengeance, the shamed individual wants to induce similarly painful feelings within the object of his hatred. It is also true that shame at one's own behavior can induce self-hatred, which may make self-forgiveness difficult. However, it is an overstatement to say that hatred is *invariably* the result of feelings such as shame, unworthiness, and loneliness, since one may have these feelings without hatred.

Hatred often appears in the form of racism, sexism, homophobia or other forms of bigotry and prejudice. Depth psychologists typically understand these phenomena in terms of the projection onto the target group of some quality of the prejudiced person, some aspect of his unconscious, or a toxic introject. The scapegoated group is usually chosen by the cultural and religious prejudices in which the bigoted person lives. A variety of forms of hatred, such as hatred of the poor or hatred of other religions or races, can be disguised in the form of political and social ideologies. Extremely sadistic forms of punishment for crimes, or extreme forms of moral indignation, may be the result of hatred which has been incorporated into the superego. Such intense hatred has biological, developmental, and social origins. During development, attachment factors such as stranger anxiety, identification with family members, and cultural prejudices play a part in the individual's development of hatred and the resulting prejudice (Parens, 2012). Human beings are biologically wired to attach to others and also to be afraid of strangers; stranger anxiety (which may be an evolutionary residue of predator anxiety) seems to be an early precursor of xenophobia, and hence "plays a key role in the predisposition to prejudice" (ibid., p. 175). However, this kind of prejudice may not take the malignant form of wishing to harm others. Parens believes that ambivalence in the child's primary relationships is "the most central and powerful contributor of the generation in humans of the wish to harm or destroy others" (p. 176). Trauma in childhood, especially when inflicted by a parent, contributes to the development of hostile destructiveness towards others, leading to malignant prejudice or hatred that is actually an unconscious form of revenge at parents. It is very difficult for a child to feel hostility towards a parent it loves and needs, because the child's undeveloped adaptive capacities cannot cope with this combination of feelings, so entrenched defenses develop. The person so affected may defend against his hatred using mechanisms such as depreciation and vilification of those he hates. The situation is worsened by educational influences which socialize the child to identify with group prejudice such as anti-Semitism. The anti-Semitic individual may have never actually met a Jewish person. Unfortunately, hatred which manifests itself as prejudice can be internalized by its victims, damaging the personality by producing shame about oneself. An example is the so-called self-hating Jew. This phenomenon can be a problem for immigrants who feel shame when subject to discrimination, even leading to subtle self-hatred or at least extreme consciousness of being different, sometimes to the extent of hiding their ethnic origins.

Hatred has important defensive functions (Akhtar, 1995); it protects against feelings of vulnerability, helplessness, dependency or fear. Hatred offers meaning and purpose, and it holds the personality together when it might be on the edge of fragmentation, in which case hatred acts like a drug that is difficult to give up. Hatred can be used to defend against painful memories or narcissistic injury, and hatred offers a way of denying one's relational needs. If we can hate the person who has been hurtful, we can avoid feeling some of the distress or humiliation caused by the offense. According to Balint (1952), we hate people who are very important to us but who do not love us despite our best efforts to win their love. We then use hatred as a barrier against our need for these people and our dependence on them; we tell ourselves that although they are important to us, they are bad, and we can do without their love. This helps to explain how love can turn into hatred, and the difficulty of changing hatred back into love. For Balint therefore, hatred is a sign of immaturity. Hatred of another person simplifies the way we think about that person and avoids complexity. Hatred of particular social groups wards off or projects one's own feeling of low self-esteem and allows us to feel superior. However, these defensive uses of hatred have the drawback of alienating others and damaging the individual's capacity for relationships.

Some writers believe that aggression is a fundamental motive in all human relationships, and that hatred becomes destructive only when it is denied; this view suggests that mature love requires the recognition and acceptance of hatred in ourselves and our partners (Goldberg, 1993). Various authors point out that the ability to hate as well as love is important for the healthy personality (Eissler et al., 2000). Gerald Schoenewolf (1991) believes that one cannot practice the art of love unless one has also mastered the art of hating; one cannot have one without the other because they are inextricably bound. Following Winnicott's (1949) paper on hate in the countertransference, Schoenewolf distinguishes between objective and subjective hate. Subjective or destructive hate is based on psychodynamic and social factors in the individual, and it affirms destruction and death. Objective or constructive hate is the result of a situation in the world which can be worked through, and so affirms life. Objective hatred involves telling the truth when it is possible and safe to do so, whereupon it may lead to resolution and genuine communication.

Many people are unable to consciously feel hatred because their parents could not tolerate their aggression, although during development hatred can be an important way to facilitate self-delineation. In infancy, Winnicott (1971) pointed out that the child needs to be able to intrapsychically "destroy" the object and discover that the object survives; a parent must tolerate the child's aggression without retaliating. This allows the child to experience the parent as separate and real. Similarly, the patient's "destruction" of the therapist allows the recognition of the therapist as a separate person. It is therefore important for the therapist to accept the patient's hatred and not avoid it. Hatred may be defended against; it may be denied or repressed because of guilt in ambivalent relationships, for example between parents and children. It is important to recognize that parents may hate their children for many reasons. This hatred may be unconscious, occurring for example because children are a burden or because they restrict their parents' freedom, or for neurotic or sadistic reasons. We see the theme of parent-child hatred in many fairy tales, such as Hansel and Gretel. Winnicott (1949) noted a number of possible reasons that a mother might hate a baby[11]. Envy of children for their health and beauty is an unconscious source of child abuse. It is not uncommon for parents to be unable to tolerate their child's advantages, leading to patterns of child rearing which Miller (1985) referred to as poisonous pedagogy because they suppress the child's subjectivity and autonomy. Hatred may be used to recruit help and support from others, or to attack others or make them feel guilty. However, the expression of hatred may be frightening, so that listening to a stream of hateful invective is often difficult. For this reason, the individual afflicted by hatred may alienate family and friends, who then tend to either encourage suppression of these feelings or they urge the individual to forgive and forget, to move on with his life, and so on. None of this is helpful. The individual often remains stuck in a painful state of mind, finding it increasingly difficult to find people who can bear to listen to his litany of hatred.

Hatred in psychotherapy

To help a person suffering from hatred, it is important to allow the expression of such feelings with as much understanding as possible, so that the individual may eventually grieve whatever happened to him to provoke his hatred. The problem is that for the patient to give up his hatred he has to feel the underlying pain against which the hatred was defending. Not surprisingly, hatred is one of the main obstacles to bonding with others, and like envy

---

11   According to Winnicott, mothers may hate their babies because: the baby is a danger to her body in pregnancy and birth; the baby hurts her by biting her; the baby treats her as a slave and has to be loved unconditionally; the baby's love is "cupboard love"; the baby does not realize her sacrifices for him, and so on. By singing nursery rhymes such as "Rockabye baby, on the tree top," the mother can release pent up hatered without actually hurting the child.

it acts as a major source of difficulty and resistance in psychotherapy. The way the individual expresses or acts out hatred is a function of character structure. Psychopathic hatred is acted out as antisocial behavior towards others, depressives hate themselves, obsessional individuals express hatred through defiance, control, and withholding, narcissistic people hate in fits of narcissistic rage, and so on. For some misanthropic, paranoid people, hatred is a habitual attitude towards the world—they feel cheated by life. Whatever its source, it is crucial for the therapist to provide empathic understanding of the person's hatred without judgment. When the relationship is sufficiently trusting, the therapist might tactfully explore the defensive nature of the hatred and the unmet needs and emotional vulnerability it serves to protect. It helps if the therapist assumes that no matter how much hatred one sees on the surface, somewhere there is a vestigial if unconscious hope for a loving connection to another person.

People who hate others will sometimes turn their hatred towards the therapist. This hatred may be expressed in a variety of ways, such as subtly demeaning remarks, resentment at having to pay a fee, or by means of overt hostility. Hatred in the transference to the therapist has a variety of sources. It may be the result of a classical transference in which feelings the patient had towards early objects are projected onto the therapist, who is seen as sadistic and tyrannical. The therapist may then be provoked to behave in such a manner. Hatred may be the result of a major selfobject failure on the part of the therapist, or by the therapist's insensitive behavior, so that the patient is hurt by something the therapist does. Narcissistic and borderline individuals may hate the therapist because he is not good enough, not sufficiently idealizable, or because an idealizing transference is traumatically disrupted by a therapeutic error made by the therapist. The patient may hate the therapist because of envy, or because of the therapist's defects, especially if these coincide with the patient's own difficulties. Hatred of the therapist may occur because the patient is dependent on the therapist and he hates his dependency. The patient then hates the very thing he needs, and this situation often leads to a poor therapeutic result.

The therapist may hate the patient for a variety of reasons. What Winnicott (1949) calls "objective" hatred is justified by the patient's hateful behavior. Subjective hatred stems from issues within the therapist, for example when the patient reminds the therapist of the therapist's hateful father. Winnicott points out that it is important to sort out which form of hatred the therapist is experiencing; if it is subjective, the therapist has personal work to do; if it is objective it reveals the nature of the relationship, and it may need to be spoken of. The therapist may be feeling the hatred towards the patient that a parent felt towards the patient, or the therapist may be feeling hated the way the patient was hated as a child, and it may be important to be able to tolerate this hatred in the same way that a parent can tolerate a child's hatred.

There are times when the therapist has to turn the other cheek, and times when hatred has to be confronted or interpreted. When hatred is intense, the therapist might need a case consultation. In the presence of a stable therapeutic relationship, countertransference hatred can lead to fruitful discussion if the patient feels safe. It is a mistake to assume that "unconditional positive regard" is always necessary, and it is impossible if the patient is offensive, excessively demanding, intrusive, or chronically negative. Ignoring these kinds of attitudes allows them to escalate, and denial of the therapist's hatred is unhelpful.

Countertransference hatred is a not uncommon cause of impasses in therapy. Maroda (2010) has a very helpful discussion of this issue, and Otto Kernberg (1992) suggests several possible outcomes. The therapist might emotionally withdraw or might view the patient as a victim and so facilitate the directing of the patient's aggression elsewhere. The therapist might masochistically submit to the patient's assault and eventually act out his aggression, or the therapist might oscillate between trying to resolve the patient's hatred therapeutically and emotionally giving up on the patient. Kernberg (1995) suggests that it is important to help the patient become aware of the intensity of his hatred and envy, which may be humiliating, and the therapist must also help the patient to acknowledge the sadistic pleasure provided by acting out hatred and envy. Eventually the patient has to learn to tolerate the guilt derived from the recognition that his attack on the "bad" object therapist "is at the same time an attack on the potentially good and helpful object" (p. 66). Kernberg also believes that behind the hateful patient's relentless attacks on the therapist, there lies an unconscious hope that an ideal good object will eventually emerge. Kernberg suggests that the patient must recognize that his hateful behavior interferes with the gratification of his own deepest wishes, so that depression after the successful working through of hateful transferences is painful but essential.

Self-hatred

The idea that one could hate oneself seems odd, but the phenomenon is very real. Self-hatred has various sources. It commonly occurs when something about the individual, something at the core of the self, is felt to be bad or wrong—perhaps a desire or need, or the person's destructiveness or sexuality. Psychotic people are particularly prone to hatred of the self and its needs because these needs cause pain (Eigen, 1986). In depressed people, self-criticism and self-hatred are often the result of the introjection of hateful caregivers. We also see intense self-hatred among addicts and people with eating disorders. Typically, the individual's self-criticism overrides his awareness of unmet needs, which are often felt to be shameful. When self-hatred is unconscious it may manifest itself in the form of self-mutilation or suicidal behavior.

Another form of self-hatred occurs when one is a member of a persecuted group struggling to live in a dominant culture, especially if reconciliation between one's own culture and the mainstream is difficult. Those who are persecuted sometimes identify with the aggressor and hate themselves—an example would be a Jewish anti-Semite. A variety of theories try to explain this phenomenon. People who suffer from social prejudice against them may develop an unconscious identification with those who hate them, or they may feel they are worthy of being hated. The persecuted person then internalizes his oppressors' opinion of him and this becomes a structural component of a harsh superego. Or, the individual feels unable to advance socially and so resents his origins, or the dominant culture makes him feel chronically inferior and ashamed of himself. Even though homosexuality is more and more socially acceptable, there remain people who are repelled by their own sexual orientation, and closeted homosexual people (some of them politicians) support anti-gay policies—apparently they hate themselves in projection. Self-hatred often leads to the hatred of others for some attribute that one possesses oneself. Self-hatred can be projected onto socially devalued ethnic or religious groups who are objectified, dehumanized, and demonized. Persecuted people tend to become prejudiced themselves.

Social factors conducive to hatred

When it was announced that the people who committed the Sept.11 attacks were fundamentalist Muslims, hatred developed towards Muslims who had nothing to do with the attack, as if people can be guilty by simply being a member of a certain group. There are many similar examples; the Hutu genocide against the Tutsis began immediately after it was announced that the Hutu president of Rwanda was killed by Tutsi rebels—an accusation that was never proved. While some forms of hatred are attributable to the psychodynamic and developmental factors mentioned above, suspicion of other groups may be an inherited evolutionary trait among humans, an aspect of our anxiety about predators which makes us suspicious of the foreign and unknown. (Michener, [2012] provides a review of the psychology of group hate.) When hatred of another group is combined with envy, fear, and the need for revenge following a group trauma such as Sept.11, and these factors are reinforced by government propaganda, hatred towards others is rationalized and seems to be legitimate, which contributes to atrocities and war crimes. Once a government declares a certain nation or group to be the enemy, especially if a war against them begins, people tend to hate that group even if they do not know them, as if they "must deserve" to be hated. Then, mass psychology and the need for group cohesion overwhelm individual judgment.

It is important for the psychologist to be aware of the many social factors that contribute to the development of culturally-approved hatred, such as mob psychology, the maintenance of social stereotypes, and the diffusion of responsibility which allows the expression of hatred when phenomena such as genocide are going on (Harrington, 2004). The importance of obedience to authority and social roles, as exemplified by the Milgram and Zimbardo experiments, are discussed on pages 96 et seq. Another important predictor of social prejudice is authoritarianism. Erich Fromm (1941) suggested that harsh parenting produces adults who are submissive yet also hostile. Theodor Adorno and colleagues (1950) investigated the characteristics of authoritarian personalities, individuals who tend to feel hatred and can incite others to prejudice and discrimination (Altemeyer 1996). These studies indicated that people who score highly on the dimension of authoritarianism tend to be submissive to authority, punitive to unconventional people and minorities, and conventional with regard to religion, sexuality, and social customs. They tend to be ethnocentric, politically conservative, anti-homosexual, anti-feminist, and oriented to law and order. High levels of authoritarianism are associated with a view of the world as a dangerous place.

An alternative way of describing hateful personalities was suggested by Hannah Arendt (2006), who believes that people behave hatefully because they are too weak and thoughtless to resist cultural bigotry and indoctrination. In her view, a major perpetrator of the Holocaust, Adolf Eichmann, was simply following orders according to the current dominant cultural ideology. His evil was not the result of psychopathology or ideological conviction, only personal shallowness; he did not realize what he was doing. However, for many people, Arendt's idea of the banality of evil does not do justice to the enormity of Nazi evil and its complex psychological and social sources. It is more likely that the Nazis knew exactly what they were doing, but they thought what they were doing was right.

Another social style associated with prejudice is described by social dominance theory, which describes social groups which have the greater share of wealth, power, and status. This theory holds that problems such as racism and sexism are natural outgrowths of social hierarchies, which inevitably develop because of the need to justify unequal sharing of resources. Individuals may support social hierarchies because they are within the upper strata of society and wish to justify being there, or because they aspire to attain that level. Racism, sexism, and negative stereotypes are legitimizing myths that justify unequal distribution of wealth, power, and status, and individuals endorse such myths to varying degrees. At the extreme, social dominators think of the world as a competitive jungle in which the strongest reach the top; such individuals oppose social welfare programs and civil rights policies. They view social hierarchies as legitimate and seek to enhance themselves at the expense of others.

There are some differences between authoritarian personalities and social dominators; the latter are self-centered and not particularly religious or dogmatic. They know they are prejudiced. Authoritarians tend to be obedient to authority, religious, dogmatic, fearful, and often unaware they are prejudiced. A small percentage of people combine the most negative characteristics of each group; authoritarian social dominators are willing to lie, cheat, and steal in order to dominate, and are "well positioned to take charge of conservative religious groups or antifeminist, antiabortion, anti-gun-control groups" (Harrington, 2004, p. 67). As a coda to this discussion on hatred, I should mention that religious patients in psychotherapy may find it difficult to admit their hatred; they have an added burden when they hate because they are commanded to be forgiving, but hatred makes forgiveness much more difficult. They may feel guilt or anxiety because of biblical verses such as: "You shall not hate your brother," (Lev. 19:17) or: "Anyone who hates his brother is a murderer" (1 John 3:15).

The suffering of a scapegoat

Innocent people may suffer because they have become scapegoats for the difficulties of others. The scapegoat is an ancient archetypal theme (Perera, 1986).

According to the Hebrew Bible (Lev. 16: 21), in ancient Israel on the Day of Atonement the sins and pollution of the community were ritually transferred onto a goat, which was banished into the desert, thus atoning for these sins and relieving the guilt of the people. (Psychologically speaking, it is as if the problems were sent back into the unconscious; no new consciousness of the shadow is possible in these circumstances.) The goat substitutes for the community, as if God needs this form of reconciliation.

Elsewhere in the Hebrew Bible, a "suffering servant" (Isaiah 52-53) suffers for the sins of others. This theme is found in many cultures; the ancient Greeks used to choose a scapegoat or *pharmakos* who could be stoned and cast out of the community in response to natural disasters such as crop failures.

Similar rituals of substitution are found around the world, sometimes using animals, sometimes objects or human beings for this purpose. During a time of plague, the ancient Hittites placed colored threads on a ram, thus symbolically transferring plague onto the ram which was then driven away (Wright, 1987). The theme of substitution is prominent in the Christian idea that Jesus is sacrificed to atone for the sins of humanity; he is the ultimate innocent scapegoat[12]. This archetypal mechanism seems to depend on the idea that one can transfer certain attributes of oneself, or one's illnesses or impurities, to another creature, who then bears the burden of one's own difficulties. In a discussion of ancient healing rituals, Wright (1987, p. 37) points out that the evil is not just transferred for the purpose of disposal: "It is transferred so that the consequences of the evil will fall on the bearer of impurity instead of the patient."

Human beings like to have explanations when things go wrong, so we often try to find someone we can blame. This paranoid stance is particularly important if we want to avoid personal responsibility or if we are trying to control or make sense of chaos. Scapegoating requires that we split the good from the bad, then project and displace the bad (such as illness or hostility)

---

12   For Christians, Jesus is a moral exemplar of self-giving love, but the psychological problem raised by the crucifixion has been pointed out by feminists who are concerned that the Christian story might glorify child abuse, might promote victimization, or might be used to justify the notion that women should patiently endure abuse (Brown et al,. 1989).

onto another person. The victim becomes a "whipping boy" on whom rage or guilt can be vented when the legitimate target cannot be attacked. The victim so chosen may be totally innocent and may suffer for no reason.

A person or another social group may be blamed for the problems of an entire community, in a way that allows the community to remain self-righteous, maintain a sense of unity, deny any responsibility for its difficulties, and maintain self-esteem and an attitude of moral superiority without the need for self-reflection, producing a fictitious social history. The group may project its own shadow qualities or its internal hostilities towards an outer enemy, or the group may choose one of its own members to scapegoat. Overall, finding a scapegoat distracts attention from the real source of the group's difficulties, but unfortunately increases the likelihood of violence. According to Girard (1997), we find and sacrifice scapegoats to channel our innate human aggression, with the hope that the death of the scapegoat will prevent retribution and increase social cohesion. Oedipus is a classical example of this mechanism since his punishment was necessary to end the plague which was afflicting the city of Thebes because of the killing of King Laius. (Girard's theory of the scapegoat is discussed further on pages 120 et seq.)

Typically, an entire social group is stereotyped and labeled according to the bad behavior of a few individuals who belong to the group, as we see today when Muslims are scapegoated in the USA or Gypsies are targeted all over Europe. Such scapegoats are chosen from outsiders on whom people can project their own failings. The scapegoats are typically underprivileged minorities and those considered deviant in some way—the classical examples are pogroms, the Holocaust, and the medieval witch hunts, but human history is replete with many others. Politicians often scapegoat certain social groups or other nations, in order to deflect blame for their own failures—scapegoating is a social as well as an intrapsychic process.

This mechanism is particularly noticeable in societies with authoritarian leaders who are afraid to lose power in a crisis. People who are imprisoned or silenced for their religious or political beliefs are scapegoats, punished in an attempt to silence dissent or "purify" the society. In a totalitarian state, this is easier than embracing a diversity of opinions. Although the victim may be entirely innocent, at times religious martyrs consciously participate in the scapegoat mechanism. These individuals invite scapegoating by making themselves stand out in some idiosyncratic manner, perhaps by their appearance or, as in the case of the early Christians, by refusing to worship the local gods. Those who scapegoat others by projecting blame are able to feel consciously self-righteous; this mechanism is particularly noticeable among narcissistic personalities who cannot tolerate any form of self-examination or shame. As well as its painful effects on the scapegoat, the mechanism of scapegoating is also deleterious to the one who is projecting his shadow, because doing so prevents the necessary consciousness and integration of the shadow.

The scapegoat complex

In a family, one particular child may become the focus of family difficulties such as conflict between the parents. By blaming the scapegoated child, the apparent cohesion of the family is maintained, and parental guilt or blame is avoided. The child then carries the disowned, projected shadow material of the whole family. The scapegoat's burden is then to struggle with whatever the family is denying or ignoring; this child is psychologically exiled, banished into an emotional wilderness, and blamed for the family misfortunes. Family therapists have long pointed out that by carrying these projections the scapegoated child may serve the function of stabilizing the parents' marriage (Pillari, 1991) and maintaining the stability of the family system (Vogel et al., 1960).

There are several reasons for the choice of the scapegoat; a particular child may seem different or disturbed in some way, or the child may exhibit a trait or behavior which one parent dislikes in the other parent. Or, the child chosen to be the scapegoat reminds the parents of some difficulty of their own which they cannot tolerate, such as a tendency to be overweight. At other times, the parent has a sibling transference to the scapegoated child; a mother who hated or envied her older sister may scapegoat her oldest daughter. This phenomenon may also occur when a child deviates too much from family expectations—for example, when the child is artistically inclined but the family only values athletics. The child is molded into the role of the scapegoat by being constantly viewed and treated as if he is the problem, until he eventually internalizes and acts out the role which becomes part of his identity. He is made to feel guilt and shame and is often regarded as the black sheep of the family. The scapegoat grows up feeling different and "bad" in some way because of the internalization of the family's criticism. The resulting personality damage and low self-esteem lead to a lifetime of suffering.

Dare (1993) points out that such children often become full of rage and hatred. He provides a helpful list of the clinical characteristics of scapegoated children. The parent's complaints about the child are non-stop; they complain that the child is defiant and ungrateful and has been difficult to understand since birth. The psychotherapist might point out that these complaints do not correspond to the child's actual behavior, but the parents insist that the child's good behavior is deceptive because others do not know what the child is really like. Any good qualities in the child are discredited, and there is no sympathy for the child. (It is important to point out however that it is a mistake to assume that emotional problems in a child always results from scapegoating.)

Family therapy can be helpful in trying to shift the focus from a scapegoated child to the family system as a whole, but this often meets considerable resistance, so that many families drop out of therapy when, for example, the focus turns towards the parents' marriage rather than their child. When dealing with an adult who was scapegoated as a child, it helps if the scapegoat story is recognized and discussed in psychotherapy, in order to allow the person to loosen her identification with the role of scapegoat and stop carrying what is not really her burden. A particular countertransference difficulty arises if the therapist was himself a scapegoat. This often leads to a tendency to blame parents for everything that ails the person, based on the stereotyped idea that family issues (mothers in particular) are responsible for all our ills. The therapist has to bear in mind that childhood often presents many difficulties for children that have little or nothing to do with parents. I hardly need to mention problems at school due to difficulties learning specific subjects or the pain of unpopularity and the cruelty of other children. Moving house, losses, and other traumas and ambiguities are often unavoidable. Parents may be loving, supportive, and nurturing to the best of their ability, yet their children become inexplicably unhappy or even self-destructive because of influences over which parents have no control. Sometimes the child simply misinterprets what is going on in the family. Developmental psychologists sometimes try to counter excessive parent-blaming by pointing out the importance of genes. Shyness, for example, is said to have a large genetic component. Given all this, the psychotherapist has to search for the patient's emotional truth with no possibility of objectively knowing what a person's childhood was "really" like.

Scapegoating is seen in group psychotherapy when the members collude to focus negative attention towards one member who seems to be vulnerable or self-depreciating, or who seems to personify the group's struggle, or who deviates from a group norm. Typically this is a role which was originally played by the scapegoated group member in his or her family of origin. When this dynamic remains unconscious, and the individual identifies with this role, he may behave in such a way as to incite the scapegoat complex, passively allowing himself to become a victim of the group's projections. The result may look as if it is the result of masochism or self-hatred.

Suffering due to poverty

Nearly half the world's population lives in absolute poverty, surviving on less than $2.50 per day (*www.globalissues.org*). In the USA, at least 15% of the population lives below the federal poverty line, and the numbers are rising (DeNavas-Walt, 2011). Some of the detrimental effects of poverty on life-satisfaction are offset if the individual has social support and good relationships with others, but nevertheless poverty causes enormous suffering, frustration, helplessness, humiliation, feelings of inferiority, and the sense that one is powerless and has no control over one's life. The health-related and educational consequences of poverty, food and housing insecurity, and the risk of exposure to violence and family disruption add to the suffering of the poor. Poverty is known to be associated with an increased risk for both physical and psychological illness because of the stress it causes. In turn, serious mental illness increases the likelihood of becoming poor. Contributing to the problem is the social perception that being poor is somehow related to personal inadequacy, so that poor people may be stigmatized and disrespected.

Psychotherapists have tended to exclude poor people from their practice, and until recently the poor have not received culturally sensitive care. Fortunately there are now increasing calls for more attention to the effects of social class in the field of psychotherapy (Appio, 2013). Many poor people do not receive mental health treatment for obvious pragmatic and logistical reasons, but when it is available, several types of psychotherapy have been shown to be helpful (Santiago, 2013). The psychotherapist working with the poor has to be conscious of the stressors and social difficulties faced by the poor which exacerbate the individual's psychological issues. These factors are often ignored in training programs.

In the past, poor people were viewed as less able to engage in psychotherapy for reasons that were considered to be purely psychological, applying middle-class stereotypes of mental health and ego strength, without taking into account the monumental practical difficulties faced by the poor. Problems of transportation, childcare, and the need for flexible scheduling because of work commitments are all important when working with this population. By taking into account these difficulties in the overall context of the person's life, the therapist's credibility and the therapeutic alliance are enhanced (Grote, 2009). However, many psychotherapists are not "class competent"; they avoid directly exploring the patient's socio-economic situation because doing so makes the therapist uncomfortable. The psychotherapist's consciousness of his own social class, his lack of knowledge of the psychosocial consequences of poverty, his assumptions about poverty, his fear of poverty, or shame about his own privilege, may all affect the countertransference. The therapist may unconsciously assume that middle-class values and world-views apply to a poor patient, and may thereby replicate in his practice the kind of "classism" found in society. The poor are sensitive to being treated respectfully, and they may be prone to shame about their situation. It is important for the psychotherapist to not re-create the power dynamic they suffer from in the larger society. The poor may withhold certain details of their life because they fear that the therapist could not possibly understand. It is important to attend to the patient's strengths and ability to cope with poverty, which offsets shame. Obviously, talking alone will not deal with many of the poor person's difficulties, and an exclusive focus on psychological factors risks making the patient feel as if he is responsible for his poverty, thus worsening his self-esteem. Some psychotherapists who work with the poor incorporate advocacy into their practice, helping them to obtain necessary resources and benefits from local and government agencies, but this is controversial since it is not the usual role of the therapist. Nevertheless, it may be impossible to maintain a traditional psychotherapeutic frame if a disadvantaged patient needs help with concrete necessities such as food stamps.

Some people have a "poverty consciousness"; they feel poor even when they are actually financially comfortable, because of the lasting effects of childhood deprivation that render the person unable to trust the reality of his or her current situation, leading to a reluctance to obtain goods that they can indeed afford.

At the other extreme, many people have a craving to possess much more than they actually need, to the extent that greed for money can be thought of as an addictive process. It is a truism that one can be wealthy but unhappy, whereas one can be completely content in average economic circumstances if one's real needs are met—needs such as relationships, political freedom, satisfying work, and adequate food, shelter, and clothing. It is now well understood that material objects, wealth, and status are often only stand-ins for psychological needs—the achievement of material success may be a consolation prize for the lack of significant relationships and for a sense that one's life is meaningless. One may feel internally empty and try to fill the void with possessions, food, sex, religion, or any other intense preoccupation which distracts one from one's emotional state.

For emotionally vulnerable people, the accumulation of possessions or money far beyond what is needed has the value of supporting a fragile sense of self, or of shoring up shaky self-esteem. The drive to keep accumulating on the outside is then a symptom of internal insufficiency, the need to prove to oneself that one is worthwhile. In emotionally healthy people, the accumulation of wealth resulting from well-deployed creative talents does not have the desperate quality found in more fragile personalities. When such individuals are in psychotherapy they do not give the therapist the sense that their wealth is being used to prevent fragmentation anxiety.

The suffering produced by desire

Desire may produce considerable suffering, not only when it is unsatisfied but even at times when it is satisfied. Desire can be seen through various lenses, sometimes disparagingly in certain religious traditions, sometimes with approval. From one point of view, desire is problematic, the result of a sense of incompleteness or emptiness. Alternatively, desire is seen as intrinsically good, an expression of the energy of life or of the vitality of the body. Desire lies on a spectrum from simply wanting a particular object to a complex emotional state such as a yearning for someone to meet an important selfobject need. Desire refers to a state of mind in which there is something we do not have but we which we wish for, sometimes with overwhelming intensity and sometimes merely as a preference. Perhaps we once enjoyed something we now desire again, or we imagine we would enjoy what we desire if only we had it, so that the imagination is a potent source of desire. Desire is a motivating force within the personality, sometimes unconsciously driving behavior or giving us reasons for actions, choices, and goals to which we aim. Interestingly, we may have desires which we wish we did not have. The nature of a person's desire tells us a great deal about that person, and the same is true for the desires of a culture; in our consumer society, much socially constructed desire is driven and shaped by advertising. This type of desire stimulates dissatisfaction because it is ultimately insatiable, and it is geared towards making us desire things we may not really need. However, these artificial desires are often experienced as if they are needs, because advertising links consumer products with authentic needs such as love and happiness. In contrast to consumer-driven desire, natural human desire is the result of both our biology and psychological processes such as attachment. We desire to be desired by another person. We desire love, recognition, and mirroring of our emotional needs, and some psychoanalysts believe we never forgo a desire for the unattainable mother of infancy. While some desire is rational and understandable, some desire is the result of conditioning, purely for the sake of pleasure or to avoid discomfort. Other kinds of desire are quite individual, such as the desire for knowledge or power, or to hear particular music and read certain literature.

It may be difficult to draw the line between need, wish, appetite, and desire. Desire may act as an incentive to fulfill real needs. "Need" seems somehow intrinsic to being human, something which is necessary for survival, such as food and water. These needs are easier to satisfy than more complex desire. Furthermore, it is impossible to ignore our biological needs for long, but one can repress or suppress desire. Unlike needs, wishes are much more based on personal experience than are biological needs, and wishes change but fundamental needs do not.

While desire can be life-affirming and enlivening, it is common for the psychotherapist to hear frustrated desire in the form of the pain of unrequited love, unfulfilled ambition, and other types of unrealized desire which can dominate or even ruin a person's life. We also see the disappointing result of desire that has been met, only for the individual to discover either that he does not really want what he has achieved, or that the satisfaction it brings is fleeting. What he desired was a mirage. This is why George Bernard Shaw (1930, p. 171) said that: "There are two tragedies in life. One is to lose your heart's desire. The other is to gain it." It is also true that we may already have what we deeply desire and not realize it. Because of our ambivalence about desire, there is a long-standing philosophical debate about whether desire is a good thing or not; would it be better to have no desires and live a life of equanimity? Is it better to control our desires or try to satisfy them? Plato (*Theaetetus*) asks whether something is good because I want it or I whether I want it because it's good. Since then, some (subjectivist) theorists suggest that human happiness depends on our obtaining what we desire, while other (objectivist) theorists believe that there are values that are objectively good for us to have, such as knowledge, friendship, love, and freedom, whether or not we consciously desire those things (Parfit, 1984).

Desire seems to arise spontaneously, sometimes for no obvious reason, and it may seem to be totally irrational, as if we have no idea why we desire what we desire. Desire may be triggered from the outside by something we perceive, or it may arise as an internal prompting—perhaps the result of a body sensation or an image or memory which arises in the mind. Then, the image and its associated desire arise simultaneously as components of a single process. Depth psychologists since Freud have pointed out that some desires are unconscious; when they emerge fully formed into consciousness, we may give them a rational explanation and perhaps justify them defensively. Desire may also remain unconscious but still drive behavior; such unconscious desire may only become conscious during psychotherapy, often as a component of the transference.

Some of the sources of our desires are unconscious, so we are unable to articulate why we desire them. For example, the desire to become rich and famous may have a variety of roots; it may be the result of grandiosity, a way of coping with a sense of inadequacy, a need to prove one's worth, or result from a need to feel safe. The intense desire for worldly success may feel like a way to hold together a fragile sense of self.

Some desires conflict with each other, especially when reason and emotion are at odds; I'd like to overeat and also be thin, or I'd like to drink wine and be able to drive home, but my reason restrains me. The western tradition has long depicted this kind of tension between reason and desire, and for the most part reason has been preferred, so that desire based on emotion has often been devalued, especially among religious thinkers, as if reason has to keep desire in check. This devaluing of desire and emotions in general, rather than according them equal status with reason or thought, seems to be partly a function of the temperament of these writers, who were thinking types in Jung's (or the Myers-Briggs) typology.

Typology has much to do with whether one's emotions or one's reason is in charge of behavior; the turbulent emotional life of the undeveloped thinking type is well known. The caveat here has been provided by recent research which suggests that our emotional life plays an important part in making what seem to be purely rational decisions (Damasio, 1994), or cognition and emotion occur together. We see a clear relationship between desire and our emotional state in depressed people who lose all interest in desire. Desire has cultural as well as personal manifestations; most religious systems and mythologies describe the desire for some kind of paradise— a Utopia or a heavenly realm where everything is perfect. Mythological images of heaven tend to compensate for the needs of the specific culture in which they arise; it is not hard to see the Garden of Eden as a place that a Bronze Age farmer would imagine as perfect. Depth psychologists might find the desire for heaven in various sources. One reflects our psychological need for wholeness. Another is the need to believe in survival after death; when all the inequities of life on earth will be rectified, we will meet departed loved ones, and good behavior will be rewarded. Yet another source for the idea of heaven might be the experience of early infantile or uterine bliss, a time of containment and safety. This experience lives on inside us as an aching nostalgia,[13] projected into the mythological idea of a lost paradise from which we have separated (Jacoby, 2006).

We reject some desires even as we feel them, because we regard them as wrong. Addictive desires for food, drugs, and alcohol may be a way of filling a painful feeling of emptiness in the sense of self, or an "empty depression," so that a psychological lack is experienced as a desperate need for something from the outside. This kind of desire seems to be qualitatively different from the desire emerging from an intact sense of self, which is felt as a creative force or power, an expression of the energy of life and of our need for connection to others. An addictive desire is unlike other desires, because most desire is for something that seems good to us, but we wish we did not have addictive desire; in some ways we see it as alien, not really me. Here we see the complexity of desire, which may lie anywhere on the spectrum from selfish greed or lustful sexuality to the desire to selflessly serve others.

Biologically based desire is natural, but it becomes problematic if this desire conflicts with reality, or when the desire overtakes our ability to choose, so that we act out the desire without regard for the consequences. The ability to control desire often seems to correlate with the ability to tolerate painful affect, so psychotherapy directed towards improving affect tolerance helps to restrain problematic desire. Desire is also a problem when it produces conflict with the desires of other people, or simply if it keeps us from feeling at ease, which is why the ancient Stoic philosophers regarded desire as futile. An

---

13   Originally, the word nostalgia referred to homesickness—from the Greek *nostos*, or homecoming, and *algos*, or pain. Eventually this word came to mean a painful yearning for the past.

example of this futility is the Sufi teaching story of Nasruddin, who surprised his friends when they found him eating one hot pepper after another while tears streamed down his face. When they asked him why he kept eating peppers that caused him discomfort, he replied that he was looking for a sweet one—the point being that desire never gives up and never learns, even if it only produces suffering.

Any discussion of the biology of desire leads to the question of the extent to which our desires are the product of our evolution. The traditional view of the evolution and structure of the brain goes back to the work of Paul McLean in the 1960's, which divided the brain into three parts or levels, each of which plays a part in human desire. The oldest or reptilian brain is the seat of instinct and biologically-driven behavior, which is repetitive, hard to change, and necessary for self-preservation. The limbic system evolved next, along with a crude memory system and the ability to generate desire based on emotion, drives, and reward/punishment systems. The limbic system is connected to the cerebral cortex, which allows desire based on conscious thought, together with some control over the more primitive levels of the brain. This model now seems oversimplified[14] but some neuroscientists believe it is still a useful way of organizing our thinking about the brain.

Presumably, certain desires evolved because they increased the organism's ability to survive. However, for many of us, the idea that evolution or genetics alone can explain complex human desire (or any other behavior) is an oversimplified form of physicalism.[15] Human beings radically transform their biology, and our more abstract human desires, such as those for knowledge, beauty, art, and spiritual development, are unique and not necessarily traceable to evolutionary pressures. Furthermore, just because animals and humans have similar behavior, such as aggression, does not mean the explanation for the behavior is the same in both cases. To explain complex human desire only in terms of evolution ignores the complexity of both our brains and human culture—for example, the politics of war and the preparation for war are far more complex than aggression in animals, and it is hard to compare gourmet cooking to animals eating their prey. A human being is not the same as his or her brain; our brains were shaped by evolution, but our desires also have other sources. (For more on neuroscience,

---

14   This is partly because the brain is so networked and interconnected that brain activity tends to involve all levels of the brain simultaneously, even if one level dominates.

15   Physicalism is the doctrine that every phenomenon has to be explained in observable, physical, spatio-temporal terms.

evolution, and human consciousness see Tallis, 2012.) Humans—and our desires—are more than our brains, genes, and the effects of natural selection, and if we are to do justice to our patients, psychotherapists must be cautious about partial explanations of human complexity.

Approaches to the suffering produced by desire

a) Psychotherapeutic approaches

Even if we understand the basis of desire in terms of human biology and its evolutionary past, by itself this knowledge does not help the therapist working with undesirable or uncontrollable desires—whether they belong to the patient or to the therapist. The therapeutic task in the face of desire which produces suffering can be thought of in terms of developing the self-structures necessary to contain the emotional pressure of the desire without acting on it. In order to help the patient with intense desire which is producing shame or other forms of emotional pain, the therapist has to help with the intense affective arousal associated with desire. A primary function of psychotherapy is to help in the integration of potentially unmanageable emotional states so they do not flood the person and threaten fragmentation of the self. When the patient is experiencing affect that is overwhelmingly intense, affect regulation is facilitated by the therapist's responsiveness when it has a holding, containing, and soothing quality. Accurate empathic attunement is crucial for this purpose. The dyadic regulation of affect in psychotherapy also requires being open and engaged without withdrawal or retaliation. At times this may mean giving painful but authentic feedback about the way in which the patient is affecting the therapist. It also helps to "mentalize" the affect produced by desire, to develop clarity about the desire, reflect on its meaning for the person, and better understand its origins.

Within dynamic psychotherapy, desire has evolved from being thought of as purely sexual to being object related and relational. One of the most difficult forms of desire is found in narcissistic character disorders who desperately desire the admiration of others, or who constantly desire more power, more money, more status, and so on. These desires, which are used to sustain and buttress a fragile sense of self, are impossible to fully satisfy because even when satisfaction seems to have been attained, new dissatisfaction and desire invariably arise. In such a case, therapeutic work involves strengthening the self so that outside approbation and success are less necessary.

b) Spiritual and religious approaches to desire

If the therapist is working with someone committed to a particular religion, it is worth being aware of the attitudes to desire in the patient's tradition. Some traditions condemn desire, while most traditions recommend the control or channeling of desire, and offer practices and rules for this purpose.

Buddhist philosophers distinguish between problematic forms of desire, such as an addiction, and wholesome desire, such as the desire for enlightenment. They point out that desire can never be permanently satisfied. Everything we desire will eventually pass away, because reality is impermanent, so in the end our desire will inevitably cause suffering[16].

When we are driven by insatiable desire which cannot be satisfied, in Buddhist terminology we become "hungry ghosts," tormented by craving, searching for the impossible. Buddhists believe that to transform desire we have to change the way we see the world; we need to work on our mistaken view of reality and change our relationship to desire rather than constantly try to fulfill it. In this view, the problem is our belief that things inherently exist, or exist concretely. In fact, "things" are always composites, the coming together of many factors without which the thing would not exist—to exist is to be dependent on an infinite number of causes and conditions. Buddhist psychology suggests that unwholesome desires can be opposed by generating the opposite, wholesome desire; if we wish to attack someone, we can counter this by generating generous thoughts towards that person. Sexual desire for an attractive person can be opposed by thinking of the unattractive parts of the body, a process which is said to extinguish sexual desire by producing indifference to the body. Or, one can imagine the body decomposing after death. By understanding the nature of desire and by investigating it with attention, desire diminishes by itself. According to this tradition, meditation and mindful awareness of the present moment are also valuable antidotes. However, a great deal of practice is necessary for desire to diminish using this approach.

Krishnamurti's attitude to desire is similar to that of the Buddhists. He (1981, 1954) points out that there is a sequence of phenomena which condition the mind and produces desire; we perceive something which produces a pleasant sensation and images, whereupon thought takes over and transforms

---

16   Perhaps this is why in western literature there is sometimes an association between desire and death, such as in Shakespeare's line from Sonnet 147, "Desire is death," meaning that when desire is impossible to fulfill, it is so painful we would prefer death.

them into desire and wanting. Desire then becomes urgent and incessantly demands fulfillment, breeding frustration, conflict, and fear of not obtaining what we want. At the same time, desire strengthens the idea of "me," which for him is the source of suffering. He points out that it is futile to suppress desire, which is actually a precious possession, part of the eternal flame of life, but it must be understood properly or it becomes tyrannical. It is possible to perceive something of beauty without wanting it. The problem for him is therefore not to try to get rid of desire but to leave it alone and understand the way it works—an approach to desire based on rationality.

Judaism, Islam, and Christianity believe that it is worth denying oneself forbidden desire in order to attain one's reward for good behavior in heaven—although there is considerable disagreement about what heaven will be like. In general, Christians believe that desire is ultimately good if it is directed correctly, if human desire is in accord with God's desires for us. The core of desire is the longing for God, and our deepest desire is satisfied in our relationship to God and in serving others in love. Christianity and Judaism are committed to the Ten Commandments, which list forbidden desire, such as to covet (illicitly desire) one's neighbor's wife or possessions. Desires such as greed and lust are also frowned upon in these traditions. The usual recommendation when faced with these kinds of temptations is to pray for the necessary strength to resist them. Community pressure may also help.

There is a long tradition of Christian asceticism, which tries to deny the desires of the body for the sake of the improvement of the soul. Sometimes the regulation of desire involves segregation of the sexes, for instance in orthodox synagogues where women and men are separated and women's voices are not heard.

For some religious writers, desire is seen as somehow antithetical to the spiritual life, or it is only acceptable if it is carefully channeled or directed towards God. C.S. Lewis (1952) believed that the desire for God suggests that God exists, because we would not be born with desires unless some kind of satisfaction of these desires exists. In his words: "If I find in myself a desire, which no experience in this world can satisfy, the most probable explanation is that I was made for another world...Probably earthly pleasures were never meant to satisfy it, but only to arouse it, to suggest the real thing" (p. 136). This is an unconvincing argument, since we may desire something subjectively which does not exist objectively. However it is true that the desire for God, or the desire for wholeness, produce an intense yearning that leads people towards a spiritual path or a path of self-exploration. Longing is a feeling of incompleteness which we try to satisfy in many ways, but the mystics believe that the source of all longing is the soul's longing for connection to the Absolute (Zweig, 2008). In this view, even the search for a human partner is really a spiritual quest for the Beloved, or all desire is actually desire for the divine. In Simone Weil's (1943) Statement of Human Obligation, she suggests that "at the center of the human heart is the longing for an absolute good, a longing which is always there and is never appeased by any object in this world." Theologians often say that such desire for God is natural, and this desire is reflected in innumerable mythological images which depict a variety of forms of human union with the divine, such as the Eros and Psyche myth or the story of Krishna and the Gopis. However, even if it is true that union with the divine is our real desire, most people are not conscious of that wish, and many would reject the idea, so in the presence of long-standing loneliness which has produced bitterness or despair, a spiritual explanation of this kind may not be much help in the psychotherapeutic setting.

Grief

There is an element or core of grief in most forms of suffering. Grief is therefore a prototypical form of suffering which illustrates many of its aspects. Like suffering in general, grief may be psychologically crippling and life-altering, or it can be transformative in positive ways.

Grief at the loss of a loved one produces intense anguish. It is important not to underestimate the degree of upheaval which occurs in the bereaved person's life. Especially when one's relationship with the deceased was relatively unambivalent, such a loss feels as if one has lost a part of oneself. The bereaved feels a combination of sadness, irritability, insomnia, preoccupation with and yearning for the lost person, and intrusive memories and images of the deceased. The shock at a death is of course much worse if the death is unexpected, violent, or apparently senseless. The bereaved person has no idea how long these feelings will last, or if they will ever improve. The bereaved is plunged into liminality (discussed further in chapter 9.)

Until a severe loss occurs, it is as if we have walked through the world unaware of one of its harsh realities. Up to the time of the loss, the world seems to be predictable and we seem to be in charge of our lives. Then the unimaginable happens. The world may seem to have become unreal, meaningless or irrelevant for the bereaved; all our vulnerabilities are exposed, and any sense or faith that we live in an ordered, safe cosmos may be shaken. The bereaved person often feels like the passive victim of fate. Sometimes the death of a loved one is additionally terrifying because it brings up the survivor's own death anxiety. When the lost love was an important selfobject, who helped the survivor to feel cohesive, the survivor may feel unglued, as if he has also died, or at least is disconnected from himself. When a loss has seriously fragmented the bereaved person's sense of self, it may be impossible to grieve until new selfobject relationships have been formed and the sense of self is becoming firmer.

Many people are surprised by the intensity of their emotional reaction to a serious loss. Some of these reactions, such as the insatiable need to search for the loved one even though we know he or she is dead, seem to make no sense. Often the bereaved experiences compulsive mental images and memories of the deceased, which although painful also seem to have a sustaining effect. It is important to be able to talk about these experiences, but they are sometimes not welcomed by others. The emotional turbulence may be so great that the bereaved may need reassurance that he or she is not going insane (Parkes, 1987).

Grieving is a work, a process, an active response to loss which may require that we change the pattern of our life in response to the loss. Habits and routines change and we have to re-learn how to be in the world. Dreams for the future may be lost; life's coherence is lost. Ginette Paris (2011) points out that grief, abandonment, and heartbreak can produce the neurobiological equivalent of traumatic shock. These experiences are hazardous to the sufferer's health, and their physical and emotional sequelae can be serious. Paris points out that, fortunately, psychotherapeutic work can modify the neurological circuits which are involved in the experience of the trauma produced by grief—these circuits cannot be healed solely with medications such as antidepressants. She points out that unless the necessary psychological work is done, one might respond to grief with bitterness, anger, and an inability ever to love again.

The spiritual traditions can offer help to the bereaved, but here an important caution is necessary; it does not help to offer spiritual consolation at the wrong time—I refer to beliefs that the deceased is in heaven, and so on. Whether or not these statements are true is not the point; if offered at an inopportune moment they can be maddening. Traditional consolations about death and the continuance of the soul may simply sound like platitudes, or they may feel to the bereaved like an attempt to avoid pain—a form of spiritual by-passing.[17] There is also a danger that suffering and grief may be suppressed or repressed in the service of dogma and doctrine. In some churches, too much light is preached; God is said to comfort the sufferer, but in practice this comfort may not be felt. Although for Christians suffering is seen as necessary because it is part of the life of Christ, the resurrection is often seen as more important. It is rarely acknowledged that those who witnessed the crucifixion were in abject despair because they did not know that the resurrection was about to happen. Transpersonal psychologists have recognized grief as an opportunity to experience realms of consciousness beyond the ego. These levels may suddenly erupt, as we hear from psychotherapist Miriam Greenspan (2004) after the death of her baby:

> Time stood still and the world fell silent. I was drawn into a vortex, and the self I knew was irreversibly shattered. What happened next: an energy larger than my body could contain broke through in a rush of strange, unfathomable syllables... What came through me, as I stood and wrapped my arms around my dead baby, was a form of speech emanating from a source deeper than personality. Though utterly indecipherable, these strange sounds were a kind of prayer. (pp. 90–91)

Needless to say, the skeptical therapist, one who does not have a spiritual orientation, would see such a reaction as a purely psychogenic response to severe grief, perhaps dissociative. I prefer to suggest that this mother's grief reduced the hegemony of her ego, allowing a transpersonal dimension to irrupt into her consciousness, and this dimension manifested itself in the form of unknown, automatic speech. One's attitude to such an experience depends on one's metaphysical commitments, or the lack of them. In order to work authentically with grieving people, the psychotherapist needs to be aware of his or her personal beliefs about phenomena such as death-bed visions[18] and the question of life after death, and be willing to share these beliefs during therapy. One does not have to have answers, but one has to be real when expressing one's views. For spiritually oriented

---

17   Spiritual bypassing refers to the use of a spiritual practice or teaching to avoid a psychological issue.

18   Death-bed visions, such as those of an after-life or spirit visitors or deceased relatives, are occasionally reported by people on the brink of death. These visions can be very comforting to the dying person and his or her family. The debate about these experiences concerns whether they are authentic, hallucinatory, or the result of physical changes in the brain. They are sometimes shared by others at the dying person's bedside.

people, acceptance of the suffering produced by grief means acceptance of the inscrutable design that reveals itself through life. Acceptance (discussed further in chapter 10) includes the need to grieve without any suppression or hiding of our feelings, but without fighting the inevitable.

Like any form of suffering, the effects of grief on the personality may be either positive or negative. Negatively, grief may produce impaired physical and mental health and disturbed functioning in all areas of life. On the positive side, grief offers the potential for developing increased compassion for others, teaches humility, and forces one to participate in the suffering of the world. Grief empties a space within oneself in a way that can allow one to open empathically to the suffering of others and expand one's capacity for love. Grief teaches courage and the value of each moment. Grief allows us to take back projections onto the lost loved one and see who they really were. However, these are long-term effects; none of this is much help during the process of active bereavement, especially if the bereaved person suffers from a paralyzing desire for the loved one to return. Often, the bereaved person continues a psychological relationship with the deceased, including the continuation of lifelong love—a need which contravenes some traditional advice about letting go of emotional ties to the deceased (so called decathexis), which is often impossible. As Attig (2000) pointed out, there is nothing morbid about the desire for lasting love for a person from whom we are separated. All loving relationships include separation, and one can love without physical presence—the lost person remains as an internal presence, and may continue to influence one's behavior. It is possible to develop new emotional investments at the same time as we grieve a loss, unless the lost person is experienced as irreplaceable, in which case despair may occur. Part of the legacy of the dead is the love they felt for us and their continuing influence on our lives, which we feel in our hearts and memories. This fulfills the desire of the dead who wanted to make a lasting difference in our lives.

One of the most painful aspects of grief is a sense of isolation, the awareness that people may have no idea how the bereaved person feels; others look at the bereaved as if he or she was the same person as he or she was before the loss, without seeing the empty center. The bereaved may feel obliged to behave a certain way, because societies usually have expectations about the ways in which grief may be expressed. In some cultures, public expression of grief is socially desirable, and intense weeping and wailing are expected, but in others there is a tendency to discourage the expression of intense emotion. In our culture, after the funeral and memorial service are over, the bereaved are expected to cope with their feelings without much help, so they are often lonely. The bereaved person's social network often finds prolonged grief difficult to tolerate, adding to the individual's sense of isolation. Too much mourning, or mourning that goes on for too long or which is too visible, is seen to be self-indulgent or weak rather than a psychological imperative. However, grief that is repressed is harmful, and may show itself as somatic illness, as we see in the case of the biblical Job, who denied his rage and grief at the loss of his children and as a result broke out in sores all over his body. Depression or numbness often result from an incomplete mourning process. Grief is characterized by conscious awareness of what we have lost, whereas depression tends to occur when we deny the reality of what we have lost, in which case the therapeutic task is to allow the bereaved to experience realistic grief and normal sadness.

Part of the importance of grief is its capacity to make us look at the meaning of death. Terror management theorists have explained the human search for meaning in terms of mortality salience, or the awareness of the inevitability of one's own death. Working with the bereaved may force the therapist to face his or her personal death anxiety.

Psychotherapy of grief

It is often difficult to grieve alone; grieving is facilitated if carried out within a relationship with another person who can listen, contain, and mirror the bereaved person's feelings. The psychotherapist therefore has to allow the bereaved to talk freely about the loss, and support the expression of emotion, without offering premature consolation. Sometimes the therapist will also help to explore the individual's choices about what to do next, and work with other difficulties produced by the loss such as a blow to the survivor's self-confidence. New meaning in life may have to be found, and sometimes a new spirituality. Unfinished business with the deceased may need to be addressed, especially if it involves anger or guilt or other hurtful aspects of the relationship. On reflection with the psychotherapist, old relational difficulties with the deceased may be viewed in a new light and re-interpreted. Needless to say, the psychotherapist will note the bereaved person's capacity for going on with life as this question arises—the issue of suicide may be in the background after a serious loss. Some of the least helpful things to do are to suggest ways to control the grief or to encourage the bereaved to "focus on the future" and similar platitudes, which indicate that the helper feels helpless and cannot tolerate the pain of the bereaved. The instinct to comfort is powerful but impotent in the face of death, and we tend to defend against helplessness by giving advice or insisting on a specific type of grieving response that seems "normal" or "uncomplicated." When the bereaved is inconsolable, the therapist is only able to mirror the patient's feeling of helplessness, but doing so is helpful. Sometimes the best treatment is the therapist's willingness to witness grief without any expectation that witnessing will help. (On the importance of the witness, see p. 173 et seq.)

A useful therapeutic approach is the grief narrative, the development of a story about the deceased person, which is helpful in dealing with grief and communicating it to others (Klugman, 2007). The psychotherapist encourages the bereaved person to tell stories about what the deceased person was like, what kind of relationship they had, how the individual died, and how the death affected the survivor. This process may reveal aspects of the mourner's relationship with the deceased that are surprisingly new—a kind of de-repression occurs in the act of telling these stories, and new levels of meaning may emerge. Listening to such stories often has a profound effect on the therapist as well as the mourner, and seems to deepen the therapeutic connection. (The overall importance of narrative and story discussed in chapters 8 and 5.)

Dreams about the dead person may be important to the survivor; these dreams are comforting when the deceased seems to be well and happy in the dream. Such dreams may lead to a therapeutic discussion about whether the dream is a visit from the soul of the dead person, when the patient's belief system allows for such a possibility. Otherwise, the dream can be understood on a purely psychological level, commenting on the relationship between the dreamer and the deceased. Many widows and widowers report waking visions of the deceased which are felt to be helpful. Others experience after-death communications such as a sense of presence, touch, or fragrance associated with the deceased, which can be interpreted either as a real visit or as a hallucination, again depending on one's metaphysical commitments. When they are considered to be real these experiences can be very comforting.

When the relationship with the deceased was ambivalent, hostile, or guilt-ridden, a complicated grief reaction may ensue (these are estimated to occur in about 20% of bereaved people), but it is not clear exactly how complicated grief differs from normal grief reactions, other than to say that complicated grief is of greater intensity and lasts longer than normal grief. Sometimes people with complicated grief avoid thoughts and feelings associated with the deceased or complain of numbness and disbelief about the loss. Some clinicians believe that complicated grief is indistinguishable from depression, especially if despair or somatic symptoms such as fatigue are present, but I believe they can be distinguished based on the predominance of either typical grief phenomena or depressive symptoms. This distinction is important because grief *per se* does not respond to antidepressants. It may be hard to discern the dynamics which are maintaining a prolonged state of grief (Howarth 2011), particularly when these dynamics are unconscious, for example if there has been a highly ambivalent relationship with the deceased, or one which was very dependent or hostile, or if the survivor is guilty about the way the deceased died. Some people experience complicated grief when they are caught between a need to release the dead person and a need to restore him. This impasse may lead to an insoluble entrapment. Particularly intense grief may occur because the immediate loss is activating grief from earlier losses in the person's life, so the psychotherapist is actually seeing the cumulative effect of multiple losses.

At times the therapist has to help someone grieve a life goal that has become unattainable, either because of external circumstances, aging or infirmity. Commitment to an impossible goal is a potent source of suffering and drains emotional resources, whereas if one can let go of such a goal subjective well-being improves. Nevertheless, at times people persist in trying to attain the impossible—a phenomenon leading to psychological entrapment in a painful situation. One example is to stay in an abusive marriage in the hope that it will get better. We see the same phenomenon when politicians maintain or escalate an impossible war, and in the gambler who cannot give up gambling. In such situations, negative feedback does not seem to make a difference. Needless to say, the psychotherapist's problem working with such an individual is to discern whether the person must let go and grieve the loss of a hoped-for goal, or whether yet more effort may actually lead to success. People may pursue a failing course of action when they cannot admit to themselves that starting the action was a mistake—they need to justify themselves at all costs. Then, the therapist has to point out that remaining committed to an impossible goal rather than grieving its loss is a way of avoiding painful feelings of defeat.

One of the problems with academic discussions of grief is that they tend to have a remote quality. Some authors try to impose order on the process of grief, as if the writer has decided how much and how long and in what way grief is normal, but this approach does not take into account the individual nature of the loss. There is no consensus in the literature about how long grief "should" last. Neither is there a correct way to grieve; the individual's response to a loss may be totally appropriate for that person. In practice the grieving process is always unique to the individual. Bereaved people may behave in ways that are incomprehensible to an observer but meaningful to the individual. Notions that there are specific constituents or stages to the process of grieving oversimplify the complexity of the experience and imply that it should have an end at a certain time. But grief is unpredictable, and it is a mistake to impose any expectation, derived statistically, on the bereaved. Too clinical an approach can be paternalistic or patronizing and ignores the individual's choice about how to react to a loss. Some therapeutic approaches are defensive, used when the therapist does not wish to be reminded that he or she will also die or suffer major loss.

The psychotherapist might have to clarify some misconceptions derived from certain self-help books directed to the survivors of bereavement. These books try to help the survivor feel better by giving good advice, such as anticipating a positive outcome and not dwelling on sadness, as if grieving is somehow a task that we can accomplish as expeditiously as possible if we set our minds to it. The process of grieving is actually chaotic; there is no particular sequence in which things should happen and no map, in spite of the books that recommend particular steps such as staying away from dark colors.

Chronic sorrow

Susan Roos (2002) uses the term "chronic sorrow" to describe the unending grief of parents living with children with life-long developmental disabilities, as these parents realize that these impairments are permanent and the parents' dreams for their children will never be realized. Many people with life-long illnesses such as multiple sclerosis and Parkinson's disease also suffer from chronic sorrow. In her eloquent book on this subject, Roos points out that chronic sorrow is often both unrecognized and misunderstood by mental health professionals. It is often confused with other types of grief as well as with major depression. According to Roos, chronic sorrow is a form of normal grief, and is not synonymous with complicated mourning.

Roos believes that chronic sorrow occurs when we live with wounds that can never be removed or healed, or with loss that has no foreseeable end but which continuously requires energy in order to adapt to the loss. She suggests that the concept should also include situations in which there is no way to know whether a loved person is alive or dead or will be permanently absent, so that closure is not possible. The families of soldiers who are missing in action may be affected in this way. Some mothers who have given up their children for adoption continue to be sorrowful for many years. These mothers develop distressing fantasies of what the child might look like and how life might have been if they had kept the child. Sadness and longing recur on birthdays, holidays, the time when the child would be expected to graduate from high school, and similar occasions. Chronic sorrow occurs when family members disappear and are never heard of again, leading to perpetual grief, or when children are kidnapped with nothing known about their fate; such a loss cannot be alleviated or resolved.

Chronic sorrow may begin with a trauma, such as the unexpected birth of a congenitally malformed baby. Roos notes that, because chronic sorrow is so stressful, it can lead to complicating factors such as depression, regression to immature forms of coping, affective overload, immobilizing guilt, poor control of anger, stress-related physical illnesses, impaired immune functioning, emotional numbing, or even psychosis. She also points out that chronic sorrow may lead to strength, wisdom, and resilience.

Although the term "chronic sorrow" has faded from the literature, it is very evocative and deserves to be retained, not least because of the dangers of mis-diagnosis, perhaps leading to the inappropriate use of anti-depressants, but also because it is a help to such individuals if the psychotherapist recognizes what they are going through. It is important not to confuse chronic sorrow with other types of grief; chronic sorrow does not resolve in the same way—by definition, the sufferer cannot make a permanent emotional adjustment to the loss. Acceptance and resolution of the loss cannot occur. Kaethe Weingarten (2012) notes that people who live with chronic sorrow need to be accompanied, by which she means that "we place ourselves alongside a person as she makes and remakes her relationship to a body/mind that is unreliable" (p. 450). The person has to be supported while she figures out how to care for herself. The person with chronic sorrow has difficulty communicating the nature of her experience to others. Pain, confusion, and uncertainty contribute to the disruption in the sufferer's "self-narrative," the ability to find coherence and meaning in one's life circumstances. According to Weingarten, who writes from the perspective of narrative therapy, the therapist's problem is to help to reduce the disruption which chronic sorrow poses to the self-narrative, one's story of oneself which is important in the formation of an identity. The therapist also has to gently work with "narrative dissociation," a failure to accept one's circumstances, perhaps as a way of protecting those around the sufferer when she believes they cannot tolerate how she feels, while at the same time warding off necessary changes. Narrative dominance may also be seen—a phenomenon in which one narrative takes over the entire personality—crowding out other ways of thinking about the self. In this case, the sufferer's self-narrative may become colonized by derogatory inner voices because the dominant discourse in our culture prefers productivity and independence so much that dependence is repellent or shameful. Weingarten suggests that the therapeutic task when working with chronic sorrow is to help increase the patient's tolerance for a fragmented self-narrative and to assist in the development of a new self-narrative which takes into account the current situation.

Mourning as a creative process

Many writers have pointed out the relationship between creativity and mourning. The literature suggests that the pain of loss can be softened by producing a symbolic substitute in the form of a creative product which allows painful feelings to be expressed. Artistic creation is then a form of restitution for what has been lost, and creative work may assist the process of mourning by releasing affect which has been sequestered. As Ogden (2000) put it, successful mourning "involves a demand that we make on ourselves to create something—whether it be a memory, a dream, a story, a poem, a response to a poem—that begins to meet, to be equal to, the full complexity of our relationship to what has been lost and to the experience of loss itself" (p. 65). The proviso here is to note that artistic work can be used compulsively after a loss as a way to avoid painful feelings rather than to try to understand and explore them.

Cruelty

Deliberate, gratuitous cruelty to others causes enormous suffering. We constantly hear of such cruelty in the form of torture, tyranny, imprisonment, bombings, and similar behavior, not to mention interpersonal acts of cruelty such as belittling others, teasing, bullying, racial prejudice, betrayal, and the like. We see both cruelty and empathy in the play of children, and even God has been accused of being cruel, for example in the biblical story of Job, who complains that God makes him suffer even though he is innocent (Job 30:21).

Many definitions and interpretations of cruelty have been offered (Baruchello, 2010). Our understanding of the nature of cruelty has varied in different geographical regions and historical periods. Beating one's children was once considered to be necessary, and slavery was not always recognized as cruel. To us, the word cruelty implies intentionally inflicting unnecessary pain or fear on another person, sometimes deriving sadistic pleasure from doing so, with the connotation that the perpetrator could restrain himself if he so wished. There seems to be something wrong with the person who constantly behaves cruelly towards others only for the sake of self-gratification—we have a strong moral intuition that makes this behavior abhorrent. Even if the cruel person does not take pleasure in his actions, for example when cruelty is inflicted purely as a form of social control or punishment, we wonder how such a person can show no mercy or pity for his victims.

Victor Nell (2006) is among those who believe that cruelty is a uniquely human trait, not found in animals, and he suggests it is a by-product of the evolution of predatory behavior, which is widespread among animals. Our early hominid ancestors had to eat meat to accommodate to the development of increased brain size and a smaller gut, necessitating easily digested, highly nutritious food, leading to the need to hunt. Nell suggests that the evolutionary precursor of predation is competitive aggression. He cites the neurobiological research of Panskepp (1998) and others which suggests that hunting and killing are positive emotional experiences for predators, and the sight of pain, blood, and death are linked to brain dopaminergic and opioid systems which are affectively rewarding and positive, sometimes linked to sexual arousal. He goes on to explain how, as a result of this evolutionary development, punitive and disciplinary cruelty emerged in human societies. Nell defines cruelty as "the deliberate infliction of physical or psychological pain on other living creatures, sometimes indifferently, but often with delight" (Nell, 2006, p. 211). This definition has been criticized on the grounds that it does not take into account passive forms of cruelty (such as animal hoarding[19]) in which the perpetrator lacks the clear intention to be harmful (Herzog et al., 2006), or

---

19   Animal hoarding is the practice of keeping too many animals in too small a space, without proper care, while denying the harm being caused to them. However, this disorder does not seem to be due to intentional cruelty.

painful medical procedures intended to be helpful. Nell rebuts this critique by saying that cruelty requires not only the intention to inflict pain but the infliction of pain *because* doing so causes the victim to suffer.

Nell's nativist or evolutionary view may explain why cruelty can be perpetrated by people who have not been socialized to be cruel, and helps to explain why we are attracted to cruelty in the media. Nell is clear that an evolutionary view of cruelty does not mean we should not condemn it and does not absolve perpetrators and their audiences of moral responsibility.

Nell's work has been criticized on various grounds. It seems rather restrictive to attribute all forms of cruelty to predation; there may be several other factors involved, such as competition for resources or intra-species aggression. Our advanced psychological development might be expected to modify our evolutionary inheritance as we invest our behavior with social, spiritual, aesthetic, and other forms of significance. Terror management theorists[20] suggest that the need to defend a particular cultural world-view and participate in a heroic triumph over evil contributes to human aggression and cruelty (Kosloff et al, 2006). Other writers believe that parallels to human cruelty can in fact be found among animals (Dallman, 2006). The territorial aggression of chimpanzees produces violence towards other groups, and a cat will toy with a mouse until the mouse dies, but we do not know if these animals *intend* to cause suffering to others in a self-conscious way—these behaviors may simply be forms of aggression.

Cruelty has no regard for the other person, so that the antidotes to cruelty are concern, empathy, and compassion. In most people, to see the suffering of another person restrains our behavior, which might mean for example that not seeing the suffering produced by bombing makes it more likely to be used. Much cruelty is the result of a lack of empathy for others, which leads to indifference to their suffering. It might seem that empathy, the ability to sense the emotional states of other people, would reduce cruel behavior, but this is not entirely true. Some sadistic people use their empathic ability to enjoy their victim's pain, but the sadist's motive also includes the enjoyable exercise of power. Human beings have an inborn predisposition to resonate with the experience of others, which suggests an evolutionary basis for empathy because it had survival value for the species, so that empathy

---

20   Terror management theory suggests that as hominids evolved self-awareness they developed awareness of death and the potential to experience dread. To manage this existential terror people create cultural world-views which offer the hope of symbolic immortality.

is based on "a very primitive biological core" (Kriegman et al., 1988, p. 271). Nevertheless, even if the capacity for empathy is innately human, empathy also has a developmental line which may go awry (Hoffman, 2000), as we see in the case of psychopathic individuals with no capacity for empathy. Just as we have evolved to be predatory, fortunately we have also evolved the ability to be cooperative and mutually caring. Reasonable psychological health requires a balance between aggression, dominance, and pro-social feelings and behavior.

Psychological roots of cruelty

It is important for the psychotherapist to understand why some individuals are able to commit appalling acts of cruelty. There is an ancient idea that people are cruel in order to exact revenge for the way they themselves have been treated. Some parents abuse their children as a way of dealing with the abuse they suffered in their own childhood (Miller, 1985), or they try to stabilize their narcissistic disequilibrium by hitting their children. Cruelty to others is then a pathological product of accumulated rage and an unconscious identification with one's early persecutors. Children who ruthlessly tease other children are often unconsciously identifying with adults who abused them, in a kind of role reversal. Sometimes a child abuser unconsciously identifies with those who abused him, while the child he is abusing unconsciously represents a split off, infantile level of himself. Not surprisingly, most aggressive criminals suffered childhood abuse. In an attempt to master the situation, other victims of childhood abuse unconsciously develop a repetition compulsion in which they repeatedly become involved in abusive relationships. Other people who were abused in childhood go into helping professions, often because they identify with someone who was kind to them at the time of the abuse. Here, it is important to bear in mind the standard warning that to understand evil or cruel behavior is not to condone it.

As well as the psychological factors at work, there are also societal and political factors which allow the transformation of ordinary people into perpetrators of extreme cruelty. Social psychologists reject the claim that only psychologically abnormal people commit cruel crimes. Societies or rulers are sometimes cruel to maintain power and social dominance. James Waller (2002) describes how ordinary people may commit genocide and mass killings, as we saw in Rwanda or Nazi Germany. Genocide requires not just an ideology or an ethnic prejudice but also organization, training, and leadership. Some people are able to resist collective pressures, but individual judgment is often submerged by being part of a large group, especially when this is combined with devotion to a charismatic leader such as Hitler. People then lose awareness of their personal identity and regress as they are swept away by the emotions and behavior of the group, behaving in ways they would not do as individuals. Being a member of a large crowd tends to produce a loss of the sense of individuality, so that the person is less likely to act according to his normal values. The sense of being part of a huge group produces a feeling of strength and security.

Ervin Staub (2002) points out several situational and social factors which motivate genocide. He lists: devaluation of a particular ethnic or political group at the direction of a despotic leadership; a destructive ideology which has a simplistic, one-dimensional view of history; uncritical respect for authority; a monolithic society; lack of real contact and shared goals with others; and the passivity of bystanders, which makes the perpetrators believe they are supported. Even if bystanders are not indifferent to those being persecuted, they may feel powerless in the face of a dictatorship deploying armed soldiers. One has to add the effects of idealizing a dangerous leader, the power of group identity which dilutes personal responsibility, thoughtless nationalism, distortion of historical truth, and religious prejudices which are manipulated by authoritarian leaders to their own ends. If one believes in a just world, the idea that everything happens for a reason, one might conclude that victims of persecution deserve their suffering because of who they are. This attitude is fostered by dehumanizing propaganda which treats the persecuted as if they were less than human. During the Rwandan genocide, Hutus referred to Tutsis as cockroaches, and during the Holocaust the Nazis referred to the Jews as rats, and believed they had a moral duty to exterminate them (Smith, 2011).

From the intrapsychic standpoint one can see racial or ethnic prejudice as a function of unconscious, primitive splitting and projection. Splitting reduces uncertainty and ambiguity, so that "we are all good, they are all bad." Extreme religious and political ideologies project all of a group's disowned negative qualities onto a persecuted group, which becomes a scapegoat, just as an individual can try to destroy his own badness by attacking it in the other. Sometimes, because guilt and painful memories of his behavior cause internal discomfort, the perpetrator comes to hate those he persecutes even more, rather than feeling remorse for his behavior. Social and ethnic prejudice allows the individual to maintain a narcissistic sense of superiority over others; in many cultures, members of other ethnicities are regarded as inferior, so that any feelings of inadequacy or low self-esteem can be evacuated by projecting them onto the devalued group. No self-reflection or self-criticism is then necessary. Similarly, we may bolster our self-esteem by making cruel jokes about or laughing at the misfortunes of devalued groups.

Several now classical experiments indicate that an individual can lose his or her autonomous thinking under the right conditions. John Darley and Daniel Batson (1973) carried out an experiment based on the biblical story of the Good Samaritan, in which a priest and a Levite ignored an injured man on the side of the road but a passing Samaritan helped the victim (Luke 10: 29-37). It is not clear why the first two ignored the man who needed help; the implication is that they did not really follow the values they professed. The researchers recruited seminary students to study this question. The subjects began the experiment in an office where they filled out questionnaires. They were then told to proceed to another building, where some were told they would give a talk about jobs for seminary graduates while others were told to prepare a talk about the Good Samaritan story. The experimenters varied the degree of urgency in the students, so that some were in more of a hurry than others because they were told they were late for their task. On the way they encountered an actor who obviously needed help. Some subjects failed to notice the man in need, even stepping over him, while others offered varying degrees of help. The results showed that the amount of hurry and urgency induced in the subject had a major effect on whether the student would stop and offer aid. Even the students who were about to give a lecture about the Good Samaritan were less likely to help if they were in a hurry. There was no correlation between the student's type of religious commitment and their behavior.

The Stanford prison experiment (Zimbardo, 1996) was a study of social roles. Students were randomly selected to take either the role of prisoner or guard in a mock prison. The participants adapted to their assigned roles only too well; some of the "guards" became abusive, sadistic, and tried to degrade the "prisoners," while the prisoners became passive, depressed, and docile in the face of abuse, and harassed other prisoners who attempted to prevent it. The experiment had to be stopped after only 6 days. This experiment produced a model which helps us understand the cruelty displayed by soldiers at Abu Ghraib. It is important to note that the researcher was unable to predict from psychological tests which guards would become brutal.

The psychologist Stanley Milgram (1974) studied obedience to authority, in order to address the question of whether Eichmann and other Nazis were following orders in a way that allowed them to override their conscience, or whether they were real accomplices in the Holocaust. The participants were paired into a "learner," who was an actor and actually one of Milgram's collaborators, and a "teacher," who was the real research subject. The learner, who was strapped to a chair with electrodes attached to him, was given a list of word pairs. The teacher tested him by naming a word and asking the learner to recall its paired word. An authority figure in white coat told the teacher to administer an electric shock of increasing intensity to the learner each time he made a mistake. The learner deliberately gave occasional incorrect answers. If the teacher tried to refuse to administer shocks, the experimenter would insist that the teacher keep on doing so in spite of the pain he seemed to be inflicting. Two thirds of the participants obeyed the authority figure and continued to administer shocks to the maximum level, inflicting what they thought was severe pain on the learner. This study showed that the approval and insistence of an authority figure allows some ordinary people to perform cruel acts. Milgram concluded that human nature alone is not sufficient to protect us from harming others if ordered to do so at the behest of an authority figure. This might include not just a malevolent government official or gang leader, but cult figures such as Jim Jones, who ordered his followers to commit mass suicide with cyanide-laced Kool-Aid.

Overall, these experiments and the evidence of history suggest that the readiness to be cruel is universally human, given the right situation; there are situations which may evoke latent sadism. At the same time we also have evolved an instinct for compassion, perhaps the result of genetically-based bonds of kinship (Panskepp, 1998). Nell (2006) points out that this combination of potentials cause us to oscillate between fascination and horror when we witness cruelty.

Cruelty to animals

Concern with the humane treatment of animals is growing. Ascione (1993, p. 28) defines animal cruelty as "socially unacceptable behavior that intentionally causes unnecessary pain, suffering, or distress to and/or death of an animal."

Ill-treatment of animals is important to the psychotherapist for several reasons: we recognize a moral obligation to treat animals properly; cruelty to animals causes unnecessary suffering; and we now realize that there is an association between cruelty to animals in childhood, personality disorder, antisocial behavior, and interpersonal violence in adulthood (Arluke et al., 1999). Ascione (1993) suggests that to commit cruelty to animals inhibits our capacity for empathy, making it easier to disregard the feelings of people as well as animals. Abused children abuse animals, perhaps to act out what happened to them, in an identification with their abusers or to gain some semblance of control (DeViney, et al., 1983). It may be that children learn to abuse animals if they witness animal abuse in their families or grow up in violent families. Multiple forms of violence occur in families, and early experience with violence predisposes to the use of violence in adulthood (Gelles, 1997)—but it is also true that some children who grow up in abusive homes become activists on behalf of animals. Husbands who batter their wives often also abuse animals in the home to further intimidate their wives (Flynn, 1999), and feminists see male violence against animals as a symptom of patriarchal male dominance (Adams, 1994). Other psychological factors which contribute to cruelty to animals include lack of empathy, poor anger control or impulsivity, and high levels of interpersonal aggression. Criminologists are now studying animal abuse in a less human-centered manner; Beirne (1999) has argued that animal abuse is a legitimate field of study in its own right, not only because it is related to human violence. It is increasingly recognized that animals suffer emotions such as grief and pain.

Human cruelty to animals has a long history. An obvious historical example is the ancient Roman practice in which large numbers of animals were killed in amphitheaters built for this purpose. Apparently the spectators identified with the excitement of a gladiator killing the animal, leading to a vicarious sense of pleasure. The same process of identification may account for our contemporary enjoyment of other forms of competitive fighting. Bullfights are a modern example; they seem to arouse the spectators emotionally, so that in his *Death in the Afternoon*, Hemingway wrote that if the matador is unsuccessful, the spectators may swarm into the arena and kill the bull themselves.

In our culture, anti-cruelty laws (which at least affirm that cruelty is wrong) are not very effective; animals are considered to be property and have no legal standing. Much legal cruelty to animals is the result of factory farming, animal experimentation, testing of cosmetics, and the use of animals in circuses and zoos. It is not clear why our society tolerates these painful practices—presumably the reasons are largely economic combined with a certain amount of denial. These factors also contribute to our cultural indifference to the cruelty inflicted on animals in slaughter facilities and medical research. Unfortunately, traditional religions see humans as superior to animals, which does not promote a humane attitude.

Human beings have always been hunters of animals, and early hunter-gatherer societies are thought to have observed rituals that reduced their guilt about their need to kill. Some modern hunters also feel guilt or grief as well as gratification at killing animals, but any compassion or guilt has to be split off at the time of the hunt, producing an empty emotional state followed by feelings of pleasure after the kill (Nell, 2006). Hunting may also be enjoyable because it allows a feeling of mastery, and not necessarily because the hunter enjoys being cruel or wishes to inflict suffering. Many hunters admire or are even fascinated with the survival skills and beauty of wild animals, and hunters attach great importance to knowledge of the natural world and their interaction with it. The human capacity for empathic identification with animals seems to account for the many people who care for their welfare. These individuals see hunting as barbaric. In Britain, there has been much debate about the ban on fox-hunting; those in favor of the ban argued that hunting is cruel and morally wrong, while those who defended hunting argued that it is a relatively human way of controlling the number of foxes who are a danger to livestock. One can also think of hunting in evolutionary terms; human beings evolved to beware of becoming the prey of predatory animals, which partly accounts for our fear of strangers and those very different than ourselves. Apparently, one way to cope with predator anxiety is by becoming predatory oneself.

Torture

Torture is understood here to be any action which inflicts deliberate, unbearable, unjustified and unnecessary physical or mental suffering on a person or any other sentient creature. This type of cruelty is often used as a form of political control in totalitarian societies, where it is used to extract information, to punish offenders, to intimidate citizens or to express the power of the state. Torture violates human dignity and it seems deeply morally wrong to most people, suggesting that it offends an inborn moral code. Even in liberal democracies however, this practice has been justified to prevent imminent and serious threat to the population, although these societies sometimes narrow the definition of torture in an attempt to sanitize or domesticate forms of torture which do not cause obvious physical damage, such as sleep deprivation, solitary confinement, degrading treatment, or exposure to extreme cold. However, all forms of torture produce serious long term physical and psychological effects such as post-traumatic stress disorder, depression, anxiety, impaired memory, insomnia, nightmares, and other serious emotional and physical sequelae (Basoglu et al, 2001).

The torture victim's imagination add to his pain; he constantly imagines the dreadful things which may happen next, including the fate of his family, and these painful fantasies may continue after the torture ends. Enduring personality changes have been reported among victims, seen in the personal accounts of survivors of torture (Ortiz, 2001), including the existential difficulty of living in a world in which torture is a reality. The survivor's family is often affected, and the consequences of torture are transmitted across generations (Daud, 2005). Some professional groups such as the American Psychiatric Association prohibit their members from participating in torture. Nevertheless, we have learned from Lifton's (1986) interviews with Nazi doctors that some physicians may abandon their personal and professional values in societies where torture is the norm.

Since torture is repugnant to most of us, of interest to the psychologist is the question of how the torturer is able to inflict pain on another human being, even if an interrogator believes the torture is justified, for example to save innocent lives during a "ticking time bomb" scenario.[21] According to their personal testimony, torturers who initially feel distress at what they are doing eventually habituate and feel nothing (Crelinsten, 1993). At times the pain and fear of the victim may escalate the savagery of the torturer, and Nell (2006) suggests that this phenomenon may have evolutionary roots, paralleling the escalating ferocity of a predator as the terror and death struggle of its prey increase.

Interviews with torturers may not provide reliable information about why they torture. Torturers use a variety of strategies to inure themselves against their behavior and block any sympathy for their victims. They dehumanize or blame the victim, or they appeal to reasons such as national security. According to Elaine Scarry (1985), in order to neutralize the moral fact that they are inflicting agony, torturers focus their attention on the process

---

21   The ticking time bomb scenario is sometimes used as justification for torture. It presupposes that a terrorist knows the location of a bomb which will soon explode in a major city. This scenario assumes that only torture will succeed in obtaining the information in time to prevent the explosion.

of questioning. Torturers rationalize their actions using euphemisms such as "interrogation" or "gathering intelligence," or they deflect responsibility onto their superiors. Some torturers may be latent sadists who are given an opportunity to de-repress this behavior. Torture then expresses the sadist's need to dominate others and to have absolute power.

Sadism was traditionally considered to be a sexual perversion, the experience of erotic pleasure associated with pain, but broadly understood, sadism simply means that the person enjoys hurting others. There is no single psychological explanation for this behavior; several factors play a part. The traditional psychoanalytic views of sadism as erotized aggression or a function of the death instinct no longer seem adequate. A more recent view suggests that the sadist is trying to overcome feelings of impotence by demonstrating his power (Rizzuto, 1999). The sadistic torturer is trying to master his childhood experience of being abused by making someone else suffer torment. He projects his own vulnerability into his helpless victim, and being in control of the situation seems to ensure that someone else will have to feel the pain he once had to endure. Torturing others may also be a form of the intense need for revenge which characterizes chronic narcissistic rage. The victim's innocence is of no help to him; the torturer is often envious of or hates innocence because of consciousness of his own misdeeds.

Torture is not only harmful to the victim but also to the torturer himself, who is depraved by this act. Torturers sometimes suffer long-term emotional problems later, even when they were given situational justification for their actions (Falk et al.,2006). The use of torture also harms the character of the society which condones the practice, by eroding its standards of behavior (Gushee, 2006), although it is true that totalitarian societies are more likely to use torture in the first place, since they use torture to impose the power of the state. For the most part, liberal democracies only torture when they feel threatened. However, McCoy (2006) points out that the use of torture is difficult to control; once torture is used in limited cases, its use tends to spread to more and more suspects. As the use of torture gets out of hand, prisoners may be tortured even when the torturers do not really believe the prisoners have any useful information. In any case, many experienced interrogators believe that non-coercive interrogation gets better results than torture, and torture may not extract reliable information (ibid.). However, torture is easy to rationalize.

101

There is an argument which justifies torture as part of the "just war" tradition, which holds that killing in war is morally permissible under certain circumstances—for example, there must be a good reason for war and the right motivation, and war must be proportional and a last resort. Within this framework, if there are situations in which torture is truly necessary to save lives, Cole (2012) argues that it takes a person of extraordinary moral character to make this judgment.

3

SACRED PAIN AND SACRIFICE

Sacred pain

Various religions and world mythologies illustrate the belief that pain, suffering, and mortification of the body can be deliberately self-inflicted in the service of enhancing spiritual development. The obvious examples are the physical austerities of mystics such as fasting, vigils in the presence of extreme heat or cold, and painful body postures. Christian saints and mystics exhibit stigmata[22], spontaneous bleeding of their hands and feet in a way that mimics the wounds of Christ on the cross. Throughout the ages, Christian devotees have scourged, whipped, and tortured themselves because they believe that self-induced suffering purifies the soul in some way, allows them to identify with the suffering of Christ, or leads to self-transcendence. Barefoot pilgrimages over rocky ground occur in several traditions, and in the Native American Sun Dance the dancer suspends himself from a pole with a pin that pierces the skin of his chest. Ariel Glucklich (2003) describes the self-torture of the 16th century nun St. Maria Maddalena de' Pazzi, who walked barefoot in the winter, dripped hot candle wax on her body, and wore a nail-studded corset and a crown of thorns. Maria not only had stigmata, she was also thought to be subject to attacks by evil spirits who would throw her down stairs and beat her.

Glucklich coined the term "sacred pain" to describe the ways in which the devout of several religious traditions seem to induce pain and suffering for the sake of spiritual power, or in the name of the divine. Glucklich believes that the task of this kind of "sacred pain" is to transform destructive

---

22   According to Lowell Gallagher (1997), the etymology of the word "stigmata" dates to the Graeco-Roman practice of engraving a mark on the face or forehead to identify a criminal. Consequently the term "holy" stigmata is often used to distinguish the wounds suffered by saints from punitive branding of the type seen in Hawthorne's *The Scarlet Letter*.

or disintegrative suffering into something positive; suffering becomes a mechanism by which the sufferer feels part of a reality that transcends his or her individual life. The wound becomes a form of communion with the sacred. Glucklich points out the enormous difference between the unwanted pain of an illness or accident and the voluntary, self-inflicted pain of the religious practitioner, which change his identity, enhances his sense of connection to God, or suppresses bodily desires such as sexuality and hunger.

There has been a long-standing controversy about whether the phenomenon of self-induced pain for religious reasons is pathological. Classical psychoanalytic theory would see self-induced suffering as a form of masochism resulting from unconscious guilt that requires punishment. Or, self-punishment alleviates the fear of being hurt by others. Psychoanalytic self-psychology might see self-induced pain as somehow enlivening or transforming a dead or defective sense of self. Glucklich believes that self-inflicted pain makes the body-self more transparent, facilitating a new sense of identity and the sense of a greater presence, whereupon the mystic finds what she set out to experience. Another way to express that idea would be to say that self-inflicted pain reduces the hegemony of the ego and allows an experience of transcendent reality to irrupt into consciousness.

Since we sometimes work psychotherapeutically with committed Christians, it is worth pointing out that penance has always been an important Christian practice. In an earlier era this involved self-inflicted pain such as self-flagellation. Indeed the roots of the words "penance," "penal," "penalty," and "punishment" are etymologically connected to the Latin word *poena*. In the history of Christianity, self-induced punishment as penance was at one time a cure for sin, a kind of medicine that ensured salvation, meaning spiritual health. The pain itself was not the goal as much as it was a medicine for the soul. Today, masochistic behavior has largely separated from religion and is now often seen as pathological.

Stigmata

Stigmata are spontaneous wounds on the body, which resemble the wounds on the crucified body of Christ. In people so affected, bleeding appears on the palms, the feet, the chest, and sometimes around the head where Christ wore his crown of thorns. Tears of blood may appear. The experience is often preceded by an ecstatic state, and the wounds may appear on a regular schedule such as Friday to Sunday. There are many interpretations of this phenomenon. Believers see stigmata as supernaturally produced on the body of a saintly person. Skeptics dismiss these wounds as hysterical, dissociative, or fraudulent, either consciously or unconsciously self-inflicted during an altered state of consciousness—a condition known as *dermatitis artefacta*. It is suggested that if the subject is powerfully identified with Christ, psychosomatic bodily changes may occur. Easy bruising and bleeding into the skin are commonly thought to be psychogenic.[23] Here we have to remember that naming is not explaining, and none of these psychological explanations disprove the subject's personal belief that her wounds are divinely given signs of connection to God. Stigmatics often see their suffering as an act of love or agape for all humanity, which connects the phenomenon with the traditional Christian theology of Christ's suffering.

The earliest known stigmata, those of St. Francis of Assisi in 1244 CE, were initially mistrusted because they seemed to infringe on the unique status of Jesus. It is worth noting that at the time they occurred Francis was physically ill, nearly blind, and in considerable emotional distress because of the political turmoil resulting from the establishment of his new order of monks. His stigmata developed immediately after he experienced a vision in which a six-winged seraph embraced a crucified man, and the crucified man seemed to pierce Francis's own body. Many stigmatics have appeared since St. Francis. St. Teresa of Àvila is said to have had invisible stigmata which took the form of a wound to her heart, which she received in a vision from an angel who thrust a golden dart with a fiery tip into her. The phenomenon continues into recent memory: Audrey Santo was a severely disabled girl who was born in 1983 in Worcester, MA and lived until 2007. She had been in a coma or a state of mutism since almost drowning at the age of 3, and because of brain damage it was never clear how conscious she was of her surroundings. Her stigmata had been witnessed by many people, and she was thought to be responsible for miraculous healings. She has been regarded as a "victim soul," one who offers her own suffering for the sake of others. There are several other contemporary examples (Felix, 2001). However, the Roman Catholic Church still has an ambivalent attitude to the authenticity of stigmata and is not comfortable with the popular interest in stigmatics, probably because of the suspicion that their lesions are either hysterical or self-induced.

---

23   These conditions are known as psychogenic purpura and autoerythrocyte sensitization syndrome (Yucel et al, 2000).

The phenomenon became well known in the medieval era among the devout. Bynum (1991) points out that for medieval stigmatics, pain and bleeding were not intended to be destructive or a punishment, but an identification with Christ at the moment of his dying (p. 131), a way of sharing his pain. Bynum tells us that during the Middle Ages the blood from Christ's wounds was regarded as analogous to milk from a mother's breast, so women who experienced the stigmata replicated Jesus' maternal role by allowing Christ's blood to flow through them to nurture others. The stigmatic's blood both purged her own soul and saved her fellow Christians by atoning for their sins. In medieval monasteries, the sound of the flagellant's whipping was said to rise to God's ears as a sweet melody. Some stigmatics were also anorexic, and took no nourishment except the Eucharistic host—so called *anorexia mirabilis*. Fasting is used in many cultures to achieve altered states of consciousness or spiritual transcendence. Because of the misogynistic treatment of women by the Church during the Middle Ages, it may be that asceticism among women religious was a way of exerting control when no other forms of power or authority were available.

Psychoanalysts usually consider stigmata to be hysterical, the result of heightened auto-suggestion. Based on the story of Thérèse Neumann (1898-1962), a young Bavarian stigmatic, Albright (2002) believes that stigmata may be a post-traumatic stress symptom in the presence of an abnormal degree of auto-suggestibility. As a result of a traumatic injury, Thérèse became partially paralyzed. She was also blind, and remained in constant pain from deep bed sores for several years. One day she heard a saintly voice which told her that she would be able to walk, whereupon her mobility improved. She then had a vision of Jesus' life from the Garden of Gethsemane to the crucifixion, followed by the appearance of stigmata on her head, hands, and feet, with tears of blood. No cause was ever established. Albright points out that even if we understand the psychological roots of her stigmata, this does not disprove her own belief that the wounds came from God.

Self-mutilation: Religiously or neurotically motivated?

Self-mutilators deliberately and compulsively mutilate themselves, often by cutting, burning, head banging, hair pulling, or skin scratching, without any suicidal intent, a phenomenon which has been called "bodies under siege" (Favazza, 1996). Like religiously motivated ascetics, many self-mutilators are also anorexic. Both religious ascetics and non-religious self-mutilators cause themselves suffering in the service of a higher goal. For both groups, the pain produced does not seem to be important, and both groups use pain to achieve some larger purpose or emotional relief. However, the religious ascetic is consciously causing pain for the sake of spiritual development, but there is no agreed-upon or single explanation for non-religious self-inflicted suffering, which is often associated with an eating disorder and with sexual or physical abuse at an early age. Temporary states of euphoria may occur during the episode, because of the secretion of endogenous opiates known as beta-endorphins (Russ, 1992). This may be a partial explanation for the lack of pain experienced by some self-mutilators, who give a variety of explanations for this behavior. Some describe emptiness, deadness, or depersonalization that is relieved by pain, which seems to release tension and act as a form of self-soothing. Self-cutting is often triggered by a painful rejection or experience of being devalued. Self-mutilation is then an attempt to re-establish a degree of narcissistic equilibrium and self-cohesion by exerting control over one's emotions and the environment, or it is a way of attacking internal bad objects.

Some psychoanalysts see self-mutilation as a variety of masochism or self-punishment for an unconscious sense of badness, or even as a form of disguised sexual gratification which at the same time punishes the person for the act (Suyemoto, 1998). Self-cutting is also seen as an effort to counteract the experience of the annihilation of the self, to restore and maintain the cohesion and stability of a precarious or fragmenting sense of self (Stolorow et al., 1980; Doctors, 1981). We might wonder if the self-cutter is trying to carve a new sense of herself out of her own flesh, as if she is trying to reach some other self that she feels or imagines to be trapped inside. Other theorists suggest that self-mutilators need to fend off a sense that they are losing their boundaries; perhaps the sight of blood on the skin acts as a concrete marker of an outer boundary, or it is simply a way of knowing one is alive. Finally, the similarity of self-mutilation to tribal initiation rituals which slice the skin has led to the suggestion that self-mutilation is an unconscious attempt at self-initiation into adulthood.

Sacrifice, suffering, and destiny

Many religious traditions stress the importance of sacrifice, which seems to be an archetypal feature of human psychology. There is a great deal of controversy about the origins of sacrifice, and no clear explanation for why, in the throes of intense suffering, people may feel that a sacrifice will make things better, as if in some mysterious way our sacrifice can control what happens. Sacrifice can be broadly defined as the willingness to put aside one's own self-interest, or to give up something one regrets losing, either in the interest of another person, for the sake of a relationship, or in the service of an ideal or a divinity. The fact that many religious traditions use ritual sacrifice suggests the belief that if we give up something of value we can influence the higher powers or affect our destiny. Many people feel that the sacrifice of something of value to them is necessary to make life meaningful, and they often hope that something good will happen in return for their sacrifice. We see this clearly not only in religious practices of sacrifice, but also in everyday sacrifices made for the sake of others, for example by parents for their children.

Sacrifice has been a fundamental component of religions everywhere—in fact, the word "sacrifice" derives from Latin words *facere* and *sacer,* meaning to make sacred. Human and animal sacrifice was carried out in most of the religions of antiquity, so that there seems to be an archetypal connection between violence and the sacred, although the purpose of most sacrifice was not the killing itself. Sacrifice was intended to appease, appeal to, or connect with the local gods, to ask for forgiveness, to ward off evil, to ensure the growth of crops, as thanksgiving, to ask for success in war, or to ensure the continuation of the values of a society. In some cultures, it was believed that humans had to give life to obtain or preserve life, so the gods were "fed" with blood in temples in India, China, South America, Africa, and ancient Greece. The etymology of the English word "altar" comes from the Latin *altaria,* meaning a burnt offering; the Hebrew word for altar, *mizbeach,* comes from a root meaning to slaughter. Many ritual sacrifices were food offerings; apparently it was believed that the gods need to be nourished by people to sustain the society. These societies either believed that if humans give to their god, he would give something back in return, or that their god needed something the sacrifice would provide, or that they had to forestall divine retribution. The Hebrew god was believed to send his fire down to consume the flesh on the altar in the Jerusalem temple (1 Chronicles 21-26). In this tradition the sacrifice was said to be a way of establishing peace between the people of Israel and the divine, and was a way of atoning for guilt. In the Hebrew Bible, the killing of an animal is also a form of consecration; the animal represented the sacrificer, who symbolically gives the life of the animal in lieu of his own life as an atonement for his sins. The sacrificer believes he connects with God by the act of sacrificing, which had to be done in obedience to God's will. It was believed that such sacrifice would be pleasing to God if it was sincere and properly motivated.

There is also an important relational dynamic involved in most forms of sacrifice. In his classic text on sacrifice, the anthropologist Edwin Oliver James (2003/1933) suggested that if a pattern of relationship to a god is broken or at risk of being broken, a sacrifice is necessary to atone for the offense, in order to re-establish a relationship that is vital to the individual or the group. This may require a suitable offering and confession, or the transference of the sin to a scapegoat animal who is then sacrificed. Religious sacrifice did not always involve killing; some people were sacrificed to God by being consecrated as servants to God, as we see in the case of the biblical Samuel, whose mother promised him to God before he was conceived (1 Samuel, 1: 11). In some traditions, parents gave their children to the temple as vestal virgins or sacred prostitutes.

The notion of necessary sacrifice is integral to the Christian story. In Christian theology, the Mass is a re-enactment of Christ's loving self-sacrifice, given as a gift of himself, and the Christian participates in this event. Christ's sacrifice solidifies the human connection to the divine. This is a complicated motif because in Christian theology the Father sacrifices his son, but the son is one with the Father, so the Father in some way is sacrificing himself, or Christ is both the one who sacrifices and also the sacrifice, so this is an act of mutual self-giving. It is difficult to say to what extent our cultural valuing of self-sacrifice is the result of the influence of the Christian tradition, and to what extent self-sacrifice is an intrinsic part of human nature which is evoked given the right cultural setting. If it is innate, self-sacrifice for others may have evolved for the sake of the survival of the group. Self-sacrifice is common in wartime, for example when a soldier jumps on a grenade to save his comrades. Whatever the source of self-sacrifice, some research suggests that when faced with a moral dilemma, a surprisingly high proportion of people believe they should give up their lives for the sake of strangers (Huebner et al., 2011). A question which arises here is how much self-sacrifice is excessive. There must be acceptable limits; feminist writers have warned that women in particular have been socialized to sacrifice themselves to others even to the extent that they lose themselves, which can lead to their subordination or abuse (Groenhout, 2006).

Whatever its source, we seem to instinctively recognize the need for sacrifice. Perhaps a paradigmatic instance is childbirth, which is painful but necessary to bring new life into the world. Development and new birth often require sacrifice. As we progress through childhood we give up earlier modes of being, such as dependence on parents, and this process of letting go of the past and acquiring new consciousness continues throughout the life cycle. Often, we feel that something has to die for something new to appear. Unless we are prepared to make the sacrifice necessary to move to the next level of consciousness, life and development stagnate. At the same time therefore, each sacrifice is not only a loss of what we had but a new beginning. In the myth of the Garden of Eden, one of the West's foundational stories, consciousness of good and evil is only obtained at the price of expulsion from the Garden, leading to suffering, toil, and death.

Psychodynamic factors involved in sacrifice

Freud's daughter was once so ill that it was feared she would die. One morning he was informed that she had begun to greatly improve and would live. Freud exclaimed "So she is going to live after all" when he heard the news of her recovery, and impulsively, without thinking, he threw a slipper which broke a marble statue of the Venus of Medici (a 1st century copy of an original Greek sculpture of Aphrodite). He does not tell us why a statue of the goddess of love and relationship was his target. He says that his "attack of destructive madness"(1901, p. 187) served as the expression of a grateful feeling towards fate, and gave him the opportunity of performing an act of sacrifice, as if by breaking the statue he felt as if he was making an offering. He notes that it is incomprehensible how he decided to act so quickly, aimed so accurately, and did not hit anything else close by. We might imagine that he was angry and frightened at his daughter's illness and was simply letting off steam, but his main point is that such acts are not random but motivated by some unconscious pressure. Freud suggests that many daily activities are actually expressions of a sacrificial fantasy. Once he was writing a letter of apology to a friend, and while writing the letter he accidentally swept his hand and broke an Egyptian figurine that was on his desk—he refers to this as a "pious offering to avert some evil" (p. 187-8). He writes that he "immediately knew that I had caused this mischief to avert a greater one." (p. 188).

Freud makes the point that we sometimes drop or break objects to express a superstitious belief that we can mollify fate or avert evil. Such an act may be conscious, such as tossing salt over one's shoulder, or it may occur "accidentally" or unconsciously. In other words, he believed that sometimes we destroy something of value to us, or even "accidentally" injure ourselves, as a sacrificial act to the power of destiny. In his *Civilization and Its Discontents*, he notes that we have to sacrifice some of our own happiness for the sake of the community. In his analysis of ritual sacrifices in *Totem and Taboo* of 1913, he suggests that the conviction of sinfulness underlies the need for sacrifice, which is why, in the Christian myth, because man's sinfulness offends God, Christ has to redeem us by sacrificing his own life. (I should add here that Christians object to a view of the crucifixion as a sacrificial attempt to placate an angry God; they prefer it to be seen as an act of selfless love.)

Psychoanalysts since Freud have not written a great deal about sacrifice. In a review of the subject, Salman Akhtar (2012) suggests that this may be because until recently psychoanalysts have been more interested in negative emotions such as greed, which is in a way the opposite of sacrifice, and they lack interest in subjects that have a religious flavor. Sándor Ferenczi (1933) described the sacrifices children make on behalf of the family: "Children have the compulsion to put to rights all disorder in the family, to burden, so to speak, their own tender shoulders with the load of all the others," and: "A mother complaining of her constant miseries can create a nurse for life out of her child" (p. 166). Melanie Klein (1937) believed that sacrifice is a form of reparation, an attempt to repair the damage that the child (in fantasy) has done to his early caretakers.

Sometimes we sacrifice ourselves in childhood because of fear of our parents rather than love of them, a dynamic which has been linked to the development of a masochistic character style. Such individuals believe that they will only obtain care when they suffer. This dynamic could contribute to the ritual/religious need to sacrifice to ward off evil. The childhood notion that "I have to sacrifice something of myself for the sake of the family" may result from the belief that there is not enough available goodness for everyone; since goodness is in limited supply "I have to give to my parents to keep them alive." (Hence also perhaps the notion that God needs something from us.) Self-sacrificing behavior to alleviate the suffering of another person could be motivated by such early childhood dynamics, or it could be motivated by real love and concern for that person. At times, self-sacrifice seems to be a way of defending against guilt or hostility towards the person for whom one is making the sacrifice. Self-sacrifice could be motivated by a spiritual commitment to compassionate action, or it could be the result of what

Donald Carveth (1992) referred to as "empathic identification," the capacity to empathically feel for others based one's conscious awareness of one's own deprived child-self. Recurrent self-sacrifice is sometimes a way of staying connected to other people, or it could be frankly masochistic, but it would surely be a mistake to pathologize all acts of self-sacrifice as nothing more than an opportunity for masochistic self-punishment.

We see overt acts of sacrifice among children; Jean Piaget (2007) tells the story of a 4 or 5 year old child who was told that his mother, who was very ill, would die in a few days. His most treasured possession was a toy horse; the thought came to him that he must give up his horse in order to make his mother better. This caused him great pain, but he smashed the horse, and on seeing his mother's recovery he was convinced that his sacrifice had mysteriously cured her. Piaget gives several other examples of children's rituals or sacrifices which were carried out to ward off fate. Apparently we are sometimes trained to sacrifice ourselves in childhood, to try to help our parents, if necessary by suffering or sacrificing ourselves in order to maintain the connection to them—this may be the unconscious underpinning of a religious need to sacrifice to connect to a divinity.

Harold Searles (1975) believes that we have an innate concern for the welfare of others. He feels that children have a deep need to give and express themselves in a loving way, and out of this love a child will sacrifice his own individuality for the sake of mother's welfare. He describes the schizophrenic patient's need to care for his therapist, but one also sees this phenomenon with less ill people in everyday psychotherapeutic situations. In fact sacrifice is often an opportunity to prove that one loves someone. Ludwig Binswanger (1958, p. 215) describes the extreme case of a delusional patient whose father was an egotistical, hard, and tyrannical individual who treated her mother like a slave. The patient decided she should persuade her father to treat her mother more considerately, so she put her arm into a burning stove, and turned to her father saying "Look, this is to show you how much I love you!" Her intention was to suffer extreme pain as proof of what love can do. Binswanger believes that the pain was also an expression of her atonement for her love for her father. Binswanger suggests that the ultimate meaning of sacrifice lies in the forming of a union with the other.

Jung's writing on sacrifice is typical of his seamless blending of the psychological and the spiritual—for him, they cannot be separated. To understand him, one has to understand his view of the transpersonal Self.

In brief, he believes that the Self is an a priori image of the divine within the personality, and that the Self prefigures the ego, or the Self acts as a kind of blueprint for the development of the sense of self. (This a priori nature of the Self contrasts with personalistic schools of depth psychology, in which the sense of self is entirely constructed from human experience.) In his essay titled "Transformation Symbolism in the Mass" (CW 11), Jung suggests that every sacrifice is to a greater or lesser extent a sacrifice of oneself, so that sacrifice always involves suffering. This is because if the object I sacrifice is mine, my ego is unconsciously identified with the object, and to be a true sacrifice the object must be given in a manner in which I have no future claim to it. Otherwise what looks like a sacrifice may only be a way of inducing indebtedness in the recipient, in which case our apparent giving to others is actually giving to oneself. The sacrificer must be conscious of his identity with his gift and have some awareness of how much of himself he is giving up as he sacrifices the gift—the more important the object is to me, the more I suffer when I sacrifice it. However, the saving grace is that if one can give oneself, at least one possesses oneself, so that an act of self-consciousness is inherent in each act of self-sacrifice and self-surrender. An act of sacrifice means the ego must relinquish some aspect of itself, and the transpersonal Self makes this happen—in fact, "...a sacrifice only takes place when we feel the self [here Jung refers to the transpersonal Self] actually carrying it out on ourselves. We may also venture to surmise that in so far as the self stands to us in the relation of father to son, the self in some sort feels our sacrifice as a sacrifice of itself" (p. 232). The ego participates in sacrificing itself in the individuation process (Jung's term for ongoing personality development), which inevitably causes suffering as the ego lets go of what feels important but must now be relinquished because of pressure from the Self. Thus, individuation may require that we voluntarily sacrifice old attitudes, a previous way of life, and our long-held beliefs about ourselves. In the process we become more and more conscious of the Self. However, it is important to reiterate that the ego, or the ordinary empirical personality, suffers from the violence done to it by the demands of the Self during the individuation process. Ideally one makes a voluntary sacrifice rather than having what must happen forced upon us. For Jung, sacrifice remains a mystery; the impulse to sacrifice arises from the unconscious, and the ego cannot fully understand the transformative process which is going on (CW 5).

At the same time as we wrestle with the demands of the Self, Jung believed that the Self is forcing itself into our consciousness in order to become more human and more conscious—this is his psychological understanding of incarnation. He points out (CW 13, para 331) that the human effort to achieve wholeness by struggling with the Self occurs in parallel to the Self's voluntary sacrifice to the bondage of earthly existence as it incarnates to form a personality. In Christian mythology, this process is depicted as the loving self-sacrifice of Christ, who for Jung is an image of the transpersonal Self. Discussing this issue, Dreifuss (1977) quotes a personal communication from von Franz: "The sacrifice to the Self, the rising of consciousness, brings suffering on one hand, but on the other hand there is joy in it, because it leads to the experience of meaning."

The psychotherapeutic implication of the need for the ego to surrender to the Self is that both the therapist and patient must make the necessary sacrifices. The patient's sacrifices are obvious in terms of time, money, and emotional investment. The therapist's sacrifices are also important; they include isolation, therapeutic abstinence, restraint of the therapist's own wishes, constant exposure to painful feelings, anxiety, occasional boredom, and "contamination" by the patient's material which stirs up the therapist's own difficulties. This is why Jung believes that the therapist is as much in the therapy as the patient, and no change is possible unless both people change. All this can be quite taxing to the therapist's physical and mental health. It is not always obvious what needs to be sacrificed for life to go on, and this discovery may be part of the therapeutic process. We may discover this synchronistically, which is an important feature of a biblical story of sacrifice illustrated by Abraham's willingness to obey God's command to sacrifice his son Isaac (Genesis 22, 1-13). Dreyfuss (1977) points out that Abraham was ready to sacrifice Isaac, but the appearance of a ram in a nearby thicket at the moment the knife was about to fall was a synchronistic event, suggesting that if we are prepared to make a conscious sacrifice, our life situation may change in a fateful way.[24] Traditional believers hold that Abraham's acceptance of God's demand for sacrifice changed God's destructive intention.

---

24   The binding of Isaac has been an important theme in religion, literature, and art for a long time, suggesting it is psychologically important. Because there are different ways to read the Hebrew, some scholars believe that Abraham actually did sacrifice Isaac, whereupon the story was edited into its present form by subsequent redactors as a defense against the unthinkable reality of father-son murder. Other authors see the story as a protest against the practice of child sacrifice, and it has also been seen as a pre-figuration of Christ's sacrifice. Psychoanalysts speculate that the Oedipus complex underlies this story, and the threat of death may have been a punishment for Isaac's incest with his mother. Abraham had betrayed his own father's religion and was afraid his son would rebel against him (Sugar, 2002). Human sacrifice still goes on in wars in which we sacrifice soldiers and civilians, so that a military culture can be seen as a sacrificial system (Marvin et al., 1999). Capital punishment has also been seen as a form of human sacrifice (Smith, 2000). We also sacrifice people for economic reasons, by maintaining environmental pollution and by marketing unhealthy foods and medicines.

Psychologically speaking, this is a mythic image of the ego's submission to the Self. Clearly, such a sacrifice requires enormous faith, and raises the issue of whether the ego might say no to the Self.

In the religious traditions of antiquity, only the men carry out animal sacrifices. Nancy Jay (1992) suggests that this exclusive prerogative of men is the result of men's envy of women's ability to give birth. When the God-image changed from being female to male, the problem of fertility had to be addressed. Accordingly, in the Bible, every firstborn male animal belonged to God (Exodus 13:12-14). Jay believes that the male God's demand to own the first born of all animals is his attempt to "re-birth" them. Even a firstborn son had to be redeemed by giving money to a priest as a symbolic exchange for the boy, or the father sacrifices an animal as a substitute for his son, thus symbolically giving the son his life, whereupon the child belongs to the father and not its mother.

While Judeo-Christian mythology stresses father-son sacrifice, in Greek mythology (at least in the powerful play *Iphigenia in Aulis* by Euripides) we see the sacrifice of a daughter by a father. Agamemnon is commanded to kill his daughter Iphegenia in order to appease the goddess Artemis, whom he had offended, so that she will bestow favorable winds for him to sail to the Trojan War. Iphigenia is willing to sacrifice herself, partly to please her father and partly for the sake of patriotism. In myth in general, fathers rather than mothers sacrifice their children, although in traditions which teach an afterlife, women sacrifice themselves as religious martyrs for their faith. Traditional Hindu women would sacrifice themselves by casting themselves onto their husband's funeral pyre, apparently as an expression of extreme grief and also as a way of purging the couple of sin and guaranteeing their reunion in the afterlife.

Suffering, self-sacrifice, and martyrdom

Martyrdom, broadly understood as religiously or politically motivated self-sacrifice, is a recurrent theme in contemporary culture because of frequent suicide bombings. Martyrdom is an ancient archetypal phenomenon, found in several religious traditions in which martyrs are regarded as heroic examples of piety and devotion to God. Martyrdom is typically found in religions such as Judaism, Christianity, and Islam which promise an afterlife, resurrection of the dead, or a reward in paradise. Political martyrs sacrifice themselves for patriotic values or a cause. A common factor linking religious and political martyrdom seems to be a commitment to an ideal perceived as more important than oneself. Because martyrdom has many sources—political, religious, and psychological—it is probably not a single type of phenomenon.

The English word "martyr" comes from the ancient Greek term *martus*, meaning "witness." Early Christians applied it to those who submitted to death as a witness to Christ. As in the case of animal sacrifice, in the case of martyrdom there seems to be a connection between violence, death, and spiritual transformation or sanctification. Christian martyrs, for instance, believed they were fostering the unity of the church, demonstrating the power of their faith over that of the pagans, and patterning their death after the death of Jesus. Early followers of Muhammad were also persecuted for their faith. In the Jewish tradition, a good example is the story of King Antiochus in the Book of Maccabees, who forbade Jewish religious traditions and tried to enforce the worship of Zeus. Antiochus offered seven sons their lives in the presence of their mother if they would eat pork. The first six refused and were tortured and killed. Their mother implored the last son to die like his brothers rather than comply. The history of all three major monotheistic traditions is replete with analogous stories (Berenbaum et al., 2004). If one believes that martyrdom ensures eternal life in paradise, at least for those who martyr themselves voluntarily, self-sacrifice in the name of God may seem like a way of escaping the unhappiness of this world. Martyrdom is often considered a form of redemptive suffering, because it was thought to reduce the penalty the martyr pays for sin. For the skeptic, in the vein of Nietzsche, martyrdom is a form of self-enhancement in the guise of piety, not really a humble imitation of Christ but rather the disguised wish of the weak and powerless to be powerful in heaven, or a wish to be among the elite saints. This attitude does not do justice to the sincerity and courage of many religious martyrs, and it does not take into account the important social justice activity of people such as Archbishop Óscar Romero and Dr. Martin Luther King Jr., for which they were assassinated. Mahatma Gandhi threatened to starve himself to death in his quest for India's independence from Britain, and Buddhist monks regularly immolate themselves to protest the Chinese occupation of Tibet. Dietrich Bonhoeffer[25] also exemplifies political martyrdom motivated by religious faith.

---

25   Bonhoeffer was a Lutheran pastor who was working at Union Seminary in New York when WW 2 was declared. He left his safe position to return to Germany in order to oppose the Nazis, who executed him. He was subsequently considered to be a martyr, although not without controversy.

Quite often, a society retrospectively confers the title of martyr on a person who suffers and dies for the group, as we see in the case of the Lakota Sioux Chief Crazy Horse, who was regarded as a martyr after being killed while in US military custody. He was subsequently treated with great reverence by his people, and later by all American Indians, because of his resistance to white expansion on the frontier. Eventually, stories about him transformed his image into legend as a kind of Sioux Christ (Hyde, 1961). It is typical for martyred figures to be remembered as icons for the ideology of their group, because such figures enhance the identity of the group. However, the status of martyr is debatable, depending on which side of the political argument one stands. Bobby Sands was a member of the Provisional Irish Republican Army who was one of ten people who died in a hunger strike in 1981 to protest their treatment while in a British prison. His death produced a surge of recruitment for the IRA and intense international media coverage. For his followers he was a hero, a blood sacrifice, and a martyr, while for his detractors he was nothing more than a fanatic and a terrorist.

Martyrdom among the early Christians had important political overtones as well as its religious underpinnings, because Christian belief directly challenged the Roman state gods, which were part of the state power structure. Today, even when someone dies for a political cause we still use the term "martyr," giving the incident a quasi-religious quality. When Matthew Shepard was killed in 1998, the victim of a hate crime, many people described him as a martyr for gay rights. Civil rights workers have also been viewed as martyrs; for some people this includes the abolitionist John Brown, following his execution in 1859, which was one of the sparks for the civil war. Brown's political struggle was partly motivated by his belief that God did not sanction slavery. Abraham Lincoln has also been seen as a martyr for racial equality.

The Palestinian Hamas movement believes that martyrdom is the epitome of *jihad* (which means effort for the sake of Allah), which has a central position in Islamic law. Combined with the religious duty to prevent wrongdoing, belief in *jihad* is part of a moral code that Hamas believes justifies attacks against Israel. Islamic radicals who blow themselves up are often referred to in the western press as suicide bombers. However, Islam expressly forbids suicide, so these individuals would repudiate that designation because they believe they are in the service of Allah, even though other Muslim scholars forbid the practice on the grounds that it is an abuse of the divine gift of life. The term "suicide bomber" is also not accurate from a clinical point of view, because the motives and state of mind of the suicidal person and the religious martyr are entirely different, and so is their attitude to death. Most suicidal people are depressed, but religious martyrs may not be. Contemporary Islamic martyrs show anger at the shame and humiliation they feel at the hands of western countries, and these feelings are well-known sources of human violence. We do not yet know enough about the developmental dynamics or mental state of Islamic terrorists to describe them well. Lester (2004) suggests that suicide bombers have the personality traits of the authoritarian personality as described by Theodor Adorno in 1950. This includes rigid adherence to conventional values, submission to an idealized moral authority, aggression, projection of their own difficulties onto an out-group, concern with strength, and devaluation of introspection. Lester believes that most Middle Eastern terrorists are raised in fundamentalist sects which foster these attitudes. Most religious martyrs are fundamentalists, and all over the world religious fundamentalists tend to be politically conservative, authoritarian, and often anti-democratic. Modern day religious martyrdom can be seen to some extent as a fundamentalist protest against modernism and liberal democracy. Many fundamentalists demonstrate intrapsychic splitting into all-good and all-bad, so that nonbelievers may be demonized and killed. Fundamentalists tend to have a punitive, judgmental image of God, a drive for purification, and prejudice towards outsiders, all of which reinforce their motivation for martyrdom (Altemeyer et al., 1992). Fundamentalism is discussed further in chapter 6.

In this context, of interest to depth psychologists is the Islamic tradition that the martyr may be given prior knowledge of his or her death in a dream or a waking vision, part of the ancient idea found in many traditions that dreams may be sent by God. This tradition continues among modern Islamic martyrs. Friends often dream of dead martyrs who reassure the dreamer that they are happy in paradise, which is very important for Jihadist ideology (Cook, 2007; Edgar, 2007). Adding to the difficulty of sharply defining martyrdom, the proportion of religious rather than political motives of Islamic radicals is not clear. Revenge for atrocities in places such as Bosnia and Chechnya adds to our confusion about motivation in a given case.

Martyrdom and masochism

When a religious martyr choses to suffer voluntarily, the question arises whether such martyrdom is a form of non-sexual masochism, because on the surface there seem to be some similarities between the extremes of moral masochism (suffering for a greater good) and religious martyrdom. In both cases, the individuals feel they are operating in the service of a larger goal, which makes their suffering worthwhile, and both religious martyrdom and masochism can be a form of protest against an oppressor. However, although these situations show some similarities, the underlying psychological motives are often very different. The masochist was oppressed by early abusive caregivers, whereas the religious martyr suffers from a religious or political oppressor. The masochist unconsciously wants his childhood abuser to see how much he is suffering, or wants his abuser to feel guilty, hoping he will at last obtain the love and relationship he needs. Or the masochist uses his suffering to stabilize a precarious sense of self. In contrast, the martyr may have an intact sense of self and only wants to demonstrate his religious or political devotion, which is more important than his own pain. The masochistic character unconsciously arranges his life so that he appears to be a recurrent victim of malevolent fate. He has an unconscious need for self-punishment which leads to self-defeating behavior, but a religious martyr may have never exhibited self-induced suffering before he or she is martyred. Furthermore, true masochistic behavior produces a sense of satisfaction, which might not be present in the case of involuntary martyrdom, where the person is made to suffer for the sake of his religion.

Alfred Adler described a "redeemer complex" to describe people who feel they must save or redeem others as a way of feeling superior. This complex is said to be typically found among ministers of religion (Ansbacher et al., 1956). Traditional Freudian psychoanalysts see religious martyrdom as a repeat of an early family situation in a way that fulfills a regressive Oedipal fantasy. They see the Church as a nurturing mother, while the divine Father-God loves the martyr and accepts the martyr's embrace by the Church-mother instead of being angry about it in the usual Oedipal manner. Instead, the Father-God is angry with the martyr's enemies (Bradford, 1990). The need to obtain the favor of the divine father is characteristic of patriarchal monotheism even today. Presumably there were psychodynamic factors operating among the early Christian martyrs, but it is difficult to know whether we can apply contemporary psychological theories to them because our culture is so different.

Self-sacrifice is essential to the true believer, a personality type described by Eric Hoffer (2002). The true believer is prepared to sacrifice himself for the sake of a movement which he believes has the absolute truth, but the true believer's motive is different than the self-sacrifice of the martyr or the masochist. Hoffer believes that the true believer has lost faith in himself or feels like a failure. He is insecure, and finds self-assurance by passionately embracing a movement. In terms of psychoanalytic self-psychology, the group and its cause become an essential selfobject which holds him together. His cause feels righteous, and he subordinates his own creativity and any original thinking to its advancement. The true believer is often (but not always) prepared to die for the sake of a coming new life, or for a better world—he may even see his struggle as part of a cosmic drama. In the service of his struggle, he feels it is acceptable for many other lives to be sacrificed. Such an extremist feels special, one of the chosen, and his movement offers refuge from the anxieties and meaninglessness of his personal existence. The individual becomes part of a "closely knit and exultant corporate whole" (p. 41); he loses his personal identity as he is assimilated into the collective movement.

The scapegoat sacrifice

In the course of human history, many societies have believed that their sins could be purged by loading them onto an innocent victim who was then sacrificed for the good of the group. The anthropologist René Girard (1977, 1987) has suggested that there is a biological basis for such scapegoating. He believed that, since human beings are naturally aggressive, and early human history consisted of an endless series of attacks and counterattacks between groups, an outlet for this aggression had to be found in the form of a scapegoat whose sacrificial death would stop the cycle of retribution. Societies then used some form of sacrifice to maintain social order. Killing a scapegoat is a controlled form of ritual violence.

Girard's theory of the origin of violence contrasts with traditional ideas that human aggression is due to scarcity and conflict over resources. He believes that conflict is the result of a core human trait known as "acquisitive mimesis," meaning that we imitate and try to acquire what other people desire—for him, our desire is always mediated by something desired by others. When a person acquires an object, people around him also desire that object and try to obtain it, generating conflict, envy, and violence. If someone had not desired the object the others might not have found it interesting—but we instinctively want what others have and we compete for it.[26] (This dark view of human nature sounds like a learned theory of behavior based on imitation.) Given this situation, Girard believes that one societal way to prevent social violence—other than by self-examination, compromise, or spiritual discipline—is to deflect society's destructiveness onto a scapegoat who can be sacrificed. The scapegoat is an arbitrary victim who is available and close at hand. Even though the scapegoat may have nothing to do with the conflict induced by acquisitive mimesis, people are very ready to follow their group's wishes and are reluctant to oppose it. Usually the scapegoat is an outsider, or someone on the margins of the society, typically members of another ethnic or religious group. The society rationalizes its violence by viewing the scapegoat as evil. Girard gives the example of Jews in Medieval Europe who were blamed for outbreaks of the plague, or women who were burned as witches. When social problems appear, the scapegoat seems to be the cause of all the problems, so the victim is sacrificed and the violence that would otherwise produce internal social conflict is dispersed. In this way, otherness is expelled and social cohesion and equilibrium are maintained until new rivalry builds up.

Interestingly, because the sacrificial victim has saved the society, he is sometimes mythologized or deified as a savior figure who was sacrificed to save the entire community. People discovered that if they vent their violence against a scapegoat, harmony results within the community, and this process becomes ritualized in the form of a regular sacrifice. Early in human history therefore, human beings were sacrificed, to be eventually replaced by animals, so Girard believes that religions are rooted in violence which is sublimated in the service of religion.[27] Girard thinks that this complex of acquisitive mimesis and violent sacrifice lies at the foundation of all human religion and culture—which may not leave much hope for our species if it is true. Girard has been criticized on several grounds, for example that his is a very narrow theory of the origin of religion that tries to reduce it to one mechanism (Adams, 2000). In his early work, Girard (1986) saw all sacrifice as an aspect

---

26   Girard is therefore able to offer an alternative to the traditional understanding of the Oedipus complex. He believes that rather than the son seeing the father as a competitor for mother, and feeling castration anxiety, the son actually innocently loves mother with no sexual desire for her or murderous rage at father. It is the father who sees his son's love for his mother as competition and who feels threatened (Williams, 1996).

27   Girard's theory has Freudian roots. In Freud's Totem and Taboo, young men (the primal horde) kill the father of the tribe and then institute a tradition of sacrifice to atone for the murder. This memorializes the event and allows the men to express a combination of sorrow and happiness at the death of the father who was both loved and hated by them. Most contemporary writers believe this idea of Freud has no historical basis.

of the scapegoat process, so he saw Jesus as a scapegoat for the maintenance of social order. Later (2008) he suggested that this mechanism belonged to pre-biblical religion, whereas Christ's self-offering was a sacrifice of a different kind—not demanded for the expiation of sin as the tradition suggests, but as an example of self-giving love that we can follow. For Girard (a Christian thinker), Jesus' resurrection allows the hope that, with divine grace, the cycle of violence in human history can cease.

On self-sacrifice and self-love

Self-sacrifice may be an important aspect of relationships (Van Lange et al., 1997). Self-sacrifice contributes to feelings of gratitude and trust in the relationship, it adds to the partner's sense of being valued by the person who makes the self-sacrifice, and increases partners' levels of satisfaction and commitment to the relationship. Self-sacrifice may be entirely altruistic, based on empathy for the other person, or it might be more narcissistic, designed to increase one's own self-esteem, or designed to increase the likelihood that in future situations the partner will reciprocate.

Many cultures believe it is honorable to sacrifice oneself for one's country or religion. To explain why people are prepared to risk their own lives for the sake of an ideology or a national cause, Routledge et al (2008) suggest that terror management theory might be relevant. This idea asserts that our awareness that we will die motivates us to invest in cultural belief systems and values which provide a symbolic sense of the transcendence of mortality. We then feel we are part of something larger than ourselves. For example, a soldier might be willing to die for the sake of his country or for democracy and freedom. Heightened awareness of death (mortality salience) increases attempts to live up to the standards of a certain world-view, allowing people to feel they are worthy of the security and perhaps life after death which it promises. Suicide bombing and Japanese kamikaze pilots come to mind in this context.

Because self-sacrifice can be excessive, Christians have sometimes struggled with the tension between appropriate self-love and self-sacrifice on behalf of others. The Christian tradition teaches self-emptying, a process known as *kenosis*, in which one's own will becomes entirely receptive to God, but the self that is emptied must be considered to be of value and must only be sacrificed for the right reason. Discussing this issue, Lippitt (2009) points out that "true self-love and love of others are often inextricably linked" (p. 132). Healthy self-esteem, the feeling that one is a worthy person, not only encourages moral action towards others but is often a pre-requisite for being fully available to others.

4

THE EFFECTS OF SUFFERING ON THE PERSONALITY

The positive and negative effects of suffering

Suffering may be helpful or harmful to the personality and its ongoing development. Suffering may make us more open to change or it may solidify our usual ways of coping. Suffering may radically change our view of the world and of ourselves, or it may reinforce a life-long pessimistic attitude to life. Suffering forces choices upon us that we would otherwise avoid, and often radically changes the course of our lives. Sometimes intense suffering reveals previously hidden levels of a person's character by breaking through defenses and making it impossible to maintain the persona behind which the individual has been hiding or masking his shadow. Suffering evokes both the light and dark side of human nature; it reveals our capacity for sacrifice, courage, resilience, and compassion, but also our selfishness, our willingness to sacrifice others, and our resentment and bitterness. Many cultures have recognized that suffering may lead to wisdom and understanding that may otherwise be unattainable. Suffering may lead to new realizations about how we want to live our life and about what really matters to us. It is important to acknowledge that suffering is inevitable, as the Buddha pointed out, and the image of the suffering of the crucified Christ is central to Christianity. However, we can explore the psychological effects of suffering without imposing a specifically religious coloring. Suffering is one of the most important themes of the literature and art of western civilization.

I believe that we can say that suffering has been helpful when it results in some of the following: increased empathy and compassion for the suffering of others; improved ability to relate to others; a deeper appreciation for the ordinary things of everyday life; the dissolving of narcissistic problems such as arrogance; a deepened spiritual life; new experiences of the transpersonal

Self; increased wisdom; increased capacity for humor; a restructuring of values; and deepened self-knowledge. The psychotherapist's task is to assist in these developments where possible.

Suffering may change priorities and make us question our belief system, which is a lens through which we interpret life experiences. Suffering often makes us lose our innocence— we lose any fantasies we may have had of invulnerability, and we feel vulnerable and afraid. We are initiated into a new state of being. When our values and beliefs are shaken because of suffering, our personal guidelines for behavior and the goals we have pursued thus far may be called into question. Such goals are important because they give us a sense that life has a purpose. Our goals are closely tied to our values, and they are important in giving us a sense of direction and meaning in life. Our self-esteem is often radically affected by the degree to which we achieve our goals. A serious life crisis makes us think about our lives and we may have to radically reevaluate our situation. Typical patterns of behavior, such as extreme independence, the need to take care of others and neglect oneself, the need to control everything, or a life-long inability to trust others, may no longer be effective coping mechanisms. Change is then forced upon the individual, although some people may collapse rather than change.

Suffering may cause tremendous bitterness, rage, increased self-absorption, and cynicism about human values. These reactions act as a protection for unbearable feelings of vulnerability. A common type of depressive reaction to suffering occurs when a life event happens which forces us to give up a narcissistic fantasy of success, power, beauty or fame, which we had been using to buttress our self-esteem. The loss of this fantasy adds to our suffering. The origin of such fantasy is found in our early conditioning about what is important and desirable in life, and much misery is the result of our unwillingness to let go of these fantasies. We also prop up our image of ourselves with realistic achievements and positions in life, and our suffering is increased if an event such as an illness makes us lose these supports. We are then forced to ask questions about who we really are and to examine our real values.

We can also add layers of suffering by making the people around us suffer, for instance by being so angry about the problem which is causing our suffering that the atmosphere around us becomes difficult for the family or for those trying to help. Or we may become envious of those who are more fortunate. Sometimes these secondary problems are used to distract the sufferer from the primary problem, and they distance us from the search for its meaning and purpose.

Many questions arise for the psychotherapist faced with a suffering individual. Can we choose how to respond to extreme suffering? Do we choose to meet suffering either with integrity and equanimity or with rage, despair, and bitterness? Suffering may harden us or destroy us; under extreme conditions, why do some people choose to struggle and others become depressed and suicidal? Our response to these questions depends on our attitude to free will and determinism, discussed in more detail in chapter 11. Suffice it to say here that, faced with serious suffering, we make a choice about how to respond based on developmental and personality factors, sometimes combined with our spiritual commitments. Secure attachment and the development of basic trust in infancy, the childhood experience of being repeatedly cared for when we were in distress, seems to remain in us like an unconscious memory which acts as a reservoir of hope and faith on which we can draw during difficult times.

Coping with suffering: Conservation and transformation

There is no best way to cope with suffering. The psychotherapist has to discern in collaboration with the patient what will work for the individual. It is not helpful for the psychotherapist to try to move the person in a particular direction, although the temptation is to subtly or unconsciously encourage the person to cope in a way that would be helpful for the therapist, or in a way which corresponds to the therapist's world view. However, there is considerable variation in the ways in which people respond to serious life situations. Regression or full-blown decompensation is likely when we are faced with a problem that greatly exceeds our ability to manage the situation, but if we feel there is a chance we can deal with the problem we face, a life crisis becomes a challenge and may even seem exciting. As long as it is not overwhelming, stress offers the possibility of new development and growth. In wartime, as well as all the pathology that results from combat, it has also been observed that when survival skills have been taxed to their limit by fear and pain, latent qualities of endurance and leadership may emerge which can later be accessed when life becomes difficult. Combat veterans sometimes say that their wartime experience has helped them learn to cope with adversity and value life. They feel more goal-oriented, less helpless, and more resilient as a result of their combat experience. (See chapter 8 for a discussion of the negative effects of combat).

In this context it is useful to look at a variety of coping strategies for dealing with stress, which are relevant to the suffering that may result from a crisis. A modern classification of responses to stress began with the distinction between problem-focused vs. emotion-focused coping (Lazarus et al., 1984). Problem-focused coping tries to deal with the stressor itself—either to remove it, avoid it, or reduce its effects. Thus, loss of a job leads to attempts to find another. Emotion-focused coping tries to reduce the distress produced by the problem, using some form of relaxation, support from others, or mental mechanisms such as denial. Obviously both these approaches may be attempted at the same time and they can reinforce each other. Another distinction is between engagement coping, which tries to actively deal with the stress and its attendant emotions, and avoidance coping which tries to escape the problem and its related emotions (Moos et al, 2003). Engagement coping overlaps with both problem-focused and emotion-focused coping, since it includes seeking support, acceptance, finding positive meaning in the situation, and replacing maladaptive attitudes with more helpful ones. One might let go of goals that are threatened by the stressor, or one might try to adjust to it in other ways. Avoidance coping tries to avoid feelings of emotional distress using strategies such as alcohol, gambling, or other distractions, even to the extent of wishful thinking or denial, as if the problem did not exist. Obviously this latter approach does not deal with the problem, and the use of addictive distractions adds additional problems. It used to be thought that active attempts at coping, such as taking charge and making changes in one's life style, are always better than responding passively to stress such as that due to illness, but overly active coping may actually be harmful in cases of heart disease and hypertension.

Our appraisal of a difficult situation is very important in our response to suffering. The emotions which arise vary with the meaning of a particular situation: anger appears if we have been threatened or hurt, especially unfairly; sadness develops from loss; guilt appears when we feel we have transgressed an important moral value (Lazarus, 1991). The importance of personal appraisal means that the same event may mean different things to different people; the physicist Stephen Hawking is almost totally paralyzed, but he copes because the disease has left him with an intact brain, which is central to his work. His example suggests that we cannot assume we can predict the effects of suffering; rather, it is preferable to try to find out how the person is actually appraising his or her suffering. Appraisal of the significance of a situation is based on our belief systems, the way we are oriented to life, and our world-view. There are culturally approved ways to cope, but also very individual ways. We may try to find something that matters to us in the situation because this can give it meaning; if we believe that a donated organ may save the life of another, and this is an important value, this may make the suffering produced by a lost loved one meaningful. In the search for meaning, much depends on our values and what we believe to be significant. This may be money, it may be a social value such as justice, it may be a spiritual ideal such as service to others, or it may be a combination of such factors. (The issue of finding meaning in suffering is discussed in chapter 8.) However, when people are overwhelmed, they may give up any such search; they stop caring for anything and shut down in an attempt to deal with intolerable pain. Some situations of total withdrawal, which look like depression, are an attempt to avoid grieving a loss which is not being acknowledged.

There is considerable variation in the ways in which people respond to serious life situations; some people cope much more effectively than others. Personality has an important influence on the way we cope with stress. (Here I draw from the review by Carver, 2010). Neuroticism (the tendency to feel prolonged negative affect states) tends to make people appraise situations as particularly threatening. Extraversion, conscientiousness, and openness make one more likely to find stressors to be a challenge rather than a threat. People who cope well with stress tend to have relationships they can depend on, they are agreeable, optimistic, have high self-esteem, the ability to trust others, see themselves as worthwhile, and have a problem-solving orientation to life. A variety of resources may be helpful in coping with suffering. Prior experience with the problem, or with adversity in general, is helpful, which is why older people are sometimes better at dealing with it than the young. The capacity for perseverance and a sense of personal efficacy are important, as is the capacity to contain painful feelings without collapse. Access to helpers (both professional and familial), adequate finances, and social support are also of help. A prior history of failures, an unsupportive family, social stigma about illnesses such as AIDS, and neurotic beliefs about oneself are unhelpful. Pessimism and fatalistic beliefs exacerbate the problem.

One of the main responses to crisis and threat is an attempt at conservation of something of value to the person. Freud, for example, refused to leave Vienna in 1939 until the last minute, convinced that he could weather the Nazi storm, because of the powerful significance of his home. To some extent this behavior demonstrates his courage, but it also illustrates a human fear of leaving the known for the unknown, and perhaps the power of denial.

Much coping in the face of suffering is an attempt to maintain and preserve what is important to us, such as self-esteem, possessions, jobs, family, a world-view, a religious belief, or health. Such attempts at conservation are an important way to cope with stress. To conserve one's values in the face of suffering, as did Nelson Mandela through years of imprisonment, requires courage and integrity.

Under severe stress our usual ways of achieving significance in life may no longer work, and may need radical transformation. To try to conserve ones old way of life in the face of major life changes may lead to chronic frustration. Transformation instead of conservation is preferable if it is attainable. After a devastating illness or injury, transformation means that people have to develop new values and new goals in life. The aspiring ball player who develops an injury which permanently affects his ability may have to give up fantasies of playing professionally, but may be able to develop a coaching career. Some of these attempts at transformation lead to defeat, but some lead to radical personality change. New things to live for and new priorities have to be found when the old ones are lost. In the process of transformation, people may go back to school, change careers, and develop new beliefs about themselves. In psychotherapy it is not always easy to decide if a patient's style of coping with suffering is more about conservation or transformation. Much depends on the patient's goals, motivation, capacity to change, and whether his social group will support radical change. The psychotherapist can evaluate success in the coping process by looking at the person's mood as an indicator, and by asking whether the person feels as if the situation has been dealt with as well as possible or if more remains to be done.

In the short term, it is sometimes more helpful to cope by avoiding than by approaching the problem, even though avoidance may not help in the long run. Denial of the seriousness of an illness, such as cancer or a heart attack, is associated with reduced anxiety or depression because denial mutes the stress response, but denial may ultimately be maladaptive if it prevents necessary life-style changes. Some styles of coping may lead to immediate discomfort but produce longer-term gains. For example, writing and talking about a trauma may make one feel worse initially, because doing so brings back memories of the event, but in the long term it is helpful.

There are times when an individual's attempt to cope does not meet with social support, for example when an abused wife wants to leave a husband but cannot find the support to do so, or when a homeless person cannot earn an adequate wage in spite of a willingness to work. Sometimes it does not matter what we do, because too much of the situation is out of our control. Only 1 in 600 people survived concentration camps in ww2 and the prisoner's response often did not affect whether he or she survived—but see the discussion of Frankl's work in this area in chapter 8.

The Effects of suffering on relationships

Significant relationships are severely tested when one member of the relationship becomes ill; sometimes the connection cannot hold, and sometimes it gets stronger. Relationship bonds can be particularly firm during times of suffering; witness the bonds which form between soldiers during combat, or between victims of natural disasters. When suffering causes relationship problems, the difficulty is not always caused by the partner of the suffering person; the sufferer him or herself may withdraw and not allow anyone to get close. At times, spouses and close friends of the suffering person are not comfortable with the possibility that radical change in the relationship may be necessary. An adverse effect of suffering is especially noticeable when commitment to the relationship was based on narcissistic needs for beauty, power, wealth or prestige which are lost because of illness or other crisis. The connection will survive if it is based on authentic love, in which case suffering may make the bond and level of intimacy even deeper as care for the sufferer then becomes a devotional practice.

Resistance to Change

Part of the challenge in helping people who suffer is the problem of resistance to inevitable change, which can be like trying to hold onto the dock while the ship is leaving. As noted above, our resistance often arises from an unwillingness to give up a fantasy of how things should be, based on idealized expectations of success, beauty, and so on. All these can be used to support our sense of self, and so they are difficult to let go of. Rather than relinquish a dream, we may become angry at life and feel sorry for ourselves. The problem is often one of insisting on the illusion that we have total control over our lives. Resistance to change is also based on fear of the unknown, especially if it threatens the individual's sense of security.

Resistance to change is a central issue in psychotherapy. Resistance traditionally referred to the patient's unconscious interference with the work of therapy, often due to the avoidance of painful affects such as shame or rage. Resistance occurs when the patient feels that some aspects of himself have to be kept hidden, especially if he does not feel safe. For example, resistance to expressing anger towards the therapist may be due to a fear of rejection by the therapist.

All theories of psychotherapy must deal with this phenomenon, because resistance can be central to success or failure in psychotherapy, but different schools of thought view resistance in their own ways. Behaviorists tend to look at resistance in terms of non-compliance or as oppositional behavior. Therapists with a Rogerian orientation tend to see resistance as a function of the therapist's poor handling of the patient's feelings, and it is certainly true that hurtful failure of the therapist's empathy is likely to increase resistance. Sometimes the therapist's behavior threatens the patient's sense of self, which may make it difficult to maintain a tie to the therapist. In the classical psychoanalytic literature, resistance was often spoken of pejoratively, but today many depth psychologists believe that resistance is often necessary; it is the result of the patient's attempt to hang on to what is left of himself as a result of his childhood difficulties. Because resistance is a healthy form of self-protection, it must be approached delicately. Rather than being confronted or interpreted head on, many therapists prefer to leave the resistance in place until the therapeutic bond feels safe enough for resistance to dissolve naturally. It important to note that the therapist's counter-resistance may occur when the patient's material stimulates the therapist's personal vulnerability, or if the therapist's relational style or world view are very different from those of the patient, so that the therapist feels uncomfortable or threatened in the relationship.

For depth psychotherapists, the ability of psychotherapy to produce change is a function of many factors, such as the nature and intensity of the patient's defenses, the therapist's ability to deal with defenses in a helpful manner, the strength of the therapeutic alliance, the nature of the transference, and the capacity for the patient's difficulty to be re-created and re-worked in an emotionally meaningful way with the therapist. The development of insight is helpful if accompanied by an appropriate affective response. Other factors are the degree of urgency of the patient's wish to change, his fear that change will lead to loss of an important relationship, his ability to contain painful affects, and his capacity for hope. An important development in the last few years has been the growing acknowledgment that emotions are fundamental, interacting with— but not secondary—to cognition. In fact, changing thinking without concomitant emotional change may have no therapeutic benefit. The idea that emotions should be the major target of therapeutic interest has long been held by clinicians of different orientations, but until the advent of affective neuroscience it was difficult to prove. It is now clear that the distressing emotions which are re-activated during psychotherapy can be changed or regulated by means of a new emotional experience with the therapist, followed by collaboratively processing the relational dynamic involved. This cycle of re-activation and re-processing of emotions, and the associated re-consolidation of emotionally-laden memories during the course of psychotherapy, seem to be essential for change (Greenberg, 2012.)

On despair, hope, and faith

Some people who seek psychotherapy are suffering from despair, feeling that there is no way out of their suffering. Life seems futile, and they are trapped in a debilitating state of mind that narrows the horizons of their life and world with no hope for the future. This state of mind is difficult to describe or explain to others, because when in despair the sufferer's experience of the world has changed, even to the extent that the world no longer seems to have any significance.

Many people alternate throughout their lives between hope and despair. What may add to the suffering of a despairing individual is the cultural pressure not give in to despair, but rather to "think positively"—part of a cultural attempt to deny the value of suffering. This may make the suffering person feel guilty about a legitimate and important developmental phase of his life, although to point this out may be to contravene the person's cultural conditioning and risks sounding as if the therapist is saying in a simplistic way that the suffering is "good for you."

Despair is not the same as depression, although the two states of mind may overlap and sometimes are (mistakenly) treated as if they were synonymous. However, one can be suffering from an existential state of despair about the state of one's life without being clinically depressed—that is, with no vegetative symptoms of depression. Despair is a more complex state of mind than depression. Steinbock (2007) points out that despair "grips me at the level of my spiritual being" (p. 448). Despair is not simply a loss of hope with regard to one particular situation in one's life; despair means that one has no hope for *anything* in one's life. Steinbock therefore points out that hopelessness *per se* is not the same as despair; one can be hopeless with regard to a particular event, but the larger ground of hope may still be still intact in the depth of one's being, whereas in despair hope has no ground at all. In despair, we give up altogether and "the ground of hope itself is groundless, and this is why every dimension of my life would be experienced as without hope" (ibid.). Because it attacks the very ground of hope, despair opens one up to suicide, "where suicide has to be understood not just in a physical sense, but in a spiritual, historical, purposive sense as well" (ibid.). That is, I may be pessimistic about the future in general but still able to keep going on with my life, or I may be hopeless about a specific problem yet keep going on with my life, but if I am in despair I cannot go on at all—there are no meaningful possibilities. Despair is "a kind of imprisonment" in the present, in which "I am unable to escape towards the future or to retreat into the past," (ibid.) because the past and future could not redeem the present.

If the individual has had few positive life experiences and few meaningful relationships, bitterness and despair may make it impossible to find any benefit from psychotherapy, and we do see people who seem to be in terminal despair. However, there must be at least an unconscious hope for relief to bring a person in despair to psychotherapy. It is important that the patient's despair becomes a part of the therapeutic process, because paradoxically an empathic response to despair may be enough to rekindle a sense of connection to the therapist, which may eventually produce a glimmer of hope. The patient may have unconscious hope that the therapist will be able to tolerate his feelings better than could his early caregivers—otherwise he would not appear for therapy. As Ogden (1979) suggests, the therapist must contain the patient's despair without wanting to end the therapy.

The therapist may be able to empathically feel and tolerate the patient's despair while at the same time keeping alive a glimmer of hope or faith in the back of the therapist's mind, even though this hope cannot be talked about without disrupting the therapeutic relationship. Without this possibility, the therapy might not survive. Hope itself has something of a checkered career in the history of thought. Opinions vary between those who point out that hope can be illusory and impractical if it prevents us focusing on the present, merely paving the way for disappointment, and those who value the helpful aspects of hope and argue that hope is developmentally important and essential for psychotherapy (see Corbett, 2011, for a fuller discussion of hope in psychotherapy.)

The attempt to counter despair with any kind of positive commentary only makes the despairing patient feel that the therapist does not realize how badly he really feels, and makes the situation worse. The therapist may simply have to acknowledge that he or she cannot see any hope at the moment. At least this conveys the feeling that the therapist can tolerate the patient's feelings and the patient is not alone with his despair, but it leads to difficult moments when the therapist is faced with a suicidal patient without knowing whether things will get better. Perhaps the most we can do at such a point is focus on the therapeutic relationship, which may offer a lifeline, and leave open the question of what may or may not happen. An important aspect of tolerating despair in a suicidal person has to do with the ability to wait, without turning away, which is demanding and frightening for the psychotherapist. Yet the very act of remaining present in such a situation, the act of witnessing and waiting with the patient may be helpful, although despair is often accompanied by a sense of isolation such that it may be difficult for the patient to feel the affective presence of the therapist. In this context, the therapist has to beware of occasions when the patient realizes that the therapist is desperate and so the patient pretends to feel a bit better in order to look after the therapist. Transformation may come out of despair, but we never know what will emerge in the individual situation. While despair may be an initiation into a new state of consciousness, there are successful and failed initiations.

By its nature, if one is truly in despair, nothing helps. The countertransference response to such despair is often a similar feeling of hopelessness induced in the therapist, who feels powerless and ineffectual, as if nothing can be done. Then, not only is the patient in despair, the therapist despairs of finding something helpful, which may awaken feelings of inadequacy in the therapist. Here the temptation is to fall back on theoretical formulations of what is happening and the search for techniques, but these are often of little value. If the patient's despair is the result of a failure on the part of the therapist, the disappointment can potentially be understood, acknowledged, and often repaired. Other types of despair are the result of the patient's life situation and not a function of the therapy itself. It then helps if the therapist can remember and get in touch with his or her own periods of despair, and can tolerate both feeling useless and being told that the therapy is not helping, without withdrawing from an intensely painful human interaction.

Therapists are somewhat more prone to despair early in their careers. In their training programs they have been led to believe that they have been given the best available techniques, and it can be a shock to discover that there are many human situations for which there are no off-the-shelf answers. This discovery can be frightening and disorienting. Only an authentic, human response is then of any value, but many beginning therapists have yet to develop confidence in themselves or in the power of the therapeutic relationship, and they have no previous similar experiences on which to draw. Yet no matter how seasoned we are, none of us are immune from this contagious emotion. The supervisor working with a beginning therapist can help by putting the problem into a larger perspective. The supervisor can explain the dynamics of the interaction, especially the value of the countertransference as a guide to the patient's emotional state, normalize and contain the therapist's emotional responses such as anxiety, and reassure the therapist that his feelings of inadequacy do not mean he has chosen the wrong profession. Although this kind of explanation and discussion are necessary, they can be over-used in supervision; the supervisor may be tempted to avoid the student's despair by focusing on theory and technique. The supervisor can help by modeling steady presence and hope, and by empathic attunement to the supervisee's feelings without avoiding them or furiously trying to do something.

Importantly, faith is not the same as hope; hope may prevent one plunging fully into the darkness of despair, but faith allows one to even let go of hope, to be in the darkness and surrender totally, with no guarantee that one will ever emerge. When faced with a patient in despair, the therapist needs faith in the therapeutic process, and perhaps it is an unconscious kernel of faith in the midst of the patient's despair that allows him to risk being in therapy. Bion (1970) uses the term "faith" to refer to the therapist's state of mind when he works without memory, desire, or understanding; Bion believes that the therapist's desire for understanding and mastery of the situation might interfere with his or her ability to be open to whatever emotional truth might emerge in the session. The therapist then has to have faith "that there is an ultimate reality and truth—the unknown, unknowable, 'formless infinite'" (p. 31). (The similarity to Jung's notion of the Self is obvious.)

It requires faith to live with chronic sorrow, disability, illness and pain, or when one is in despair because of a gap between who one is forced to be and the person one imagines one could be. People sometimes reach their limit, and then consider suicide.

Suffering that leads to suicide

According to the Centers for Disease Control, in 2011 there were 39,518 deaths from suicide in the USA, a rate of 12.3 deaths per 100,000 people. Worldwide, nearly a million people a year die by suicide. Many of these people have had no contact with a mental health professional, and friends and family may know nothing is wrong until the suicide happens—there is often no warning. Not all suicides are the result of depression; some are impulsive acts during moments of desperation, but certainly the potential for suicide is one of the psychotherapist's main concerns when working with an individual in despair. The literature on this subject is large, so I want to focus here only on the suffering of the suicidal person and the suffering of his or her family members. People commit suicide for a variety of different reasons, usually with despair as the final common path. The sources of despair are typically severe depression, chronic pain, terminal illness, addiction, relationship or job failure, or any other situation that makes the individual feel emotionally bankrupt. It is useful to recognize that if a close family member has committed suicide in the past, the power of that memory in the individual's mind may influence the decision to commit suicide under situations of extreme distress.

The motives for suicide are complex—a mixture of conscious and unconscious psychological factors combined with social and genetic influences are involved. Suicide offers the despairing individual a way of ending unbearable suffering; the therapist occasionally hears such a person say that she is comforted by the knowledge that she can control how and when she will die. This seems to be important to people who suffer because their lives feel out of control, or because they cannot live with what seems to be a greatly reduced quality of life. Sometimes people suffer because they feel so tormented, trapped, and powerless that they can find no other way of asserting themselves or changing their situation. Many suicidal people feel totally helpless, and they recover when they experience themselves as effective. Adolescents in particular have a relatively limited perspective on life, and may therefore feel that a lost relationship or other failure can never be replaced or repaired. Lack of family support, isolation, drug and alcohol use, and social factors in the life of the adolescent such as unemployment or a violent neighborhood, all seem insoluble and add to the adolescent's sense of despair and powerlessness to change his situation.

For each suicide, it is estimated that six family members are left bereaved. The suicide of a family member may cause prolonged, intense suffering among the survivors, especially when the death was unexpected (Ness et al, 1990). We do not have good social supports for helping people with a suicide in the family. A great deal of shock and self-reproach are common, and family members may either try to find a scapegoat to alleviate their guilt or blame themselves for not preventing the suicide. Sometimes the family feels socially stigmatized and withdraws from social interaction because the situation is too painful to talk about. The social stigma around suicide may prevent survivors from obtaining help, and occasionally this stigma leads to secrecy or denial that the death was due to suicide. A number of people with chronic illnesses consciously or unconsciously allow themselves to die because they are in intolerable life situations, and the illness gives them a way out.

A part of the process of grieving a suicide includes anger at the dead person, often in the form of impotent rage which may be difficult to express, leading to a complex grief reaction or incomplete mourning. Sometimes the anger is directed at the therapist or psychiatrist who was treating the deceased, or at insurance companies who would not pay for adequate treatment. In addition to grief, an exacerbation of chronic physical illnesses such as colitis or rheumatoid arthritis often occurs among survivors. Depression, suicidal ideation, or self-destructiveness are also frequent responses. Sometimes a survivor will feel relief at the death, which may be difficult to admit and may incur harsh judgment from other family members if they become aware of it. Questions such as "why did this happen?" and "could I have made a difference?" are commonly raised in psychotherapy, as survivors search for explanations for the suicide. The therapist must listen for fears that the survivor was responsible for the suicide or failed to notice or act on signs of distress. Suicide often leads to concern for the emotional stability of other people in the family; children in particular may believe they were responsible for a parent's death, or that they should have tried to prevent it. Some children identify with the suicidality of their parents and are convinced they will die the same way. The loss of a child's parent to suicide may lead to severe depression, anxiety, self-destructive behavior, psychosomatic difficulties, disruptive behavior, and academic and social difficulties, although we also see obvious denial of emotional pain. The child is often worried about losing the remaining parent. Honest responsiveness to the child's grief is very important, but in some families evasion or blatant deception about the nature of the death occurs in an attempt to protect the child. Some parents will not allow the child to talk about the death, or the child is given conflicting accounts of it. This may lead to the survivor reaching adulthood with unresolved grief that is uncovered years later while the person is in psychotherapy for some other loss. The emotional stability of the surviving parent is important in determining how a child will react to a parent's suicide; if the surviving parent experiences serious difficulties, these add to the child's burden. Parents who lose a child to suicide suffer enormously from guilt, shame, and a feeling of failure. They are often subject to social blame. They may feel rejected and abandoned, and they have lost whatever hopes they had for their child. Mothers are particularly likely to become depressed, and suffer additionally from the social and professional prejudice that tends to blame mothers in particular for their children's distress.

A suicide in the family may radically affect family dynamics, sometimes accentuating conflict or other problematic family relationships or creating new relationship difficulties for which family therapy can be helpful. It is also important that relationships among the surviving family may be strengthened after a suicide if the family can offer mutual support. There is usually intense family communication after a suicide, as people gather to try to understand what happened, but there is also a fear of saying too much to avoid being hurtful. In the treatment of survivors, the therapist will utilize his or her preferred model of psychotherapy, but there are some generally applicable suggestions in the literature (Kaslow, 2004). It is important to avoid blaming anyone, including the deceased, for the suicide. It is important to prevent a conspiracy of silence, estrangement or emotional isolation within the family, and to foster mutual support and comfort from other family members. Friends, survivors support groups, web sites, survivor hotlines, and where appropriate religious organizations may also be valuable. It is useful to educate family members about the normal grief process and the importance of expressing grief. The development of a shared family narrative about what happened can be useful. This can be done in a way that maintains self-esteem and prevents excessive guilt and shame.

Motivation for suicide

We often do not understand the reasons people commit suicide. Suicide notes are sometimes left, but they can often be interpreted in different ways. Psychoanalysts since Freud have developed a range of theories about the motivation for suicide (Maltsberger, 2004). Freud originally speculated that the urge to inflict suffering on family members played a part, and it does seem that some suicide is the result of the wish to punish others. Freud also suggested that suicide represents an attack on a loved person with whom the individual has identified, so that suicide is an unconscious form of homicide. Early theorists believed that a harsh superego, or punitive self-judgment, is important, especially when the person feels he deserves punishment. Later writers realized that suicide is related to intolerable, unmanageable mental distress, which has a destructive effect on the organization and structure of the self, leading to the sense that the self is fragmenting. Sadistic, critical introjects are also important, acting as hostile internal presences in the person's mind; suicidality may occur as a result of the perception that someone in the family wants the person dead. This perception may be accurate, and the suicide may actually be an enactment of this wish.

Winnicott (1960) believed that the False Self—the personality the person had to adopt in order to cope with his family—is always searching for conditions which will allow the True Self to come into its own. When these conditions cannot be found, the False Self has to find new defenses against the exploitation of the True Self. To avoid annihilation of the True Self, suicide organized by the False Self may be the only defense against betrayal of the True Self. For Kohut (1977), in mid-life the sense that one has not achieved one's ambitions and personal ideals may lead to shame-based despair and suicide. Suicide is then an attempt at remediation, because of the feeling that one has failed and does not have time to remedy the failure. In people with a fragile sense of self, severe narcissistic injury following the disruption of an important selfobject relationship may precipitate suicidal ideation, perhaps in an attempt to evoke a re-connection to the lost selfobject or to experience a degree of self-efficacy or self-regulation.

Hartmann (2000) has pointed out some of the countertransference clues to the risk of suicide which are connected to the patient's motivation. He notes that suicidal people often feel a loss of agency combined with despair and helplessness. People with a fragile sense of self develop ambivalent relationships with their therapist, and they sometimes develop a transference which takes the form of an attack on the therapist or on the setting of the therapy. Because of intra-psychic splitting, the attack may be subtle and uttered in a friendly tone, but it produces a feeling of helplessness or powerlessness in the therapist or the sense that his self-worth is threatened. The therapist may then become defensive or wish to get rid of the patient, or even wish that the patient might die. However, Hartmann believes that such an attack is not intended to destroy the therapist; it is actually an effort to make contact with the therapist or to feel effective by affecting the therapist, because this strengthens the selfobject tie and allows the patient to feel more cohesive and lessens his suicidal ideation. Self-harm in borderline people is sometimes an attempt to regulate unbearable affect, or they feel it is the only way to communicate inchoate distress. Many people with borderline personalities attempt suicide at some point because they experience a rejection by the therapist or they detect the therapist's countertransference hatred.

Some suicidal people have grandiose fantasies in which they desperately try to achieve control of life and death (Maltsberger et al, 1980). By getting rid of the body, as if the body were not a part of the self, they feel they will be able to escape their impossible situation or unbearable pain. Maltsberger (1997) points out that manic patients sometimes commit suicide in an ecstatic state, and he gives examples of suicides which occurred in states of ecstasy among religious martyrs such as Christians persecuted by the Romans in the early years of Christianity. Whereas suicide is forbidden in most religious traditions, there are warrior cultures such as the Samurai in which defeated soldiers committed suicide to regain their honor. Many of their descendants were Japanese Kamikaze bombers in WW2. In 73 C.E. at Masada, a group of Jewish soldiers defeated by the Romans committed collective suicide, and there are many recent examples of suicidal warriors such as the Tamil Tigers in Sri Lanka (Lakatos, 2010). Whether the current spate of suicide bombings should be defined as martyrdom or suicide is discussed further in chapter 3.

Can suicide be rational?

An important debate centers around whether moral judgment can be passed on the act of suicide, and whether it can ever be rational. This remains a matter of opinion. Some people who seem quite rational, suffering from no emotional illness, can be suicidal under certain circumstances. Suicide is considered to be rational if the person feels that his quality of life is impossibly impaired, usually due to illness, and there is no significant emotional disorder such as depression which is impairing his judgment. The suicide must be an informed choice that has not been coerced. However, this is a complex problem; it has been pointed out that if rational suicide were to become accepted as a person's right, it might intensify pressure on some ill people who feel they are a burden on their families; the option to commit suicide would then feel like an obligation. Family members sometimes withdraw from terminally ill people, which adds to the ill person's distress and isolation, so that what seems to be a rational suicide may actually be a response to a sense of abandonment.

Notes on the treatment of suicidality

The assessment and management of suicidal people is dealt with in all psychotherapy training programs, and need not be rehearsed in detail here except to mention some points that are sometimes neglected. One of the main difficulties in working with suicidal people is that the therapist must be able to contain the person's wish to die without being overwhelmed with anxiety, not only because the therapist feels responsible for the life of another person, for a person that he or she cares about, but also for the possible legal consequences. The therapist's own death anxiety may be stimulated by a suicidal patient, and the therapist's own conscious or unconscious suicidality may affect the countertransference. These factors may lead to the therapist's aversion to a suicidal patient, which only makes things worse for the patient. One has to be conscious of one's own fear of death to really help someone with suicidal feelings without being incapacitated by anxiety.

A problem for the therapist is that, although most suicidal patients do not commit suicide, and a trusting therapeutic relationship often keeps them alive, there are no infallible predictors of who will commit suicide, and we cannot help all suicidal people. What the therapist can do to prevent suicide is to help explore the reasons for the person's suffering in detail, since some suicidal people cannot see a way out of their distress even if the possibility actually exists. It is worth trying to help the person find meaning and purpose in his life when there seems to be none. We can ask the suicidal person what has kept him from suicide so far—this often gives the therapist a clue about what is important to the person, and may be the beginning of a conversation about whether life is worth living. Most importantly, we can hear the cry for help. The therapist must understand the patient's perspective and avoid insisting on the therapist's view of things. Rather than try to talk the person out of suicide, time is better spent empathically exploring in detail the wish to suicide, so that the patient does not feel alone with his feelings. Occasionally, one discovers unconscious feelings of loss and grief. Exploration of the fantasy of what will happen at death and the reaction of relatives to the patient's death may be helpful.

The therapist must convey that she realizes the patient is in unbearable emotional pain. This kind of empathic connection with a therapist is often enough to prevent suicide, but at the same time suicidal people are very sensitive to the therapist's behavior; they look and listen for signs of caring and emotional availability. Signs of the therapist's indifference or irritation as part of the countertransference may literally be fatal. These signs (which are present in micro-expressions on the therapist's face or in his tone of voice) may be unconsciously discerned by the patient, and they may be unavoidable if the therapist becomes defensive or angry with someone who seems to resist everything he offers, which may lead to the therapist behaving in a vengeful or withholding manner. One of the crucial things that stops people from committing suicide is the presence of another person who believes that the suffering person is important, that he or she really matters, someone who does not give up on the sufferer. The patient's search for signs that the therapist really cares becomes a problem if the therapist cannot find much to like about the patient, so the therapist has to make an effort to find some aspect of the suicidal person which the therapist can genuinely appreciate. If the therapist cannot find anything to value it may be that the patient's positive attributes are split off in some way, and this situation can be tactfully explored.

The therapist may recommend hospitalization, perhaps only because of the medico-legal risk, but the patient may see this as an abandonment or a rejection, and it is not clear that hospitalization reduces the long term risk for chronically suicidal people. The traditional arguments about the prevention of suicide revolve around whether doing so interfere with the autonomy and freedom of the individual. On these grounds, in the 1980's, psychiatrist Thomas Szasz argued against coercive attempts at suicide prevention. Today, most people believe that intervention is justified if the person is not able to make a free choice because of overt mental illness or impairment. Nevertheless, as discussed above, there is a view that suicide can be rational under certain circumstances.

In studies of the dreams of people on the verge of suicide, Litman (1980) found that the person in such dreams is affected by earthquakes, explosions, and other disasters, reflecting panic over the sense that the self is disintegrating. Sometimes, before attempting suicide, the individual dreams of beautiful surroundings or a serene experience of merger with a higher power—the Jungians would see such dreams as an attempt at compensation for the distress of the empirical personality, or they may be seen as premonitory of death.

Apart from our legal and ethical obligations and our concern for the patient's welfare, the psychotherapist's response to a patient's suicidal crisis also depends on his or her personal attitudes towards suicide, and perhaps more deeply on his or her world-view. Traditional Judaism, Islam, and

143

Christianity all forbid suicide, while many existentialists believe that suicide may be the result of a conscious and free human choice. Camus, in his *The Myth of Sisyphus*, suggests that the question of suicide is the one truly philosophical problem, because it asks whether life is really worth living. He makes the point that many people feel that life is absurd—God is dead and there are no eternal values in this view—but Camus believes that suicide is wrong partly because it would be a denial of the absurdity of existence. We have to choose life as a revolt against the meaninglessness of existence, and new possibilities may emerge in the future. However, many of us would deny that life is entirely meaningless even if it has some meaningless aspects to it, and even if its meaning is ambiguous and sometimes ephemeral.

Based on his interviews with survivors of people who jumped off the Golden Gate Bridge, David Rosen (1975) found that the impulse to suicide means that the old sense of self needs to die—the wish to commit suicide is a desire for a psychological rebirth, "egocide," or a radical transformation of the personality. The therapeutic task is to help the person distinguish between ego death and physical death.

The suicide of a patient often has a profoundly painful effect on the psychotherapist. Trainees are particularly affected by the death of a patient. In one study of psychotherapists in this position, Jane Tillman (2006) found the expectable shock and grief combined with a sense of humiliation and professional injury, a narcissistic wound with enduring and sometimes devastating consequences. The event is often traumatic for the therapist, leading to intrusive thoughts and dreams about the deceased which are often gruesome. The therapist often scrutinizes the quality of the therapeutic alliance with the deceased patient, searching for what the therapist may have missed. Contact with the patient's family may be helpful if painful, although the therapist is often a target of the family's rage. Colleagues, supervisors, and personal therapy are usually helpful sources of support in this situation. Fears of legal action are significant sources of distress, especially when the therapist had been very dedicated to the patient and being sued seems to destroy any recognition of this dedication. A professional crisis may then arise which may lead to doubts about staying in the profession, worries about professional competence, a crisis of faith about the value of psychotherapy, or sometimes an unwillingness to work with suicidal patients in the future. Some therapists fear the judgment of colleagues or adversely compare their form of psychotherapy with psychopharmacology or other modes of treatment.

Finally, it is worth noting a common misconception; it has long been noticed that people often kill themselves as they begin to improve, rather than when they are in the very depth of depression. Traditionally this was understood to be the result of returning energy at the same time as the individual is still depressed. A more likely explanation is that depressed people feel better once they have decided to kill themselves because they know their suffering is coming to an end.

The enjoyment of tragic stories: Why do we enjoy watching the suffering of others?

Images of terrible suffering are now common in our newspapers and television broadcasts. Why is it that we are so fascinated with the suffering of others that we constantly want to read and hear about it in the media and in our literature, photography, and art? This interest is rather like our fascination with evil; we watch terrible events such as wars and earthquakes, but we also want to be able to turn them off. There are a variety of explanations for this fascination, ranging from sadistic enjoyment of others' pain to automatic empathy or compassion, or even a purely aesthetic enjoyment of the story. We can watch the suffering of others while appreciating our own privileged position, safe in the knowledge that there is nothing we can do to help, appreciating our own innocence if we are hearing about an atrocity. Watching suffering in the media can therefore teach us something about ourselves.

The representation of suffering in the media is a mixed blessing; we must keep informed about human suffering, yet at the same time it feels wrong to turn suffering into entertainment[22]. However, the confrontation with another person's suffering is an ethical problem which demands a response. In her *Regarding the Pain of Others*, Susan Sontag points out that although we need to know what is going on in the world, there is also an inherent danger in being a passive spectator: our sympathy allows us to feel we are not accomplices and reassures us that we are impotent to help. In spite of our good intentions she believes sympathy can be impertinent—but

---

22   Here I am following Adorno (1962) who was concerned that when suffering is turned into an art form such as theater, it becomes entertainment for people who have not lived through similar suffering, which re-violates the victims. He did not mean that art should not address suffering, but he wanted to stress how difficult it is to truly represent intense suffering. The problem is that if we transform a horrifying trauma into an aesthetic product such as fiction or art, we may reduce the horror of the event. Adorno was addressing the Holocaust, but I think the principle holds in general. Many people believe that severe trauma is essentially unrepresentable.

her notion of sympathy here is more like condescending pity. At the same time, there is a real danger that when faced with the suffering of others we often cannot help feeling relief or even pleasure at our own safety and comfortable distance from it.

When sadness is evoked watching a tragic drama on stage or film, this emotion, based on empathic resonance, makes us particularly involved in the story and enhances the spectator's sense that the story is real (Ahn, 2012). Yet sadness is an unpleasant affect, so why are we so attracted to this genre? Tragedies such as Shakespeare's *Othello* and movies such as *Titanic* have a powerful emotional effect on us. It is as if the sorrow we witness resonates with something insides us, and at the same time also has a kind of enjoyable effect, so that we regularly seek sorrowful media as entertainment.

No one has fully explained the paradox of why we enjoy watching other people's sorrow, but many attempts have been made (Ahn, 2012). In his *Poetics*, Aristotle suggested that tragedy allows the cathartic expression of pity and fear, which has a purging effect on these emotions and so reduces their intensity or refines or changes them. However, it has never been clear if or how this works, and many theories have emerged since Aristotle. Whatever the mechanism, by its nature tragic drama does produce an emotional response or catharsis in the spectator, and the catharsis we experience watching a sad performance is in some ways analogous to the catharsis we see in psychotherapy. In their *Studies on Hysteria* of 1895, Breuer and Freud first noticed the importance of making traumatic memories conscious, whereupon catharsis occurs. Freud believed that when this happens it is important to put words to the painful emotion being expressed, because he felt that the recovery of memory and insight would then be curative. He did not fully recognize what we know today, which is that the presence of an empathically attuned, containing therapist is important for this process to be successful. The traditional theory suggests that repeated catharsis of painful memories allows a working through process, meaning it takes time and repetition for a person to assimilate painful affects and overcome resistance to expressing them. Eventually, with frequent repetition combined with cognitive processing within a holding therapeutic relationship, people are said to become less reactive to the expression of traumatic memories, and their perspective on the memories changes. However, catharsis has become a controversial topic; it is sometimes considered to be useless or even counterproductive, on the grounds that once emotions are stimulated they tend to reinforce themselves rather than disappear, so that catharsis might worsen an emotion such as aggression. Accordingly, catharsis is not much spoken of in the contemporary psychotherapeutic literature. Nevertheless it remains a component of some approaches to trauma even though we recognize that other major factors, such as repair of low self-esteem and shame in the trauma victim, are not helped by catharsis.

In his *The Interpretation of Dreams* (1900) Freud wrote that we enjoy tragedy because it fulfills repressed wishes; the spectator wants to be a hero, and identifies with the tragic hero. That is, the story stimulates and gives us access to something in our unconscious—tragedy touches our own wounds and helps us understand it. Later, Freud (1915) attributed the enjoyment of tragedy to sado-masochistic identification; either the spectator masochistically imagines himself being punished in the place of the hero, or the spectator imagines himself sadistically punishing the hero. This seems like a description that would only apply to a limited number of people, but the more general point is that some kind of identification occurs with the tragic figure when we watch a sad story. We empathically share the tragic figure's emotional experience, even imagining it to be happening to ourselves, but from a safe distance. This might be especially true when the hero has a tragic flaw such as hubris, which we can see in ourselves, or when the sad situation on screen matches a theme in our own life, or when we fear it might happen to us. If we can empathically identify with the protagonist in a film or play, so that his or her plight resonates emotionally with us, we are likely to enjoy the spectacle. We may be inspired by the hero's courageous response to a tragedy, or perhaps we enjoy the feeling of compassion for a tragic hero, especially if he or she is particularly soulful or superior in some way, or he is suffering in an undeserved way. Here it is worth noting that some people enjoy watching horror movies, presumably because the danger and the gruesome events are experienced as not threatening to the watcher, who enjoys the physiological agitation the movie produces. It may be that the constant images of death in our movies allow us to find a safe distance from death; it is as if we can witness it from a detached place; it looks real but we know it is not. Perhaps our curiosity or our death anxiety is vicariously satisfied when we see death in the movies. When we experience a traumatic episode in fiction, the trauma is highly contained, so any feelings we have are safe and tolerable, but we are able to participate emotionally because the drama is going on in Winnicott's (1974) transitional or play space. Pleasant emotions stirred by the story may allow us to feel that life is meaningful, while the existential anxieties that the story stirs in us, such as the fear of death, can be worked through much more readily in a story than in real life. It may be that we watch tragic media because we feel better about ourselves when we see someone suffering more than we do. Or the sad story makes us value our own life, or makes us feel we understand something about life in general. We can use a tragic movie or play to think about the meaning of life, so that we appreciate the work even if we don't exactly enjoy it. In this context, mythic stories such as the story of Oedipus are particularly powerful because they illustrate archetypal patterns which are important to humanity in general, and it is pleasing to find order and patterns.

Perhaps the problem with frequent exposure to suffering in the media is that, while such exposure has the potential to bring the problem home to us, it also tends to de-personalize suffering or inure people to it, so that we start to take suffering for granted. On the positive side, to witness suffering by means of the media can allow communion with those who suffer, strengthen national bonds during a national tragedy, and mobilize compassionate action. Furthermore, cultural products such as movies and literature allow us to see evil being committed in the form of a story. While this may incite predisposed individuals to commit evil, for most people watching such a story, by engaging the imagination the symbolic expression of evil may be sufficient to prevent evil being literally enacted in a destructive way.

5

HELPING OTHERS WITH SUFFERING

Altruism

What is our motivation for helping others who are suffering? Are human beings altruistic simply because of empathy or compassion, or is our motivation for helping others usually more self-interested, a way of enhancing the helper's self-esteem?

The word "altruism" is derived from the Latin *alter*, meaning other; the sense of the word is to care for the other. Batson (1991, p. 6) defines altruism as "a motivational state with the ultimate goal of increasing another's welfare." Some authors add to this definition the proviso that the helping is carried out without conscious regard for the helper's own self-interest (Hoffman, 1978), but others believe that such pure altruism does not exist, because every altruistic act is fundamentally egoistic—it makes the helper feel self-satisfied, or it is done because it leads to social appreciation and enhanced social standing. Of course, there is no reason that one cannot help someone else altruistically while at the same time enhancing one's own sense of self or receiving some personal benefit in the process.

Kristen Monroe (1996) therefore suggests a continuum of human behavior which oscillates between the poles of self-interest and altruism. She contrasts pure altruism, helping another even at the risk of oneself, and particular altruism, or helping only particular groups of people we perceive as worthy, such as close family. Another aspect of this debate hinges around whether an act has to involve a degree of self-sacrifice to be considered altruistic; otherwise, if both parties gain, the act may be simply a form of cooperation and not altruism (Sigmund et al., 2002). In contrast, Batson (1991) points out that if we make self-sacrifice an essential part of the definition we are focusing on the consequences of the act rather than the helper's motivation.

Since most people who become psychotherapists are interested in helping others, the question of why human beings are altruistic is important to us. The literature on altruism is evas, and has largely engaged social and developmental psychologists and a few psychoanalysts. Many developmental psychologists believe that altruism is a product of socialization; children exposed to altruistic behavior in their families tend to become altruistic, and people who experienced secure early attachment find it easier to respond compassionately to the suffering of others (Mikulincer et al., 2005). However, children also demonstrate an innate wish to help others, so indifference to others may be a learned response resulting from family and cultural behavior which desensitizes the growing child to the suffering of others.

In his *Civilization and Its Discontents*, Freud suggests that we are in conflict between our struggle for our own happiness and the needs of the community; for him, altruism develops either as a result of guilt about being selfish or as the introjection of social standards. Ever since Freud wrote that altruism conflicts with our innate desire for pleasure seeking, psychoanalysts have typically been skeptical about altruism or any kind of pro-social behavior that seems to be motivated by concern for others. At the extreme, giving to others altruistically without expecting anything in return is seen by some psychoanalysts to have masochistic or neurotic underpinnings. Anna Freud (1946) uses the term "altruistic surrender" to describe a patient who, because of a harsh super-ego, would not allow herself to be aware of her own wishes, and instead devoted her energy to taking care of others. She took great satisfaction in the achievements of others but she actually wished these achievements for herself. Vaillant (1977) saw altruism as a mature defense, so that a person who cannot experience pleasure by fulfilling himself can experience vicarious pleasure by helping others. There are people who are compulsive caretakers, whose apparent altruism disguises a masochistic need to take pride in their self-sacrificial behavior.[23] Or, they control others by taking care of them. The problem is that even healthy forms of altruism, which are based on empathy for the suffering of others, can be used in the service of enhancing self-esteem, especially if we need a response of gratitude and admiration from the one we help. It is therefore not surprising that altruistic behavior is self-reinforcing; we enjoy the feeling of self-satisfaction, which altruism produces in us.

---

23   Students of the Enneagram will recognize type 2, the Helper, people who go out of their way to help others, often feeling this is the only way they will be loved. In the extreme they can be overly self-sacrificial in their care for others.

Just as altruism can support vulnerable self-esteem, good self-esteem allows us to feel we have something to give. One may see oneself as a powerful protector or guardian of the weak, in a way that is narcissistically gratifying and crucial to our self-image. However, this may be a somewhat skeptical view of altruism, since altruism may simply be evoked by empathy for a suffering person rather than for purely narcissistic reasons (Dovidio et al., 2006). Surely it would not be possible to dismiss all attempts to care for others as nothing more than the attempt to satisfy one's own needs. To accuse someone in this way might be a projection of the accuser's own selfishness. Are there not some people who are genuinely altruistic, perhaps only expecting a word of thanks as a reward? One difficulty here is that our motives for being altruistic may actually be selfish but repressed, so we only believe we are selflessly altruistic. However, theories that suggest that acting to help another person is really a mode of self-gratification do not take into account phenomena such as the rescuing of Jews from Nazi persecution. There seems to be no self-interest in such behavior; many of these rescuers worked in secret and were not expecting to be treated as heroes. They risked their own lives and were in danger from both the Nazis and their neighbors. Many of the people they rescued or hid in their homes were complete strangers. In contrast, many non-rescuers in Nazi-occupied Europe claimed to not know what was happening to the Jewish population, and in fact did not want to know. On this basis, Kristen Monroe (1996) concludes that truly altruistic people are bonded to others in a way that encourages altruistic behavior and self-sacrifice. This behavior can hardly be described as egoistic or self-serving.

In her study of 20 healthy altruistic individuals, Nancy McWilliams (1984) found traits of helpfulness, sociability, and natural warmth. Her subjects were all compulsive—they maintained self-esteem by doing things, and they would sacrifice themselves trying to help others. They saw their own unconscious needs in the needs of others, so that giving to others was a way of coping with their own needs—a defense mechanism known as reversal. They projected their own dependency needs onto others who could be helped and cared for in the way the subjects unconsciously wished for themselves. McWilliams also found that their altruism could be a way of undoing unconscious hostility. They had difficulty saying "no" to unreasonable demands, and they could not tolerate seeing themselves as demanding or greedy. McWilliams believes that some humanitarianism is motivated by unconscious guilt over the feeling that one is selfish. Each of her subjects had experienced love and care early in life followed by major loss or deprivation at an early age, and she postulates that they had a strong model of altruistic devotion available to them at the time of the early loss, with whom they identified, so that they took on the attributes of a personal savior. All her subjects were religious and found religious models such as Albert Schweitzer or Martin Luther King to be important. McWilliams believes that the pain of their early developmental stress was transformed into a prolonged humanitarian commitment.

Our theories about any human motivation are partly conditioned by our view of human nature. If we are skeptical, we believe that an altruistic act is only done for the helper's personal gain, whether this be direct or indirect, in the present or the future (Khalil, 2004). Thus, because we feel distress when we witness the suffering of another person, our desire to help may sometimes be a way of relieving our own distress and sense of obligation. But surely, to suggest that consciously or unconsciously we expect something in return would not fully explain human empathy and compassion, given the fact that the urge to help another person in distress often arises as a kind of reflex, without thought, even to the extent that people risk their own lives to help others. Some economists believe that people only behave in terms of a rational and personal cost-benefit analysis that will maximize their own welfare and self-interest, but this would not account for *pro-bono* work carried out by many professionals as a public service. In his study of blood donors, Titmuss (1970) suggested that not only do we need others, we have a human need to give to others.

Altruism and sociobiology

Sociobiologists believe that human behavior is largely the result of evolution, and they try to derive explanations of human nature based on our evolutionary inheritance. Sociobiologists[24] look at altruism from the point of view of the survival of the species and its genes and do not deal with the moral or psychological aspects of altruism. However, sociobiologists and evolutionary biologists have had difficulty understanding why animals should behave in

---

[24] If human behavior is largely determined by evolution, it is not easily changed by social factors, so that many aspects of human nature can at best be modified but not eradicated by education or training. It has been claimed that sociobiology can lead to a system of ethics based on our biology, in contrast to religious, moral, and ethical ideas which are unrealistic or difficult to implement. In this view, aggression, for instance, cannot be eradicated, and it is natural for some people to dominate others because inequality is a biological given. The prevailing social order is somehow biologically necessary. Many sociobiologists are biological determinists. A weaker version of sociobiology sees biology and genetics as setting constraints on behavior such as altruism or selfishness, but not being their ultimate determinants.

self-sacrificing ways; the theory of evolution might suggest that selfishness would be favored by evolution. However, some writers believe that the instinct for survival at the expense of others is balanced by an instinctual feeling of solidarity with others. The Russian zoologist and evolutionary theorist Petr Kropotkin suggested that mutual help is a basic trait of all living beings, and that this trait is stronger than egoism and not due to culture. Nevertheless, an altruistic act does not seem to be helpful in propagating one's own genes, and so from a strictly evolutionary viewpoint one would think it would be avoided, especially if it involves the risk of one's own life. However, many sociobiologists believe that an organism would risk its life for the sake of another organism if the helper shares genes with the one it is trying to save—the helper is then also contributing to the survival of its own genes. (This is the theory of "kin-selection," first suggested by Darwin himself to explain why members of the same tribe would help each other. Relationships have evolutionary significance.)

A competing theory (hotly debated) is that altruism is the result of group selection. This theory points out that, in contrast to selfish individuals, those who cooperate in groups are likely to enhance the survival of their group. Group selection suggests that human beings have an inherited tendency to communicate, bond, and cooperate with each other, producing social intelligence. Sociobiologists also postulate "reciprocal altruism," the idea that we will help others who are likely to return the favor; human beings typify this behavior (Trivers, 1971). However, people sometimes help others with whom they have no familial or social connection, even when the helpers have no idea if they will ever be helped in return. Altruism then simply looks like a core human value, and it is possible that the human capacity for altruism is not entirely a function of our genes and evolutionary history. Because altruism is found in all cultures, cultural and psychological factors may also be involved even if it is "primed" by our genes to develop in a normal environment. If there is a genetic component, since some people seem incapable of altruism it must be a highly variable trait. Erikson's (1997) idea of generativity is a form of altruism which describes the satisfaction we obtain by contributing to the welfare of future generations, which he thought would help the survival of the species.

Social psychology and altruism

Most social psychologists believe that pro-social behavior is learned from the individual's cultural norms, from cultural values such as benevolence and responsibility for others, and from relationships (Bierhoff et al., 2004). People with a strong sense of community, who feel that they belong and that mutual benefit results from community, may be particularly altruistic. Situational factors are important in this respect; people are more willing to help after a large-scale disaster has occurred than they are in everyday situations (Piliavin et al., 1990). Some evidence from social psychology (known as attribution theory) suggests that the environmental aspects of a situation may be better predictors of certain behavior than the characteristics of the person performing the behavior. Thus, as discussed in chapter 5, when a person is in difficulty on a street, the possibility of getting help is higher if the number of bystanders decreases (Ross et al., 1991). One might think that in this kind of situation the number of people around is morally irrelevant, but apparently such circumstances can affect one's altruistic motivation. The research on circumstantial factors has been said to discount philosophical accounts of altruism, which have tried to identify what it is about morally good behavior that makes it worthy (Beardman, 2012).

Is there an altruistic personality?

It has been suggested that certain personalities, such as those people who helped persecuted Jews in Nazi-occupied Europe, are innately altruistic (Oliner et al., 1988). In her study of people who rescued Jews in World War 2, at great risk to themselves, Monroe (1996) showed that there was no difference between those who did and did not rescue Jews in terms of religion, family background, or social factors. Accordingly she rejects socio-cultural explanations for altruism and believes that some people simply have an altruistic or moral perspective on life, a sense of our shared humanity. Their altruism was a reflex, something that they felt had to be done in the circumstances. Intrinsically altruistic individuals are "other-centric," empathic and generous, with a strong sense of self, an internal locus of control, and minimal need for social approval. However, the view that there are intrinsic altruists or pro-social personalities is controversial, and the egocentric view of altruism remains popular. Perhaps this is a function of our societal attitudes.

Parenthetically, it may be worth mentioning the theory of selfishness proposed by Ayn Rand, who sees altruism as nonsensical. She believed that only self-interest would motivate people to take risks. For her, altruism is a waste of energy, and the ultimate moral value is the individual's personal well-being. This point of view ignores the empirical work of Monroe and others.

The suffering of others calls us to respond to it, but sometimes we question how much we should help when we see people who have put themselves into a harmful situation—for example by drinking and driving—so that it seems their suffering is self-imposed, or they are irresponsible. We feel more inclined to help when someone is suffering through no fault of their own. However, all these people are suffering, and we cannot distinguish between the deserving and the undeserving because we rarely have the level of understanding of a person's life that would be needed to make this judgment. Suffering does not call for judgment; it calls for empathy, which can motivate altruism. (For a review of the research suggesting that empathy produces altruistic motivation, see Batson, 2010). I subscribe to the school of thought which says that altruism or responsibility for others is part of human nature, that our hearts can be spontaneously generous, and that sometimes at least we want to serve the needs of others. Here the philosophy of Emanuel Levinas has been very influential for some psychotherapists.

The importance of Emanuel Levinas to psychotherapy

Levinas is an important thinker for anyone concerned with human suffering, because he believes we have an absolute and unlimited moral responsibility to engage with the suffering of others, however demanding that might be for our own resources (1998a). For him, ethics is the foundation of all philosophy: ethics means a compassionate response to the vulnerability and suffering of another person, and compassion is the supreme ethical principle. Levinas's emphasis on the *primacy* of the suffering of the other distinguishes his philosophy from much of the mainstream of western thinking. The relationship between oneself and the other is at the heart of his thinking; in fact, he believes it is only in recognizing our relationship to the other that we can understand ourselves as ethical beings. Our freedom is limited by the ethical demands that our responsibility to the other places on us.

Levinas's (1998a) view on suffering differs sharply from the view of writers such as Jung and Frankl, who find meaning in suffering. For Levinas, suffering is the denial of meaning, with one exception; the only time we can say suffering is meaningful is when we take responsibility for the suffering of another person—if suffering has any meaning, it is that it opens us to respond to help the suffering person. Otherwise, Levinas believes that innocent suffering is intrinsically useless—in his words, it is "for nothing" (p. 93), by which he means that innocent suffering serves no purpose; suffering cannot be justified or rationalized in any way. He suggests that my own suffering is useless in itself but it can take on meaning if I suffer for another person. Levinas describes compassion as "non-useless" suffering or love, which does have meaning; unlike useless suffering, compassion is not for nothing.

For Levinas, suffering restricts our freedom and hurts our humanity. Suffering is the bearing of the unbearable that can be expressed as moaning or a cry for help, but cannot really be communicated. Suffering cannot be transferred; it is primordial, irreducible, and we cannot decline it. It is the very uselessness of the other's suffering that makes us responsible for the other. The cry for help exposes to an ethical duty, with no expectation of receiving something in return. One believes that to wait for a redeemer in the Christian sense who will take over responsibility for the suffering of another person is an avoidance of own responsibility. Consequently, he believes that any attempt at theodicy, (the attempt to justify God in the presence of evil and suffering, discussed further on chapter 6), or any attempt to justify suffering based on the necessity for some social good, would be an immoral attempt to make meaningless suffering somehow significant. Because theodicy is no longer possible after Auschwitz, our own responsibility for suffering is now demanded. Suffering is essentially gratuitous, unintelligible, absurd, and arbitrary, and to try to justify suffering in any way might allow us to forget how useless suffering is to the sufferer. Or, an "explanation" for suffering might be used to justify the pain of others or legitimize our ignoring it. To justify the suffering of the other, for Levinas, is "the source of all immorality" (1998a, p. 99). Not only is suffering an evil, in fact all evil refers to suffering, and because suffering is evil, if we were to justify suffering with a theodicy we would justify evil.

According to Levinas, the suffering of the other person calls into question my own agenda and my sense of certainty and security. In fact, our quest for security often causes the suffering of other people. In his words, "justification of the neighbor's pain is certainly the source of all immorality" (1998a, p. 9). For Levinas, whatever I do to take care of myself may conflict with the needs of others or cause their suffering. Levinas is skeptical that we can rationalize the priority of any individual's rights at the expense of a person who is suffering. For Levinas, the other person is infinitely transcendent, beyond my ability to understand, and certainly beyond my ability to master.

It seems in Levinas's work that we only come to know ourselves as a subject by our exposure to the other person and by our sense of absolute responsibility for the other, indeed by our subjection to the other's needs. It is as if the self is only allowed to emerge as a self by the other who confronts it; selfhood is based on our responsibility to others. I realize that for some psychotherapists, this account of our selfhood might seem too de-centered or too passive, as if the self has no central sense of identity by itself, or only has meaning in relation to another. However, Levinas's idea is best seen as a call to serve the needs of the other.

Levinas was partly reacting to the tendency in western psychology and philosophy to focus on the centrality of the ego and the freedom of the individual, a focus which he believes to be too self-centered, leading to a society full of conflict. For Levinas we live in a world of others, which leads us beyond ourselves, so he tries to ground human subjectivity in the self's connection with the world. However, he does not believe that the self entirely loses its identity in a merger with others (Peperzak, 1993); he says that the appreciation of otherness "is possible only starting from me" (Levinas, 1969, P.40). That is, a real relationship with the other has to start from having an autonomous sense of self. At the same time it must be admitted that Levinas does not offer much guidance to the complexities of relationship, compared to the guidance provided by contemporary relational psychotherapy.

Levinas challenges models of thinking which stress competition with and domination over others. To dominate another person is an exercise of power, but for Levinas (1969,) "the face [of the other] speaks to me and thereby invites me to a relation incommensurate with a power exercised." He also challenges utilitarian ethics which teach that what is right is what produces the greatest good for the greatest number of people. The problem with this notion is that it may justify excluding or even victimizing a few people for the sake of the general good. We see this clearly in the way totalitarian regimes rationalize their oppressive behavior. Levinas criticizes any form of "totalizing" thought (overarching ideologies, the attempt to force everything into categories or fixed meanings) because it does not attend to the suffering of the other; this failure makes it violent.

It seems obvious that traditional standards that measure the rightness and wrongness of actions (so-called normative ethics) do not prevent the suffering which is intentionally inflicted on people in our own country and round the world. These standards do not prevent large-scale indifference to suffering, as we saw in the case of Germans who colluded with the Nazi genocide. The majority of European Christians ignored what was happening to their Jewish neighbors. Their ethical system failed to prevent the atrocities which took place, just as many contemporary religious people ignore the enormous levels of suffering in our own society.[25] Our current social and political structures sometimes allow us to dehumanize people as if they were expendable. We do not always try to prevent innocent suffering. For Levinas, such indifference to the suffering of others denies their vulnerability, compounds their suffering, and is evil. What he calls our "inter-human responsibility" stands before any social contract. In his *Otherwise Than Being*, Levinas even says that the other has priority over my own self-seeking; I am a hostage to the needs and suffering of the other. The vulnerable face of the other reveals a responsibility that is non-reciprocal, asymmetrical, and not regulated by any law or first principle. The face of the other reveals the other's vulnerability and does not allow me to be indifferent. The face of the other is much more than simply an object see; it tells me that the other is beyond thought, it exceeds anything can know about the other, and it approaches the infinite; it is "manifestation of the height in which God is revealed" (Levinas, 1969, p. 79). Levinas wants us to realize that the ordinary human level and the infinite level are present at the same time. Or, we approach the infinite by means of the human other. For him, the ethical level of the relationship is more fundamental than the ontological level, or the level of everyday activity in the world.

Levinas believes that our responsibility to the suffering other is so great that we should if necessary give the sufferer the bread from our own mouths (1998b, p. 74)-we are, as it were, held hostage to the other's suffering. The relationship is not reciprocal. The psychotherapist can legitimately question this attitude; it may require an excessive or masochistic self-sacrifice, and the suffering person might not want the therapist or any other person to feel such obligation—we often want mutuality. Some ethicists might point out that we should not take care of the sufferer in a way that contravenes other moral

---

25   Levinas would say that those Christians who did protect Jews were becoming themselves in the act of being responsible for the other. For him, selfhood does not depend on the ontological primacy of being, but on the enactment of our responsibility to the other.

principles or in a way that harms others or oneself. It may also be argued that we have a prior duty to family and friends rather than to strangers. Levinas himself points out that our responsibility for others has to limit itself; the ego can "be called upon to concern itself also with itself" (1998b, p. 128), and I am an other for the others. But the face of the suffering other may weigh more heavily than these reasonable arguments. Clearly, Levinas's argument is not "evidence-based" or grounded in empirically-based psychology, but what Levinas is taking about seems so fundamentally human it does not seem to need testing in a laboratory. Furthermore, the distance between Levinas's approach to care and the kind of therapy allowed by insurance companies, where decisions are made by an administrator who does not actually see the suffering on the patient's face, is stark (Huett et al, 2012).

The bystander effect

The bystander effect is a term used by social psychologists to describe situations in which someone in a public place is suffering or in danger, but bystanders do nothing to help. The phenomenon came to public attention in 1964 when Kitty Genovese was stabbed to death in New York. The exact details are uncertain, but some newspaper accounts of the assault suggested that her neighbors ignored her cries for help or even witnessed it without intervening.[26] The subsequent research suggested that a person's likelihood of being helped in a critical situation decreases when a crowd of bystanders is present, rather than a single individual. No one in the crowd helps because they assume that someone else will do so. This effect is therefore an important phenomenon to understand in our review of helping others with suffering, since it is not always clear what prevents our helping others. Needless to say, at times bystanders have intervened heroically to help others.

The original researchers postulated that in order for the bystanders to intervene when a person on the street is in trouble, bystanders have to notice that the situation is critical or an emergency. They must feel personally responsible to help, they must feel able to help, and then must decide to help (Latané et al.,1970, 1981). The research found three psychological processes

---

26   Her assailant attacked her on three occasions over the course of half an hour. News of the attack led to a great deal of societal outrage because no one helped her, but the media may have mis-reported the incident. The stabbing took place in the middle of the night, and apparently no one in the surrounding buildings could clearly see what was happening. The people who heard shouting may have thought it was nothing more than an argument.

that might interfere with helping. There is a tendency to divide responsibility among the bystanders; the more bystanders there are, the less the individual feels personally responsible to intervene and the less he feels responsible for a negative outcome to the victim. Another factor is apprehension about being evaluated or judged by others when acting in public, and a third factor is the tendency to rely on the behavior of others in an ambiguous situation. If everyone believes that no one else sees the situation as an emergency, the bystander effect is maximal. Subsequent research (reviewed by Fischer et al., 2011) suggested that this effect is true for both men and women and across all age groups. Bystanders who are friends of the person in need are more likely to intervene, especially if he or she is part of their group, while we are less willing to intervene to help strangers. Some recent research suggests that the bystander effect is less marked in situations of extreme danger, even if the helper might expect a high personal cost if he or she intervenes. This may be because the emergency is recognized more quickly, and in the presence of danger the bystander's distress increases and is reduced by helping the victim. In an emergency it may be clear that only the cooperation of several people could resolve the situation.

Prevention of personality damage caused by suffering

There are a variety of ways in which the psychotherapist may try to prevent suffering from causing damage to the personality. We may caution against the patient adding to his or her suffering by reacting to it in ways that add layers of additional problems to the primary problem, such as excessive self-pity or self-reproach, unreasonable blame of others, prolonged "if only" ruminating, or an unnecessary catastrophizing of the situation with fantasies of the worst possible outcome. Reactions such as rage, envy, and hatred act as protections for unbearable feelings of vulnerability, but therapeutic softening of such protective mechanisms is a difficult process in people in whom feelings have always been disavowed or difficult to contain or regulate. Prolonged empathic responsiveness to the person's experience is helpful in dissolving this shell of negativity, and occasionally a transpersonal or numinous experience is helpful.

Both patient and therapist need the wisdom to discern which suffering is due to a problem that can be changed and which suffering simply has to be accepted. Suffering that cannot be changed does not need to be approached with an attitude of resignation; we can investigate its meaning, and sometimes radical acceptance is possible (see chapter 10). Acceptance of suffering about which nothing can be done requires a particular attitude. It helps if we believe that we are in the grip of a transpersonal process, such as a dark night of the soul, which is beyond our understanding. One then has to be affected by the situation but not resist it, because resistance usually makes things worse. But the psychotherapist has to be careful not to collude with an attitude of masochistic submission, as we find in some theologies that suggest that we deserve our suffering as a punishment for sin, which projects a parent-child psychology onto the situation.

It is possible to believe one is helping a suffering person while actually maintaining or reinforcing the individual's suffering. Unhelpful attempts to help may occur for several reasons, apart from simple ignorance about what is required. We might respond to suffering in a way that prevents the sufferer from accessing his own resources or confronting self-destructive behavior. This may occur for example when one spouse is chronically depressed and helpless and the partner takes over more and more responsibilities, reinforcing helplessness, often leading to a cycle of resentment in the partner and more depression in the spouse. Such overprotective helping may result from a fear of abandonment in the helper, or from the helper's masochism, or from the helper's need to give to others what the helper himself needs. Sometimes a helper needs the suffering family member to depend on the helper, so the helper perpetuates the sufferer's helplessness. The helper may feel that not helping will lead to a loss of love or approval, or because of difficulty saying no, or from a real difficulty discerning the level of help which is appropriate. The helper may be helping as a reaction formation to hostility; helpers who resent helping, consciously or unconsciously, may help the sufferer in a passive-aggressive manner. Salvador Minuchin (1978) described "psychosomatic families" in which the family is organized around helping one suffering family member, whose suffering has become essential for the family's stability. This dynamic may make it difficult for that person to benefit from psychotherapy.

The psychotherapist can prolong the patient's suffering by using psychotherapeutic theory in a way that avoids the patient's real-life problem, in the service of commitment to working according to a particular technique. We saw this occasionally among the classical Jungians who focused exclusively on dreams while the patient's life situation deteriorated, or among classical Freudians who tried to explain everything in oedipal terms. In both cases narcissistic issues such as grandiosity or a fragile sense of self were ignored or misunderstood, to the detriment of the patient's real-world relationships.

161

A rigid psychotherapeutic technique of any kind can be used in a way that makes the patient's suffering worse. This is true even of core concepts such as the transference. Thomas Szasz (1963) suggested that although the transference is a real phenomenon, Freud also developed this concept so that he could deal with his patients' erotic and aggressive feelings towards him within the real relationship, without taking them personally. By assuming these feelings are purely transference-based, the therapist is protected from the full impact of the patient's personality, or from real-life involvement with the patient. Thus, if the patient dislikes the therapist, the therapist can reassure himself with the belief that this attitude is really about an early object of the patient, and not the result of the therapist's behavior. However, sometimes the therapist may be behaving in a way that re-traumatizes the patient, producing an appropriately negative reaction which is then attributed to the transference. Fortunately, developments in psychodynamic theory today have rendered this critique less relevant to practice, as it is now well understood that the therapist's actual behavior and not only the transference influence the patient's experience of the therapist.

Psychotherapy with caregivers of suffering people

It is well known that family members who care for physically and cognitively impaired relatives often suffer physically and emotionally (Monin et al., 2009). This situation is particularly difficult when the caregiver is unable to do much to alleviate the suffering of a loved one, leading to helplessness and anguish in the caregiver. The distress of the caregiver is alleviated to some degree if he or she is able to be helpful; indeed sometimes being able to alleviate suffering has positive effects on the caregiver. However, it is difficult to be constantly exposed to the suffering of a loved one without one's own health, or at least one's emotional equilibrium, being negatively affected, sometimes severely (Schulz et al., 2008; Beach, et al., 2000). It is particularly difficult to see a loved one in constant pain, or to witness the spiritual and existential suffering of family members, for example when one sees that their lives are restricted and unfulfilled because of illness (Coyle, 1996). Because of the effects if suffering on the personality, suffering may so radically affect the individual's identity that the person we thought we knew may become unrecognizable. The prospect of losing a loved one who is suffering adds to the caregiver's distress. The experience of caring for more than one family member, either simultaneously or in the past, has an additive effect on a caregiver. When a loved one is institutionalized, the resulting guilt and possible financial anxiety may cause great suffering in family members. Sometimes the empathic caregiver responds with the same painful emotions as the suffering person, such as anxiety or depression, but if the sufferer's distress is too much to handle, the caregiver may respond defensively with anger or frustration or even by blaming the suffering person as if the problem is self-induced. A negative reaction to a sufferer, revealed for example by not acknowledging the true gravity of the suffering person's pain, is likely to occur if the relationship between the care recipient and the care giver was ambivalent or hostile before the care was needed. Some dysphoric affect in the caregiver seems to be the result of projective identification, which leads the caregiver to experience the split-off emotions of the suffering person.

The psychotherapist working with a caregiver may be helpful by clarifying what the caregiver can realistically do and not do, helping the caregiver to identify in which ways the situation is truly out of her hands. There is a place here for mindfulness approaches which decrease emotional reactivity in the helper without suppressing painful feelings. At a deeper level, it is also valuable for the psychotherapist to help the caregiver look into the dynamics of his or her relationship with the suffering person, especially working with unexpressed guilt or anger. In psychotherapy, a useful distinction can be made between "caring for" and "caring about" (Jecker et al. 1991). Caring *for* means that we respond to a person's needs, which can sometimes be done relatively unemotionally. Caring *about* involves an emotional response to the person, which becomes part of the countertransference. It is nearly impossible to be deeply involved with the care of suffering people with little emotional reaction. Some writers therefore suggest that these two types of caring cannot be cleanly separated; "caring about" is inextricably a part of "caring for"; without caring *about* a person, care *for* that person suffers (Boleyn-Fitzgerald, 2003).

Compassion, sympathy, empathy, pity, and consolation

Words like compassion, empathy, and sympathy tend to be used colloquially as if they are interchangeable, but the meaning of these terms can be distinguished, and there is a good deal of debate about how to define them among researchers in several fields.[27]

Empathy

For psychotherapeutic purposes, empathy means that to varying degrees we feel what the suffering person feels—at times, even sensations of somatic pain. Kohut (1984) referred to empathy as "vicarious introspection," or the ability to "think and feel oneself into the inner life of another person," a mutually shared internal perception of the same feelings (p. 82). (The German word for empathy is *Einfühlung*, which literally means feeling-into.) Kleinian writers see empathy as a benign form of projective identification.[28] Empathy allows us to be emotionally attuned to the other person; it is a mode of perception and an important way of understanding others. In psychotherapy, empathy operates in both directions—therapist and patient empathically understand each other. What we perceive empathically may then be elaborated cognitively.

Importantly, as Kohut (1984) pointed out, empathy is value neutral; empathy can be accompanied by a helpful or a malevolent attitude to the sufferer—we can use empathy to hurt or manipulate someone, because we can take pleasure in knowing someone is in pain. We can be empathic without feeling sorry for the sufferer, without any moral response to his suffering, without endorsing the feelings we experience, and with no desire to help. A small number of people are either unable to utilize the therapist's empathy or they actually find it unpleasant, either because they lack the childhood experience of finding empathy helpful, or because it makes them feel weak and pitied, or because it forces them to face a feeling they would rather disavow.

Without empathy, other people become objects rather than human beings. Batson (2010) suggests that empathy evolved among higher mammals

---

27   For historical review of the use of these terms in psychoanalysis, see Black, 2004 & Pigman, 1995. For the debate between developmental and social psychologists, see Nakao, 2008. For a review of the importance of empathy in philosophy rather than psychotherapy, see Stueber, 2008 and Agosta, 2010.
28   Empathy is usually attributed to non-verbal communication, sensing the other's facial expressions, tone of voice, and body language, but there is also evidence for extrasensory perception which is ignored by "respectable" materialistic scientists.

as part of the instinct to parent, because parenting requires empathic inferences about the desires and feelings of the child. Empathy is essential to our humanity; it motivates pro-social and moral action, it is a major means of communication between people, and it has the effect of diminishing or even abolishing the emotional distance we feel from a suffering person. As a result of empathy, a shared emotional field arises between the participants. Empathy flowers in normal development unless environmental factors, such as those seen in the families of future psychopaths, inhibit its appearance. Empathy appears to be built into the human nervous system, as fMRI studies seem to confirm (Jackson et al. 2005), but it is too simplistic to reduce empathy to the firing of mirror neurons,[29] which is part of the attempt to reduce the psyche to the brain. fMRI studies of human brains measure large sections of the brain containing many neurons which are interconnected with other areas of the brain. Most of the research into mirror neurons has been done on single cells in monkey brains, and these studies cannot be replicated in humans. This is not to mention the fact that monkeys do not have culture or language as complex as that of humans. There are other problems with the notion that mirror neurons allow us to empathically understand the actions of others. For example, we can understand actions done by others which we are unable to perform ourselves, and at times we can understand another's emotion without actually feeling it empathically. The problem of the complex personal meaning of an emotion to each individual further complicates the issue, so that empathy is more than a matter of a specific type of localized neuronal firing. (For a review of current knowledge about mirror neurons, see Kilner et al. 2013.)

Some very young children seem to be temperamentally or innately empathic. Children as early as two years old may show the ability to understand the emotional states of other people and wish to alleviate their distress, so it may be that human beings are to some extent genetically programmed to help others. Nevertheless, it takes some years for the child to learn how to actually

---

29   Mirror neurons are neurons that replicate in an observer's brain the same neuronal activity that is going on in the brain of the individual performing an action. Mirroring of neuronal firing also occurs in cortical pathways when we observe someone having an emotional sensation such as disgust. This observation has led to the claim that we understand other people's emotions because the same neurons fire in the observer as would fire if the observer were the one actually having the emotion. However, there are various difficulties with the attempts to correlate brain activity with psychological processes. One is in the nature of our instruments; different types of brain scans lead to different conclusions about where the brain activity underlying a given mental state is located. fMRI studies have the limitation that they measure neural activity several seconds after neuronal activation, so the precise anatomical areas involved in a mental process may not be clear. Another problem is that understanding a brain mechanism that seems to underly a mental event does not tell us about the meaning of the event to the person in his socio-cultural setting (Gergen, 2010).

comfort others. It is not clear to what extent empathy is teachable—many educational theorists are interested in how this may be done, but the idea is controversial (Schertz, 2007).

Empathic concern for others affects our moral behavior as much or more so than our reason affects it, so that a wicked person may be quite rational but indifferent to the suffering of others. It may be that the capacity to be empathic determines whether or not one can be a caring person, and the combination of one's capacity for caring and empathy radically affects whether one is capable of moral behavior—in short, whether one is a decent person. Empathy also enters into our concepts of right and wrong, good and evil, and accordingly it is important in our political system and society in general (Slote, 2010). Lack of empathy contributes to society's ability to ignore the suffering produced by poverty, homelessness, and other social ills, and contributes to racial and religious prejudice and conflict.

Sympathy

Unlike empathy, sympathy may occur without the sense that we are actually feeling what the sufferer feels, and unlike empathy, sympathy is not value-neutral; sympathy adds the feeling of concern for the other person, the feeling that we care about the sufferer. Sympathy has therefore been referred to as "feeling for" rather than empathy's "feeling with" (Snow, 2000). That is, one can feel sorry for someone at an emotional distance, without feeling empathy (Chismar, 1988). There is a difference between feeling the same distress as another person and feeling sorry for that person without feeling any distress oneself. Sympathy can have moralistic overtones, and can even be accompanied by a feeling of horror or revulsion at the suffering of the other, so that one can be sympathetic without any of empathy's sense of the emotional merger of oneself with the other. Because of this, sympathy can backfire when a suffering person realizes that the person attempting to sympathize does not really understand the situation, and this increases the suffering person's alienation. Suffering people often hide the depths of their despair because it is too painful to reveal. They may also feel that only a person who has had their experience can really understand it.

For classically-trained psychodynamic psychotherapists, the word "sympathy" has been under a cloud and tends not to be used in the literature because it implies the wish to help directly, which many practitioners are trained not to do. This may be because Freud (1912) told his adherents that they must model themselves on the surgeon who puts aside feelings such as sympathy. However, the surgical model has been abandoned by most contemporary psychotherapists, who see themselves as collaborators in a journey of exploration and mutual understanding.

Compassion

Compassion is an emotional response to the suffering of another person which is characterized by benevolence, the sense we are personally addressed by the sufferer, and the wish to relieve his suffering without expecting anything in return (Gelhaus, 21012). Compassion requires that we are not afraid of the other person's suffering and we do not distance ourselves from it. In fact, part of the spiritual value of compassion is that it unites us with others. Polly Young-Eisendrath (1996) suggests that compassion is an antidote to our own suffering because it counteracts the alienation produced by suffering. Suffering may act as a bridge to a profound connection to another person, a sense that one has touched a sacred place.

Compassion is obviously a valuable attribute for the psychotherapist, but compassion is not something we can invoke at will. We cannot control the feelings which arise in psychotherapy. Compassion may arise spontaneously within the countertransference, with some patients more than with others. However, to expect the therapist to always be compassionate runs the risk of burn-out, or at least risks placing overly high demands on the therapist. Burn-out tends to happen when the therapist feels empathy but at the same time feels too exhausted to be helpful. In this context, it is well known that empathy for others tends to decrease as medical students and other trainees in the health care system progress through their education. Apparently the intense emotions stirred up by constant exposure to the suffering of others may lead to repression or disavowal of these feelings because they are unbearable, so that the individual becomes inured to suffering. In practice, distinctions between empathy, sympathy, and compassion cannot be drawn too sharply; one cannot be sympathetic or compassionate at all without the presence of at least some degree of empathy. Caring and compassion are normal human responses to suffering, but these are not always possible for the therapist. Working with a suffering person can be overwhelming, so that it is not unusual for the therapist to defend against too much emotional immersion in the inner life of the sufferer. This might occur when, through a process of identification, one imagines oneself in the patient's situation and protects oneself by disavowing its emotional intensity, or one responds from the fear that this generates. Helping others can be uplifting, but empathy can make one unbearably vulnerable. If we feel our empathy fading, the best we might be able to do is stay engaged and present, so that the suffering person does not feel abandoned, which suffering people often feel.

Reduced emotional responses to the suffering of others may also occur among individuals with high levels of social power, which is sometimes associated with reduced empathy and compassion (van Kleef et al., 2008). People with more power are sometimes less motivated to respond to those with less power, or they respond selectively to people with less power, especially when doing so furthers the goals of those with more power. The social and political implication of these findings for the care of those in need is obvious.

Consolation

Consolation has always been an important aspect of human relationships; the attempt to console seems to be an innate response to the suffering of others. It is clear that consolation sometimes helps, but it is not clear exactly how it helps. Empathy is a pre-requisite for the ability to console a suffering person; one has to be able to feel, or at least to imagine that we feel, what the other person is experiencing. Then, the addition of consolation and comfort offers relief by offering one's own strength, which may penetrate the suffering person's darkness (Morse et al, 1995; Alfredsson et al., 1995). Yet consolation for suffering is not always easy to find or to offer: words fail us, or words seem to be inadequate, especially when one has nothing hopeful to offer. It is useful at these times to remember that even if what we say is no use in itself, the suffering person may benefit from the recognition that the therapist is trying to help.

It is painful to witness another person suffer intensely and feel helpless to do anything useful. The psychotherapist's personal vulnerability is often stimulated in such situations, and one may find oneself working on one's own sorrow at the same time as one listens to the grief of another. Accordingly it requires courage and a certain faith in oneself for a psychotherapist to venture deeply into the suffering of another person. One has to be able to put one's own concerns aside for the moment, to know when to talk and when to be in silent communion because the other's suffering is beyond words. Here the word "communion" is used in the sense expressed by Gabriel Marcell (Glenn, 1984), who describes communion as a sense of unity or "enveloping." This kind of communion produces a shared suffering and sometimes the feeling of a shared sacred dimension.

Consolation may be difficult to accept; sometimes a suffering person has difficulty expressing feelings or disguises his or her feelings in order to protect others. Many people dislike appearing to be needy, making them hesitate to reach out for help. Jung's typology can be useful here; some introverted people do not express their feelings readily, and psychotherapists with introverted feeling may feel profound empathy but have difficulty expressing it verbally, which can lead to accusations that the therapist is cold or unfeeling. However, sensitive people can sense another's caring even in silence; often when nothing can be said, nothing needs to be said.

The suffering person may either project or accurately perceive that the psychotherapist is emotionally unprepared to deal with the situation, and indeed the therapist may be unconsciously signaling that he or she does not want to hear too much of the patient's pain—a form of counter-resistance. When the therapist takes on a suffering person, a kind of tacit promise is made which may be difficult to fulfill in a consistent way if the person needs frequent contact. It is common for people to rush to the aid of a friend or neighbor at the moment of a crisis, but then the would-be helpers fail to sustain their attention after a few weeks.

While it is true that consolation may alleviate painful feelings, it is also true that suffering people are not always ready for consolation; the sufferer may experience attempts at consolation as intrusive. This tends to happen when the sufferer is offered what feels like a platitude, or if the suffering person senses that the one attempting consolation is actually defending against his inability to tolerate what has happened to the sufferer.

Consolation has always been a part of health care (Norberg et al, 2001), and research into the process of consolation has become very important to the nursing community because comfort and consolation are central to nursing care, but burn-out is an ever-present danger for nurses (Glasberg et al., 2007). Importantly, burn-out may mimic depression, and may indeed be a form of depression based on a combination of exhaustion, high expectations, lack of recognition for the work one does, and a hostile work environment in which economic concerns are valued more than human concerns. Eventually this may lead to disengagement, feelings of hoplessness, or even indifference to the people the individual cares for.

The psychotherapist may be able to ask or discern what would be consoling to the patient. Otherwise, empathic listening, showing interest, and accepting and witnessing grief and vulnerability may be all one can do—but these may be very helpful (Langegard et al., 2009). The experience of a psychotherapist trying to deeply understand the person may itself be helpful, and the shared search for meaning has a therapeutic effect. When true consolation is offered and accepted, the experience is rewarding to the one who consoles as well as to the sufferer. It is important that the psychotherapist does not fall back on notions that what helps is only a function of the transference; when working with a suffering person, mutual openness and direct, heart-to-heart contact are necessary. Anything that sounds bookish or technical becomes reductive, diminishes the reality of the person's suffering, and is fatal to the authenticity of the relationship. In other words, the ability to console is not a technical matter that can be learned; it emerges spontaneously as a human potential in the face of suffering. The true witness cannot appeal to theory; one can only allow oneself to be affected by the suffering of the other person, and a response may—or may not—emerge spontaneously from the psychotherapist's unconscious.

Concern

There are occasions when the psychotherapist's state of mind is best described as concern for the welfare of the other rather than empathy, pity or sympathy. The importance of concern has been overshadowed by psychotherapeutic interest in empathy, but although these two states often coincide, they can be independent of each other; one can know how a person feels but have no concern for him, and one can be concerned without empathy. I should note here the (rather neglected) work of Ian Suttie (1935), who believed that concern for others is innate in human beings and not the result of developmental factors. In this tradition today, relational theorists believe that we are wired to respond to other human beings, especially to faces and voices. Concern for others may have evolved to become part of human nature because of its survival value, although concern also seems to be partly a developmental achievement since it means that we must recognize the other person as a separate subject with his own inner world. Not surprisingly, secure attachment styles allow increased concern for others.

Winnicott (1963) is one of the few psychoanalytic writers who directly address the issue of concern. For him concern means that we both care and also feel and accept responsibility for another person. In his early view, he believed that a baby develops concern for its mother as it realizes that the mother is separate from the baby and is capable of having her own feelings, whereupon the baby develops guilt for hurting her. Concern then develops as a desire for repairing this damage to mother. Later Winnicott suggested that the baby also feels grateful because he can feel any way he wishes towards his mother, including hostility, and mother survives, so concern can be motivated by joy and love as well as anxiety and guilt.

Pity and self-pity

When the psychotherapist works with a suffering person, pity rather than empathy may arise, and the distinction is important. In the ordinary sense of the word, pity suggests that one feels sorrow for the suffering of another person and one may be moved to help. However, on closer inspection, pity is a more complex emotion (Solomon, 1993; Geller, 2006). There is some debate about whether pity is an admirable human feeling like care or compassion, or whether pity is not so noble because it can include a tinge of contempt or an attitude of superiority on the part of the one who pities another, so that Nietzsche even charged people who pity with arrogance. These latter feelings are not a part of true compassion, which is one way we can distinguish between them. Nevertheless, in its positive aspects, pity can foster forgiveness and mercy and stimulate compassion, and there are surely acts of pity that are not tainted by condescension. In its problematic aspect, pity can at times feel humiliating or devaluing to the one who is pitied, so that one may hear a suffering person say "I don't want your pity." This attitude can become exaggerated; some individuals hear any of the therapist's attempt at caring as a demeaning form of pity, as if the therapist's caring implies that he or she sees the patient as weak. Other people feel that they do not deserve the therapist's concern.

Ben-Ze'ev (2000, p. 328) points out that "we can pity people while maintaining a safe emotional distance from them." One can feel pity for a victim of famine depicted in the media and at the same time feel relief that one is not in such a parlous situation oneself. Furthermore, one may resent feeling pity when one feels manipulated by it, which may happen if one feels that a story is being told in a deliberate attempt to evoke pity. Karen Horney (1937) noted that some people in therapy use appeals to pity as a way of disclaiming responsibility for their actions or as a manipulative attempt to gain affection. Usually this dynamic will provoke a countertransference feeling of resentment, but the therapist does not resent the empathy or compassion that arises spontaneously in response to genuine suffering. The difference seems to be partly based on our judgment that some people deserve compassion because of their tragic situation, while others are less deserving because they have brought misfortune on themselves, even though we may in such cases feel a degree of pity for the person. When we believe the suffering person is at fault for what has happened to him, we tend to initially feel blame and reproach, but we may also feel compassion if the person is seriously suffering, although we feel this to different degrees; some of us are more soft-hearted than others. One can be angry with a person who seems to be exaggerating his difficulties, being rather too helpless and needy, while feeling pity and even dislike at the same time. Our social disdain for someone who seems too self-pitying is seen in sarcastic remarks such as: "Get off the cross; we need the wood." Pity is therefore more remote than true compassion—one can pity someone and feel aloof or even disgust at the same time, so that pity has been described as a spectator sport. Buddhists believe that pity is a "near enemy" to compassion, meaning that pity can easily be mistaken for compassion. Pity however means we are sorry *for* someone, whereas compassion arises when we are sorry *with* someone, so that a kind of suffering exists within oneself because of the other's suffering. The Buddhist Steven Levine (1982), contrasting pity and compassion, says that pity means that we meet another's pain with fear or aversion to the sufferer's predicament; we then want to alleviate the sufferer's pain in order to alleviate our own. For him, compassion means that love touches the other's pain.

There are times when, trying to help another person, the psychotherapist experiences the sufferer as too full of self-pity, too dependent or too manipulative. Manipulation of others is either an attempt to elicit help by a person who feels his needs will not be addressed if he asks for help directly, or it is a strategy of the psychopath who must win at all costs. Exaggerated self-pity, or self-pity that seems to be going on too long after a tragedy, tends to alienate others and has a bad reputation in our culture; it implies that one is masochistic, a moral martyr, not taking responsibility for oneself, or one is simply inadequate. This kind of self-pity may be motivated by developmental factors, and it is essential for the therapist to understand the psychodynamics of these individuals in order to treat them empathically. Usually these forms of coping occur when, in development, the individual could not elicit appropriate responses from caregivers and had to find other ways to survive. Frequent self-pity tends to occur when there has been a recurrent failure of empathic, comforting responses from selfobjects in childhood (Wilson, 1985), so that the person is left with a weakened sense of self that lacks resilience under stress. Then, after any kind of distressing event or injury the individual feels as if he is alone with no help. He can only try to comfort himself and be empathic with himself, leading to self-pity. When a person with a fragile sense of self suffers a wound to his self-esteem, self-pity may arise as an attempt at self-comforting and self-consolation, or as an attempt at reparation, a way of putting oneself back together after being hurt. We can all experience self-pity at times, after a rebuff or failure of needed attention. However, when self-pity is an overly prominent feature of the personality, the individual tends to convey a feeling of being always a victim of fate or injustice, seeing himself entirely controlled by outside events, and angry that people are not being helpful enough. These individuals tend to see themselves as emotionally isolated even when they are not socially isolated (Stöber, 2003). This defensive organization can act as a powerful resistance to change. When trying to help someone with these dynamics who suffers from self-pity, it may feel as if anger is directed at the psychotherapist, as if the therapist is somehow responsible for the individual's suffering. This happens within the transference as if the therapist is a new version of the original selfobject who failed the sufferer. Complicating the picture is the fact that self-pity is sometimes accompanied by envy of others who are more fortunate, and it is sometimes part of a more encompassing depressive state.

There are circumstances in which one is in a very tragic situation, such that a degree of self-pity is almost inevitable. This kind of self-pity is based on realistic empathy for oneself. However, the psychotherapist also sees people who cannot be empathic with themselves, so that they do not have the capacity for appropriate self-pity. Because of the indifferent attitudes of their childhood families, some people minimize their legitimate suffering and see any expression of distress as weak and self-indulgent. Others grew up in abusive families, and as children assumed they deserved to be abused, so they feel chronically guilty and unable to be empathic with themselves. The therapist may need to help such a person appreciate that his tragic situation is not of his own making and a degree of pity for himself is warranted.

Bearing witness

There are many occasions in psychotherapy when one can only witness the suffering of another without being able to change the situation causing the suffering. In such situations, one of the important functions of the psycho-therapist is to act as a witness to what has happened. People often need to give testimony to their experience. Indeed Masud Khan (1981) believed that the human need for psychic pain to be witnessed silently and unobtrusively by another person is so important that it has led to the creation of an omni-present God in world religions. This is an exaggeration, but it points to the importance of addressing the isolation that suffering produces. Such isolation may occur because survivors feel that what they have been through cannot be expressed and may not even be believed—we see this in concentration camp survivors who will not talk about their experience. The sense of being witnessed and believed by the therapist may prevent a life-long attitude of silent resignation to suffering. It is important to add that silent witnessing of the suffering of another person benefits the therapist as much as the patient, because it enhances the therapist's capacity for empathy and his understanding of the human condition. Witnessing is an important component of the beneficial effects of therapy, but the psychotherapist cannot witness without at the same time participating in a mutual experience. Witnessing is not a passive process; it means that we empathically grasp the emotional significance of what is being said and we are affected by it, but we do not interfere. We observe what-is without judgment. This silence is a form of active presence and active listening, allowing the soul to be heard. This often means that we listen not only for the surface meaning of what is being said, but also for a more muted level of meaning. A good way to do this is to encourage story-telling, because stories always have multiple layers of meaning. The process of telling a story leads to the appearance of previously unseen tendrils of meaning which can be gently encouraged to further emerge. The act of telling stories that bind events into a narrative thread seems to make experiences more meaningful than would be the case if events were to be seen in isolation with no connection to each other. Telling stories about oneself also clarifies one's sense of identity and reveals the evolution of the personality. Lorraine Wright (2005) sees ill people as "wounded storytellers" (p. 157) who need to tell stories to make sense of their suffering, which has a healing effect.[30] The act of witnessing seems to catalyze the patient's experience, or sometimes makes it possible for more levels of it to be experienced. Sometimes a person does not know what she feels, or cannot make sense of something about herself, until what she feels is said in the presence of another; witnessing allows the patient to really believe that what she says is valid. This is not simply about offering comfort. It *matters* to people that someone else deeply understands how they feel and recognizes

---

30   Narrative approaches are part of postmodern constructivist theory, which views individuals as active agents who co-create the meaning of their experiential world.

what has happened to them, even if nothing can be done about it. Neither is this simply a mirror transference phenomenon; when the therapist is silently witnessing a patient's anguish the therapist is engaged as a real person, not only as a mirroring selfobject, although these functions may be inseparable.

Witnessing might be particularly important if the psychotherapist is working with someone who has been the victim of evil. In a way the psychotherapist then stands in for society as a whole, acknowledging that the evil should not have happened. If the witness-therapist can help to contain the pain of these memories, they become better able to be integrated. Sometimes we are then privileged to witness the emergence of an aspect of the person's soul that has long been unavailable; sometimes we can witness a truth about the person that he or she cannot see him or herself. An unobtrusive, holding silence, combined with the therapist's emotional investment, are required for witnessing what the soul wishes to say. Holding here means allowing space for emotions to emerge in a way that feels contained and safe. The witness must have no agenda, no judgment, and must not be committed to a particular outcome. A witnessing attitude requires receptive silence on the part of the therapist, which may mean that the therapist must sacrifice his wish or need to say something.

The act of witnessing opens the therapist to the unknown; it requires courage and faith, because as we witness we have no idea what may emerge next. The psychotherapist empathically senses feelings such as terror, rage, or helplessness, and must respond in a way that signifies she is affected but not overwhelmed. It is painful to see a person's suffering, but the witness's discomfort must not be avoided, although it sometimes leads to a posture of detachment in would-be caregivers who cannot tolerate what is stimulated in themselves as they witness the other's pain. To stay with the suffering of the other person is to suffer oneself; suffering invariably stimulates our own vulnerability and our own difficulties. At the same time, the therapist-witness has to be careful to manage his own feelings and not burden the patient by inducing in the patient an obligation to look after the witness. Nevertheless, one cannot help but imagine oneself in a similar situation, even though one may not be able to truly know what the other is going through. Sometimes the best we can do is to be a companion in the person's suffering, without the sense that we are trying to take away his or her pain.

True witnessing is not detached; to witness is to take in as fully as possible what is happening to the other and to be a part of what is going on, which is an act of mercy, love, and sacrifice (Helin, 2003). Somehow, the act of witnessing expresses an important human value. We take a risk when we witness silently; we face great uncertainty, but we may discover something very important; a new understanding of life and new values may emerge. To be a witness is to truly see the other in all his vulnerability, which evokes our responsibility to the other and consequently our own vulnerability. According to Levinas (1985), the face of the other person awakens an ethical responsibility in us and a wish to care for him. For Levinas, to care for the other's suffering before one's own is the height of a person's humanity, the highest form of human selfhood, and an ethical imperative. For him, it is incumbent on us to respond properly to the suffering of another person, regardless of whether others are also doing so. Levinas suggests that when a person stands in front of the other and says "here I am," he acts as a witness of the good, the Infinite, or God; when a person is at the disposal of another, he is a witness that there is "something beyond." Levinas believes that witnessing has this spiritual character provided that the witness is in contact with his or her own spirituality. Levinas describes a profound form of spirituality in which one might recognize infinity in the face of the other; this face points to the beyond because the absolute otherness of the other cannot be grasped or understood, and so opens the door to infinity. At the same time, the face of the other makes the otherness of the other concrete, which is essential to witnessing. Looking at the face of the other, being caring and understanding, are all one. The therapist's silent caring is an act of love, which may be all we can do to alleviate suffering. This love is transmitted silently by means of one's facial expression, tone of voice, and eyes. Even when the therapist is silent, the patient consciously or unconsciously perceives subtle changes of emotion in the therapist's face, which powerfully communicate to the patient that he is affecting the therapist.

An interesting paradox about the process of silent witnessing in psychotherapy is that it reflects the patient's ability to differentiate himself from the therapist, and to individuate, but at the same time to experience a deep level of connection. These should not be thought of as opposites; they are part of a unitary process of development. We are alone with our difficulties but present with the other at the same time.

There is of course a dark side to the process of witnessing—not everyone is able to listen to serious emotional pain or trauma, and sometimes the witness feels she must say something; she cannot keep silent and has to offer advice. However, it is unhelpful when the witness says something in a way which minimizes or deflects the severity of the sufferer's pain, which makes the sufferer feel even more isolated and hopeless. In other words, talking about trauma without being properly received and witnessed is itself traumatic. It is important for the psychotherapist-witness to remember that intense suffering may make it difficult for the sufferer to have much empathy or caring for others, so that the witness herself may become the subject of undeserved bitterness and anger, as if she were responsible for the sufferer's pain. The witness may have to simply accept these projections, or they may be interpretable in a usable way in relatively healthy individuals.

I should note that we may use an art form such as music, theater, poetry, cinema, or painting to witness or express sorrow and to find some ways to assuage it. We use music to sooth our suffering because music has a unique ability to convey and express emotion non-verbally, which is why music is often used to express mourning, grief or remembrance in funeral requiems, spirituals, laments, and so on. Music can also provide a sense of hope and comfort and seems to offer a kind of safe container or mirror for painful feelings. The very transience of music mirrors the impermanence of what we have lost. When we play music that is or was particularly important to a loved, one, the music allows a sense of connection with that person, which is also why some music is too painful to listen to after a loss.

Therapeutic Presence and the transpersonal Self in psychotherapy

People return to the next therapy hour because they receive something important, something they need. But this may not be anything verbal; silent presence is a powerful medicine. Therapeutic presence is essential for meaningful psychotherapy to occur, but real presence is elusive and hard to describe. True presence is not passive; it can be thought of as spiritual attention, which may be strongly present even if we are silent, just as it is possible to be talking but not emotionally present. Therapeutic presence waxes and wanes in intensity; it is conveyed and detected by tone of voice, facial expression, body language, gesture, and by a subtle atmosphere in the room. Presence is about how we are with the other person, how available and open we are to what is happening, combined with the ability to pay sustained attention. Presence is not the same as charisma, although charismatic people do have presence. However, one can be present without charisma, which at times feels narcissistic and cloying. Some individuals seem to have a healing presence, which induces an experience of peace and comfort in suffering people. Healing presence has not been well studied. It has been considered to be part of the placebo effect—what Jungians might call the constellation of the inner healer. In addition, most healing traditions also assume the effect of a spiritual component that is independent of the subject's cognitive processes. When healers are asked for the components of healing, they typically list factors such as: love; grace; focused awareness; openness to healing; creativity; imagination; relatedness; intention; belief; direction of energy; listening; and reconciliation (Jonas, 2004). Love is said to provide healing energy, while intention provides its direction.

Therapeutic presence is an important aspect of psychotherapy, one of the common factors found in all schools of thought. Presence can have a healing effect in its own right, and may be essential to an effective therapeutic relationship (Geller et al., 2002). One definition suggests that therapeutic presence is the state of having one's whole self in the encounter on many levels—physical, cognitive, emotional, and spiritual all at the same time, so that one is attuned and responsive, with a "kinesthetic and emotional sensing of the other's affect and experience as well as one's own intuition and skill and the relationship between them" (Geller et al., 2012, p. 7). Paradoxically, to be fully present one has to empty oneself of egoistic investment in the outcome of the situation, allowing an internal space inside oneself to be filled with the presence of the other. To let go of the ego also means that one has to let go of one's theories, presuppositions, diagnoses, and so on. Presence is more important than the therapist's theoretical orientation; in fact, to be fully present is the opposite of working with a specific technique. One has to be absorbed, fully in the moment with no goal in mind, only interest. Then, when one is truly present, one feels psychologically as if one is physically very close to the other person, even though there is the usual physical space between us.

There is more to presence than the presence of the body; presence seems to extend beyond the body, like a subtle but palpable extension of the body. The therapist can use the body in order to be present, by focusing on the breath, one's level of muscle tension, and on a sense of internal stillness and somatic awareness. This practice may have a calming effect on an anxious patient. Full presence requires a radically open form of listening with close attention, without judgment, without trying to make something happen, without listening for anything in particular, without interpreting or needing something, while allowing oneself to be totally affected by what is happening. There is then a sense of timelessness and lack of spatial boundaries. This is a kind of unconditioned listening. It makes one realize how attached we are to talking—in fact, if one is talking it is harder to be fully present, because talking is a distraction.

For people with a spiritual orientation, one can conceive of three presences in psychotherapy; the patient, the therapist, and the transpersonal Self or the archetypal or spiritual dimension. The presence of intense emotion due to an activated complex indicates the presence of the archetype experienced in the body, because the archetype embodies by means of the emotional tone of the complex, which has an archetypal core, and emotion is mediated by the brain and autonomic nervous system. Very often, the only meaningful response to the analysand's intense emotion is silence, which is an important mode of experience of the Self (Corbett, 2013). Words often do not do justice to the pain which is going on, and we often sense we are part of a much larger process that we cannot fully understand. Silence then emerges with the realization that there is nothing the ego can say or do; one can only be present to the moment.

At moments of intense pain and helplessness, the psychotherapist will have to take into account the sufferer's stance on spiritual issues if it looks like these are important to the individual. A religious individual may feel abandoned by God or closer to God as a result of his or her suffering. It is worth asking whether the person feels that his or her suffering is the will of God, a divine punishment, and so on. The therapist may personally believe that spiritual attitudes to suffering are defensive, but the therapist has to work within the patient's frame of reference. If the sufferer is committed to an established religious tradition, this spiritual meaning of his suffering can be dealt with by a minister, who can offer the wisdom about suffering found in his or her spiritual tradition, when a traditional solution fits with the sufferer's personal psychology. These possibilities are discussed in Chapter 6. If the person has a personal spirituality but is not committed to a particular tradition, the therapist may become a *de facto* spiritual director (Corbett, 2011).

The importance of presence is found in the work of the contemporary psychoanalyst Daniel Stern (2004), who writes about "moments of meeting" during psychotherapy, in which an experience is expressed by means of vitality affects. These are dynamic shifts in the sense of self, a rising and falling of affective intensity such as a sudden rush of anger or joy or "a wave of feeling evoked by music" (p. 64). These affects mostly operate outside awareness except in moments of intense experience such as blushing or having a temper tantrum. Stern believes that these moments offer the greatest potential for authenticity and change; this is where "the magic in a therapy session or in intimate relations" (p. 67) resides. These moments of presence are experienced as a sense of vitality. Sometimes these moments are almost imperceptible, when the therapist suddenly and unexpectedly grasps something of special importance. Such moments of affective attunement have a core of feeling that cannot always be put into words; often they are silent moments, based on eye contact alone, in which the therapist has direct access to a quality of the other soul. The relational field then suddenly changes. During these moments we are both equally vulnerable. An important dream may follow such a moment. During these moments of presence, theory is at a distance; only the immediate connection is important. The emphasis is on affective experience rather than cognitive meaning. Attention to these here and now micro-moments is a radical change from the broader focus of classical psychoanalysis with its emphasis on the past and life narratives.

Psychological aspects of helping

The psychotherapist's intention to be helpful, combined with the patient's perception that the psychotherapist is trying to help, are important factors in addressing suffering. Consequently, it is important that the psychotherapist look into his or her motive for wanting to be of help to others, in order to avoid using the patient to meet the therapist's personal needs. Certain elements of these dynamics are well known; typically the therapist had suffering parents, or parents who were physically or psychologically ill, so the future therapist was trained to be a caretaker early on. Or, according to Kleinian theory, one becomes a therapist in an unconscious attempt to repair the damage we fantasize we did to our early objects. We may become therapists because of an unconscious wish to understand and cure ourselves; many therapists were abused as children or had lonely, difficult childhoods. They take up this work to meet their needs for attention and intimacy. Therapists are usually psychologically minded, intellectually curious people who need to understand others (Farber et al., 2005 provide a fuller review of this literature).

Unless the therapist understands at least some of his motivation to be a therapist, certain types of countertransference reactions become particularly troublesome. The need to help others may itself act as an impediment to the therapeutic process, because this desire becomes too much a part of the therapist's personal agenda. Any form of neurotic compulsion to be helpful distorts the process of therapy. For example, the therapist may feel he has to be helpful in order to feel loved, or he needs to be admired and valued, or he needs to feel superior or in control, or he harbors grandiose fantasies of being a healer. Some psychotherapists sacrifice themselves masochistically to the needs of others, which often leads to difficulty maintaining boundaries with very demanding patients.

Personal suffering allows the psychotherapist to develop the internal capacity to help contain the suffering of others, but it is important for the psychotherapist not to use his caring for others as a substitute for necessary personal work. It has long been recognized that helping others is sometimes a way of defending against one's own suffering. It is then as if we work on our own suffering by working on the suffering of others. Some people in the helping professions devote their lives to giving to others the care they would like to have themselves, although those who help others often have difficulty accepting help when they need it themselves.

One of the dangers of being in the socially sanctioned role of helper, such as that of minister, social worker, therapist or physician, is that these roles can become too rigid and formal. We can become too attached to the role if we need it for a neurotic reason—to feel important, to support self-esteem, to avoid being lonely, or to assuage guilt. Such an individual is overly invested in his position and too identified with his persona; he is not doing the work simply to be helpful—not that there is anything wrong with a benign sense of satisfaction in helping others. Another danger for highly trained professional helpers is to allow technical considerations to overshadow the helping relationship itself; the patient then becomes nothing more than a diagnosis, and spontaneously arising compassion is submerged by knowledge which substitutes for understanding. It is important to participate in a helping role without identifying with it and losing our humanity.

The therapist's negative responses to suffering: Burnout and compassion fatigue

The psychotherapist who empathically feels the full impact of the suffering of another person makes a sacrifice which requires faith in the psychotherapeutic process, because caring can be emotionally costly for the caregiver. Over-exposure to the suffering of others may lead to a variety of responses in the therapist. The phenomenon of burnout is well known among psychotherapists and other health care workers in hospitals, hospices, and nursing homes who become emotionally and physically exhausted by the day-to-day needs of very ill people, and hence risk becoming desensitized to their suffering. Burnout refers to the sense that one has no emotional resources left to give to others (Schaufeli, 1996). Health care workers have to deal with patients' negative feelings, problematic behavior, and often an inability to be of any help. In these situations, as a defense against feelings such as impotence, or simply due to being overwhelmed, patients are often depersonalized or treated with indifference. Burnout can lead to negative attitudes towards those who are suffering and also to a devaluation of the caregiver's own work, and concomitant guilt about feeling this way. Our hearts begin to shut down, and we become apathetic as we feel we have nothing left to give. The irony of the situation is that we started out trying to alleviate suffering but only managed to increase our own. This phenomenon may also occur among family members who take care of people with chronic, severe illness such as dementia, cancer or multiple sclerosis. The caregiver is expected to support the ill family member without receiving much emotional support in return, which may lead to resentment, especially between spouses when the marital relationship is poor (Ybema, 2002). On the other hand, if the caregiver feels that he or she is being helpful to the suffering person, care-giving may be a positive experience.

It is helpful to acknowledge that we feel burnt out, and not try to soldier on, blaming ourselves for not being compassionate enough. Constantly dealing with suffering is difficult, and the psychotherapist has to be gentle with himself, acknowledging his limits and his own needs. Psychotherapists and nurses commonly suffer from "compassion fatigue" as a result of insufficient self-care. This phenomenon reduces our ability to contain the suffering of others. In the etiology of compassion fatigue, Figley (2002) lists a combination of factors; the therapist empathically feels the patient's distress—she is motivated to be helpful but she is under the constant stress produced by direct exposure to suffering people while trying to relieve their suffering. Another contributing factor is that helpers often have unconscious motives for helping, such as the need to be needed, which can become frustrated, leading to disappointment. Excessive fatigue and self-doubt may be important indicators that introspection is indicated. While it can feel like a privilege to be allowed into the inner world of another person, if we are too stretched emotionally we may also become irrationally angry at the suffering person and his situation.

In psychotherapy, anger at a suffering patient is often a complementary identification with the patient's parents who found their child too burdensome, while helplessness in the therapist may be a concordant identification with the way in which the patient was made to feel as a child. These countertransference feelings can be usefully explored in the therapy. The therapist may become angry and frustrated with himself if the patient's suffering goes on for a long period and shows no sign of abating, often because the patient is frustrating the therapist's need to be a helper. For these kinds of reasons, psychotherapists often become angry at patients who seem to be self-destructive with alcohol or drugs, and therapists who have difficulty acknowledging their own limitations are prone to reject the patient who makes demands that seem unmanageable. All these factors, combined with guilt and self-blame, predispose to burnout.

Clinicians who treat trauma survivors are greatly affected by this work, and they open themselves to profound personal transformation. Constantly working with traumatized individuals may produce extreme distress in the psychotherapist, a phenomenon that has been called "vicarious traumatization" (Pearlman et al. 1995a) or Secondary Traumatic Stress (Figley, 2002), which is similar to PTSD except that it results from prolonged exposure to the trauma suffered by another person combined with the responsibility of care. This phenomenon may lead to changes in the therapist's world-view, her spirituality, relationships, and core beliefs about the world. Pearlman (1995b) points out that these developments are not the result of immaturity or unresolved countertransference; they are an occupational hazard when we are constantly immersed in human suffering.

Compassion fatigue can be helped by good supervision or personal therapy when needed, good professional training, the ability to distance oneself from our patients' suffering between sessions, respite or breaks between sessions, social support, relationships with colleagues, a sense of achievement and satisfaction in one's work, acknowledgment of one's limitations, reduction in the number of traumatized people one works with, and attention to personal stress management. Unfortunately, therapist self-care skills are not always stressed in psychotherapy training programs, and the personal needs of psychotherapists may be ignored by bureaucratic institutions. However, unresolved vicarious traumatization can induce despair in the therapist, producing a kind of spiritual wound. If this is pursued it can lead to a deepening of the therapist's emotional life, sometimes because there is nowhere else to go. It is also helpful if we can cultivate an attitude of not needing to know exactly what to do in all situations—what Keats referred to as "negative capability." To help others is potentially transformative for the psychotherapist, putting us in touch with our own suffering and thereby increasing our self knowledge to help others puts us in touch with our own suffering and thereby increases our self-knowledge. That is the gift that the suffering person gives to the helping person.

The suffering of others seems to awaken an instinctive need in us to help. At the same time as we feel a spontaneous opening of the heart, as noted above we may also discover in ourselves a need to be useful and needed, praiseworthy, wise, and strong. The therapist may therefore choose to work with a certain type of suffering person whom he finds gratifying, because the patient's difficulty corresponds to the psychotherapist's need to shine in a certain way, perhaps because of special training in a certain area. At the same time, we may be afraid of those who suffer in a certain way because they may demand too much of us, leading to a simultaneous resistance to helping. This mixture of motives in the psychotherapist may lead to a degree of internal conflict. We compromise by setting limits on what we can do and by establishing professional boundaries, which are often ethical necessities to protect the patient, but boundaries are also important to protect the psychotherapist from being overwhelmed. Boundaries allow the therapist to titrate how much she can tolerate. However, patients sense the therapist's self-protection or distancing, just as they know when the therapist's caring is just professional and not really felt. This feeling often repeats early trauma with indifferent or exhausted parents. Sometimes it is more useful to acknowledge to ourselves our fear of being overwhelmed and our need for distance, instead of protecting ourselves by being too removed. It is hard to deal with someone else's vulnerability if we cannot acknowledge our own.

Professional helpers are often people who give what they need; instead of asking for help ourselves, we give it. Similarly, we may expect that others will respond to suffering in the way that we respond to our own, or we may respond to other's pain in the same way as we respond to our own. These attitudes may or may not be conscious; we may think of our suffering as random misfortune or as well-deserved, we may judge ourselves for it or feel humiliated by it. We may be ashamed to ask for help, or we may insist on help; we may become angry, we may become martyrs, or we may be able to accept help graciously. These styles or personal attitudes to suffering may all color the therapist's countertransference. When faced with a suffering person, given a normal capacity for empathy, we may involuntarily imagine how we would feel in that situation. We therefore have to know how we react to our own suffering, because a problem arises if the therapist unconsciously assumes that what the patient needs is based on the way the therapist would react himself if he were to be in the patient's situation. Or, if we unconsciously over-identify with the suffering person we may increase his or her burden; the patient then has to take care of the therapist. It is important that the suffering person not be invaded by the therapist's emotional reactions. The therapist has to be willing to allow the suffering person to suffer in his or her own way, with no preference on the part of the helper about how this is to happen. Even when the therapist feels overwhelmed by the intensity of the patient's suffering, it is most important not to abandon the person, since even a hint of this may produce hopelessness and worsen the sufferer's sense of despair.

Commonly, when the therapist feels (perhaps unconsciously) that he could not tolerate being in the patient's situation, or if the patient's story is too similar to that of the therapist, the therapist tries to deal with his own distress by giving the patient a diagnosis which objectifies the person and provides a little distance. Or, instead of owning our own suffering stirred up by working with a person in great distress, we blame our inability to tolerate the patient's suffering on the patient himself, often for ostensibly technical reasons; the patient is seen as too resistant, too dependent, insufficiently motivated for psychotherapy, or not suited for the type of therapy we offer.

Therapeutic action

We often begin psychotherapy with no clear idea of what will happen or exactly what the person needs. Even at the end of a successful therapy we may discover that what actually helped was not what the therapist initially believed would be the helpful factor. There are many non-specific processes, which are helpful and common to all schools of thought (Jørgensen, 20014).

All theories of therapeutic action can be approached from the point of view of the alleviation of suffering as their primary goal. The well-known therapeutic mechanisms include the selfobject transferences, the development or repair of internal structure, the development of new associational networks, affect regulation, the provision of a new perspective, and so on, which need no further articulation here. Some of the broad differences of opinion about what is happening during psychotherapy are affected by the therapist's fundamental view of the nature of the self. Some psychotherapists believe that human beings have an intrinsic essence, which is trying to express itself. This may be conceived of as an a priori spiritual essence or as a kind of innate, genetically determined nuclear program. Suffering results when the environment does not allow its expression, in which case it remains in a kind of cold storage from which it can be recognized and liberated in psychotherapy. In contrast, psychotherapists with a more postmodern approach believe that there is no such essence to the person, and our sense of self is entirely constructed by relationships with others and with society. The psychotherapist's approach to suffering people is therefore affected by whether we feel we are trying to discover or repair what has always been there, some essential truth of the person, or whether we are trying to build something that has never fully developed—or some combination of these. The relational or mutual influence approaches in psychotherapy suggest that what emerges in the therapeutic dyad is co-constructed by both therapist and patient. A competing view suggests that people have an intrinsic nature, and they have minds that are not completely determined by the therapeutic interaction. Whichever position we hold, it is most helpful to understand the patient's suffering from the patient's point of view, without allowing the therapist's theoretical perspective to have too much influence. Excessive adherence to any particular perspective is inimical to deep understanding.

It may become clear during the therapeutic process that the patient's suffering has damaged an important aspect of his personality, such as his faith in human nature or his hope for the future, which had been helping to sustain the individual. In that case, the therapist may help to restore that feature of the personality. At other times, understanding why a person is in distress requires that the therapist try to grasp some aspect of the person, perhaps an inchoate feeling or belief about himself, that he has never before articulated or even been conscious of. This is often an intuitive or empathic process. A further possibility arises when the cause of the individual's suffering is clear, but he will not let go of it.

Holding on to suffering: The case of Philoctete

Sophocles's (409 BCE) recounting of the myth of Philoctetes is a good example of a person who holds onto his suffering for complex reasons, even when it becomes possible to relinquish it. There are political and spiritual dimensions to this story, but here I wish to focus only on the psychological issues involved in Philoctetes's bitter rejection of the possibility of relief from suffering, because this is a dynamic which psychotherapists still encounter.

Part of Philoctetes's suffering is due to the fact that he did nothing of his own accord to deserve his wound. On his way to fight with Odysseus and the Greek army against the Trojans, he inadvertently walks into the sacred precinct of the goddess Chryse and is bitten by the poisonous snake who guards it. His cries of pain are unbearable, and they prevent his comrades offering sacrifices to the gods, which would be dangerous to omit just before a battle. His maggot-ridden wound festers and emits a horrible stench which his fellow sailors cannot tolerate. Consequently Odysseus is ordered to abandon Philoctetes, leaving him stranded on the desolate island of Lemnos for nine lonely years while the Trojan War goes on without him. (By the standards of the time, this is probably understandable behavior.) Philoctetes can hardly walk, he has fits of agonizing pain that render him unconscious, and his clothes are covered in discharges from his wound. He feels helpless and ashamed of his plight. Whenever visiting sailors land on Lemnos he begs to be taken back to Greece, but no one can tolerate being near him, so appalling is the stench of his wound. He survives because he had been given the gift of a magic bow by the dying hero Heracles (Hercules). This bow never misses its mark, so Philoctetes is able to hunt and stay alive. Heracles had given Philoctetes the bow in return for lighting his funeral pyre, when Heracles wanted to die because he had been poisoned and was in constant pain. After his death, Heracles became a god and was worshiped throughout classical Greece.

When a seer announces that Troy would never fall unless Philoctetes and his bow re-join the Greek army of his own free will, Odysseus and a young man named Neoptolemus are sent to Lemnos to bring Philoctetes back to Troy. Odysseus tries both trickery and the threat of force to induce Philoctetes to go to Troy. At first, Neoptolemus colludes with an attempt to deceive Philoctetes, but his conscience pricks him and he has a change of heart when he realizes that he has betrayed his own integrity by trying to deceive Philoctetes. In a moral crisis, Neoptolemus gradually comes to pity Philoctetes and tells him that the oracle announced that the Greek physicians in the cult of Aesculapius could heal him if he returns to Troy, and he will become a hero. Nevertheless, Philoctetes is so full of spite and bitter, narcissistic rage at Odysseus that he wants revenge, even if it means his own suffering will continue and the Greeks will not take Troy. The only thing that would make him feel better is to see his enemies suffer as he has done. He hates Odysseus, he curses him and wants his betrayers dead. Nothing will persuade Philoctetes to forgive Odysseus or make Philoctetes go with

Odysseus to Troy; Philoctetes says he would rather commit suicide. The chorus criticizes him for blaming fate and choosing suffering instead of a heroic life among his people—after all, they say, Odysseus was ordered by his commanders to abandon Philoctetes.

Philoctetes's refusal to go to Troy has other possible motives, not least of which is Odysseus's lack of compassion for him—Odysseus wants only the bow, not the man. It may be that Philoctetes believes he deserves his suffering because he agreed to kill Heracles, who was a kind of symbolic father to him. His refusal to go to Troy is a desperate attempt to assert some personal power, to cope with intense shame at being so helpless, combined with intense hatred of the men who betrayed him. Gottleib (2004) suggests that Neoptolemus is kind and empathic to Philoctetes, and is willing to examine his own mistake at trying to trick him—and these qualities open Philoctetes to a vision of Heracles, which appears just as it looks as if Neoptolemus will take Philoctetes back to Greece instead of to fight at Troy. Heracles insists that Philoctetes voluntarily returns to the battle. Philoctetes agrees, perhaps because the vision of Heracles, his idealized hero and mentor, gives him permission to do what part of him unconsciously wanted to do, partly because of Neoptolemus's empathy, and partly because the vision of the god is so numinous. Unfortunately however this divine intervention precludes any personal reconciliation with Odysseus.

The relevance of this story to the psychotherapist is that there are patients who refuse to get better in order to spite their therapists, sometimes out of envy or some form of transference hatred, which may lead to the therapist's countertransference hostility and need for revenge (Gottlieb, 2004). Melvin Lansky (2003) believes that Philoctetes's hatred, rage, and inability to forgive arise from his unbearable shame at having been abandoned by his comrades. They have dealt an enormous wound to his self-esteem, so that he feels the humiliation resulting from the discrepancy between the state he is in and his ego-ideal, and from the fact that his revolting wound makes him impossible to be with. His enduring hatred diverts his attention from his shame and onto the guilt of his betrayers, but this hatred also prevents forgiveness. Lansky suggests that Philoctetes's belief that his comrades deliberately abandoned him because they devalued him is a paranoid fantasy in which it seems that others gloat over his misfortune. This paranoid shame holds him in place emotionally and must be resolved if he is to be re-united with his comrades. However, Philoctetes is unable to forgive those who have hurt him. He never inquires about the meaning of his suffering and he constantly protests and bemoans his fate. His story shows an archetypal sequence; apparently meaningless suffering that will not heal, isolation, rage, hatred at those who caused his wound, agony at the injustice of his situation, and rejection by the sufferer's friends who cannot tolerate his suffering but end up needing him for their own purposes.

A modern-day Philoctetes in psychotherapy who wanted to forgive his comrades would have to let go of his hostility towards those who harmed him. Elsewhere, I have suggested some of the dynamics and therapeutic processes involved in forgiveness (Corbett, 2011, pp. 95-102). Briefly, the therapist would have to remind Philoctetes that forgiveness need not be complete or immediate, it could be conditional on his not being injured again, and forgiveness is not the same as pardoning in the legal sense. Forgiveness might happen if he could be empathic with his comrades' reasons for abandoning him, if he could imagine himself doing what they did in a similar situation, and if his self-esteem and shame could be repaired in the therapy. Finally, forgiveness is more likely if he is open to and were to receive a sincere apology.

6

SPIRITUAL AND RELIGIOUS APPROACHES TO SUFFERING

Introduction

When a psychotherapist is working with a suffering person who is committed to a traditional religion, it is important for the therapist to understand that religion's approach to suffering, since it often affects the person's attitude to his or her difficulty. Sometimes these attitudes can be traced back to early childhood influences from Sunday school and the individual's family of origin. Even when these religious teachings are repressed or disavowed, they may be exerting an influence. In this chapter, I describe various religious responses to suffering, both from our major traditions and also from some important but independent religious thinkers such as Krishnamurti and Simone Weil.

Faced with suffering, religious people characteristically invoke transpersonal or spiritual forces, either to explain the situation or to call for help with it. Sometimes these unseen forces are understood in terms of a traditional image of a deity or a figure such as the Buddha, and sometimes they are seen in uniquely individual terms. In either case, some form of spirituality is important to many people. In a 2010 poll, 80% of Americans rated religion as "fairly" or "very" important to them.[31] The importance of religion is increasingly recognized among mental health practitioners, and a good deal of research suggests that religious belief is beneficial to the individual's physical and mental health (Lee et al., 2005). People often turn to religion during times of distress, partly because religion gives people a way to make suffering meaningful and helps them to cope with it. Religion offers consolation and an explanation for suffering. In fact, if a religious

---

31   Gallup Poll (2010). Retrieved from http://www.gallup.com/poll/1690/Religion. aspx

tradition fails to console the individual, it fails one of its most important functions. As Jung (CW 18, p. 162) points out, religions can be thought of as psychotherapeutic systems, or ways of dealing with suffering. Religions also respond to the great "who am I?" and "why am I here?" questions that are stimulated or intensified by suffering. It is also true that the problem of suffering causes people to lose their religious faith entirely (Ehrman, 2008).

Not only do all religious traditions address the problem of suffering, with some justification it is often said that suffering is a major stimulus to the development of religion, because religion gives us a way to understand and deal with what would otherwise be inexplicable (Bowker, 1970). The problem of suffering is therefore a source of one of the great divides between religious individuals who find an answer to suffering within their tradition, and atheists who regard such answers as illusory palliatives. Freud, for example, in his *Future of an Illusion*, suggested that religion came about in an attempt to deal with our fear of death, to protect us from our helplessness in the face of nature, and to reconcile us to the difficulties we experience by partaking in civilization. Religion is then nothing more than a defense or a way of coping with life. However, even when religion is used defensively, even when faith is used to cope with existential anxiety, those dynamics do nothing to disprove the reality of a spiritual dimension of reality. We all try to find a world-view that provides us with an orientation and comfort in the face of our suffering and existential dilemmas. For some people this means religion, for others the pursuit of money or power, and so on. Here it is worth noting Beck's (2004) idea that while defensive religion is deployed to deal with death anxiety and offer consolation for suffering, what he calls existential religion is a mode of faith that is not defensive. This mode acknowledges the inevitability of death at the same time as it consciously struggles with the doubts and anxieties that accompany faith. When this reality-based religion emerges in the therapy room, even if the psychotherapist is an atheist, it has to be taken at face value as the patient's reality, and not reduced to nothing but a defense.

There is no answer to the problem of suffering that satisfies everyone, but perhaps struggling with the question is one way of coping with the problem. Philosophers of many orientations have offered interpretations about human suffering. Thinkers of antiquity tend to approach this problem by giving good advice, pointing out for example that death is universal and frees us from life's difficulties—although to us at least, these forms of consolation are not particularly helpful. The classical work of this genre, the 6th century

Boethius' *Consolation of Philosophy*, is the approach of a thinking type who falls back on reason. Written while he was awaiting his execution for false charges of treason, Boethius argues that everything happens in accord with the divine governance of the universe, and so must be viewed *sub specie aeternitatis*, from a universal, eternal perspective, as part of an impersonal cosmic order rather than from a worldly viewpoint (Duclow, 1979). Christian and Jewish thinkers point to the promise of resurrection, eternal life in the world to come, and the idea that whatever happens is God's will. However, such attempts to spiritualize suffering, although satisfying to sincere religious believers, also have their dangers; they often lead to skepticism when they fail to be helpful, and they risk denying the actual harshness of suffering. Furthermore, religious explanations do not make suffering less real—thus, promising a future benefit in heaven may not be very helpful here and now. There are levels of suffering, such as we saw in the Holocaust, Hiroshima, or the Japanese Tsunami, that seem to be beyond explanation by any religion, but for the truly faithful, explanations are not really necessary. Nevertheless, all religious traditions attempt to understand suffering in the light of their own beliefs. The psychotherapist reading the following traditional attempts to deal with suffering might find some more credible than others, but of course the psychotherapist's personal beliefs have to remain in brackets as he or she works with a suffering individual.

In this context, it is worth remembering William James's distinction between morbid and healthy-minded religionists, which is a kind of typology or classification of religious temperaments. This distinction has not persisted in the literature, but I find that it does correspond to people we see in psychotherapy, and it might make a difference to the way in which we approach a suffering person. The healthy-minded or "once-born" individual (meaning they do not need a conversion experience) is, James believes, congenitally happy and enthusiastic whatever their living conditions or the theology into which they were born. He suggests that the tendency to ignore the negative side of life is the essence of "healthy-minded" religion that refuses to "make much" of the "evil aspects of the universe" (1902/1958, p. 125). Healthy-mindedness is a tendency to see all things as good. James includes in this category writers such as Emerson and Whitman, and people who believe that we can stay healthy by focusing on the positive aspects of life. James points out that this is an incomplete orientation "because the evil facts which it refuses positively to account for are a genuine portion of reality; and they may after all be the best key to life's significance, and possibly the only openers of our eyes to the deepest levels of truth" (ibid., p. 160).The healthy-minded person does not adequately address sorrow, pain, and death, and such an orientation may not be helpful during intense suffering. By contrast, James pointed out that what he calls the sick soul has trouble seeing beyond suffering and sin. The sick soul or the "twice-born" personality (who has had a conversion experience) is painfully conscious of the amount of evil and suffering in the world, and lives in a world in which "every individual existence goes out in a lonely spasm of helpless agony" (p. 142). James's historical examples of the sick soul include Martin Luther, St. Augustine, and Leo Tolstoy. James points out that the religion of the morbid-minded brings with it self-contempt, dread, and melancholy. Just as the healthy-minded religious enthusiast minimizes evil and believes it is not an essential component of the world, so the sick-minded person is forced to ignore goodness. According to James, while healthy-minded people are happier, because of the way they deal with evil and suffering, the sick souls have greater insight into human experience. Pawelski (2003) has pointed out that the modern field of positive psychology is a development of James's study of healthy-mindedness. It is not clear whether positive psychology is a helpful approach for morbid-minded individuals.

Theodicy

For believers in the traditional monotheistic image of God, the experience of suffering and evil, especially among innocent people, may produce a crisis of faith or a collapse of meaning. Some religionists believe that suffering and evil are a divine mystery that cannot be understood and have to be accepted in faith. Others have developed theodicies—attempts to explain why an omnipotent, just, and all-loving God would allow apparently meaningless suffering and evil (Furnham et al, 1995; Hall et al., 2002). This question may arise when working psychotherapeutically with a religious individual.

People who believe in a God who is benevolent, loving, and all-powerful, struggle to understand how such a God allows apparently innocent people to suffer. Many parts of the Bible grapple with this issue (Laato et al., 2003) and it is still much debated (Davis, 2001). The typical dilemma that arises is: If God cannot prevent suffering and evil, God cannot be omnipotent, and so cannot be of any real help to us, but if God is omnipotent and *could* prevent evil and suffering but does not do so, how can God be all good? When these questions arise during psychotherapy, it may be useful for the psychotherapist to be aware of the range of theodicies that have emerged because sometimes they are satisfying to particular individuals. However, they all have weaknesses and some of them are too abstract to be much use to people who are actually suffering. Some theodicies offer an ancient world-view, so that they clash with the way we now see the world and with contemporary modes of thought, which have been so affected by modern science.

A typical theodicy points out that the world as a whole is good, even though there are parts of it where suffering and evil occur; the problem is the limitation of the human mind, which cannot see the big picture. The difficulty with this argument is firstly that it is not clear that the amount of good in the world outweighs the amount of evil, and even if this were the case that would not explain individual instances of suffering and evil. It may be of no help to a suffering person to say that overall the world is good. Furthermore, to insist that what we call evil is actually for a higher good is of no use if we cannot see the higher good, and this argument can be turned around, so that what seems to be good may actually be evil.

Some traditional religionists believe that suffering is a punishment for sin, suggesting that God operates on the basis of reward and punishment. This obviously anthropomorphic argument fails in the face of the suffering of children and animals, and also because innocent people suffer disproportionately or for no obvious reason. It seems absurd to say that God starves people to death or makes them die of malaria in order to discipline them. God is traditionally depicted as a loving father, but then it makes no sense to say that a loving father would at times torture and brutalize his children for the sake of making them adhere to his commandments or to test their faithfulness. To many of us it seems meaningless or even obscene to say that large scale famine, disease, or war affecting millions of people could be a punishment for sin. However the view that suffering is the result of sin is found throughout the Hebrew Bible, for example when Moses tells the people of Israel they will be cursed by God if they disobey him: "The Lord will smite you with consumption, and with fever, inflammation, and fiery heat, and with drought...they shall pursue you until you perish" (Deut. 28: 22). The Hebrew prophets constantly threaten punishment for sin, and this is also a classical Christian view, found in several places in the New Testament, for example when St. Paul says that we have all sinned, but Christ takes our punishment on himself (Rom. 3: 23-25). Many adherents of religious traditions try to minimize the gravity of suffering by explaining it away in terms of their theology. Thus, it is sometimes argued that suffering is necessary for spiritual development—suffering brings us closer to God, it is educational, and it makes us understand our lives better. For example, Psalm 119: 71 says: "It is good for me that I was afflicted; that I might learn thy statutes." Another popular theodicy suggests that evil and suffering must exist in order that we can make free choices about how to behave; without the existence of evil and suffering, free will and morality would be impossible. However this argument does not take into account that we could choose between different degrees of goodness, and does not explain the sheer amount of evil and suffering in the world. Neither would the invocation of free will be any use trying to explain the suffering produced by earthquakes and tsunamis. From a psychological point of view, the invocation of free will ignores the fact that much behavior is driven by developmental factors which are unconscious and completely out of the individual's control.

It is not surprising that some theologians reject the entire intellectual project of theodicy, believing that it struggles with the problem at the wrong level, which should be a personal response to suffering (Tilley, 2000). This argument suggests that the functions of religion is not necessarily to explain suffering or to promise divine intervention, but to give us the emotional strength to cope with suffering and appreciate the goodness of life in spite of it.

Some theologians adhere to a school of thought known as process theology, which influenced Rabbi Harold Kushner's influential *When Bad Things Happen to Good People*. For this approach, the divine has two natures, a transcendent, timeless, perfect aspect and also an immanent nature. At the immanent level, God is not necessarily omnipotent and the source of everything that happens in the world—God is only one factor among many which influence events. There is creative power in the world that is separate from God. Some principles of the universe are inherent in the nature of things, and even God cannot change them, so that things must be as they are. God is as much in the process of becoming as are human beings, and as the capacity for good increases, so must the capacity for evil. According to Kushner, suffering happens to good people because the laws of nature do not distinguish good people from bad people—it is therefore a mistake to think that suffering invariably comes from God. There are chaotic, random events, and natural disasters which God does not and indeed cannot control, because they are aspects of the world that are independent of God—we are essentially on our own in the face of morally blind fate. God gives us intelligence and freedom to do good or evil, but does not interfere with our choice. The best we can do in the face of suffering is to try to find meaning and to decide how we will respond. Kushner therefore retains the traditional idea of God as all good, but rejects the idea of divine omnipotence. This approach produced a cry of protest from traditional religionists who would accept nothing less than the possibility that God restrains his own power in order to allow human free will. By saying that God cannot stop our perpetrating evil without taking away human freedom, by allowing for the autonomous laws of nature, and by remaining with the evidence provided by experience, Kushner was trying to make traditional theism compatible with modern science.

Here I would like to mention the discussion of theodicy in the work of Emmanuel Levinas, described more fully in chapter 6. Briefly, he believes that the age of theodicy came to an end with Auschwitz; for him, the Holocaust and the other horrors of the 20th century are so beyond all measure and reason that no theological justification of such evil and suffering is now possible. The Holocaust virtually confirmed Nietzsche's comment that God (at least the traditional image of God) is dead. For Levinas, the Holocaust cannot be assimilated into any meaningful conceptual system. This attitude contradicts Christian theologians who interpreted the ability to survive the suffering of the Holocaust as a spiritual victory in the face of extreme abuse. Other post-Holocaust writers also believe that the Holocaust is so conceptually unmanageable that our traditional ways of thinking about evil no longer apply. As Cohen (1981, p. 4) puts it, the Holocaust "has no meaning, because it denies meaning and makes a mockery of meaning."

Levinas believes that the suffering of another person "solicits me and calls me," and "this attention to the suffering of the other…can be affirmed as the very nexus of human subjectivity, to the point of being raised to the level of supreme ethical principle—the only one it is impossible to question..." (Levinas 1998a, p. 81). Levinas goes on to say that attention to suffering people is so incumbent on us that waiting for an all-powerful God to act is impossible "without lowering ourselves." Theodicy for Levinas is an ancient temptation to invoke "supra-sensible" perspectives, such as God's grand design, in an attempt to discover meaning in suffering, whereas suffering is actually gratuitous and absurd (p. 82). The temptation of theodicy is to try to make God innocent, but the suffering of the prisoners of Auschwitz showed the disproportion between suffering and every kind of theodicy. To try to explain this kind of suffering as the result of sin (the response of some ultra-orthodox Jews) is "impossible and odious." For Levinas, the Holocaust means the end of theodicy, and it is outrageous for us to justify suffering in this kind of way.

An alternative approach to the problem of evil and suffering is to suggest that God is not all good. One may then attribute suffering and evil to the dark side of God. The notion that the divine itself may produce evil and suffering is found in the Hebrew Bible, where God admits that he both makes peace and creates evil (Isaiah 45: 7). The biblical God causes (or at least allows) a great deal of suffering; for example, the prophet Amos (3: 6) acknowledges: "Does evil befall a city unless the Lord has done it?" In Christian theology, in contrast, the divine is typically described as only light and loving, and darkness is projected onto the devil. Exceptions are Christian writers who believe that God is at work in events such as Hiroshima (Garrison, 1983), and the avenging angels pouring out the wrath of God in the book of Revelation. Jung insisted that our image of God (the Self) must include both a light and a dark side, since the divine must contain all the opposites within it. After all, God creates the serpent in the Garden of Eden and God allows Satan to make the biblical Job suffer terribly, apparently for no good reason.

A few other preliminary notes are important when discussing psychotherapy with religious individuals. First, it is important that spirituality can be incorporated into a variety of psychotherapeutic approaches, including psychoanalytic, Jungian, cognitive behavioral, humanistic, and others (Sperry et al.,2005). There is no association between psychopathology and religious affiliation or religious belief. In fact, people who belong to religious communities tend to find that the community's social support, prayer, and relationship with the divine are all psychologically helpful (Larson et al., 1992). However, it is true that because of concern that a psychotherapist may not share their values, deeply religious people often attempt to get help for their emotional difficulties by first consulting a member of their clergy, and only when this fails do they seek psychotherapy. The person's spiritual values and beliefs often become a part of the therapy, so that the psychotherapist must be aware of his or her countertransference to religious material, which may be influenced by the therapist's childhood experiences in religious schools or with religious parents. Work with religious patients may require that the psychotherapist explore his or her personal religious beliefs.

Working psychotherapeutically with fundamentalists

The fundamentalists of all traditions can be difficult to work with in psychotherapy. In this section I describe some of the psychological structures common to many fundamentalists, and some of the psychodynamics that predispose to fundamentalism. This phenomenon is often seen as a response to modernity or to the decline of religion in the world and increasing globalization (Armstrong, 2001), but these societal explanations do not take into account the inner world of the fundamentalist. In general, fundamentalists believe that theirs is the only valid religious tradition, to which they must strictly adhere, and those who disagree with the fundamentalists are regarded as evil. Paradoxically, since most religious traditions teach humility, the fundamentalists are often self-righteous and take pride in their special knowledge of the divine intention. The teachings of their tradition, and especially its sacred texts, are regarded as infallibly true divine revelations. Accordingly, these teachings take priority over secular thought and science. Often there is an attempt to return a tradition to its original founding principles, as if its contemporary practices are a departure from an original purity. In general, fundamentalists seem to have a great need to avoid uncertainty and complexity, so that they reject any interpretation of their sacred text other than its literal meaning, rather than in terms of metaphor and symbol. They cannot tolerate any questioning of their beliefs, so they also reject the notion that truth may not be single. They reject modernity because of its moral relativism and tolerance of alternative life styles, and instead espouse a kind of simplistic absolutism. When the sense of self is fragile, uncertainty causes anxiety, and adherence to the tradition is then used to buttress the cohesion of the sense of self. It is reassuring to belong to a group of like-minded people who mirror one's values and meet one's need for twinship.[32] Hatred of non-believers may lead to violence, partly because non-believers carry the projection of the believer's unconscious doubt about his tradition. Non-believers also carry the projected, rejected aspects of the believer or of his internalized toxic objects. In order to maintain the purity of their own tradition, fundamentalists split humanity into us-versus-them; our goodness versus their evil. This kind of splitting reduces fragmentation anxiety and acts as a shield against the uncertainties of modern culture, but makes fundamentalists feel separate from people of other traditions. Many fundamentalists are very fearful or even despairing at the Godless world, and at the extremes tend to form enclaves of safety that minimize contact with the wider community.

Certainty reduces complexity and makes life seems simpler, but the price paid for certainty is some loss of individuality, loss of self-expression and

---

32   The twinship or alter-ego need is the need to feel that one is like other people, who reflect oneself.

novelty, a narrow view of what life may offer the individual, and a restriction of the imagination when this would lead to too much anxiety-provoking personal choice. The attempt to maintain cognitive simplicity may be a defense against tumultuous affects; self-hatred or low self-esteem may be experienced simply as a sense of being sinful. Fundamentalists often see human nature itself—not just their own nature—as fatally flawed in some way.

Strict adherence to a set of religious rules of behavior allows the fundamentalist to maintain a sense of omnipotence and mastery of anxiety. This need may result from a fragile sense of self, or fragile internal psychological structures such as a limited capacity to tolerate painful affect. In this context we might note their insistence on the inequality of men and women; fundamentalists of some traditions ban the education of women, prevent women from having public power, and are obsessed with controlling women's sexuality. Summers (2006) suggests that female sexuality is threatening to the fundamentalists of many traditions because women evoke desire which threatens to reveal weakness. Sexual desire for a woman gives her power and threatens the male's omnipotent defenses. The resulting shame produces rage at any woman who exposes his fragility. The assault on women's sexuality reassures the fundamentalist of his own strength. In general, the attempt to sublimate sexuality and other desires for the sake of spirituality gives rise to suspicion among dynamically-oriented psychotherapists. The usual assumption is that when these processes are repressed, denied or split off, they manifest themselves in a neurotic form. Some research suggests that the more reactionary a religious system becomes, the more it flourishes, whereas religions that are more progressive and accommodating to modern life tend to be less successful (Berger, 1999). The fear of the modern world may account for the sense of impending doom or the apocalypse for which many fundamentalists are preparing (Almond et al., 2003). Fundamentalists often seem fearful, and their sense of certainty helps to defend against their fear. One can only speculate about the internal dangerous objects or personal shadow material that the fundamentalist is projecting onto the outer world, which makes the world seem dangerous. Any badness within themselves, and any doubt about their beliefs, can easily be evacuated onto unbelievers and fought out there, as a war if necessary, rather than within the self. If they need justification, it is easy to invoke God's will, to which they feel they have special access.

When suffering emotional distress, fundamentalists typically seek help from their clergy before considering psychotherapy (Wamser et al., 2011). They may see their emotional distress from a religious point of view, for example as a punishment from God, or in extreme cases as the result of demonic possession. Some religious individuals believe that depression is a sign of lack of faith, and so may deny it, or they may feel that if they have faith God will intervene on their behalf, so they are likely to first seek help from a spiritual director or minister who will assist in this process. Others are more flexible about the possibility of psychotherapeutic help because they believe that God has given human beings the ability to solve their own problems (Phillips et al, 2004). In general, fundamentalists tend to fear that a secular psychotherapist will devalue their faith or at least not understand it, so they prefer practitioners who belong to their own tradition. Their perception of mental health professionals is sometimes quite negative compared to their view of clergy (Schindler et al. 1987)—in part this is because of the traditionally negative view of religion held by psychologists.

Religious approaches to suffering

What follows are broad descriptions of some religious approaches to suffering. It is useful for the psychotherapist to be aware of these beliefs when working with a person who belongs to one of these traditions, since they may be an important background presence in the therapy even if the person never articulates them. Even unconscious religious beliefs, assimilated in childhood, can color the individual's current psychology. For example, the monotheistic traditions often see suffering as a punishment for sin, and it is not unusual to come across a suffering person who assumes that his suffering is a punishment—as in the mournful, oft-heard complaint "what did I do to deserve this?"

In very general terms, religions that emphasize a creator God, such as Judaism, Christianity, and Islam, believe in an initial earthly paradise, free of suffering, which was corrupted by a particular event—the "fall" of Adam. Suffering and evil are seen as the result of human choices. The Buddhist tradition simply sees suffering as an integral part of the nature of reality and does not offer explanations in terms of a creator God. Like Buddhism, the Hindu tradition also sees suffering as the result of the accrual of karma from past lives while also acknowledging a divine reality.

Approaches to suffering within Judaism

Judaism today consists of several branches, on a spectrum ranging from very liberal to ultra-orthodox, and there is a corresponding range of Jewish approaches to suffering. In general, the tradition believes that the divine manifests itself in history, first by means of creation and also by means of revelation which is found in the Torah, a book of law and guidance given by God. The divine also manifests itself in the lives and teaching of special individuals and in ritual practices and the study of sacred texts. Certain major historical events, such as the Exodus from Egypt, are thought to be the result of the divine will. Early in the Hebrew Bible, the God of Israel clearly participated in the lives of the people. A covenant was established in which God offered protection and help in return for faithful adherence to his law. This was a kind of treaty, somewhat analogous to those which existed between nations. Suffering was seen as the direct result of divine intervention, sometimes as a punishment for deviation from the law, an attitude which is still thought to be the case by many people within the strictly orthodox community. Suffering is also seen as a discipline, a judgment, or a test of faith. Suffering can be ennobling, purifying or purging, or a call to examine one's behavior and repent. Orthodox Jewish patients may adopt the Talmudic notion (Babylonian Talmud, *Berachot* 5a) that inflicting pain and suffering is one of the ways in which God expresses his love for certain people, as long as the person consents. Martyrdom is the extreme example of this love made manifest as affliction.

There is also a line of Jewish thought which suggests that suffering can be redemptive, leading to better things; events that seem terrible at first are actually for the good in the long run. Therefore one cannot judge isolated instances of suffering, because one cannot see the whole tapestry of creation. Another strand of thought says that even when suffering seems to make no sense to us, it is important to remember that human beings simply cannot understand divine providence, and in various places in the Hebrew Bible suffering brings about later salvation, so in the long run something good comes out of it. The fall of Jerusalem to the Babylonians in 586 BCE was a serious crisis in the history of the Jewish people and in their faith in God. The book of Isaiah predicted that this event would lead to the eventual restoration of the land of Israel, which would prove the supremacy of their God. The nation's suffering was therefore redemptive, the foundation for greater things. Nevertheless, the anguished prophets Jeremiah, Habakkuk, and the writer of the book of Ecclesiastes questioned the suffering of the innocent and the prosperity of the wicked, and found no real answer; they simply had to cling to the idea that God is in control and has some purpose. The problem of unexplained suffering permeates the Bible, and up to the present day the need to somehow salvage a benign image of God persists. The books of *Job* and *Ruth* have similar themes in which a pious person suffers for no obvious reason, apparently repudiating the idea that suffering is a punishment for sin. Nevertheless, this idea persisted in the rabbinic literature, along with the idea that suffering purges or atones for sin and is a way in which we are drawn closer to God.

The distribution of suffering seems uneven and unfair. In response to this problem, belief in life after death appeared in the later biblical literature and continued after the biblical period, when the rabbis postulated that any apparent injustices in this world are resolved in the next world. There is also a Jewish doctrine of reincarnation, or the transmigration of souls, although it is not universally accepted within the tradition. Where it is believed, reincarnation is thought to include suffering so that the soul can be purified of a sin in a past life.

Within Judaism, the Holocaust is of course the touchstone for any discussion of suffering and evil, and here a range of opinions has arisen. Some ultra-orthodox groups see the Holocaust as divine retribution because the people were not sufficiently observant of the law, while others in this community deny this possibility and see the Holocaust as simply beyond human explanation. Some writers regard the Holocaust as the necessary precursor to the state of Israel, while others believe that the Holocaust means that God is no longer involved with humanity. Still others attribute the Holocaust to human evil alone, which God allows so that we can have free will. The Holocaust has also been said to be a form of vicarious atonement for the sins of the world, so that its victims are the "suffering servant" mentioned in Isaiah. An alternative and controversial view is that God is not omnipotent and so could not prevent the Holocaust. For some writers, the Holocaust means that after all there is no God, while yet another view suggests that the original covenant with God is no longer in effect. Overall, the Jewish tradition insists on the reality of the presence of God in people's lives, in spite of the disasters which have occurred in Jewish history.

Jewish fundamentalists believe that the written and oral law are divinely given and have been directly transmitted by God, so that that the biblical lands are non-negotiable. Fundamentalist or ultra-orthodox Jews tend to see dynamic psychotherapy as in conflict with their beliefs, so they are often reluctant to engage in psychotherapy. Sometimes this results from a reaction to the classical psychoanalytic tendency to reduce all religious belief to infantile dependency or an obsessional neurosis, as Freud described in his paper on obsessive actions and religious practices (Freud, 1907; Strean 1994). The suspicion of psychoanalysis found within the orthodox Jewish community is understandable, for example when circumcision is understood by some psychoanalysts to be a sublimation of homicidal impulses or a symbolic castration or infanticide (Rubenstein 1968). This kind of interpretation would probably prove to be disastrous if deployed in the average psychotherapeutic situation. Ostow (1959) points out that both Jewish religious practices and psychoanalysis are concerned with the control of unconscious, irrational human behavior, but unlike religion psychoanalysis does not dictate which of these urges should or should not be expressed.

Orthodox Jews who participate in the Jewish mystical tradition point to other forms of psychoanalytic reduction of their beliefs and practices. Ostow (1988 p. 40) reduces mystical experience, such as the experience of unity with the divine, to an "illusory haven," based on an infantile wish to return to the womb or for parental comfort; mysticism is a defense or an avoidance of harsh reality. In fact, Ostow sees mystical experience as a sign of serious emotional disturbance, and would like such individuals to relate to reality in more traditional ways—for the orthodox Jew, this means a return to the support of the community and traditional rabbinic teaching.

Because of the tendency of classical psychoanalysis to reduce religious experience to neurosis, orthodox Jews sometimes feel that psychotherapy might lead people away from the observance of traditional Jewish practice, perhaps by excusing improper behavior by attributing it to unconscious drives for which the individual is not responsible (Klein, 1979). (This attitude ignores the fact that psychotherapy actually assists in the mastery of such impulses.) Furthermore, if behavior is driven from the unconscious and by our genetics, the importance of divinely-given free will is undermined (Schimmel, 1977). Ultra-orthodox Jews may feel ashamed at the need for psychotherapy, partly because there is still a degree of stigma against emotional disorder in that community, and the need for psychotherapy is seen as a sign of failure to live up to community standards. Usually therefore, Orthodox Jews prefer to approach emotional difficulties using traditional rabbinic teaching. For example, Amsel (1976) believes that the rabbinic concepts of the good and evil impulses represent the two sides of human nature, one rational and the other irrational, and one can deal with one's evil by deciding to behave rationally and in accordance with traditional observances. In the struggle with one's evil impulses, one is helped by Torah study, focusing on one's character development, and the use of the appropriate ethical teachings under the guidance of a rabbi. As Mariam Cohen, et al.(2004) points out, essentially these authors are advocating a behavioral form of psychotherapy. Moshe Spero (1992) has addressed such simplistic models of the mind in a series of books which describe the ways in which dynamic psychotherapy is compatible with traditional Judaism, suggesting that both are valid ways of viewing the world within their own realm of discourse. He points out that psychotherapy can be similar to the process of confession and repentance which are greatly valued in Judaism—the psychotherapist is then in the role of ethical mentor. Spero also makes the important point that the reality of one's relationship with the divine cannot be reduced entirely to parental projections and has its own reality which must be addressed on its own terms.

Unless the therapist is a member of that community, before embarking on psychotherapy with an ultra-orthodox Jew, to be culturally sensitive it is worth reading the paper by Howard Margolese (1998), which details the cultural and religious beliefs of these individuals with particular relevance to mental health treatment.

Christian approaches to suffering

For believing Christians, what looks like a total defeat—Jesus' crucifixion—is actually a new beginning and a victory. The whole edifice of Christianity rests on this belief. In fact, the crucifixion, which is the epitome of suffering, is seen as a glorification. Christian theology says that, because of the crucifixion and resurrection, Jesus conquered suffering and death by allowing himself to be killed out of love for humanity. He is said to repair the connection between God and humanity which had been torn because of sin. No amount of suffering can eradicate the importance of the resurrection, even if the necessity for suffering cannot be explained. This assertion is central to the Christian response to suffering, but it is important to note that over the course of history Christ's crucifixion has often been emphasized more than his resurrection.

These beliefs are vitally important to the believing Christian when suffering occurs, because suffering may produce a crisis of faith and cast doubt on her relationship with God. The suffering Christian may ask: "How can the God who afflicts me be the same God who promises to save me?" The Christian in the depths of despair must reconcile his suffering with what may feel like the absence of God. There are a variety of responses to this problem. For example, Christianity teaches that God always works for the good, and God is present with the sufferer. Christ can be encountered by suffering people, or God somehow works by means of our suffering. The tradition says that Christ voluntarily took onto himself the burden of human suffering, out of love; by taking on human sin, he expiated this sin, which redeemed humanity—his suffering thereby brought a victory over evil. That is to say, suffering can be redemptive.

In the Gospels, much as in the Jewish tradition, suffering is thought of as a test of endurance or faith, a punishment for sin, or a discipline or trial that will be character-forming. However, in her critique of the patriarchal God-image and the notion that God causes suffering to punish, test or teach obedience, Dorothy Sölle (1975) points out that this doctrine is a form of theological sado-masochism. She believes there is a correlation between this kind of repressive theism and social repression. She also points out that the doctrine that suffering is deliberately inflicted by God for pedagogical reasons may explain why Christians may avoid noticing suffering and become insensitive and indifferent to the suffering of others.

There is a sense in the Gospels that even though we do not understand the necessity for suffering, or why it is unequally distributed, we can trust God in spite of it. It is clear from the Gospel story that Jesus knew that his life might end painfully, and he prayed for this to be otherwise, but because of his unshakable connection to God he was able to accept what was to happen. Perhaps this is why, at least for some people, Christ's suffering is the exemplar, and to be a follower of Christ inevitably involves suffering. For many authentic Christians the cultural emphasis on immediate relief of suffering is too shallow; their lives may be given meaning by suffering. In fact the Christian may identify with Christ especially when suffering, because to be a disciple involves bearing suffering patiently. To suffer is to participate in Christ's suffering and also the comfort he brings. A glorious end to suffering is anticipated when a new era will be ushered in, so that although suffering is real, it is not the last Word. Our suffering will eventually be compensated. The next world will be better, and if there was no suffering we would have no incentive to prepare for it. There is also a sense in the Gospels that suffering may be caused by the devil, so that when Jesus heals he sometimes describes the sick person's suffering as the effect of an unclean spirit. He was able to do so with great authority, power, and compassion; Christians who truly follow him draw on these qualities and follow his example of compassion for those who suffer.

Clearly, the traditional Christian approach to suffering is comforting to believers. However, thoughtful Christians are often puzzled by various questions which may arise during the process of psychotherapy. Why would God create a world with so much suffering? If God chooses to suffer voluntarily for the sake of humanity, how can a perfect God suffer in his perfection? The problem of why a good God allows suffering cannot be solved, in spite of many attempts to do so, but for many Christians the practice of compassion outweighs such questions.

There has been a historical tendency within Christianity to idealize suffering, but we do not hear much about the importance of suffering from some of today's Christian churches, which prefer to emphasize morality, charity, faith, and sometimes affluence as a sign of God's grace. Some preachers minimize the suffering in the story of Jesus and focus only on the resurrection, as if the suffering is somehow not important in its own right. Furthermore, it may be that the emphasis on a heavenly father inflicting suffering on his son is unconsciously connected to images of child abuse, about which we are now very sensitive. Not surprisingly, a feminist critique sees some aspects of Christian theology as glorifying suffering. Feminists point out that Christianity has approved of and perpetuated the oppression of women, and that the Christian image of God the Father makes God the ultimate bloodthirsty child abuser, demanding the death of his own son (Brown et al, 1989). Another problem is that the traditional emphasis on sin as a cause of suffering has too moralistic a tone for many people. James Hillman (1997) points out that the image of Christ crucified dominates our cultural relationship to suffering as if this were the only model for suffering, whereas in fact there are other ways to suffer: "We need many models, besides the Christian one, to locate our psychological experience" (p. 97). We should remember that the Christian attitude which became dominant was not the only one; within Gnostic Christianity, in a text titled The Acts of John, Christ says that he did not suffer on the cross; only a phantom Jesus was there (Barnstone, 1984).

Christian fundamentalists often live in a kind of closed system which is suspicious of others. (For a review, see Thurston 2000). They believe in the literal inerrancy of the Bible and its historical accuracy, and they see the Bible as a source of divine guidance. They believe in the divinity of Christ, his resurrection and immanent return. Many of them believe they are duty bound to evangelize the rest of the world, including the psychotherapist, because Christ will return one day and judge everyone. Because non-believers will be permanently separated from God, this is an urgent matter. Many fundamentalists strive for personal holiness, so that they avoid activities such as dancing and gambling, and they often judge the larger culture as "unchristian" and so may separate themselves from non-believers, for example by home-schooling children. Fundamentalist Christians may ask if the psychotherapist is a Christian. Usually this is a probe to try to discover whether they will be understood and whether their religious views will be respected. It is advisable to answer directly, with straight-forward discussion of the person's concern that the therapist will try to talk them out of their beliefs. A therapeutic relationship can be developed, even with an atheistic therapist, if the therapeutic couple can find common values such as relationship, love, and forgiveness.

Christian fundamentalists tend to look to religious authority or church elders for direction in how to live, and they may see psychological problems such as depression or addiction as the result of sin. It is not unusual for a fundamentalist clergyman to discourage a person from taking antidepressants on the grounds that doing so reveals a lack of faith. Sexuality is often a source of guilt, and gender roles are sometimes rigid. Many fundamentalists believe in creationism and prefer to take the word of the Bible over scientific accounts of evolution, as if to take evolution seriously would harm their beliefs. Revealingly, in spite of their claim of the literal truth of the Bible, Christian fundamentalists selectively ignore many biblical commandments such as the Bible's tolerance of slavery and the commandment to put to death those who work on the Sabbath, while paying special attention to biblical attitudes to homosexuality. At times, a fundamentalist clergyman may encourage behavior such as child abuse on biblical grounds, in which case the psychotherapist may need to encourage alternative spiritual guidance. Not surprisingly, given these beliefs, there is a tendency for psychotherapists to over-pathologize fundamentalists (Gerson et al, 2000). When one hears outrageous claims, such as the biblical idea that women should be submissive to men, the psychotherapist's response is often one of protest or bewilderment at the fundamentalist's view of the world. However, the problem for the psychotherapist is that to openly challenge such an idea may feel like a challenge to the person's entire belief system or even to the person's sense of identity. Accordingly, one usually has to wait for the development of a firm therapeutic relationship before tactfully questioning or confronting such claims, or a premature termination is likely.

Recovery from Christian fundamentalism is often difficult and prolonged, leading to what has been called the "shattered faith syndrome" which produces depression, isolation from family and friends, self-doubt, and a sense of being lost with no sense of direction (Yao, 1987). With a person in such a state, the therapist has to be careful not to be critical of the person's past beliefs, which are often a source of shame. Instead, these beliefs can be explored for their psychological meaning; it is preferable to take the position that these beliefs were once developmentally understandable but are no longer helpful. Psychotherapeutic repair of damaged self-esteem, which membership in a fundamentalist community was used to buttress, is often necessary. Feelings such as anger may have been split off, since these are sometimes seen as "unchristian," and have to be acknowledged. Guilt about sexuality may remain a problem, and when personal authority was relinquished to religious leaders, the therapist must help this to be re-claimed. With regard to theological issues, consultation with liberal clergy may be useful, and some communities have self-help groups such as Fundamentalists Anonymous, which are a useful support for former fundamentalists.

Christian teachings provide a good example of the ways in which religious solutions to suffering may be unhelpful, because even when the traditions give high-level spiritual advice, the human level of the problem may remain untouched. Jesus' advice not to resist evil but to turn the other cheek (Mat. 5: 39), which is at the very least a call to humility and non-violence, is only helpful if one's narcissism is firmly under control. The implicit message is that only the ego is wounded when we are offended, whereas the spiritual essence of the personality, the Self, is not affected by anything. This is a very advanced teaching, from which most of us are insufficiently spiritually evolved to benefit. Giving such advice to a person with a narcissistic personality with a vulnerable sense of self, or to a borderline personality disorder who is full of unassimilable rage, would be insensitive as well as a waste of time. Spiritual advice that only addresses consciousness and ignores the unconscious tends to be unusable, even if it is good advice.

One of the reasons that Christianity has lost its grip on so many people is that its promises do not seem to bear fruit, and the therapist occasionally hears disappointment when working with an erstwhile Christian. Thus, the New Testament tells us that the meek will inherit the earth (Mat. 5: 5), which seems highly unlikely given our present political system, and unless we have unusually strong faith, it is cold comfort to tell us that if we are hated and ostracized for our faith our reward will be great in heaven (Luke 6: 22-23). It is not helpful to workers being exploited by ruthless employers to be told that servants should obey their masters in all things (Col. 3: 22-24). Needless to say, such teachings can be used defensively, as a way of avoiding responsibility. It is worth remembering Marx's critique that religion can tranquillize oppressed people so that they do not protest their exploitation.

Islamic approaches to suffering

The Qur'an forms the basis of Islamic life and thought. Muslims believe that the Qur'an is the final and purest revelation of God, which occurred through the prophet Muhammad. The Qur'an is considered to be the culmination of the same tradition in which God appeared to Abraham, Moses, Jesus, and other prophets, but Muslims interpret biblical stories, such as the crucifixion of Jesus, very differently than do Christians, and the stories of the Hebrew Bible are told differently in the Qur'an. Islam assumes that, since the sacred texts of Judaism and Christianity differ in their messages, Jews and Christians must have corrupted the revelation which was given to them; their Bible cannot be the final revelation of God, who is a unity.

In the Islamic tradition, the teachings of the Qur'an are applied to all instances of suffering. Suffering is thought to be always a part of God's purposes, since God has power over everything that happens; God's omnipotence is particularly stressed within Islam. Accordingly, an explanation for suffering is essential, because God is also believed to be loving and compassionate. Suffering can be a punishment for sin and evil, but this is not always the case; sometimes suffering is a test of faith or belief. Suffering must be alleviated when possible and otherwise accepted and endured patiently. Suffering in the service of God is commendable, builds character, enhances spiritual development, and will be rewarded either in this world or the next, while fear of suffering is a sign of insufficient trust in God. Because God is absolutely just, the apparent problem of the unfair distribution of suffering will be balanced in the world to come. Sometimes, suffering is seen as a sign of spiritual development, so that the more saintly the person is, the more he or she suffers. Suffering in the service of God is commendable—an attitude that is particularly found in the Sufi tradition, a mystical branch of Islam, which stresses voluntary suffering for the sake of God because pain and suffering make one aware of God.

Muslim fundamentalists believe that they should interpret the Koran literally and replace secular law with Islamic law. They believe that accommodation to secular democracy and civil authority in the western sense would harm Islam. Like fundamentalists of all traditions they selectively ignore some parts of their sacred text and focus on parts of the text that reflect their own psychology.

Buddhist approaches to suffering

The problem of suffering lies at the heart of Buddhism. The English word "suffering" does not fully translate the Pali term that the Buddha actually used; the word *dukkha* does not mean any specific type of suffering—it has the larger connotation of the generally unsatisfactory state of affairs in which we find ourselves. The Buddha tried to show the causes of suffering and the way it can be dealt with. Buddhists point out that suffering may be obvious or it may be concealed beneath experiences that may be superficially pleasant but which may lead to pain later on. The satisfaction a pleasant experience produces may not last, or we may be constantly afraid of losing it. We may become too attached to or dependent on an experience. Our desire is therefore a major cause of suffering and may cause others to suffer.

For Buddhism, suffering occurs on many levels: life is transitory and subject to impermanence, change, and decay so that our nature is to suffer. Even if we attain what we desire, we cannot hang onto anything permanently. Our own sense of self, who we think we are, is also subject to this process of change. The root of suffering is that we crave or cling to things as if they were permanent entities, not realizing that everything which exists depends on everything else, and everything changes. In the same way, we also cling to our sense of self as if it were an entity that we own. An essential element of the Buddha's insight is that this self is in fact not a separate essence or thing to which events happen. The self is made up of various constituents that combine together, giving the illusion of being an entity or a permanent individual, but the sense of self is an aggregate of matter, sensations, mental states, and consciousness which produce the experience of self-awareness. These aggregates seem to constitute a person, but in fact they are impermanent and not an abiding entity; they cannot be separated from the gradual process of the body's decay or from the larger environment in which we are embedded. They are all part of the change and flow of things. Therefore, according to the Buddhists, although suffering as such exists, there is no distinct sufferer. Our existence is not as a solid entity but a series of rapidly changing events moving from one moment to the next, like the separate frames of a film, which give the appearance of continuity when projected rapidly.

Because of the law of *karma*, or cause and effect—a chain of events in which what happens depends on what went before—particular instances of suffering are the result of preceding causes in the chain of existence. Each lifetime is related to the previous ones, just as a new candle is lit from another candle. Continuing re-birth occurs because craving for things and for existence in general makes us try to cling to something in the stream of change as though there were something substantial to hold onto. Selfish clinging or craving causes suffering and rebirth.

Suffering can be brought to an end when clinging and thirst stop—this state is known as *nirvana*, a state that is impossible to describe in which there is no passion, aversion, longing, or confusion. Buddhism assumes that since the Buddha and others have achieved this state, it can be attained by practice. The Buddha taught that the way to the cessation of suffering is the Noble Eightfold Path. This consists of correct understanding, thought, speech, action, livelihood, effort, mindfulness, and concentration—in other words, morality or ethical conduct, meditation or mental discipline, and wisdom. Buddhists believe that one has to know or realize these truths to be liberated from suffering—non-attachment is a psychological attitude. There did not seem to be much emphasis on social or political sources of suffering in traditional Buddhism, but in recent years, recognizing that practice is more important than theory, a socially engaged Buddhism has developed, in which Buddhists attempt to improve local living conditions and work towards peace. For a few people, some of the time-honored approach to suffering, such as the great teaching stories of the religious traditions, may be of value if they can help the person re-frame his situation. The Buddhists tell the story of the woman who asked the Buddha to restore her dead son to life. He agreed to do so on condition that she could find a house where no one had died, which she could not do, making her realize that death is inevitable. This genre of story is unlikely to be helpful today.

Hindu approaches to suffering

There are many Hindu traditions, philosophies, and approaches to divinity, so that it is impossible to summarize them all, although there are a few points on which there would be general agreement. In general, the Hindu belief is that one is born again and again until the supreme goal is achieved, which is merger or identity with the Supreme Reality, known as Brahman. This achievement of release or *moksha* requires a long process of development, maturation, and purification of the mind, which requires multiple births to achieve. Suffering is the result of actions one has carried out in previous lives; it is the result of one's *karma*, a Sanskrit word which refers to the inexorable law of cause and effect. Actions bring fruit, either in this life or another, in the form of happiness or unhappiness, pleasure or pain. Each time we are reborn, we bring with us the fruits of all the actions of previous lives, and we accrue more karma in this life. Each individual has his or her own *dharma*, the law of one's own being, which means that one has to behave in a way that is appropriate to the circumstances in which one finds oneself. One has to develop an even disposition and a degree of detachment in the face of both suffering and happiness, and carry out one's karmic tasks without attachment to the outcome, realizing that the true Self (the Atman) cannot suffer or be harmed. There are various paths or yogas by which detachment and an approach to the divine can be achieved, each suitable to a different temperament. One is the path of work, carrying out action in the service of others without concern for the outcome; another is the way of discrimination, using the mind; a third is the path of devotion to God, while another is the path of meditation.

In the Upanishads, the sacred texts of the Hindu tradition, suffering is seen as the result of misperceiving duality in what is actually a non-dual reality. Existence is a unity, and everything that is, is a manifestation of Brahman, or Being itself. This unity exists behind all the apparently manifest forms of the world, and whatever happens, including suffering, is a manifestation of Brahman. The body suffers, but not the Self which inhabits it. Suffering occurs when we are attached to objects, pleasures, or our lives as if they were ultimate reality. The apparent individual is actually a manifestation of Brahman, and our suffering has to be seen in this larger perspective; suffering is real but it is not the ultimate truth about reality. A degree of detachment from suffering is then possible, but this must not be allowed to slide into acceptance of the status quo and indifference to others, by dismissing suffering as nothing but one's karma.

Krishnamurti

Krishnamurti is regarded by many people as one of the major spiritual teachers of the 20th century, but he deliberately did not identify with any specific religious tradition. In fact, he believed that man-made religious organizations and ideologies are harmful because they divide people and produce conflict. He would often point out that at the deepest level we are simply human beings and not Christians, Jews, or Muslims, and we are psychologically identical in our experience of suffering. He therefore tried to make his teachings universal. They are the result of his own insights into the human condition, and the problem of suffering was one of his major preoccupations. There are hundreds of references to suffering in his talks and texts. Although I try to summarize his attitude towards suffering here, he would probably protest at any attempt to talk conceptually about suffering, believing rather that one can only come to terms with it as a direct experience.

There are endless forms of suffering, so that Krishnamurti wants to find an approach that is generally helpful. He therefore tries to understand the nature of suffering rather than focusing on individual instances of suffering. Essentially, he (1981) believes that suffering and conflict are the result of duality; instead of seeing the unity of existence, we think we are separate from the rest of reality and from others. Because our (mistaken) sense of separation comes from our ego, to understand suffering we must understand the nature of the ego or the sense of "me" which thinks it is separate. The ego is made up of the past; it is constituted by memory, ideas, and other mental contents—all of which Krishnamurti refers to with the shorthand term "thought." All this thought is conditioned, and suffering occurs when we identify with our conditioned mind, which has preferences, likes and dislikes. When reality—which Krishnamurti refers to as "what-is"—threatens or challenges the ego in a way that causes pain or works contrary to our preferences, we suffer. We try to avoid pain and maintain pleasure as much as we can, but what-is constantly intrudes into the ego's thought-created image of how it would like the world to be. The problem of suffering is not what-is itself, because what-is, is the nature of the universe, which he would say is grounded in Intelligence and a larger, a priori Order. (He would not use the word "God.") The problem of suffering arises from our reaction to what-is, our resistance to it, or our interpretation of it, which is a function of our conditioning. Pain, for instance, is a part of what-is, part of the natural order

214

and a signal of malfunction. Suffering occurs when we resist pain instead of seeing it as a signal and trying to understand it. For him, the essence of suffering is therefore the self-centered, limited ego with its hopes, fears, desires, and conflicts. When we can be with what-is with equanimity, we feel peaceful. With no ego to protest, there is no suffering (1983). When a situation arises that demands understanding and insight, these may be obscured by the ego because of its own preferences and fears. The ego tends to want to move away from what-is when it causes discomfort, but Krishnamurti insists on the importance of staying with what-is and observing it with full attention—he believes that the necessary action will arise from clear perception. He refers to this process as choiceless awareness, which requires moment-to-moment mindfulness, watching the activity of the mind without judgment. Only with full acceptance and clear perception can we transform the situation we are in (1954). I should add here what he does not say, which will be obvious to the psychotherapist, that this attitude requires considerable tolerance for painful affects, which of course is not always possible. Krishnamurti seems to have been a thinking type who was able to cope with his emotional life by means of his considerable intellect, and one of the criticisms of his teaching is that it is too intellectual.

Krishnamurti does not think that trying to find the cause of one's suffering is enough to relieve it; he believes that this effort, and even searching for a solution, may be an evasion of the suffering itself. He believes it is preferable to stay with the suffering and see where it leads—which is knowledge of oneself. Krishnamurti suggests we remain with the suffering, observe it closely, give it total attention without trying to suppress or escape it, and without thinking about it in terms of prior knowledge and experience—that is, without the ego's interference. Otherwise, if we respond to suffering in terms of our past conditioning, in terms of our desires, preferences, pre-existing ideas and ideals, we are merely reacting to suffering and gain nothing from it. He points out that much religious belief, desire, ambition, and so on, are attempts to escape from suffering, but escape does not work, or only does so temporarily. Making efforts in these directions often causes more conflict and suffering. In fact thought itself, in the sense of responding out of what we have learned in the past, is often responsible for suffering. For him, the essence of suffering is self-centeredness; suffering is "the expression of the me" (1981, p. 181).

The corollary of this idea gives Krishnamurti a particular understanding of the relationships of suffering and love. As long as we feel separate from others, and respond to others based on our own conditioned mind, there is no love in the way he uses the word, which is a transpersonal quality—akin to divine love in the mystical traditions. Love is essentially non-dual; it means the ego is not involved. The conditioned mind which feels separate cannot love in this way, because it is always self-centered. Suffering is the result of thought, meaning the workings of the ego or the conditioned mind, but transpersonal love has nothing to do with thought or the conditioned mind. Because suffering invariably means the presence of the ego, suffering has no relationship to love, so Krishnamurti makes the extraordinary statement: "Where there is suffering you cannot possibly love" (1981, p. 181). By this he means that suffering is an ego phenomenon, and where there is ego there is no real love in his sense of the word. He also notes that action which arises from suffering is based on thought and is self-interested, but action which arises from love is entirely different than action which arises from suffering.

Simone Weil

Simone Weil was a French philosopher who was highly regarded as an independent religious thinker. She remained outside any formal religious institution, although she was deeply influenced by Christianity. Weil makes a case for the presence of God even during the most intense affliction, which she believes can be a way of giving total assent to God if the affliction is accepted (Weil, 1951). She distinguishes between affliction and ordinary suffering. For her, affliction is much broader than suffering— affliction includes the physical, emotional, and social dimensions of the person's life, including social degradation or the fear of it. She suggests that pain which is only physical does not affect the soul, but affliction affects both body and soul; it "deprives its victims of their personality and makes them into things" (p. 125), and could make God appear to be absent. "A kind of horror submerges the whole soul. During this absence there is nothing to love" (p. 120-121). There are no words for real affliction, which is "one of those blows that leave a being struggling on the ground like a half-crushed worm" (p. 120). Those who have never had this experience have no idea what it is, because true affliction is impossible to describe, as sound would be to a deaf person. Affliction is an "uprooting of life, a more or less attenuated equivalent of death" (p. 118). For her, the *Book of Job* is an authentic expression of affliction. Because we hate affliction and we are revolted by it, everybody despises the afflicted, although we may not realize it.[33] Nevertheless, according to Weil, despite being afflicted, the possibility of exercising human freedom remains intact, and the afflicted can hear the word of God from the depths of affliction. Because, for Weil, love is a direction or an opening of the soul towards God, not simply a state of the soul, the afflicted can continue to love God by opening to God; in fact, only then is the height of the love of God reached. This is because the unconditional love of God is only possible when one feels totally abandoned by God. This is Weil's theodicy, her solution to the question of why a loving God would allow affliction, which is therefore "a marvel of divine technique" (p. 135).

Many people would see Weil's view of suffering as too extreme. For example, in her *Gravity and Grace* (2002) she makes the startling claim that misery, distress, crushing poverty, exhausting labor, cruelty, torture, violent death, terror, and disease are all manifestations of divine love. She believes that God withdraws from us out of love so that we can love him, because we could not tolerate the direct radiance of his love, which would destroy us without the necessary protection of space, time, and matter. Therefore, we must consent impartially to everything that exists; indeed we must love the harshness of this necessity because it is given by God. She does not believe there is any answer to the "why" question of affliction, because the world is based on necessity and not on purpose—there are no final causes (Weil, 1968). The world is impersonal, and matter behaves according to blind necessity, but we can give the world meaning by loving the apparent absence of God, which is actually a secret presence. Suffering has no significance, but if we do not accept it, we do not love God (Weil, 1976). That is, if we think of God as a cosmic emperor we are not loving God.

For the depth psychologist, Weil's insistence that suffering is so necessary for a relationship to God, combined with her personal asceticism and indifference to comfort,[34] could suggest an underlying masochistic element in her character—which, it is important to add, does not necessarily invalidate her thought. The skeptic wonders if she tries to rationalize the intractable problem of suffering by turning it into a spiritual virtue. However, Weil is a model of the way in which one can transform one's suffering into something

33   If Weil is correct that the afflicted are hated, this may help to explain why marginalized groups such as the homeless are badly treated. The idea is reminiscent of Victor Turner's point that people going through liminality are regarded as polluted.

34   Weil left a teaching appointment to work for a year as a deprived, unskilled worker in a French factory, often going hungry. She wished to experience affliction first hand. Living in London, she often refused food, eating no more than the official ration for people living in German-occupied France; a combination of malnutrition and overwork led to the decline of her health.

meaningful to the individual by developing a personal myth. She suffered all her life from agonizing headaches which often made ordinary life difficult for her, but her pain helped her to understand and identify with the suffering of others and provided her a connection to the passion of Christ. Indeed, she had a mystical experience of Christ at the height of a severe episode of pain (Helsel, 2009). To people with a religious sensibility, Weil's reflections on the divine-human relationship are profoundly moving.

Suffering from a non-dual perspective

Suffering, grief, and loss are approached in a unique manner within non-dual spiritual traditions such as Taoism, Advaita Vedanta, and Buddhism. Non-duality teaches that reality is a unity; there are no independent entities or people disconnected from the totality of reality. Non-dual thinking does not divide reality into opposing categories such as good and bad, illness and health, sacred and profane, or mind and matter as if these apparent opposites are fixed essences. Subject and object, or self and other, are not separable, and although we appear to have a separate self, there is no such entity. Our true nature is often conceived of as transpersonal Consciousness or Awareness, which is absolute, infinite, ubiquitous, unbounded, indivisible, not relative to anything else, and with no relationship to time. Here is where language fails us; the Absolute is not an it, because it is not an entity. "It" is not a being in the theistic sense, and it is not a thing; nor does it have parts. There is nothing it relates to, since it is the totality. In this tradition, the sense of a separate "me" that was born and dies is a perceptual mistake—a story resulting from intense conditioning. The non-dual perception of reality therefore requires a radical shift in perspective; it seems to contradict both everyday experience and commonsense.

Experiences of non-dual reality, or the unit of Being, may briefly irrupt into anyone's life, although only enlightened beings are able to sustain this level of consciousness. However, the empirical evidence for the non-dual, unitary nature of reality is not accessible to most people. Furthermore, this experience cannot be described conceptually, because it transcends all categories of thought and language and it cannot be compared to anything. Yet, one can have an intuitive understanding of it, which can be transmitted from mind to mind. This understanding has a liberating effect because it diminishes fear and weakens attachment to "things" or to the notion that there is an independent ego.

The non-dual traditions typically do not believe in a creator divinity who offers punishment and reward, who must be obeyed or placated, because these are dualistic notions in which the divine and the human are two different things. Non-dual traditions do not stress asceticism, because self-inflicted hunger, cold, and pain or the abjuration of self-will do not necessarily dissolve egocentricity and desire—in fact these practices are often disguises of the ego. Only understanding the nature of reality has the necessary effect.

Devotional traditions such as traditional Judaism, Islam, and Christianity are essentially dualistic. They tell us that humanity and God are distinct, whereas for non-dual traditions enlightenment means the realization that there is no boundary between the divine—or Absolute Reality—and humans. Thus, Judaism and Christianity acknowledge that God is beyond thought, but their image of God is a Being distinct from humanity. However, there are hidden non-dual strands of both Christian and Jewish thought, although each tradition colors non-duality in its own way. Wendy Farley (2011, p. 140) quotes the attempt of the anonymous 5th century Pseudo Dionysius to dissolve the mind's dualistic attachment to names and concepts by asserting that the divine nature "is not soul nor mind nor does it possess imagination, conviction, speech, or understanding…it is not wisdom, neither one nor oneness, divinity nor goodness, nor is it spirit… Darkness and light, error and truth—it is none of these. It is beyond every assertion and every denial." Farley also quotes the 14th century Marguerite Porete's *Mirror of Simple Souls*, which gets beyond conceptual thought by insisting that because God is so utterly ineffable "everything one can say or write about God, or think about him, God who is greater than what is ever said, everything is thus more like lying than speaking the truth" (p. 141). But this approach is not common; as Farley puts it, because of subjection to institutional authority "Christians only rarely ventured to speak the truths of sapiential monotheism: institutions cannot deliver transformation, ultimate reality is not confined to the expression of any historical tradition, the duality of divinity and humanity is an illusion, truth does not sign its name with violence" (p. 144). Similarly in the Kabbalistic Zohar, the *Ein Sof*, or the divine prior to manifestation, is our true reality, and the Chassidic tradition teaches that God fills the whole world.

From a non-dual viewpoint, we feel as if we are an ego, but since the ego is not an independent entity, although suffering is going on there is no separate "one" who is suffering. To cope with suffering, non-duality begins with radical acceptance, letting go of struggling. (I say more about radical acceptance in chapter 10). This is not a prescription for resignation or passivity; everything necessary and sensible to alleviate suffering is tried, but there may come a point where nothing more can be done, and the situation must be fully experienced without judging or rejecting it. At that moment of surrender, one may feel a level that is beyond the suffering itself. Brian Theriault (2012) describes such a moment as his wife was dying:

> And so suddenly, in that instance of full stop, I felt a swelling of energy emerge and expand in the centre of my chest. I felt like I was being opened up from the inside out. This was not a traumatizing experience in the least; rather it was like deep currents of energy were passing throughout my body and it felt incredibly refreshing. I was clear and alertly aware. As I accepted the entirety of my experience in the moment without any desire for escape I experienced a thinning away of my usual sense of self and replaced by a vast spaciousness that I had never experienced before. I was truly stunned. I realized that the essence of my pain was fed through my desire to be rid of it. Strangely, my search for healing was an underhanded way of perpetuating its existence. (p.355)

From a nondual perspective, our ego, or the personal sense of self, is a highly conditioned level of consciousness based on everything we have been told by family and culture, but this self is not an entity and it is not our true nature. The nature of our true nature is a matter of debate among the traditions. Some describe a spiritual essence, often called the transpersonal Self, others find a Void or emptiness or pure Awareness—but these differences are a matter of scholarly discussion which is outside the province of psychotherapy. Non-dual philosophers point out that attempts at self-improvement, such as psychotherapy, help with the reality of suffering but they are not ultimate solutions to suffering. Neither, by the way, is much spiritual practice; Chögyam Trungpa (1973) has described various forms of "spiritual materialism" which turn spiritual practice into ego-building activity. This includes participation in traditional religious practices, grasping after special states of mind, or accumulating teachings, all of which may only solidify the ego. When the therapist works with someone using his spirituality in this way, therapeutic judgment is necessary about whether and when to confront the situation.

From the non-dual perspective, our fear of death is fear of the loss of the ego or the personal sense of self, which is frightened to let go of control and terrified of non-existence. Most teachers believe that the only way to deal with this fear is total surrender to it, at which time people describe a kind of silent, empty fullness or peace that is impossible to conceptualize. Instead, many religious teachings, such as reincarnation, and many spiritual practices, regardless of their validity, are deployed as defensive operations to deal with this fear.

Non-dual approaches to psychotherapy are now emerging (Prendergast et al., 2007). Traditional psychotherapy is based on strengthening or re-structuring the sense of self, but non-dual psychotherapy challenges the very existence of a separate self. Non-dual psychotherapy assumes the existence of a level of transpersonal Awareness; if one can rest in that level there is no fear and nothing is wrong with how we are. The task of psychotherapy and the way to work with suffering is then to facilitate the awakening of this unconditioned level of no-self consciousness. Non-dual psychotherapy sees no boundary between therapist and patient; fixation on roles or techniques are inimical to the experience of non-dual awareness because they reinforce the ego. This approach requires radical acceptance of whatever emerges in the moment, openness, and spontaneous responses, with no expectation or hope for change. Needless to say, doubt and any hint of narcissistic investment are impediments to this process. Finally, like all spiritual approaches, this one too can be used in the service of the denial of suffering.

The approach to suffering from atheism and Western secular culture

While traditional religions try to explain suffering in terms of their own teachings, at some point the therapist is likely to work with an avowed atheist. In this world view, there is no creator; the origin of the universe is not known, and nature is impersonal and indifferent to human beings, who only exist as the result of the chance concatenation of random events, which happened to produce life over billions of years of chemical and physical combinations. Evolution explains the appearance of humanity, and our goal is to control nature as much as we can. Suffering is an amoral fact of life with no necessary meaning, the result of random physical events, natural forces, the struggle to survive, our response to threats, human mistakes, and the like. Death is an end to the body, whose brain is the source of consciousness, and there is no after-life. Suffering is distributed randomly, and is the result of the laws of nature taking their course—it is part of the human condition, and our task is to try to help. For atheists with this orientation, suffering has to be explained in naturalistic terms without invoking anything supernatural.

The atheistic existentialists believe that life has no intrinsic meaning or that we have to find our own meaning. Moral values can be derived from human experience, and they need no theological sanction. We are uniquely free, we define ourselves and become individuals based on the choices we make, and we have the responsibility to make choices. For writers such as Albert Camus, suffering is purely random, and the problems of suffering and evil are insurmountable obstacles to belief in a God who is both omnipotent and benevolent. These writers understand the appeal of religion in the face of suffering, but they do not believe that religion is an acceptable solution. Camus is concerned that the suffering of Christ can be used to condone or even justify suffering, and he believes Christians identify too much with it. Camus cannot accept any world-view that could justify the suffering of the innocent—for him it is impossible to account for the suffering of children. Religion could also be used to escape personal responsibility for atrocities such as Auschwitz. Atheistic existentialists such as Sartre believe that it is contradictory to say that both human beings and God are free, and since Sartre was convinced that human beings are completely free to decide what they will become, there can be no God. The idea of religious faith is problematic if one insists on complete freedom to make one's own choices. In his writing which stresses human freedom, Sartre did not have to take into account modern sociobiology, which views human beings as a product of evolution which produces biologically determined patterns of behavior, and he ignored the influence of the unconscious on behavior and the choices we make.

Numinous experience during episodes of suffering

Numinous or mystical experiences often occur in settings of intense suffering, trauma, or despair (Hardy, 1979; Corbett, 1996, 2007).

Apparently the continuous pressure that suffering imposes on the ego and its defenses allow the archetypal or transpersonal dimension to erupt into consciousness. It is as if intense suffering produces a crack in the boundaries of the self, through which the spiritual level may enter.

This may be why intense spiritual practices such as mediation, fasting, or various forms of asceticism predispose the person to spiritual experiences— suffering reduces the ego's capacity to keep out other dimensions of consciousness. Sometimes this happens after a prolonged period of suffering, and sometimes in moments of great danger. A man whose car was hurtling out of control experienced the following numinous vision just as it crashed:

> Time slowed and I remember thinking I may die. In a completely unconscious, spontaneous moment, I raised my hand heavenward and cried out "Jesus Help Me!" Instantly I was surrounded in what I can only describe as the most peaceful, warm, protective cocoon that somehow I knew extended to the immediate space around my body. There was a certain golden light to the cocoon and all worry vanished. I was utterly at peace and in awe, with an absolute knowledge I was being held by an Other. I just felt utterly safe and protected, like what it must have been like in the womb. There was no fear, no worries, just utter peace...I didn't have a single bruise or scratch on me... I was completely unhurt and my car was completely demolished. The cocoon had vanished when the car came to a rest but I was still in awe of the experience.

It is not unusual for traumatized children to experience the manifestations of angelic helpers, often in the form of figures of light (Kalsched, 2013).

The spirituality of Alcoholics Anonymous

Intense suffering motivates many addicts towards recovery; in fact, some therapists believe that the more intensely addicts suffer, and the more they feel their lives are out of control, the more likely they are to enter therapy. Addicts suffer from intense psychological pain, especially anxiety, depression, hostility, emptiness, helplessness, and rage. They also suffer because of the social, familial, and bodily consequences of addiction. This suffering may not end even when the addict remains abstinent.

Addiction and the recovery process have an important spiritual component. In a letter to Bill Wilson, the co-founder of Alcoholics Anonymous, Jung (1975) writes that the formula for the treatment of alcoholism is *spiritus contra spiritum*, or spirit against spirit—the idea being that addiction is a concretized expression of a spiritual thirst, or the thirst for wholeness, which can be cured by authentic spirituality. Indeed, involvement in spiritual practices of all kinds and religion in general are associated with decreased use of alcohol and drugs (Larson et al., 1998). However, the mechanism of this protection is not clear; it may be due to religious principles, social support of the community, or mystical experience of the kind described by Bill Wilson[35] and many other alcoholics, which can produce dramatic changes, acting like a conversion experience. However, neither these experiences nor any kind of spiritual awakening may happen spontaneously, which is why researchers some decades ago used LSD to produce a religious experience when treating alcoholics. The theory was that a glimpse into cosmic consciousness would reverse the course of active alcoholism, and this sometimes proved correct. Contemporary reports suggest that ayahuasca may produce the same effect.

When their suffering becomes unbearable, many alcoholics turn to 12-step programs, which are an important form of spirituality for many people who are alienated from traditional religions. Empirical studies find that some form of spirituality and the discovery of meaning in life are crucially important in decreasing the intensity of negative emotions among addicts (Chen, 2001). The lack of a sense of meaning in life is a well-known association with alcohol and drug use (Black, 1991).

To participate in Alcoholics Anonymous, the individual must admit that he or she is powerless over alcohol and must then surrender to a "Higher Power," whatever that means to the person. Alcoholics Anonymous therefore demonstrates an important exception to the cultural distaste for surrender, because surrender is central to its philosophy of treatment. Therapists should not underestimate how difficult the acknowledgment of powerlessness over one's addiction can be; given our cultural mores of individualism and self-sufficiency, it may be very difficult to ask for help. The process of surrender is understood to require not just submission or resignation, which have a grudging and halfhearted quality, but radical acceptance of the situation, felt at the level of the heart as well as the head (Tiebout, 1949). Those alcoholics

---

35   During treatment for a binge in 1934, Wilson had this vision: My depression deepened unbearably and finally it seemed to me as through I were at the bottom of the pit. I still gagged badly on the notion of a Power greater than myself, but finally, just for the moment, the last vestige of my proud obstinacy was crushed. All at once I found my crying out, "If there is a God, let Him show Himself! I am ready to do anything, anything! Suddenly the room lit up with a great white light. I was caught up into an ecstasy which there are no words to describe. It seemed to me, in the mind's eye, that I was on a mountain and that a wind not of air but of spirit was blowing. And then it burst upon me that I was a free man. Slowly the ecstasy subsided. I lay on the bed, but now for a time I was in another world, a new world of consciousness. All about me and through me there was a wonderful feeling of Presence, and I thought to myself, "So this is the God of preachers!" (Alcoholics Anonymous comes of age, p. 63). I should add here that there is some doubt about the authenticity of this vision.

who are able to surrender tend to be less narcissistic, exhibit less overall psychopathology, and are able to remain sober for longer periods (Speer et al., 1998). It is a well-known paradox that acceptance often allows change that attempts at control would prevent (discussed further in chapter 10).

One can view alcoholism through a standard clinical lens, as an illness, and at the same time one can see alcoholism as an invitation to embark on a journey of transformation, both spiritual and psychological. Jungian writers have seen the Greek god Dionysus as an image of the mythic background to alcoholism; in antiquity he was the god of the vine, and came to represent ecstasy, intoxication, disruption of acceptable social standards, self-destruction, and in particular, transformation. This god has been seen as a liberator or loosener; he produced episodes of both ecstasy and madness in his devotees. Metaphorically, the alcoholic is devoted to this ancient deity—the psychological point being that the alcoholic is possessed, or in thrall to archetypal forces which have the gripping power of a divinity.

A combined spiritual-psychological approach to addiction is useful. There is no longer any reason that psychotherapists should keep spirituality and psychology separate, since spirituality is an important motivation for human behavior. Alcoholics Anonymous stresses the importance of spiritual qualities such as humility, acceptance, and forgiveness, aspirations which may be worked on at the same time within psychotherapy.

Suffering and a depth psychological approach to spirituality

One of the great divides in our approach to the suffering person arises from the question of whether reality has a spiritual dimension. Some patients in psychotherapy are committed to a traditional spiritual path, and when they suffer they will apply the teachings of that tradition to their own situation—to varying degrees they will spiritualize the problem. The psychotherapist does not need to pay attention to this aspect of the patient's life unless it seems to involve denial or the use of spirituality as a way to avoid a psychological issue. Other people have a personal spirituality but they are not committed to any particular religious tradition. These individuals may benefit from a depth psychological approach to spirituality, which is not dependent on any form of theology, doctrine or dogma (described in Corbett, 2007, 2011). This requires attention to the individuation process, to dreams, synchronicities, and other manifestations of the transpersonal unconscious or the Self.

New Age thought

Adherents to New Age spirituality occasionally find their way to psycho-therapy, often inclining towards Jungian or transpersonal therapists whom they assume will be sympathetic to their beliefs. New Age thought is a mixture of eastern and western wisdom traditions, shamanism, occultism, depth psychology, the human potential movement, and ecology, combined with ideas such as the oneness of reality and the underlying unity of all religions. These ideas are often combined with idiosyncratic interpretations of quantum physics that physicists decry as over-simplified. Most New Age thought is critical of mainstream culture, and would like to replace it with a new planetary culture which focuses on harmony, self-realization, and the attainment of a higher level of consciousness. Some of these ideas, although overly idealistic, are valuable, but New Age approaches have an important shadow side. We sometimes hear advocates of New Age spirituality insist that we are responsible for our own suffering, as if we become ill because of faulty attitudes, implying that suffering would disappear if we could change our thinking. This attitude is problematic for several reasons. One is that although our emotions may contribute to illness, the pathogenic material is usually completely unconscious. The ego has no control over negatively toned unconscious material and cannot change it with an act of will. Asking someone why he or she "brought on this illness" is a way to blame the victim for something out of his or her control and is a moralistic stance that is not helpful. Although it now looks as if gene expression can be affected by our emotions and beliefs, we cannot determine our genes themselves. As well, our emotional lives are heavily conditioned by psycho-logical structures which are not easy to change, and our health is affected by environmental factors such as pollution, racism, and socioeconomic problems over which the individual has no control. The New Age attitude can make us less sympathetic to the suffering of others if we believe that somehow they are responsible for their own suffering, allowing us to be self-righteous and judgmental. It is also true that many adherents to New Age thinking rely on magical thinking[36], and the therapist often gets the impression that believers use this mental mechanism to cope with dysphoric affects. Mel Faber (1996) typifies the skeptical approach to New Age thought;

---

36   In psychoanalytic thought, magical thinking is the assumption that thoughts can directly affect the physical world, because some power or force connects thought and matter. Crossing one's fingers, touching wood, belief in lucky charms, or similar superstitions are examples. For the skeptic, magical thinking simply increases people's confidence in their own ability.

he believes that New Age adherents are absorbed in a regressive merger with the environment, infantile omnipotence, and narcissistic inflation. He points out that their magical thinking erases the reality of separation and loss. A more sympathetic approach suggests that the problem for the therapist is essentially the same as it is when dealing with any spiritual belief; even if the belief is used defensively, that does not prove it is invalid. The therapist has to put aside his or her personal metaphysical commitments and decide whether it is important to confront a New Age belief or ignore it, depending on its function in the psychological economy of the person.

Does the divine cause suffering and evil? Do religions tend to ignore the dark side of the divine?

Many traditional adherents of monotheistic religious traditions prefer to think of the divine as only good and loving, while moral evil (as distinct from natural evil such as earthquakes) is attributed only to human beings. These traditionalists will often refuse to acknowledge what Jung pointed out, that our experience of the divine includes a dark side to it.

Suffering may occur when an individual has been raised to take seriously the biblical promise that good behavior and good people will be rewarded, whereas wickedness will be punished. Typical of many such statements is this one, from Proverbs 3:33: "The Lord's curse is on the house of the wicked, but he blesses the home of the righteous." This is manifestly untrue, and when disaster strikes good people who have believed this kind of maxim since childhood, the world no longer seems to make sense. Deeply religious people then wonder if they are in fact being punished, or if they have been misled by their religion, or if God is not just after all. The therapist may need to remind the individual of the biblical story of Job, which makes it very clear that there is no relationship between one's behavior and whether or not one suffers in life. In such a situation a new image of the divine is required, such as Jung's idea of the dark side of the Self.

7

COMPARATIVE PSYCHOTHERAPEUTIC APPROACHES TO SUFFERING

The assumptions and presuppositions underlying theories of psychotherapy

All schools of psychotherapy attempt to relieve suffering, although different approaches use radically different philosophies of treatment. All theories of psychotherapy are based on a certain view of human nature and a certain worldview. Practitioners who work within any particular approach make an implicit commitment to its underlying philosophy, whether or not they do so consciously. I believe that students of psychotherapy are better informed about their chosen school of thought if its underlying assumptions are made clear. Otherwise, students may unwittingly commit themselves to a view of humanity that is not in accord with their values. The psychotherapist's image of humanity and his or her ideological views are deeply ingrained but often unexamined, and they tend to blend with the therapist's theoretical approach. For example, there is a tendency to either give more weight to a biological view of human nature[37] (biological determinism gives primacy to genes and evolution) or a view based on the primacy of the environment (social determinism), even though it is clear that these interact. Classical psychoanalysts saw human beings as struggling to control instinctual forces while living in a society which wants to constrain their expression. These clinicians were constantly trying to reveal the patient's lust and destructiveness in order to bring these biological forces under the control of the ego, so that the therapeutic process was colored by an assumption of defensiveness or even antagonism. This is a somewhat pessimistic view of human

---

37   The concept of "human nature" is ambiguous. Part of the debate centers around the extent to which our nature is fixed or changeable. While much of our nature is constrained by our biology and evolution, we also make meaning and we use our biological endowment creatively. There is currently concern that our knowledge of the human genome will alter our concept of human nature and lead to biological engineering of human beings—so-called "neo-eugenics."

nature. More modern views see human beings as primed for connection, response, and attachment to others. These attitudes lead to radically different treatment approaches.

In this chapter I would like to examine some of the often hidden assumptions which underpin two important treatment approaches, namely cognitive-behavioral psychotherapy and psychotherapy based on depth psychology, or the psychology of the unconscious. Today, the majority of mainstream psychotherapists use some form of cognitive-behavioral therapy, while a minority of practitioners use a depth psychological approach, with historical roots in either the Freudian or Jungian traditions.[38]

Cognitive-behavioral approaches to suffering

Cognitive behavioral therapies (hereafter CBT) tend to be structured, goal directed, and focused on problem-solving. The therapist is very much in the role of an expert who knows what is likely to help. He relies on techniques that can be applied broadly to many people with the same type of problem. CBT appeals to policy makers and third party payers because it seems to be quickly effective and based on empirical evidence. It also seems very rational.

Most mainstream psychologists using cognitive-behavioral approaches have adopted "evidence based" practice or "empirically supported" treatments. Most investigators in these areas prefer quantitative research, which assumes that we can measure and objectify the important aspects of human psychological life, and that we can somehow transform human subjectivity into something observable. The assumption is that external observation and measurement tell us about the subjective quality of human experience, which is a dubious proposition. As Stanley Klein (2014) points out in his trenchant critique of this view, to describe subjective reality in terms of the vocabulary of physiology or contemporary psychology "is likely to truncate (or eliminate) the phenomena under description" (p. 46). He points out that it is doubtful whether complex states of experience such as suffering, love, hate, jealousy, and beauty can be described in physical terms "without suffering serious loss of content and meaning" (p. 46). As Klein puts it, quantification comes at the expense of the phenomena.

---

38   For the sake of space I will ignore Interpersonal Therapy which uses a mixture of psychodynamic and cognitive-behavioral methods.

In the history of psychology, aspects of human subjectivity such as dreams, the nuances of relationships, the unconscious—and certainly consciousness itself—were ignored by behaviorists because they could not be observed or measured. Often we do not know enough about these experiences to know what we are measuring, or at least these measurements only give us one perspective on the question. It is doubtful whether these psychological phenomena are in fact empirically measurable, because they are not sufficiently manageable or controllable (Trendler, 2009). However, for the depth psychotherapist, these states of mind are all extremely important even though they are not measurable. Instead of trying to objectify these experiences, the depth psychologist tries to participate in them within the psychological field generated in psychotherapy. We try to gain access to the inner world of the other person by means of empathic attunement, by attention to intuition, by listening to dreams and fantasy, by attention to resistance and defense, and via the transference-countertransference, rather than by using measurements or rating scales. These are unashamedly subjective experiences in which the therapist is immersed as much as the patient. They are not the kind of phenomena which can be quantified, but in many psychotherapeutic situations they are all we have. Much depends on what the therapist considers to be important; these subjective phenomena are crucial to the depth psychotherapist but much less so to the CB therapists.

An approach to emotional suffering based on specific treatments for specific clinical syndromes—whether through medication or CBT—assumes that our emotional and existential difficulties fall into particular categories analogous to diseases, leading to all the problems of the medical model approach to psychotherapy. Many psychologists have uncritically accepted the use of psychiatric diagnostic categories, such as "major depression," as if these are actual entities, which is a dubious assumption (Pilgrim, 2009). For example, a person might be justifiably depressed because of factors such as racial prejudice, unemployment, and loneliness, at the same time as he meets all the DSM criteria for major depression. Depression in such a situation can hardly be considered to be a *primary* mental disorder. Focusing on the depressed mood would only be partly helpful and would not intervene at the level causing the problem.

The depth psychologist is less interested in diagnosis than in the way in which the patient's problem emerges within the therapeutic relationship. The depth psychotherapist is more concerned with what is unconsciously motivating behavior than with behavior alone, because the same behavior may be driven by different unconscious factors. Statistical truths or generally valid laws of behavior may not help us with the individual.

Adherents of empirically-supported treatment sometimes decry psychoanalytic and Jungian psychotherapy on the grounds that they lack empirical evidence of therapeutic efficacy, although this assertion is incorrect (Shedler, 2010; Leichsenring et al., 2013; Roesler, 2013). Critics of depth psychology assume that scientific knowledge grounded in physicalism, rational thought, and objectivity are superior to other ways of understanding the world. This attitude reflects the dominant power structures in our society. However, it is now well understood that a given research approach, the choice of research topics, and the use of research results are greatly affected by the interests and values of elite power groups in society. The dominant scientific world view takes for granted various questionable assumptions. Many of us would dispute the metaphysical view that physical accounts of reality give us all we need. Feminists have pointed out that apparently value-neutral, impersonal science is often biased against women (Rossides, 1998). Some important values, such as compassion and self-understanding, and some ways of knowing the world such as the tacit clinical knowledge provided by long experience, intuition and feeling, are obscured by attempts to be impersonal, objective, and precise.[39] Tacit knowledge, part of the art of clinical practice rather than the science, is rarely mentioned in the literature, perhaps because it seems too subjective, as if that automatically disqualifies it. The implication is that only externally verifiable experience is a reliable source of knowledge, although all observations are formed in complex contexts; background beliefs and assumptions are crucial in deciding which evidence seems to confirm which theories (Longino, 1990). "Evidence" is often colored by economic and political interests and by one's social perspective. Because of the contemporary stress on evidence in the psychotherapy literature, I would like to discuss some of our major psychotherapeutic paradigms from this point of view.

---

39   Polanyi's notion of tacit knowledge means that we know more than we can articulate or explain. Physicians often make accurate diagnoses even when they cannot explicitly account for how they did so.

The issue of evidence in Cognitive-Behavioral, "evidence based," psychotherapy

Cognitive-behavioral psychotherapy includes a range of treatments for emotional suffering. This family of approaches has a variety of theoretical bases, but all of them are ultimately based on the idea that the way we think and process information, including our erroneous way of interpreting reality, are responsible for maladaptive behavior and emotional distress. Some CBT theorists see thinking and information processing as essentially biological processes in the brain, while others invoke traditional learning theory to explain the source of cognitions. In either case, faulty cognition, or faulty cognitive schemata, are linked to psychopathology; for example, depression is considered to be the result of persistently negative ways of thinking about events in the person's life. The CB therapist suggests new patterns of thinking to try to alter faulty cognition, which it is hoped will change distressing patterns of behavior and affect. The possibility that deviant cognitions are secondary to psychopathology rather than primary is not always admitted, although in the case of depression it is entirely possible that depressive thinking is the *result* of depression and not its primary cause. The depression may have its origins in sources other than thinking itself, and the meaning and subjective experience of depression to the person are not given by a number on a rating scale. A person may be depressed because of a life situation, and his thinking about his difficulty may be entirely accurate and appropriate—perhaps he is in an oppressive social situation that has nothing to do with his cognitive processes. There is not much empirical evidence that abnormal or distorted thinking always precedes the onset of a period of depression. Some depressed people are simply sadder and wiser than the average person—depression may then not be a disorder at all.

The student psychotherapist may not be told that, like any psychological theory, CBT is fraught with ideology and hidden assumptions. All of these imply certain values and beliefs. For example, CBT privileges quantitative and experimental approaches to suffering, but when we assume that these approaches to human beings are the best ones, we are unconsciously adopting a positivist philosophy and an objectivist theory of knowledge. Positivism is the doctrine that only what can be objectively observed and measured empirically is really knowable, and questions about the meaning of life are not meaningful. Objectivism means that people and the world in general have objective meanings which are independent of the ways we think about

233

them—thus, a patient in distress can be seen to be distorting his perception of a single, objective reality and must be helped to perceive it more accurately. These approaches assume that there are empirical, experimental methods which will lead to universal truths or laws of behavior, which are value-free and which transcend their historical and social context. However, such views are not very helpful when trying to understand the complexities of personality and subjectivity, some levels of which are not amenable to this kind of consideration—think of love, faith, compassion or other spiritual dimensions of the person. Positivism often ignores the subjective meaning of events to a person and the fact that human beings do not necessarily behave according to universal laws of behavior; we try to make sense of the world creatively, and our behavior is often unpredictable. Furthermore, a strictly empirical approach cannot decide between right and wrong, except relatively, or in terms of contemporary social standards. Traditional empiricism tells us that only what is observable is real, and CBT urges us to think rationally about the world as if the world is fully knowable, but our experience is that the world is both mysterious and often non-rational.

The modernist philosophical assumptions of positivism and objectivism, which underlie cognitive-behavioral approaches to psychotherapy are incompatible with postmodern perspectives on the human condition (Hammack 2003). Phillip Hammack points out that because so many aspects of postmodern thought are in conflict with the positivist ideology of modern psychology, most psychological research resists the implications of postmodern thought. In a series of publications, Gergen (2001) has summarized the postmodern attitude by pointing out a) that science reflects social processes within the culture, b) that language constructs, rather than only reflects, our perception of reality, c) that culture and context construct some properties of our mental life, d) that all methodology is value-laden (there is no pure objectivity), and e) it is illusory to think that scientific progress will progressively accumulate definitive truth. What we call "reality" is a perspective, so that we do not have an objectively knowable, universal reality; reality is subjectively and socially constructed. Furthermore, the notion that the patient is irrational in his thinking ignores the fact that human beings often do not use reason, evidence, and logic to make decisions—witness the fact that smoking goes on among people who know it is dangerous. There are other ways of knowing beside the cognitive processes assumed by CBT theories. Some people are more intuitive, more affected by feelings, or they think in a spiral or non-linear mode. Overall, the student who trains in a program in which CBT is taken for granted is socialized into its underlying philosophical assumptions, and so are the practitioner's patients.

Evidence-based practice has obvious virtues, but clinical ethicists have pointed out its shadow side; it is rigid, leaves little room for variation from patient to patient, and it serves the corporate interests of cost containment and efficiency by standardizing care (Mills et al. 2003). Nevertheless, many student psychotherapists are introduced to evidence-based, cognitive-behavioral approaches to psychotherapy as if it were taken for granted that this approach to emotional suffering is the gold standard. However, from the point of view of depth psychology, CBT has major deficits. It gives too much weight to thinking and not enough to emotion; the sense of self is radically affected by affective transactions during development, and it takes time and new relational experiences for these patterns to be changed. By ignoring the unconscious, CBT radically oversimplifies the complexity of the inner world. Traditional CB therapists have ignored the transference, although recently many CB practitioners have begun to acknowledge both unconscious cognitions and the relational dynamics of their work. This development may conceivably lead to a convergence of dynamic psychotherapy and CBT, for example if negative cognitive schemata have their origin in unconscious psychodynamic factors.

Reductionist interpretations of human beings lead to their being treated in a restricted manner. When one reads CBT literature, one sometimes gets a narrow sense of the person, who is described only in terms of symptoms and behavior. The symptom is seen as the main problem, so that the therapist does not always take into account the person's ethnicity, gender, socio-economic status, and other contextual aspects of the person's life. But people live complex lives and have complex emotional states, some of which are affected by their unconscious and by their culture and social situation. Nevertheless, the patient is often treated as if he or she is expected to follow instructions based on a treatment protocol which may not attend to this larger context of the person's life.

The use of a specific manual to treat an emotional disorder tries to force psychotherapy into a model in which a particular medicine is effective for a particular symptom. However, for the depth psychologist the presenting symptom is not the main problem—it is the attempt of the personality to deal with the problem. Unless the patient is able to place the symptom in the larger context of her life, including her relationships, family, occupational and spiritual life, the symptom cannot be understood at all deeply. Human lives cannot be reduced to small units that can be measured, without the psychotherapist losing a sense of the whole human being. Approaches that use a fixed protocol or manual do not encourage the patient to talk about his or her life in a broader context than the symptom or the manual allows. Following a manual makes the therapist ignore his own thoughts, feelings, and ideas about the patient, and restricts his creativity and autonomy. The therapist may have a feeling of certainty at the cost of the patient's truth, thus distorting the relationship—the worst possible situation for a person who desperately needs a genuine relationship.

A further difficulty with CBT is its assumption that cultural standards are invariably healthy. Culture-bound assumptions can masquerade as value-neutral, but feminists have pointed out that white, middle-class male standards cannot be used as a standard of healthy psychological development for everyone. Nevertheless, some CB theory assumes these standards to be normative criteria and that patients should conform to them. This is a socially conservative philosophy which risks putting the therapist in the position of promoting conformity to the social order, as if that adaptation equals psychological health. However, some people are not willing or able to adapt their behavior to the standards and values of the dominant culture. In particular, gender, race, and factors such a poverty and discrimination must be taken into account. (For a feminist critique of psychological theory and research, see Unger, 1984). Psychological values such as self-actualization and autonomy have been criticized on the grounds that these are middle class concepts which are simply not relevant or possible for people without social power (Lerman, 1992). While some CBT approaches recognize the larger context of a person's life, others ignore these factors by assuming that behavior is entirely within the control of the individual. It is important that the psychotherapist not unwittingly serve the socially dominant power groups rather than the individuation process of the individual, who may wish to swim against the tide. Liberation psychologists have pointed out that cultural factors such as sexism and the devaluation of women play an important role in the development of difficulties such as the borderline personality disorder. I should add that psychoanalysis and humanistic psychology have also been criticized for ignoring the patient's social context and focusing too much on adjustment to existing conditions.

"Evidence-based" approaches to psychotherapy are problematic for other reasons. Philip Cushman et al. (2000) point out that they entail "abhorrence of ambiguity, complexity, uncertainty, perplexity, mystery, imperfection, and individual variation in treatment" (p. 993). These approaches ignore the uniqueness of the psychotherapist and patient, the nature of their relationship, their creativity, and the complicated existential contexts of their lives. If we allow it, something completely unpredictable usually emerges in each treatment. This does not mean that evidence-based theory is unhelpful; it means that such theory must be used with discretion and without claims to absolute knowledge on the part of the psychotherapist. We often have to improvise to be helpful, and manualized treatments make this more difficult. There are times when sticking to a standard treatment may be the worst thing one can do because of the deadening effect on the therapist's spontaneous, human responses.

It is often claimed that the efficacy of empirically supported therapies validates their underlying theory. However, people may recover for reasons other than the reasons given by the theory underlying any particular therapy. There is a difference between showing that a treatment works and knowing *how* it works. All schools of thought have their own theory of therapeutic change, but the actual process of therapeutic change is not always clear because of non-specific factors common to all schools of thought. These commonalities are those such as patient and therapist characteristics, the quality of the therapeutic relationship, shared expectancy, the effect of facing emotional pain while being supported by another person, overcoming demoralization, providing an experience of mastery, and the stimulation of the patient's hope and self-healing ability. This means we cannot pinpoint any single factor as responsible for change. The CB therapist may believe her technical interventions help, while from the patient's point of view the therapist's empathy, caring, and capacity for relationship may be even more valuable. Similarly, the psychoanalyst may believe she is helping the patient by dealing with unconscious conflicts or deficits, although at the same time she is desensitizing the patient by repeatedly exposing him to anxiety-provoking material in a safe relationship while also strengthening his sense of personal efficacy. Based on empirical studies of the psychotherapy research literature, Michael Lambert (1992) notes that factors common to all therapies, such as catharsis, identification with the therapist, mitigation of isolation, the therapeutic alliance, therapist warmth, empathy, and acceptance account for about 30% of patient improvement. He estimates that patient factors such as ego strength and environmental change account for about 40% of the variation in treatment outcome, and expectancy and hope for about 15%. This means that technical difference between types of treatment are minimally important, contributing only about 15% of the total improvement. The notion that all forms of psychotherapy are equally effective has been referred to as the "Dodo bird verdict" (from *Alice in Wonderland*), which is that all have won and all must have prizes. It makes intuitive sense that we might be able to achieve the same results using different approaches. To complicate the issue, when different types of psychotherapy are compared, unnoticed bias may creep in; the results of studies comparing different treatment modalities have been shown to correlate with the affiliation and allegiances of the observer (Luborsky et al., 1999).

Having trained intensively in one approach, some practitioners become less and less able to view their patients through a different lens. Other experienced psychotherapists gradually adhere less to their training and develop their own, individualized approach to patients. These practitioners are then working with a therapeutic sensibility that widens the gap between academic research and clinical practice. However, the insurance industry has a vested interest in controlling the type of psychotherapy it will reimburse, even though there is a good deal of evidence that different types of psychotherapy produce similar results (Asay, 1999). The claim that some forms of therapy are particularly effective for particular disorders is offset by research suggesting that for most forms of psychopathology there is a lack of unequivocal evidence in favor of one particular approach. This is true despite the rhetoric of the insurance industry which uses the notion of empirical evidence in order to control costs. The implication of insisting on a specific approach is that all patients with the same diagnostic label, such as depression, require the same treatment—which is manifestly not true, given the uniqueness of the individual, the many causes and types of depression, and the consequent need for therapeutic flexibility. People with the same DSM diagnosis may be at very different developmental levels and may have different personality structures.

The question of evidence

Obviously some kind of evidence is needed for the practice of psycho-therapy, since we need to be sure we are doing something helpful, but it is important to discuss the question of what we actually mean by evidence, since "evidence" is a notoriously ambiguous term. The question of what counts as valid evidence is a long-standing discussion among philosophers of science, who are looking for ways in which we can support or discount our belief in a hypothesis. Evidence must be data which has some bearing on the truth or falsity of a theory, but it is important to note that the concept of truth is complex, and there are different types of truth and different types of justification for asserting that evidence is valuable.[40] The conceptual problem is how to decide what kind of data or clinical findings provide evidence in favor of a particular theory, whether some kinds of evidence carry more weight than others, and if so, who decides which kinds are which. We must also remember that raw data are not evidence; data has to be interpreted, and data only become evidence in the light of a pre-existing paradigm, theory, or metaphysical framework.

We need the right kind of evidence for the kind of question we are asking; some questions lend themselves more to qualitative than quantitative approaches. The type of evidence we need within the natural sciences is different than the type we need within depth psychology, which does not have laws of the kind found in physics or biology, with the exception of principles which apply to all living systems. Many research psychologists only accept evidence based on randomized controlled trials of specific techniques, but rigid techniques are often not applicable to psychodynamic psychotherapy. Furthermore, randomized controlled trials presuppose particular conceptual categories (such as diagnoses), which may not be applicable to a particular psychotherapeutic situation, and this approach may prevent discoveries outside the dominant paradigm. Empirically-based psychology requires that evidence can be independently observed and verified, but this is not possible for some of our most deeply held experiences such as the subtleties of our relationships, our feelings, and values such as religious faith, which are purely subjective and not amenable to objective verification even though they radically affect behavior. CBT's preference has always been for quantifiable measurement, but it is surely a mistake to insist that only what can be measured counts as reliable evidence; systematic observation and case studies are also forms of evidence, in the sense that they give us knowledge or information about the question at hand. In depth psychology, the relationship between the psychotherapist and patient is another important and often reliable source of evidence, as is the practitioner's personal life experience, clinical experience,

---

40   Some contemporary philosophers believe that the evidence of experience directly provides the researcher with subjective justification for his beliefs, and this evidence can be mediated either by observation or by introspection or intuition. Others claim that justification for a belief is derived from the use of a reliable, observable method—the manner in which the evidence is obtained is more important than merely having evidence.

and her tacit knowledge based on years of practice. These kinds of evidence, which form a network rather than a hierarchy (Bluhm, 2005), can be made explicit, articulated, debated, and verified or discounted by the community of the psychotherapist's peers. Evidence from the accounts of patients who have been in this kind of psychotherapy is also important. These kinds of evidence, which are qualitative approaches, are often devalued by empiricists who believe them to be merely anecdotal, too idiosyncratic and subject to personal bias, but in many psychotherapeutic situations they are all we have. In all cases, empirically-derived research evidence inevitably has to merge with the practitioner's knowledge and clinical experience, not all of which is empirically based. Even among practitioners who are most committed to the scientific method, the patient's gender, occupation, intelligence, and similar factors affect clinical decision making along with empirical data. It is important to look at the ways in which evidence is actually applied in practice. As well, it is noteworthy that the subjectivity of the researcher is often ignored during randomized controlled trials, as if the researcher is always independent and purely rational, so that any other researcher using the same method is bound to obtain the same results. This completely ignores both the existential situation of the subjects and the researchers' and subjects' transferences to each other, not to mention the resulting placebo effects.

Some researchers are primarily interested in discovering what works, but here much depends on what one means by "works," and for whom and in what context something works. When we consider symptom removal, or the treatment of a particular state of mind such as depression, empirical validation means showing that one form of treatment leads to a better outcome than another. However, for depth psychology, the situation is more complicated. We are not simply interested in changing behavior or removing symptoms; we are interested in the development of the personality and relationship to the unconscious or to the Self. For Jungians, depression is a signal from the unconscious that something needs attention; from this point of view, depression is purposeful and may lead to an important course correction in a person's life. Accordingly, for the depth psychologist, therapy that removes the symptoms of depression without attention to its underlying meaning does not work at all.

Partly based on experience with their personal psychotherapy, and partly based on the qualitative evidence outlined above, depth psychologists believe that depth psychotherapy fosters personal development and self-understanding as well as producing symptom relief. Since the effects of this therapy on the individual's individuation process may unfold over many years beyond the duration of the therapy, and may affect members of the patient's family, just when should we judge its effects, and how could we find a matched control sample? If we were to apply the question of the efficacy of depth psychotherapy to studies of large populations of people who have been in such therapy, we might find results that apply to particular individuals but not to others. Whether or not the results were statistically impressive for the whole population would be irrelevant to the individual. Statistically derived knowledge always has to be interpreted in terms of the individual patient; what is good statistically may not be good for a particular individual, and visa versa. Even research-based evidence is often provisional, subject to different interpretations based on political, moral, economic, and cultural forces, and the data provided by research may only support a hypothesis to a degree. Not only is empirical evidence socially and historically constructed, it always has to be integrated into the psychotherapist's existing knowledge and then particularized in the context of an individual patient. Even in biological medicine, it is sometimes difficult to apply the results of statistically-derived empirical data into the complexities of the individual case. A rigid insistence on evidence-based medicine or psychotherapy may not value clinical intelligence.

To exemplify the problem of research in the area of depth psychology, I would like to outline the controversy about the empirical basis of psychoanalysis, which for many years was based more on clinical conviction than on publicly testable and repeatable empirical data. The value of psychoanalysis was often seen to be a matter of faith rather than science. Psychoanalysts were seen to be elitist, even cultist, detached from the mainstream of psychology, and lacking an agreed-upon canon of interpretation of clinical observations or a unified theory of cure. Not surprisingly, given the dearth of empirical evidence in the early literature, philosophers of science have roundly criticized psychoanalysis. Karl Popper (1963) believed that psychoanalytic theories cannot be falsified and are therefore not scientific; for him psychoanalysis is a pseudoscience or a mythology because it appears to explain everything but cannot be predictive. In 1984, Adolf Grünbaum announced that although psychoanalysis has heuristic value, psychoanalytic concepts are by their nature not empirically verifiable and cannot meet the criteria for scientific evidence because the psychoanalytic situation does not allow the necessary objectivity. For example, psychoanalysts are accused of suggestion, or of subtly directing the course of the patient's associations by means of the analyst's responses, which are based on theoretical expectations. In response, critics of Grunbaum (Edelson, 1984) point out that it would be impossible to rigorously research the nuances of a therapeutic relationship and impossible to design adequate comparative studies that control every variable and eliminate alternative explanations for the changes which occur in the therapy. Personality factors in the psychotherapist, expectancy, hope, and other non-specific factors play a significant role in the psychotherapeutic process but are difficult to control for. Psychoanalysts believe that intensive listening to a person's life story provides empirical evidence at least about its subjective veracity, which is what matters. They are skeptical of the experimental evidence provided by academic psychologists whose laboratory-derived statistical data seem superficial.

Psychoanalysis is often dismissed as a pseudo-science which lacks testable hypotheses and empirical data, and many psychologists and psychiatrists regard psychoanalysis as outdated, implausible, insulated from and insensitive to advances in other branches of psychology. The influence of psychoanalysis in academic departments of psychiatry and psychology is now almost non-existent, as psychopharmacology and cognitive behavioral approaches have replaced it. However, reports of the death of psychoanalysis are premature; there has recently been a convergence of psychoanalytic ideas, neuroscience, attachment research, and cognitive and developmental psychology (Luyten et al., 2006.)

In recent years there have also been attempts to demonstrate an empirical basis for psychoanalysis, in spite of methodological problems such as psychoanalysts' unwillingness to use standardized diagnoses, intangible patient variables, the lack of precisely defined procedures, the difficulty of controlling for the analyst's level of experience, the difficulty of measuring the subtlety of the therapeutic interaction, and the problem of finding meaningful controls with which to compare an index case. In spite of these difficulties, many studies show the effectiveness of psychoanalysis, and many of its assumptions have been shown to be valid (Fonagy, 2002). These studies have increased its scientific respectability, although there is an ongoing debate between theorists who insist that psychoanalysis is a purely hermeneutic (interpretive) discipline, emphasizing meaning and purpose and focusing on individual case material, as opposed to those who try to apply the methods of the natural and social sciences (Luyten et al., 2006). The former theorists stress the unique individual and believe that psychoanalysis belongs in the humanities, along with disciplines such as philosophy and literature, which have their own procedures. Psychoanalysis relies on a hermeneutic approach and it cannot live up to the rigorous standards of proof found in the natural sciences; yet, it provides a different type of knowledge.

For these writers, psychoanalysis seeks a coherent, narrative truth which may or may not be objectively accurate. Other psychoanalytic writers believe that this attitude represents a kind of intellectual retreat, because it ought to be possible to give the patient a truthful account of his situation, and this will lead to psychological health. These writers search for general laws that apply to many people.[41]

Much of this debate also applies to Jungian psychology, which has always been a minority discipline, largely separate from academic departments and often quite isolated from other schools of thought. Although there have been recent attempts at reconciling Jungian ideas, neuroscience, emergence and chaos theory (Tresan, 1996; Knox, 2004), many Jungians remain rather insular. Like the psychoanalysts, Jungians are often resistant to research because they believe empirical studies cannot capture the subtlety of the analytic process, and they are afraid that the research would influence the analytic process. However, Roesler (2013) has shown that this is not the case, and points out that we have an ethical requirement to study the efficacy of this work.

Kotsch (2000) believes that Jung's psychology can be located in the tradition of William James, because Jung's approach is pragmatic, pluralistic, and radically empirical. Kotsch also argues that Jung's psychology is consistent with many ideas within contemporary philosophy of science and cognitive science. These disciplines are currently approaching human experience in ways that Jung articulated many years ago. Kotsch points out that Jung rejects the idea that there can be an absolutely objective, Archimedean point from which we can study human experience. Jung believes that the psyche is the invariable link between our experience of the world and the world itself. Jung therefore rejects two extremes; the notion that everything we perceive exists outside us independent of our minds, and pure idealism, the idea that everything we see is nothing more than a mental image. By insisting that our image of the world is not a direct copy of the world, but is partly conditioned

---

41   People who see psychoanalysis as a hermeneutic method use the concept of the "hermeneutic circle." Here, we need knowledge of the parts to understand the whole, but the meaning of any part can only be understood as an aspect of the whole, since this gives each part its meaning. According to Ricoeur (1977), validation and proof in psychoanalysis are given by its coherence, internal consistency, and narrative intelligibility. Individual parts and the whole are in a constant dialectical movement. Some people in the hermeneutic tradition have given up the idea that psychoanalysis searches for an absolute truth or proof of its concepts; rather, it looks for the best possible narrative that will encompass the individual's symptoms and behavior. Whether this approach is an abdication of the field's responsibility as a rigorous academic discipline is a matter of opinion.

by the mind's activity, Jung's epistemology mediates between these extremes. For Kotsch, Jung's meta-psychological position is similar to the doctrine of internal realism which is embraced by many cognitive scientists. In this view, our experience of the world and its division into our categories is a function of the human mind. Order and meaning are not entirely external to human beings and independent of human experience. There is a transaction between human mental and physical processes and the real world outside us, of which we are an inextricable part.

For most Jungians, positivist-physicalist research is not appropriate for their clinical work, so most Jungian literature is qualitative, phenomenological, and hermeneutic rather than empirical, quantitative, or statistical. The research focuses on individual case studies, the process of psychotherapy, archetypal imagery, typology, mythology, religion, and the humanities. As I have discussed elsewhere:

> The dearth of empirical research in this field may also be attributable to the type of personality that is attracted to Jungian psychology. Most Jungians are introverted and intuitive, with a Romantic and religious outlook on life, preoccupied with their own individuation process and not drawn to quantitative research. These factors contribute to the alienation of Jungian psychology from the mainstream of academic psychology, which views Jungians as too soft-headed. Jungians in turn view the academy as too soulless and ignorant of the transpersonal levels of the psyche. (Corbett, 2013.)

The risk faced by this attitude is that new evidence from related fields such as cognitive science or neuroscience may require revision of some long-standing convictions. However, at the moment, most writers have concentrated on the ways in which the findings of Jungian psychology and recent developments in neuroscience are consistent with each other. For example, Wilkinson (2003) has clarified some of the relationships between the understanding of trauma in contemporary neuroscience and Jungian psychology. MacLennan (2006) has suggested the compatibility of Jungian psychology and evolutionary psychology. There are attempts to explain the notion of the archetype in neurobiological terms, which has led to the fear of reductionism.

Jung himself always claimed to be an empiricist who restricted himself to the observation of phenomena, and he claimed he was concerned with observable facts. However, he realized that empirical knowledge cannot be independent of the human mind or of culture and the human imagination. Depth psychology does have empirical evidence as long as we do not restrict the word "empirical" to quantifiable data. Otherwise, disciplines such as history would also be considered to be non-empirical. The empirical evidence for the existence of archetypes is that there are innumerable examples of similar imagery found in mythology and religion across the world. However, we do not have measurable proof of the existence of an archetypal process underlying this imagery; at the moment, such processes seem to be observable but not measurable. Consensus among many observers is all we can achieve.

There is a two-way relationship between facts and theories; theories are developed from observations, but every "fact" is unavoidably laden with theory. Only a person trained in a specific discipline can interpret data, selecting what is relevant based on previous theory combined with social and personal factors in the researcher. Observation is therefore not a neutral, unbiased process free from previous knowledge and concepts. Theories only work within certain frameworks, and the complexity of the psyche in its interaction with social and biological factors renders simplistic empirical accounts unreliable or only partially true. The value of theory is that it unifies a range of phenomena which otherwise would look as if they have no connection to each other. A theory postulates underlying principles (which are often hidden) which all the phenomena have in common, and this principle helps us to explain the phenomena. So any field can have its theories, and must find methods which are suitable to test them. The insistence that measurement and falsifiability are the best method for psychotherapy is an ideological attempt to force the field into a natural science, physicalist model. Depth psychology has its own theories and its own questions for which it needs its own methodology, its own criteria of evaluation and proof, and its own language. We describe and try to clarify what goes on intrapsychically and in relationships, and we try to understand other people empathically. In the process, we try to build or repair a sense of self. We try to discern what is not manifest or known to the patient that influences his behavior, and we search for the meaning of experience. We rely on what Polanyi (1964) calls tacit knowledge, a non-verbal sense of our subject which arises from deep immersion in it. These methods lead to the criticism that we are not doing science, because science deals only with what can be observed—but that is a specific definition of science that is not relevant to much of what goes on in depth psychology. We do not have absolute truth, and it may well be that any good results we obtain are actually by-products of what we think we are doing and not the real reason that people improve.

8

SUFFERING AND THE DISCOVERY OF MEANING

The importance of meaning

When suffering begins, we find ourselves at the threshold of a new status in life, whose outcome may be very uncertain. Questions of the meaning of our suffering, or even of the meaning and purpose of one's whole life, then come to the forefront for many people and are sometimes raised during psychotherapy. The psychotherapeutic inquiry into meaning is often stimulated by questions such as "why is this happening to me?" or "what have I done to deserve this?" It is not unusual for intense suffering to call into question our fundamental assumptions about reality. Janoff-Bulman (1992) points out that many of us have an underlying belief in a moral universe; we tend to assume that the world is a good place, that people are largely benevolent, and that we get what we deserve and deserve what we get. It is therefore not surprising that unexpected suffering calls such beliefs into question and may stimulate a radical re-evaluation of our sense of meaning in life. At times the discovery of meaning in suffering is closely tied to the meaning we have always attributed to our life, but at other times radically new meaning may emerge. Suffering or a life crisis can therefore provide important developmental possibilities.

The psychology of meaning has become a major field of study with a growing literature. (For a comprehensive overview of current psychological thinking, see Markman et al., 2013, & Wong, 2012; for a philosophical approach, see Wolf, 2010). Although the discovery of meaning is helpful in stressful situations which disrupt one's life, it has been quite difficult to define exactly what "meaning" really is (Park, 2010). One approach (Baumeister, 1991) is to see meaning as "a mental representation of possible relationships among things, events, and relationships. Thus, meaning *connects* things" (p.

15). Meaning then refers to seeing a pattern, or making connections between events in one's life that otherwise would seem disparate. One might see connections between one's current situation, developmental factors, and one's long-standing psychological structures. Finding meaning may not only mean we make sense of the situation but even that we have an intuition of why the situation must be as it is. Often, the future implications of a life crisis become as important as the problem itself. "Meaning" is also an attempt to understand one's suffering in a larger context, such as the sense that we are connected to something larger than ourselves, as described in the spiritual traditions. We may find meaning in a vocation, in our attempts to preserve the environment, work for social justice, help underprivileged people, and the like. Clearly therefore, one's life can be meaningful but not necessarily happy, as long as we feel that our life has a purpose and value. Sometimes, finding meaning may simply mean that one can find enjoyable activities and relationships despite one's suffering. Finding meaning means that life matters to us. Ultimately, the presence of affect tells us that something or someone or an event is meaningful.

Are there objective values or criteria—such as happiness—by which we can decide that a life is meaningful? Or could the question of whether life is meaningful be a meaningless question? Some writers believe that to ask whether life is meaningful is to ask what we should seek, or what our purpose should be. The moral philosopher Susan Wolf (2010) suggests that meaningfulness (here meaning having a reason to live) is not reducible to happiness or morality. She believes that doing what we care about makes life meaningful, but this action may be independent of our moral obligations or what makes us personally happy. We might make sacrifices for others whom we love in a way that does not promote our own good. She points out that we act out of love when we pursue impersonal activities such as art or music or gardening. We are then driven by the perceived value of what we love. Wolf (1997) admits that such love can be misplaced, and we may attend to an object to a degree that is disproportionate to what the object merits, but she feels that "[m]eaning arises when subjective attraction meets objective attractiveness" (p. 211). Wolf admits that there is some connection between meaning and happiness, because a person who finds life meaningless is also unhappy, whereas people who are happy are engaged in activities that give their lives meaning. However, she believes that happiness itself is neither necessary nor sufficient for meaning; one can be happy with a meaningless life and unhappy with a meaningful life. She notes that thinking about the meaning of one's life is neither necessary nor sufficient for attaining meaning, and many people live meaningful lives without thinking about this issue.

Our subjectivity is important because if we are bored or depressed, then even objectively valuable activities would not make our life meaningful. Objectivity is however important for Wolf: if we are actively engaged with a worthless object (such as memorizing the dictionary or smoking pot all day), our life is meaningless. Wolf feels that although there is no final authority on the question of which things have value, this is an important question, and she thinks that we could all agree that some activities are more worthwhile than others. For her, a meaningful life involves "creating, promoting, protecting (worthwhile) things, from helping people one loves and people in need, from achieving levels of skill and excellence, from overcoming obstacles, from gaining understanding..." (ibid., p. 212). Wolf believes that while we can be subjectively mistaken about the value of a project, part of the reason that certain projects are meaningful is that their value comes from outside ourselves— a meaningful project can be recognized as worthwhile by others, even though it is impossible to find objective values that we would all agree on. Here we run into the obvious difficulty that our judgments about which activities and lives are meaningful are rather arbitrary and very much a matter of personal taste. For this reason, some writers prefer to define meaning purely in terms of subjective interest, while others insist that a meaningful life must try to attain objective values and ends such as beauty, goodness, truth, and love.

Religious people might argue that their life is meaningful if they have a relationship with the transpersonal or spiritual dimension of existence, whether that is conceived of in terms of a personal God or in some other way. Traditional monotheists believe that their life is meaningful if they behave in a way that conforms to God's commandments, and these individuals may feel there is no meaning to life if nothing happens after death. In contrast, the philosophy of naturalism denies that one needs to invoke a God or a soul to make life meaningful; one can find life meaningful if we achieve our personal goals, because our subjective sense of meaning is most important. There are exemplary lives such as those of Gandhi or Einstein which are objectively meaningful and do not depend on a God or a soul.

A boring or frustrating life tends to be meaningless. The philosopher Richard Taylor (1991) points out that Sisyphus cannot have been satisfied with endlessly rolling his rock up a hill unless something came of his work, for example if the stone was used to build something, or unless he enjoyed rolling the stone up the hill. In old age, looking back on one's life, one might take subjective pride in having raised healthy children, or in one's service to others, so that life seems to have been meaningful. Other writers believe that because there are objective criteria which make life meaningful, constantly rolling a rock up a hill could never provide meaning in life.

Suffering may make us realize that we have been living a life that is not right for us, a life that is not an authentic expression of who we are, or a life that seems empty of purpose and value. This state of mind may come upon a relatively healthy person during a period of depression or other existential crisis, and is often temporary. However, even for people in good emotional health, the question of meaning cannot be taken for granted; today there is a good deal of collective uncertainty about whether life is meaningful, especially for those for whom traditional religion has lost its power. Because of the increasing number of people who can no longer believe in traditional religious teachings, we are going through a cultural transition; whereas traditional religions used to provide answers that would address all of life's problems, this is no longer the case. Those of us in that position have to search for meaning individually, and this search often produces turmoil or crisis. For some people this prospect is too terrifying, and they become fundamentalists, either religious or political, clutching to a pre-formed set of answers to life's difficulties. Dogmatic people tend not to search for meaning because they think they already have it. But for more open-minded people the search for meaning may become a difficult night sea journey,[42] although I should note that for some people there is no need to search for meaning because the human nervous system naturally generates meaning—it is built into our brain structure.

The search for meaning can be seen as a healthy process, or this search can indicate psychological distress such as a crisis of faith or even depression (Steger, et al., 2006). Individuals in such a crisis may continue to carry out their ordinary daily activities but at the same time they feel that their life and pursuits have become pointless or hollow. They may continue in an occupation or relationship while feeling that it has become meaningless, as if much of their life has been wasted, leading to regret, anhedonia or bitterness and an urgent need for something new. Such meaninglessness can

---

42   The night sea journey is an archetypal motif found in many myths and fairy tales; the protagonist is a hero who must undertake a difficult journey, often into the belly of a monster from which, if successful, the hero returns reborn or healed.

be triggered by a personal crisis such as an illness or loss which disrupts the person's values or makes his or her goals unattainable, and at the same time destroys his or her sense that life is worthwhile. Everything may then seem pointless, even in the absence of depression. The psychotherapist also sees characterological pessimists who are not in any particular crisis but who have always felt that life as a whole is meaningless, that life consists of more misery than joy, that values are arbitrary, that human nature is intrinsically evil, and so on.

Some philosophers suggest that from the point of view of the cosmos as a whole, in terms of the vast time and distances involved or *sub specie aeternitatis,* we are so small that our lives are meaningless. From this perspective we can only find personal meaning in the limited context of our own lives (Rescher, 1990; Blackburn, 2003.) Thomas Nagel (1986) suggests that when we look at life from this larger perspective it does not seem to matter who exists, even taking into account people like Mozart or Einstein. He contrasts this impersonal viewpoint with our subjective, personal perspective, pointing out that the contrast between these two perspectives can be moderated but not eliminated. Similarly Albert Camus (1969) argues that from the point of view of the stars, in ten thousand years the work of Goethe will be dust and his name will be forgotten, so we should be concerned with what is immediate. Atheists typically see our lives as having arisen by chance, and see humanity as nothing more than a brief spark in the infinite blackness of space.

In spite of this very large perspective, which we can bracket if not deny, there is no doubt that at the ordinary human level our lives can *feel* meaningful. Religious believers have no difficulty seeing life from the point of view of eternal truth, and atheists may also find considerable meaning in daily life on their own terms. Neither is there any need to compare ourselves with Mozart or Einstein in order to feel that we make a meaningful difference to those close to us. We can develop our own standard of meaningfulness, at any time of life but especially when we are suffering. The discovery of meaning then allows a sense of coherence and order in what would otherwise feel like a chaotic or random situation. The search for new meaning is often helpful in our adaptation to painful events such as loss or illness (Neimeyer, 2001), which can threaten our sense that life is worth living.

So important is the question of meaning that chronic illnesses of various types such as cancer, depression, autoimmune disorders, and various social pathologies have been referred to as "diseases of meaning" (Jobst et al, 1999).

Some theorists believe that illness may be an unconsciously chosen way of getting out of a "life trap," a situation which has become unbearable to the individual but which it seems impossible to escape. This situation may result from an abusive marriage, a meaningless job, or similar dilemmas.

The discovery of meaning allows the suffering person to continue to care about living, but the search for significance and meaning may be unsuccessful. People may try to find meaning for years after the death of a loved one, a spouse or child, and may never make sense of their situation. When the search for meaning is unsuccessful, unpleasant consequences may follow, such as alcohol abuse or suicidality (Heisel et al., 2004). The specific answer we find is less important than whether any answer at all is found.

The discovery of meaning in life has many positive ramifications—it increases life satisfaction, reduces dysphoria, and improves general health (Steger, 2012). In contrast, chronic states of meaninglessness are demoralizing, and serious demoralization itself seems to adversely affect disease processes. Prolonged negative affect states such as despair, helplessness, and resentment are believed to activate the recurrence of illness and to adversely affect the prognosis in patients with malignancies and heart disease (Frasure-Smith et al., 1995). Conversely, states of hope, purpose, gratitude, and joy seem to protect against the recurrence of many illnesses (Lamers et al., 2012). Cancer patients who report high levels of meaning in their lives can tolerate more severe physical symptoms than patients who report lower scores on measures of meaning, and patients with a high sense of meaning report higher satisfaction with their quality of life, despite their suffering, compared to those with a low sense of meaning (Brady et al., 1998). A serious illness such as cancer will sometimes stimulate positive psychological changes and an improved sense of meaning in life (Andrykowski et al., 1993.)

Negative and positive meaning in suffering

It is important to acknowledge that the meaning we discover when we suffer may be negative as well as positive. Broadly speaking, events that have positive meaning are those that foster well-being. The discovery of positive meaning allows us to affirm the value of our lives, gives us a goal, a sense of what is important, and a sense that life is at least somewhat predictable and coherent. However, growth is not the only possible outcome; one may also discover negative meanings in suffering, such as bitterness, cynicism about life, or an inability to trust people. Sometimes people feel to an unreasonable degree that their suffering is a punishment for a misdeed, or it is purely the result of their own thoughtlessness. Negative meaning may prevent normal growth and creativity and lead to feelings of powerlessness and dysphoric affects such as hopelessness, which seem to predispose to illness.

One situation of suffering that may have positive or negative effects on the personality is combat. In his *War Is a Force that Gives Us Meaning*, Chris Hedges (2003) suggests that war gives purpose, meaning, and a reason for living, and compared to the soldier's experience in combat, the rest of the his life seems too shallow. Some of the meaning found in war has to do with the sense of aliveness and the close comradeship that results from combat. However, even when war was intensely meaningful, some combat veterans are eventually haunted by the realization that they found meaning in killing, even as they find return to ordinary civilian life quite difficult. It may be difficult for them to find anything as meaningful as war, even if their feelings about combat produce guilt or shame. If one does search for positive meaning in war, perhaps one of the main values of combat becomes the increase in self-awareness and the change in the veteran's attitude to life that combat produces.

I should note here that war is meaningful for some people because war can represent a valid spiritual path, the path of the archetypal warrior who is willing to die for an important cause—his family, his country, or his version of goodness in the fight against evil. Being a soldier can be seen as an exercise in spiritual self-effacement; the warrior has to submerge his individuality, face the mystery of death, and be part of a larger whole. Most of the world's religious traditions recognize the path of the holy warrior, such as the Samurai or the Knights Templar. The Martial Arts traditions of the East were used to develop spiritual qualities, sometimes even to develop compassion for one's enemies. The biblical Yahweh, the Greco-Roman Ares or Mars, Hercules, Jupiter, Mithra, and the gods of many religious traditions are often invoked in wartime. In antiquity, Athena supported the Greeks, and Hera supported the Trojans, the crusaders believed they were fighting the enemies of Christ, and the tradition continued when the Angel of Mons appeared to Allied troops in 1914.

Sources of meaning

Many of us find meaning in friendships, in work that fits our natural abilities and enhances our sense of identity, or in an avocation, in family, or in commitment to a cause. For some people, meaning is given by acquisitions, status, power or money because these shore up a fragile sense of self. For others, meaning is given by the sense that we have something real to do, some work that is important, some person who matters to us, some reason for being here rather than living a banal, day to day existence. One may discover that one's own suffering allows one to be helpful to others with similar difficulties. It is as if one's own suffering has created an internal space in which one can contain the suffering of others. Altruistic behavior, such as that of Mother Teresa, always seems to be intrinsically meaningful. (For a further discussion of altruism, see see chapter 5).

Meaning may be given by a single experience that is deeply moving, such as a powerful dream, an aesthetic experience, or a numinous or transpersonal experience such as a near death experience, as a result of which the person realizes that his or her life is purposeful. Suffering makes people who have always been very rational more open to the reality of spiritual experience. With grace, the sufferer may have an experience of the transpersonal psyche that might point the way, such as a numinous dream or vision. This could be quite an orthodox manifestation of the sacred, or it could be unique, recognizable by its emotional quality (Corbett, 1997). Contact with the transpersonal dimension seems to automatically give a sense of meaning. We then feel part of a whole, we feel that there is a supra-ordinate order going on behind the scenes and that life has a pattern to it. We are not an isolated consciousness. Sometimes meaning appears spontaneously as a kind of revelation, an internal knowing which feels absolutely convincing. There is no way to be certain whether the meaning that is found in a situation of suffering is really given by a spiritual source, or whether the suffering individual simply makes it up as a way of coping. For atheistic psychotherapists, the search for meaning in a religious or spiritual context may appear to be purely defensive. Such psychotherapists then have to be tactful and respectful when working with a religious person.

An important type of meaning is found in synchronistic events. Jung used the term synchronicity when a psychological state meaningfully coincides with an event in the outer world, for example when we dream of an event such as a plane crash which we discover happened at the same time. The mental state and the physical event do not cause each other, but the inner and the outer events are linked by a common meaning. The question which arises here is whether the meaning of a synchronistic event is purely subjectively derived. Jung (CW 8, para. 915) takes the position that as well as a subjective meaning there is a level of objective or inherent meaning in such events which is a priori, outside of the person, that we can discover because there is a transpersonal background to the event. Causal explanations of events are often inadequate or they lead to an infinite regress, and Jung would like us to consider the importance of teleology, or the future goal of an event. Synchronistic events often give us the impression that something has happened which is so improbable that it cannot be attributed to chance but must be the result of a larger background process in our lives, as if the event was "meant to be." There is an obvious connection between the experience of synchronicity and the sense that fate is playing a role in what happens.

In this context it is worth noting the literature on "turning points," moments in time in which a sudden, life-changing event occurs which is beyond the individual's control (McAdams et al., 2001). Such an event may be either positive or negative. A turning point—which is often a synchronistic event—may lead to "counterfactual reflection," wondering about what might have been if the event had not happened (Kray et al., 2013). Such an event may make us feel that life is full of meaning, as if it was our destiny for it to happen; the event becomes an essential part of our life narrative, part of our personal myth which gives life meaning.

Meaning and spirituality

Some people find meaning in traditional religion, which offers believers a way to make sense of suffering and also guidance about ways to make life meaningful.[43] The meaning provided by religion tends to reduce anxiety, for example by explaining suffering as the will of God or as our necessary karma. Religious traditions often teach that it is meaningful to dedicate one's life to the service of others, and they offer the possibility of finding meaning by transcending everyday concerns—sometimes overly devaluing

---

43   I should note here that religion buffers emotional distress to different extents within different denominations. Religious coping seems to be related to lower stress among Protestants more so than among Roman Catholics, perhaps because of theological differences between the traditions. Much depends on whether the individual is conflicted about his or her tradition, and whether one focuses on forgiveness and grace or on penance and sinfulness.

the body and the human realm in the process. Whether the psychotherapist sees such religiously-derived meaning as illusory, a defensive rationalization, a way of coping with death anxiety, or the result of a need for structure is a matter of opinion. Certainly the desire for meaning may increase the need to discover a spiritual explanation for suffering, rather than seeing it as random or purposeless.

It is now well established that high levels of religious involvement and practice protect against depression and enhance the ability to cope with terminal illnesses (Nelson et al., 2002). Nevertheless it is worth noting that some people who have a lifetime commitment to a religious tradition become bitterly disappointed when their prayer seems to have no effect on illness or pain. Overall however, it feels helpful to believe that a larger power is controlling the situation, even if one has no control oneself. Even people who do not consider themselves religious in any formal sense may nevertheless admit that they believe that what happens to them is the result of fate, which consciously or not implies some kind of transpersonal background to their lives. Rationalists consider explanations in terms of fate as superstitious, or merely the result of an intense need for closure.

Many Jungians find meaning in their relationship to the Self, the intra-psychic God-image, or to the transpersonal unconscious, where this is taken to mean an irreducible, transcendental background to human consciousness. In this tradition, the word "unconscious" actually refers to a super-consciousness or a spiritual level of consciousness. Jungians might see an episode of suffering as a call from the transpersonal Self, as an entry into liminality (see chapter 9), or as an initiatory process presaging a new level of consciousness. The patient may eventually come to see herself as a wounded healer, able to help others with similar experiences.

Finding meaning

There is widespread agreement that to find meaning in suffering is preferable to allowing suffering to embitter one's life, but it is not always clear how this meaning can be found. One approach is to either find or construct a coherent story about the situation. Here I say "find *or* construct" because some people believe that the meaning of a situation is inherent in it, as if the meaning is given by a background spiritual process and has to be discovered, while others believe that meaning is created within the person, because we read or project meaning into the situation by finding a comforting story. We cannot be too rigid about this apparent dichotomy of approaches, since they are both problematic if carried to extremes. If we believe that meaning exists outside of the person, provided by a deity, there is probably only one true meaning, either leading to an inflexible attitude or to uncertainty about whether we have found the truth. Alternatively, if meaning resides only in human beings, so that different people attribute different meanings to the same event because we are all creating our own reality, there are no absolute standards and morality becomes relative, which is a controversial position partly because it cannot decide between conflicting viewpoints.

The question of the validity or historical "truth" of the patient's story is not necessarily important. Although we realize that memory is unreliable, and is constructed out of a mixture of what actually happened colored by the patient's hopes, fears, and fantasy, the story provides the immediate data for psychotherapeutic work, and it may change.

If one believes that meaning is objectively given by a spiritual intelligence operating in the background, such as the transpersonal Self, so that meaning is implicit in a situation of suffering, this meaning has to be discovered by a process of discernment. This attitude, which many Jungians hold, implies that the personality has a specific destiny, a goal or *telos* to which the suffering is directed. (I discuss the issue of fate and destiny in Chapter 11). Then the meaning of suffering is partly connected with its purpose for the future. The role of the psychotherapist is to assist in the discovery of what the suffering might be pointing to—we ask where the situation is taking the person that he or she would otherwise not go. The psychotherapist who is skeptical about teleological theories will see them as an attempt to make sense of randomness or to increase the individual's sense of mastery. Whether such an interpretation would be helpful clinically is a matter of judgment. For the atheist, there is no need to invoke a transpersonal level of suffering—it may be thought of as the result of chance or bad luck.

Whether we begin with a religious or an atheistic position, many psychotherapists believe that at best we (psychotherapist and patient) co-construct a satisfying story about the individual's suffering. The therapeutic couple decide on a narrative that fits with the dynamics of the individual's personality, a story that makes sense of the person's life as a whole (Shafer,

1982[44]). Many contemporary psychotherapists believe that our understanding of a person's childhood is never more than a narrative creation, and is partly a function of the therapeutic relationship. Any meaning we derive from this narrative can only be relatively and not absolutely true—in contrast to classical psychoanalytic claims that we can learn "the" truth. The truth of the story must remain provisional and subject to revision.

Nevertheless, even though the story we develop may be nothing more than an attempt to smooth out the ambiguities of our lives and achieve coherence, the meaning it allows can be helpful.

The role of the psychotherapist is to assist in the development of this story without imposing meaning derived from the psychotherapist's theoretical orientation, although sometimes the only thing that allows meaning is the way in which psychotherapeutic (or philosophical) theories make sense of suffering. The problem here—if it is a problem—is that one can always find multiple meanings in human behavior and multiple motivations for it. This is almost inevitable, since the discovery of meaning often requires interpretation, with all its obvious biases. One danger in trying to find meaning in the context of psychotherapy is that we can use words and concepts which make sense theoretically but which are removed from lived experience. As well, any meaning the psychotherapist attributes to a person's situation may be colored by the therapist's subjectivity and theoretical orientation. Different psychological theories stress particular meanings; when looking for the main motivators of a person's behavior, Freudians tend to find sexuality and aggression, Kohutians find the need to find others who will help sustain the cohesion of the self, and attachment theorists believe that attachment is fundamental, and so on. For relational theorists, meaning is created as a function of the interactive field created in psychotherapy by both participants; meaning is not discovered within the patient's material alone.

To tell another person one's story is an important mode of connection to others. The discovery of meaning allows one's suffering to be incorporated into the overall story of one's life, which is one's "narrative identity,"[45] so that the suffering somehow seems to make sense, or even has some value

---

44   Shafer (1982) suggests that "each account of the past is a reconstruction that is controlled by a narrative strategy" (p. 77). He believes that the development of a story is less abstract than the language of metapsychology. Many writers point out that we cannot be sure about the truth of our reconstructions of childhood—we only find narrative truth.

45   Narrative identity means that we form our sense of who we are by integrating all the experiences of our life into a story which explains how we came to our present state and where we might be going. Such a personal narrative may add meaning and purpose to life.

and provides an opportunity for further development. I do not wish to minimize the existential challenge involved in developing such meaning, but the psychotherapist does see people whose life takes a new, important direction as a result of suffering, in a way that would not have otherwise happened. Suffering makes one see and understand the world differently. A good example is given by Kay Jamison (1997), a psychiatrist who describes how she suffered from a serious mental illness. She writes that, given the choice, she would chose to have her illness: "Because I honestly believe that as a result of it I have felt more things, more deeply; had more experiences, more intensely; loved more, and been more loved...I have been aware of finding new corners in my mind and heart" (pp. 218-219). She sounds as if her illness was crucial to the development of her sense of self.

A cautionary note about the search for meaning

We often have to go through an intense or prolonged period of self-questioning to discover meaning in suffering, as a result of which suffering allows us get to know ourselves in a way that few other processes can. This can be a particularly difficult process for older people, since it means that they must look at the discrepancies between the way they wanted life to unfold and the way it actually developed. Needless to say this takes courage, since it may mean a hard look at the person's illusions and the need to grieve disappointments and goals that will never be met. On the other hand, sometimes an event causes suffering at the time it occurs, but not until much later can one see its meaning and importance, or why it was necessary at the time. There is no particular technique that is valuable in this search; open-ended questions about what the person has learned from the experience, what it means to him, and how he has responded to it so far, seem to be the most helpful.

Other cautions are appropriate to mention with respect to the psychotherapeutic search for meaning. One problem that may arise is that the psychotherapist may try to superimpose a cognitive framework onto serious pain or distress, thereby defensively avoiding the harsh reality of the suffering person's situation. There are forms of suffering, such as imprisonment in a concentration camp, that seem to be meaningless and have no possible justification, even though rationalizations of such suffering may be attempted. At such times it seems presumptuous for the psychotherapist to try to find meaning in another person's intense distress. The attempt to do so could feel to the sufferer as if the psychotherapist does not really understand the intensity of his or her pain, or that the psychotherapist is being simplistic or patronizing or is trying to avoid the real issue. Even when the timing seems right for the question of meaning to be discussed, the psychotherapist can only create the conditions in which meaning might be found, by being open and receptive—not by knowing in advance what meaning will emerge, and not by means of technical approaches which are often ego-driven and require that the patient submit to the psychotherapist's agenda about how to proceed. Manualized approaches in particular tend to inhibit therapeutic creativity and may not allow the emergence of something unexpected. It is preferable for the psychotherapist to wait for the meaning of the situation to emerge organically.

To start a conversation about meaning with a person in psychotherapy, the psychotherapist may ask what is sustaining the patient through the difficult period and what gives hope and comfort. We may ask what the patient is grateful about, in what way her life really matters, whether she has a sense of purpose in life, or what she feels that her life is really all about. For people with a spiritual orientation, suffering can be seen as an invitation from the transpersonal dimension to initiate this kind of inquiry. For atheists, especially those with an existential orientation, suffering may also stimulate a personal search for meaning, albeit without any transpersonal background.[46]

Often, the discovery of meaning requires imagination rather than logical thought; the meaning of an experience may not emerge cognitively or through words; rather, it may come as a fantasy image which changes our perspective. The imagination, which is an important source of our creativity, allows us to interpret a situation in unexpected ways, and so may free us from being trapped in it. For example, there is a long-standing association in Western thought between melancholia, inspiration, and the imagination. Although melancholia may be paralyzing, it may also bring unique creative insights. It is as if one needs the forced introspection that melancholia brings in order to access deep truths about oneself and the world. Just as melancholia may be a stimulation for the imagination, so the imagination may be a way of working with melancholy, which is why creativity is a valuable resource for melancholic artists and writers, and why Jung urged us to cast our mood into an image and dialog with it.

---

46   Just as the atheistic psychotherapist must respect the views of the spiritually-oriented patient, it is important for the spiritually-oriented psychotherapist to remember that many atheists try to find meaning and behave well in life in the absence of belief in divine authority, or when there is no particular reason to do so, just for the sake of doing the right thing. We have a long tradition of moral philosophy and ethical humanism which offers guidance in this area.

The importance of appraisal

The more that our appraisal of the meaning of our suffering challenges our core attitudes and overall orientation to life, the more distressed we become. If a new appraisal of our suffering clashes with usual assumptions about ourselves and the way the world works, we face a crisis of meaning, which is often accompanied by emotional distress. We then have to find a way to restore a sense that life is meaningful and worthwhile (Park, 2010). Because the discovery of meaning in suffering may be tied to the meaning we attribute to our life in general, this discovery may require a re-evaluation of a person's entire life story in order to put the new situation into a meaningful context.

As part of the process of appraisal, we may look to the past to see if we can find causes or antecedents that allow us to make sense of the event, or we may turn to a traditional religious explanation. If we cannot reconcile the event with the way we have looked at the world so far, our philosophy of life may have to change to accommodate what has happened. We then have to revise our goals, values, and belief system. Or, if the situation is overwhelming and cannot be assimilated in any form, rather than discovering authentic meaning people may develop defensive optimism, denial, false hope, rationalizations or self-deceptive, illusory beliefs about their situation. Thus, the manner in which a person searches for meaning can be an indicator of psychological problems or health. When suffering does seem to be meaningful, it is important to ask whether the meaning one arrives at is authentic; it could be a rationalization or a defense against an unbearable situation. One can find meaning in a pathological manner; psychotic people find delusional meaning that is used to shore up a fragmenting sense of self, but their delusional belief bears no relationship to consensual reality. If one's self-esteem is tied up with being in control of one's life, one may rigidly alter one's life-style to try to cope with the situation. A more mature way of dealing with (unavoidable) suffering is to develop radical acceptance (see chapter 10), with gratitude and appreciation for the people in our lives and for ordinary, everyday events that can still be enjoyed. This attitude may be enough to at least soften the painful effects produced by suffering. Here it is worth remembering that the Latin root *passio* means both to suffer and to endure—and the opposite gives rise to the English "apathy." People who experience suffering and eventually find meaning in it show better recovery than those who find no benefit from adversity. Two of the most important authors who stress the importance of finding meaning in suffering are Jung and Frankl.

Jung

Jung makes much of the need to find meaning in suffering. He consistently wants us to explore what suffering wants to tell us. For him, a symptom always has a purpose; without the suffering produced by an emotional difficulty, one would not discover something important about oneself. As he puts it, "Hidden in the neurosis is a bit of still undeveloped personality, a precious fragment of the psyche..." (CW 10, p. 167). Also: "We should not try to 'get rid' of a neurosis, but rather to experience what it means, what it has to teach, what its purpose is...We do not cure it—it cures us" (ibid., p. 170). By this he means that there is some split-off aspect of the personality that needs to be integrated—so the symptom is not an enemy as much as a signal, or a first step in a healing process. Here Jung is trying to get past the ego's limited frame of reference so that we can see things in a larger perspective. He believes that symptoms such as anxiety or depression are messages from the transpersonal Self, or from the unconscious, that something needs attention. If we take this view, we can trust our suffering, but otherwise our symptoms are nothing more than something to get rid of. This points to a major problem with forms of psychotherapy that only try to remove symptoms; we may do so in a way that eliminates what the psyche is trying to tell us—rather like trying to treat a fever as if it were the disease itself. Jung believed that to simply try to get rid of symptoms would ignore our relationship to the transpersonal dimensions of the psyche. Elsewhere, he writes that emotional suffering cannot be reduced to childhood difficulties alone, "for we know today that everyone has them...We ask rather: "What is the task which the patient does not want to fulfill? What difficulty is he trying to avoid?" (CW 5, p. 100). That is, we suffer when we cannot deal with an important life task, or take a necessary developmental step.

Jung (CW 11, pp. 121-122) believed that some of the people who consulted him "have no clinically recognizable neurosis"; their difficulty involves fundamental questions of existence—they suffer because of their religious, ethical, or philosophical beliefs. Accordingly, psychotherapy has to "spread into regions that were formerly the province of priests and philosophers." He notes that about a third of the people who consulted him were suffering from "the senselessness and aimlessness of their lives" (ibid., p. 41). He believed that the soul suffers when it stagnates spiritually, and the psychotherapist has to find "the meaning that quickens" (CW 11, p. 331). As well: "Meaninglessness inhibits the fullness of life and is therefore equivalent to illness. Meaning makes a great many things endurable—perhaps everything" (Jung, 1965, p. 340). Aniela Jaffé (1971) believed that Jung's stress on meaning had been elevated to a mythic level, because he believed that humanity's metaphysical task is the continuous expansion of consciousness, which will make life meaningful. For individuals who have lost any sense of meaning, it is important that what the psychotherapist does "is less a question of treatment than of developing the creative possibilities latent in the patient himself" (CW 11, p. 41).

Jung (*Letters*, vol. 1 p. 236 and p. 247) was clear that suffering is an intrinsic part of human life, and without it we would never do anything; happiness and suffering are a pair of opposites that are indispensable for life, and we could not have one without the other. We have to be able to endure suffering, and the principle aim of psychotherapy is to help the patient to "acquire steadfastness and philosophic patience in the face of suffering. Life demands for its completion and fulfillment a balance between joy and sorrow" (Jung, CW 16, p. 81). He believed that the process of individuation, becoming the person one was destined to become by realizing our full potentials, invariably involves suffering, and requires a series of initiatory experiences and ordeals.

In this context it is important to note that, according to Jung, individuation, or the full development of the personality, is a process by which the transpersonal Self incarnates within the personal self. The Self acts as a blueprint for the developing personality[47]; that is, the Self is the archetypal basis of the empirical personality and it continuously embodies itself over the course of one's life by becoming more and more conscious. However, this incarnation invariably causes suffering. For example, suffering occurs when we experience the painful emotions produced by a complex, which has an archetypal or spiritual core. (For a fuller discussion of this issue, see Corbett, 1995, pp. 128-139).

Jung distinguished between neurotic suffering and conscious suffering (CW 17, p. 78). For example, a hysterical conversion disorder, in which intolerable emotional pain is converted into a physical symptom, is actually a way of avoiding a deeper level of more authentic suffering which the physical symptom is masking. Or, depression might be a way of avoiding even more

---

47   This idea of Jung corresponds to Kohut's (1984) notion of a "nuclear program" for the development of the self. Jung's notion of the Self implies a kind of a priori essence, which is not popular in academic circles today. Many psychoanalysts believe that the self is shaped only by intersubjective experiences.

painful grief. Neurotic suffering therefore conceals a level of "natural and necessary suffering which the patient has been unwilling to bear" (CW 16, p. 81). This means that for the psychotherapist to remain at the level of removing symptoms deprives the patient of an opportunity to develop an unrealized aspect of the personality (CW 10, p. 167).

Viktor Frankl

For Frankl, striving to find meaning is the most important motivation in human beings. During his time in Nazi death camps, Frankl noticed that prisoners were more likely to survive if their survival had a meaning, such as helping other inmates, or if they had a purpose such as re-uniting with a loved one or some other goal in life. Prisoners who were able to retain a degree of hope, a reason to live, or some vision of the future tended to have a better chance of survival than those who had lost all hope. He believed that even in the terrible conditions of the camps, people had a degree of choice about how they would respond to their suffering, and that even in such a situation, people have the freedom to create meaning. For Frankl, a crisis can be an opportunity to discover new meaning in one's life. Life has meaning in all situations, and discovering meaning in suffering may allow us to use suffering creatively. To find meaning in suffering prevents despair. Very similar to Jung in this respect, Frankl goes so far as to say that suffering "ceases to be suffering at the moment it finds a meaning" (1959, p. 135). For him, despair stems from doubt that the person's suffering is meaningful: "Man is ready and willing to shoulder any suffering as soon and as long as he can see meaning in it" (Frankl, 1967, p. 56). He believes we can choose our attitude to our suffering because people are radically free and self-determined. We can find meaning in our work and deeds, by living out some important purpose in life, through love, or in an encounter with another person. This search is a spiritual search, but this does not necessarily involve a search for God in the traditional sense. Frankl believes that meaning can be discovered if we create something as a result of suffering or if we have an experience of goodness or beauty, perhaps in everyday events that previously went unnoticed. An unexpected attitude of courage or transcendence may then develop.

Eventually Frankl developed Logotherapy, which teaches that we have an innate will to meaning and that many forms of psychopathology result from a lack of meaning in life. Frankl would see much addiction and suicide as attempts to escape from a meaningless life. For the logotherapist, the goal is to help the person discover meaning that he or she can accept (Lukas, 1986).

Frankl's approach has been used with inpatients with advanced cancer, using meaning-centered group psychotherapy (Breitbart et. al 2003; Greenstein et al., 2000), designed to help patients develop or enhance a sense of meaning and purpose in their lives. Many other psychotherapists with an existentialist orientation subscribe to this view of suffering. Rollo May (1969) has described suffering as an intolerable form of powerlessness, as an inability to experience oneself as responsible. Irving Yalom (1980) believes that engagement in life, making a willful act of commitment while choosing to forge meaning and value, is the only real cure for suffering and the only way to generate authentic meaning in the midst of suffering.

Some critics of Frankl point out that one has to take on faith the idea that life is meaningful, because this is not empirically or scientifically demonstrable (as if this were the only criterion that makes an idea important). Logotherapy has therefore been criticized for being too similar to religion, or even being a form of secular religion, because the word "meaning" has spiritual implications. Even the word "Logo" in the name Logotherapy is etymologically related to the Logos of the Gospel of John, meaning the word of God. However, although Frankl stresses the spiritual dimension of existence, he does not fall back on belief in the Judeo-Christian God or in an after-life. He is more of an existentialist; he says that the suffering person is "alone in the universe" (1959, p. 99), an attitude which deviates from Judeo-Christian notions of suffering. Frankl insists that logotherapy is not a form of teaching or preaching; he encourages the patient to find his own meaning, an attitude which would not be acceptable to religionists who have biblical standards of meaning. For many psychotherapists, this spiritually eclectic aspect of his theory is actually an advantage rather than a problem.

Frankl's idea has also been criticized as only relevant to his personal way of coping, not necessarily generalizable to others in situations like concentration camps (Pytell, 2006, 2007). Some people cannot find meaning in suffering and some people find negative meaning in suffering, so this endeavor is not invariably helpful. A serious critique argues that is not clear that loss of meaning is really the root cause of emotional disorders; it is possible that these disorders have other sources and the loss of meaning is secondary to being distressed. It is also true that some patients in psychotherapy are unable to find meaning but still need therapy. Other critics point out that

Frankl's "will to meaning" as a motivational force governing behavior is too essentialist, postulating an essence or attribute which is a necessary aspect of being human, somewhat like Freud's will to pleasure.

An important critique of the search for meaning outside of a religious tradition is that anything, or any kind of behavior, even evil, can be meaningful to an individual. The existentialists insist that we are free to make our own meaning—for example, in his 1943 *Being and Nothingness* Sartre asserted that "it amounts to the same thing whether one gets drunk alone or one is a leader of nations" (p. 9). In this view, goodness and other values are purely subjective. Many existentialists argue that life has no ultimate meaning, especially given the level of evil and suffering in the world, so that at best we can only act as if life has meaning. Some psychologists believe that questions of meaning and purpose are not amenable to scientific study because they are by nature philosophical and essentially subjective. However, all schools of psychotherapy make implicit or explicit philosophical assumptions about human nature and the nature of reality, whether or not these are admitted. Thus, in a sense, all psychotherapists are practical philosophers. In this view, one's ideas about meaning reflect one's ideology, for which one cannot find objective proof. However, I do not believe that for the practice of psychotherapy the search for meaning can be reduced merely to an ancient philosophical bone that can be gnawed indefinitely. The stress on meaning in the work of writers such as Jung and Frankl adds an important psychotherapeutic dimension to the problem of suffering.

Meaning and chronic pain

Chronic pain, or pain from a non life-threatening condition lasting more than six months, is a complex phenomenon with emotional, physical, social, existential, and spiritual dimensions, and can only be understood by taking all these levels into account. The effects of such pain are not limited to one region of the body; the whole person is affected by it. Chronic pain is very common, among children as well as adults.[48] Its intensity varies from being a nuisance to the point of unbearable suffering, sometimes leading to suicide or a wish

---

48   One estimate is that chronic pain affects about 30% of the American population, or 95 million people, leading to huge economic and human costs. (Institute of Medicine of the National Academies Report (2011). Relieving Pain in America: A Blueprint for Transforming Prevention, Care, Education, and Research. Washington DC: The National Academies Press.)

for euthanasia.[49] Pain is a private phenomenon whose quality or intensity may be impossible to describe, even though we need to do so. Chronic pain seems meaningless, or it removes any sense that life can be meaningful. Such pain isolates the sufferer, interferes with many aspects of ordinary living, and may make it impossible to enjoy life because all available time and energy is taken up struggling with pain. Pain has a debilitating effect on the sufferer's capacity to work, and so may cause financial stress. Increasing numbers of chronic pain patients become addicted to or dependent on narcotic analgesics, alcohol or benzodiazepines, which causes an additional set of problems which overlay the underlying pain problem. Many people with chronic pain see a multitude of internists, surgeons, physical therapists, psychiatrists, and psychotherapists, only to receive so many conflicting opinions that they become confused and angry. These patients are sometimes belittled or at least treated without much sympathy by health care providers, for several reasons. Pain patients are frustrating, partly because pain is subjective and difficult to assess objectively, and partly because pain patients often induce feelings of failure in those trying to care for them. Needless to say, to be accused of whining or constantly complaining increases the patient's suffering. This is particularly a problem when the pain complaints are not consistent with what is known about the severity of the patient's illness, or when no somatic source of the pain can be objectively identified, so that the pain is considered to be psychogenic. However, pain is a unified mind/body experience, and the most useful approach is to accept the patient's subjective experience of the pain, taking into account that existential issues, anxiety, or depression may either be lowering the patient's pain threshold or expressing themselves as pain. One has to bear in mind that what the pain means to the doctor is quite different than what the pain means to the patient.

Unlike acute pain, which warns of tissue damage, much chronic pain seems to offer no biological purpose, and often no clear cause can be found. A large variety of emotional disturbances have been found among chronic pain patients, including depression, irritability, anger, guilt, anxiety, relational problems, masochism, and hypochondriasis. Obviously these may occur in the absence of pain, or may be the result of pain, so their relationship to pain in a given person may be difficult to evaluate. Family conflicts, abuse

---

49   One way of avoiding the suffering of intractable pain is voluntary euthanasia. Here it is worth noting Michael Hyde's view that suffering people who oppose euthanasia still find meaning in life, whereas those who wish to die voluntarily refuse to remain hopelessly debilitated by meaningless suffering. (Hyde, M. (2001).

and neglect in childhood are common concomitants of chronic pain, but no specific personality profile has been found among chronic pain patients (Gamsa, 1994). It does seem that people vary greatly in both their threshold for feeling pain and in their reaction to pain; emotional distress seems to lower both tolerance of and reactivity to pain.

Recent research focuses on a resilience model of care, attending to the patient's strengths and resources rather than vulnerabilities, so that what is working in the person's life can be maximized to support well-being. Resilient individuals are able to remain positive and recognize that their lives are meaningful in spite of their pain. They develop coping strategies and tend to be optimistic, accepting their pain as a part of their lives. They believe they can manage their pain, they learn to function in spite of pain, and they are able to regulate their subjective emotional state to maintain a positive affect so they are less controlled by their pain (Strurgeon et al., 2010).

Most of the psychotherapeutic literature in this area uses a cognitive-behavioral approach, which can be helpful, although some patients do not benefit from it (Turner, 2007) and much of its value seems to be in helping people to live with their pain without catastrophizing about the future. If misapplied, behavioral approaches may blame the victim by suggesting that the pain complaints are reinforced by attention from family members, time off work, and so on, as if these were the main factors causing the pain. Recently, cognitive-behavioral approaches have been combined with mindfulness, which teaches people to closely observe their pain and be accepting, non-judgmental, and curious about it instead of fighting it. This has become a valuable approach for both chronic pain and somatization disorder (Lakhan, 2013). When successful, mindfulness reduces the tendency to ruminate about pain or make it seem worse than it is.

Attachment theorists suggest that chronic pain may represent a plea for help with early trauma which disrupted secure attachment (Anderson et al., 1994). Most psychoanalytic literature on pain was written during the heyday of drive theory, which now seems dated. Freud showed that pain can be a symptom of conversion hysteria, but modern pain patients do not show the classical *belle indifference*[50] he reported. A classic paper by Engel (1959) suggested that there is a pain-prone personality, with psychodynamic factors which include an unconscious need to suffer, and pain as a response to real or

---

50   La belle indifference is the term used to describe an apparent lack of concern for a significant disability.

fantasied loss. Engel associated chronic pain with early childhood deprivation, parental alcoholism or early abuse and trauma, and this observation sometimes seems to be correct, but we do not know when childhood abuse will predict the adult onset of chronic pain. Engel's approach (described by Taylor, 2002) was to think of pain as a subjective experience which, once it has been represented mentally, no longer requires peripheral stimulation to be provoked. The pain is projected into a part of the body as if it had arisen there. In general, early psychoanalytic attempts to interpret specific physical symptoms in terms of their unconscious symbolic meaning were not effective, even though it seems to be true that pain is an important form of communication. Some clinicians still believe that the site of the pain may be symbolically significant; thus, back pain is often considered to be due to being overburdened, and so on. The concept of psychogenic pain has faded in recent years because clinicians now realize there is no good way to distinguish "organic" from "psychogenic" pain. All pain ultimately becomes a psychological phenomenon however it begins. Pain may arise because of emotional difficulties in the absence of tissue pathology, and pain, which is clearly somatic has emotional consequences. In the end, the individual's experience of suffering is more important than the diagnosis.

Contemporary psychoanalysts see pain in several ways: as the somatic expression of the affect produced by a threat to a needed attachment, as a cry for help in which the sufferer's selfobject needs are not met, or as the result of unprocessed traumatic memories stored in the body. In situations where one cannot untangle the emotional and physical components of pain, rather than trying to prioritize mind or body it is useful see the psychological issue and the pain as two different expressions of the same inseparable mind-body.

The Jungian approach to chronic pain would not focus exclusively on the pain, because the pain is seen as symptomatic of a larger problem; the pain is a message from the psyche, or from the unconscious, drawing the ego's insistingthat the ego pays attention to something it is neglecting. Pain is then a call from the soul, the deepest subjectivity of the individual. The physical pain and the concomitant psychological suffering are the same situation synchronistically expressed in two modes. This does not mean that the psychological problem *causes* the physical pain, since the synchronistic connection is acausal; the physical pain and the psychological situation express the same meaning. We may learn this from dreams which comment on the situation, or the patient may be encouraged to carry out active imagination (Cwik, 1995). In this process the pain is personified, or allowed to take the form of an image with which one can have an imaginal dialogue, allowing the image to speak as it will, so that the pain has a voice. The subject consciously participates in this conversation but without attempting to guide the image in any way, so that what emerges does so spontaneously from the unconscious. A related process is guided imagery, in which the subject takes an active part in determining the behavior of the image, which is also a valuable technique in pain management (Pincus et al, 2009).

Pain raises the philosophical conundrum of the mind-body problem because we still do not understand the relationship between the physiology of sensation (eg, conduction along nerve fibers leading to brain activity) and the subjective experience of pain. There is no fixed relationship between the activity of peripheral pain receptors and subjective pain experience; pain intensity and quality may not reflect the intensity of the painful stimulus (Moseley, 2007). It is common to find a discrepancy between overt tissue damage and the severity of pain.[51] It is quite difficult to detect and measure pain without a subjective report, and this situation has serious consequences, not least for animals or for people who cannot tell us how they feel. The obvious sensory component of pain is modulated both by the context in which it occurs and the affective state of the subject, so that during a battle or an important game an injury might not produce pain until some time later—there is no clear relationship between injury and pain.

It broadens the psychotherapist's understanding if we see pain from the point of view of different disciplines, acknowledging the neurological and philosophical issues involved as well as the psychological situation. It is possible to see pain as the perception of objective damage to the body, indicating that something physical is happening which is separate from the subjective experience of pain. In this view, when we have pain we are perceiving something which objectively exists, so that pain is similar to other perceptions such as sight and sound, where the object being perceived is external to the perception itself. Like other perceptions, the perception of pain may be accurate or inaccurate. Thus, according to Witonsky and Whitman (2006), phantom limb pain (the experience of pain in a limb that has been amputated) is an inaccurate perception, analogous to a visual illusion, in this case produced by irritation of peripheral nerves in the stump of the amputated

---

51   In 1965 the Gate Control theory of pain proposed that pain signals can be altered before they reach the brain by thoughts and feelings which modulate pain transmission. Because the interpretation of pain is very important, there is no clear distinction between the mental and the physical aspects of pain, or pain has both components.

limb. In contrast, changes in the brain might cause hallucinatory pain that may respond to a neuroleptic medication. These authors believe it would help to reduce the anxiety of a patient in chronic pain if he understands that while it feels as if there is tissue damage going on, actually there is no serious damage. At the same time, even if the pain is inaccurately perceived, the patient's complaints of pain must be taken seriously. This external, objectivist approach to pain is consistent with the definition of the International Association for the Study of Pain, which describes pain in terms of the perception of tissue damage. The clinician who holds this view might privilege an objective assessment of tissue damage in his or her decision about how to treat the pain, treating concomitant anxiety and depression secondarily.

One problem with the view of pain as a perceptual experience in the same sense as seeing and hearing is that pain has much more important affective, cognitive, and motivational components than ordinary perception. Pain is modified by the degree of attention we pay to it, by our mood, and by our past experience with pain. Furthermore, there is no specific environmental factor (such as light for seeing or sound for hearing) that stimulates pain, so that pain can be thought of as quite different from ordinary sense perception. As mentioned above, one can have injury that does not cause pain at the time it occurs, and some pain is not associated with injury.

An opposing view is that when we experience pain we are experiencing a state of awareness inside the mind—we are interpreting a perception in a particular way. An analogy would be the way lighting conditions change the apparent color of an object, so that we experience the object as a function of the way the mind is experiencing the color rather than in terms of the object's actual color. In this view, pain is a holistic experience in which psychological, existential, and physical components are inseparable. This approach holds that pain is whatever the patient says it is (McCaffery, 1972). This view does not separate the patient's experience of pain and his anxiety or depression; one has to see the patient's subjective experience of pain as a totality.

The medical diagnosis is obviously important but does not address the meaning of the pain to the person and its implications for the sufferer's life and sense of self. It is clear that personality as well as purely biological factors greatly affect the individual's emotional and behavioral response to pain. Pain is always elaborated within a particular character structure and has different meanings within an individual life; the sufferer's beliefs about the pain, conscious and unconscious, add to its meaning, and these belief systems can emerge during psychotherapy, so that psychotherapeutic work with chronic pain offers the patient an opportunity for self-understanding. The patient may need help with the expression of unprocessed abuse or traumatic memories, which are stored in the body. Many such individuals have been repressing or denying painful emotions. It is not unusual, for instance, for pain to begin after a bereavement that is not grieved, as if the pain is a somatic form of affect buried in the body that is expressed by means of pain. In this context, separations, or other psychological triggers for pain are worth exploring. The psychotherapist may discover for example that the patient believes that his pain is a punishment for past behavior—he is living out the myths of Sisyphus or Prometheus, who suffered eternal punishment. This association is not surprising, given our cultural and religious heritage in which themes of pain, guilt, and punishment are connected.

Here it is worth remembering Levinas's (1998a) idea that, unlike ordinary sensations, severe pain undermines the possibility of the sufferer having a coherent and meaningful experience of the world. Pain undermines our capacity to think and to unify our experience; it makes us passive, it undermines the subject and radically incapacitates our autonomy. However, unlike the position I take in this chapter, Levinas does not believe that pain is meaningful; he thinks that if we try to give it meaning we exacerbate the suffering it produces.

The sufferer often has an intense need to understand and explain the experience of pain, so that spiritual concerns such as acceptance, hope, and meaning figure prominently in pain research. Like many forms of suffering, chronic pain often forces people to reflect on their lives. Depending on one's beliefs, pain may be seen as an enemy or a challenge to be overcome, which may even strengthen the person. Various authors suggest that among pain patients the expression of love and forgiveness towards others are signs of spiritual health, while isolation, guilt, and anger are signs of spiritual distress (Newshan, 1998). The inability to invest pain with meaning has also been seen as a sign of **spiritual** distress (Burnard 1987), but it is possible to reach a state of meaninglessness because of the sheer emotional and physical exhaustion produced by chronic pain (Harrison & Burnard 1993). These individuals may find it impossible to find meaning in their suffering—life makes no sense at all.

Terror Management Theory and Meaning

Terror management theory (Greenberg et al., 1986) suggests that despite finding life meaningful, human beings are also very much aware of our eventual mortality. This awareness can be terrifying, and this fear must be managed to avoid constant anxiety. One way we buffer this anxiety is to have faith in a shared cultural worldview that gives life meaning—for example, to believe in a religion that teaches life after death. Or, we develop self-esteem based on the perception that we are meeting our own or our culture's values and standards. In terms of this theory, any activity which is meaningful, or any search for the meaning of life, may be geared towards mitigating death anxiety.

Philosophical Counseling as an approach to suffering

Philosophical counseling is an attempt to ease suffering by applying the insights of the world's greatest thinkers to human problems (Louw, 2013; Sivil, 2009; Marinoff, 1999). The field is based on the age-old idea that our difficulties in life are of a philosophical nature, and philosophers have much to say about the suffering produced by painful life circumstances and ethical dilemmas. Philosophers have always been interested in the art of living and the meaning of life and death. In fact, until the latter part of the 19th century, what we now call psychology was indistinguishable from philosophy, but since then the two disciplines have separated, and philosophy became an academic practice in which some branches are removed from personal concerns.[52]

The philosophical counseling movement has provided a degree of re-integration of philosophy and psychology by applying the insights of the great philosophers to practical problems of living. The practice of philosophical counseling is only a few decades old,[53] but its roots go back to the philosophical schools of ancient Greece, China, and India, all of which saw philosophy as a way to reduce human suffering and increase personal freedom. In modern times, the philosopher Wittgenstein believed that philosophy itself is therapy, and "the philosopher's treatment of a question is like the treatment of an illness" (quoted by Louw, 2013, p. 63).

---

[52]   Analytical philosophy, or the attempt to precisely analyze concepts, language, mathematics, and logic, is not particularly helpful with the problems of living suffered by ordinary people, or with non-rational subjects such as spirituality. In contrast, the historical tradition of philosophy going back to Plato and Aristotle, which includes existentialists and phenomenologists, is particularly interested in experience, the imagination, and subjectivity.

[53]   The field began in Germany in 1981 with the work of Gerd B. Achenbach.

All forms of psychotherapy implicitly or explicitly propose philosophical attitudes to life, but philosophical counseling avoids any standard theoretical framework of the kind found in schools of psychotherapy. Many philosophical counselors deny that any method is necessary, so there is a lack of uniformity among practitioners. There is some debate about whether or not this really is a form of psychotherapy and to what extent the practitioner is actually a teacher or a problem solver. In general, no diagnosis is made, nor is any definition of normality implied. The process used by philosophical counselors is restricted to systematic inquiry into the individual's thinking, perception, worldview, and values, and sometimes engagement with philosophical texts to see how others have dealt with the individual's situation. The counselor often applies a Socratic approach, asking questions in a way that helps the person to discover her own insights and solutions. At times the philosophical counselor will add her personal commitments, leading to a dialogdialogue, in order to encourage the person to critically examine his or her beliefs with a view towards increased self-awareness. Philosophical counselors often assume that our problems and behavior are a function of our philosophy, and are a statement about how we see ourselves and the world. By becoming critically aware of what we actually think, we can discover problematic or unexamined assumptions, values or beliefs, and come to our own truth and peace of mind. The philosophical counselor therefore encourages questions such as "who am I?" or "what do I want from life?", and assists the person with the necessary critical analysis so that he can discover his own standpoint. In this process of discovery we can come to understand our situation differently, revise our thinking and perception, and develop a response to difficult situations, thereby reducing the suffering they produce. For example, if one is a victim of racial or sexist discrimination, one can look at the nature of prejudice, what causes it and why it is wrong, with the goal of being better able to deal with it and gaining wisdom in the process.

The philosophical counselor might suggest that peace of mind can be achieved by suspending judgments about events because it is difficult to have objective knowledge of reality. A conclusion about whether something is good or bad can always be opposed by an opposite argument and an opposite conclusion that is equally credible. Thus, if I cannot know whether something is good or bad, my fear of losing it is as irrational as my joy at obtaining it. Alain De Botton (2000) provides several examples of philosophical consolations for various forms of unhappiness. When we are concerned about how others see us, he points out the example of Socrates, a good man who was judged to be evil, showing that one can be right even though he may be hated by the majority. If one is concerned about not having enough money, the philosopher Epicurus taught that true friendship and freedom are far more important; extreme wealth does not guarantee that one will be happy. Nietzsche pointed out that suffering is essential for a fulfilled life; we cannot produce art or anything valuable without a degree of "pain, anxiety, envy and humiliation" (ibid, p. 215). The important points are the way we respond to difficulties while remaining committed to what is important to us.

I should note here that the conscious examination of one's assumptions about reality or about oneself is one of the main approaches of both philosophy and cognitive-behavioral psychotherapy, which looks for cognitive distortions or automatic inferences which lead the patient to pathogenic conclusions about himself. However, while cognitive psychotherapists deploy empirically based knowledge, philosophical counseling is not empirically based—if anything it is based in texts and argument. Philosophical counselors approach their clients by defining important terms, by correcting problems in thinking, questioning hidden presuppositions, and pointing out contradictions. If we suffer from a relationship problem, the philosophical counselor could help us examine what we mean by relationship, by asking "what does it mean to be happily married?" or "what is a successful marriage?" In the course of discussing such questions philosophically, we may discover that our concept of relationship is causing the problem. If we are in ethical dilemma, we may need to re-evaluate our values or our concept of right and wrong. If life has become meaningless, we could investigate the possibility of finding meaning in existence.

Problems with philosophical counseling

If a question about the meaning of life should arise in the midst of a suicidal crisis, it seems questionable whether philosophical counseling would be as helpful as traditional psychotherapy. The depressed person is often unresponsive to logic or common sense. Or, what looks like a relationship problem on the surface may be the manifestation of a significant personality disorder that would be better treated psychotherapeutically. Just because an emotional problem has a philosophical component to it does not mean that the primary problem is a philosophical one, just as philosophy itself cannot cure a headache. There are situations in life that cannot be approached logically or by explaining where someone is irrational. One can be rational and intensely unhappy, and one may suffer from an internal conflict between two opposing positions, each of which is rational. Different aspects of a person may want different things, so there is no necessary, logical response to a life dilemma that can be arrived at by thinking clearly. Human beings are not logical machines; we have many internal contradictions or opposing feelings. Even when a person can understand the philosophical implications of his difficulty, he may not have the "mental muscle" or emotional wherewithal to benefit from such analysis. People suffering from developmentally early emotional difficulties, such as borderline personalities, suffer all their lives from an internal, painful sense of emptiness combined with emotional turmoil, and such states of mind are not amenable to reasoned discussion; our genes do not always allow us to follow the dictates of reason. There is a major difference between a severe anxiety disorder and what existentialists call existential "angst," the anxiety that arises from the experience of human freedom or the possibility that life is meaningless. Panic attacks probably have a genetic component; existential angst does not, so panic attacks are not amenable to philosophical analysis. It is true that some classical Greek philosophers believed that reason can allow us to control our passions and appetites, but today this seems overly optimistic. Traditional cognitive-behavioral psychology held that emotions are derived from cognitions, which are primary, but this is by no means certain, because contemporary research suggests that affect and cognition are highly interdependent or inseparable. Affect may arise as the primary response to a situation independently of cognition, or thought may arise secondarily to affect, which may regulate cognition.

When one reads accounts of successful philosophical therapy, it is not clear whether the client improved because of the philosophical counseling itself or whether an idealizing transference to the philosopher developed. Such transferences often produce "transference cures," improvement that only lasts as long as the relationship with the psychotherapist is intact. Case reports do not always tell us whether the philosopher was particularly empathic, supportive, a good listener, and fully present—all of these are psychotherapeutic process skills, which could enter into philosophical counseling and be partly responsible for any change which occurs, beside the content of the discussion which takes place. I know of no research that tries to untangle such variables. At the moment therefore, it seems to me that philosophical counseling is of most value to reasonably healthy people who are suffering from questions that can be addressed philosophically because they do not seriously impair the individual's emotional equilibrium. We should however remember Jopling's (1998) warning that a person may be led to "overphilosophize" his or her problems or even create problems that were not there in the first place. It is not difficult to find philosophers of equal stature who have diametrically opposite opinions about the best way to live.

9

SUFFERING AS LIMINALITY

Liminality

In this chapter I suggest that a useful model for thinking about suffering is to see it as a transitional or liminal period between different stages of one's life, a period which will lead to a new state of being or a new consciousness. Anthropologists use the word "liminality" to describe the transitional period of people in tribal cultures whilst they are undergoing initiation into a new status. The word "liminal," from the Latin "*limen,*" means a threshold, as in the threshold of a house. The notion of liminality is an archetypal paradigm for understanding major transitions and radical change. This model views suffering as purposive rather than random, and as a form of initiation.

In pre-modern societies, rituals of initiation into a new social or spiritual status have been shown to occur in three phases, which Arnold van Gennep (1908/2010) described as separation, transition or liminality, and reincorporation. The individual is first taken out of his or her usual situation, followed by a liminal period in which he is neither fully out of the old life nor into the new one, until finally he or she is re-incorporated back into society in a new status. The middle or liminal period is the most difficult time, because the initiate does not know where he or she is going or what the outcome will be, so it is a period fraught with suffering. Tribal cultures consider rites of initiation to be essential for the individual's development, for movement into a new social or religious status such as adulthood or marriage, for spiritual re-birth, and for the continuity of the culture. Jungians believe that we can learn about the process of transition by studying anthropological descriptions of these rituals. These descriptions reveal the archetypal dynamics involved, some of which are relevant to our psychotherapeutic work with suffering individuals. The psychotherapist can see the patient's suffering as the liminal phase of a rite of passage into a new status which will radically change the individual's identity. This approach offers a mythic or archetypal framework for the individual's situation, instead of seeing suffering as merely random misfortune. Many spiritual traditions believe that suffering is necessary for transformation, so that suffering can be viewed as a form of sacred wounding.

In tribal societies, the separation phase of the rite of passage involves physical separation from the individual's usual surroundings and confinement within a sacred space, outside ordinary society, often in a forest or cave. This symbolically and literally separates the initiate from his or her previous life, with all its attendant beliefs and practices. The initiate is then thrust into the transitional or liminal period, which is when the most intense suffering is experienced. The initiation rituals in pre-modern societies for both men and women are quite brutal, humiliating, and terrifying, often involving very painful scarification of the body, operations such as circumcision, and other ordeals or trials of strength. The ritual is carried out by elders who are themselves initiated, who understand the process, and who can guard the boundaries of the sacred place. The ritual often has a symbolic death-rebirth theme, as if the initiate must die to his previous life to be re-born into a new life, so the initiate may be told he will be killed by the tribal deity, and may be buried alive in a tomb-like place.

During the ritual the liminal individuals are often naked, to symbolize their lack of any social role, or they are treated as if they are infants or neither male nor female, or painted white as if they are dead (Eliade, 1965; Turner, 1995). Because the ritual has so much emotional power, the initiates are in a vulnerable and receptive mental state, and it is likely that this facilitates transmission of the culture's ideology and values to them. Importantly, the time of liminality is considered to be sacred time, and the place of the ritual is thought to be sacred space, where the transpersonal dimension reveals itself.[54] The sacred stories and sacred objects of the society are revealed to the initiates, who are told the privileges and responsibilities of the new stage of their life. They are encouraged to think about their society and the powers that sustain them. The initiated person is then re-incorporated into his or her society in his or her new status.

---

54   Modern anthropologists dispute the idea that the purpose of ritual is to produce a spiritual re-birth; it is now thought that rituals are ways in which the initiate is made to conform to social expectations. Ritual is then a form of indoctrination, a social enactment of a maturational process that happens naturally. Some of the problems with tribal initiations are that they marginalize those who are handicapped, narrowly define what it is to be a man or woman, and prevent social change.

In our culture, there are many forms of liminality, which often produces a complex changes in our sense of identity and a feeling of disorientation. Major life transitions such as loss, divorce, tragedy, or trauma separate us from the usual order of our lives and from our usual emotional state, and throw us into a period of transitional turmoil and suffering. The world then looks and feels different. The onset of serious illness thrusts the individual into liminality; not only is there pain and disability, but our usual methods of dealing with stress, such as relationships with others, the ability to hope, a feeling of control over one's body and one's life, and a sense of purpose, are all threatened. When a person becomes seriously ill, his or her sense of self may undergo a radical change or disruption, and he or she is thrown into liminality. After organ transplants, liminality may take the form of experiencing some change in identity; in the recipient's fantasy, a transplanted organ may feel as if it belongs both to the donor and the recipient, almost as if the donor is alive in the recipient. The transplanted organ may then seem to be a transitional object in Winnicott's sense (Goetzmann, 2004). Another important liminal experience is the experience of preparing to die; many traditions have ritual processes for helping this period, such as the Roman Catholic Anointing of the Sick. Today, the liminal period of the dying process is often prolonged by medical treatments that stave off death. Another type of liminality is experienced by immigrants and their children, who live in a bi-cultural home in which they may develop a liminal sense of identity.

An important example of liminality is the mid-life period, typically beginning in one's late thirties or early forties, which is often turbulent. A person who has had an apparently successful life hears some kind of internal call for change and starts out on a quest for transformation. This period may produce a change in the organization of the personality, even to the extent that people may begin to wonder who they have become. The person often feels bored and disillusioned, perhaps depressed, regretful or nostalgic, with a sense of the transience of life. There may be loss of interest in the individual's career and often a feeling of defeat. The old sense of self is gone, but a new one has not yet formed. During this liminal period, which goes on for a year or two, the person feels lost or drifting, somewhat insubstantial. Midlife is a period when we question what we have achieved so far, and our energy wants to flow in a different way. People in this situation often dream of moving into new houses, knocking down old buildings, or changing furniture, all of which represent internal change. However, there is not much cultural support for this transition. For some people, psychotherapy is then a helpful way of containing painful affective states and exploring the new ideas and imagery that arises, so that psychotherapy is a modern version of an initiation process. When this period is navigated successfully, people feel more solid as they re-constitute a new self-organization and integrate the new situation; people go back to school or take up new careers.

Depression is an example of a liminal period that is potentially transformative. The onset of any emotional disturbance, such as anxiety or depression, can be seen as a liminal period. For Jung these are a signal from the unconscious that something needs attention, or they are the attempt of the unconscious to stimulate the development of a neglected aspect of the personality. For this to occur, a forced period of introspection and reduced activity is necessary, although this might be difficult to achieve in our culture, which has little tolerance for the necessary withdrawal. Esther Harding (1970) described depression as potentially creative, and Emmy Gut (1989) also noted that depression can be productive or unproductive; productive depression produces useful learning or maturation, while unproductive depression leads to arrested development. It may be a mistake to think that the treatment of depression is to replace it with positive thinking, which may restore the ego's sense of comfort but does nothing for the soul's development.

There are many lenses through which one can view depression. It can be seen as a biological disturbance due to a genetic predisposition, or as a normal response to loss. In addition, one can view depression as a period of liminality in which the psyche is purposefully trying to move the personality into a new state of consciousness. Major life transitions often require a kind of deconstruction and reconstruction of aspects of the personality, and depression is a good example of this process. Rosen (1976) describes the way in which the pull to suicide is a demand for an ego-death, meaning the need for a radical change in attitude or for a new sense of self. Unfortunately, this demand is often mistakenly experienced as a wish for the death of the body. In other words, to see depression as nothing more than a disorder is reductive—depression is potentially regenerative.

The descent into liminality can be seen from either a spiritual or a purely secular point of view. If the psychotherapist is interested in the spiritual dimensions of psychotherapy, this period can be seen as motivated by the transpersonal Self, as part of the necessary destiny of the individual, part of a spiritual or archetypal process such as the dark night of the soul described by John of the Cross. The psychotherapist then has to bear in mind that initiation into a new consciousness often requires both suffering and patient submission to powers higher than oneself. Indeed, the spiritually-oriented therapist may see suffering as one of the ways that the transpersonal dimension claims our attention. This provides another perspective on suffering beside the everyday egoic perspective. For the psychotherapist with a purely secular sensibility, the concept of liminality is simply a useful way to talk about transitions.

Needless to say, there is a legitimate question about the extent to which we can compare social processes in our own culture with tribal societies that are so different, but it seems that there are some striking similarities with respect to the human need for initiation and help with transition. In our society, it is well known that people are prone to emotional breakdown during transitional periods of development such as the movement into adolescence, into midlife, or into old age, or when one is thrust into a transition by bereavement or other losses. These situations all produce liminal periods in which one is not quite out of the previous status but not yet adjusted to the new one. At these times of "betwixt and between" or ambiguity, people suffer anxiety and uncertainty. They may find themselves stuck, unable to take the next step in a necessary developmental sequence. Major changes are occurring in our sense of who we are, but we have no idea where we are heading. Victor Turner (1995) calls a person in such a state a "transition-being." Liminality is a time in which the individual has an uncertain status, which is why in some tribal rituals the liminal period is likened to being dead or in the womb.

Turner (1967) notes that because tribal cultures tend to regard the person in the liminal state as somehow polluting, people who have contact with them may be contaminated, which is why the initiates are always secluded from the rest of the tribe or they are disguised in masks or costumes. Perhaps analogously, because our culture does not acknowledge the value of suffering, we tend to isolate poverty, old age, and death so that we don't have to constantly face them. The unconscious fear that suffering is infectious, combined with the terror that what has happened to the sufferer may happen to oneself, may account for why certain people and some political views seem to despise those who suffer, as if suffering is somehow equated with badness or a sign of divine disfavor. At the same time, those who are afflicted may hate themselves and induce this feeling in others. Envy of those who are happy may make it uncomfortable to be with the suffering person. These psychological factors may contribute to the political reasons that we do not have adequate social structures for helping people who suffer.

Turner (1987) regards liminality as a state of "pure possibility, whence novel configurations of ideas and relations may arise." He points out that liminality may generate new thought, consistent with the observation that suffering may help us understand who we really are; the liminal period may act as a bridge to a new orientation to life, or to who we might become. "Liminality may be partly described as a stage of reflection" (p. 14). Surely this process of reflection is also important to those in our culture who suffer.

Liminal processes in our culture

Our culture is much more complex than traditional tribal cultures, and there is no standard form of initiation into adulthood. Our rituals such as Bar Mitzvah, First Communion, or passing the driving test may be formalities without much spiritual intensity. Most of us find our own forms of initiation, often based on experiences that cause intense suffering. Jan Bauer (1993) suggests that the pain of "impossible love" is a form of initiation, and Zoja (1989) describes the initiatory aspects of addiction. It used to be the case that the draft into the army was a type of initiation for men, but that is no longer true for most men, for whom initiation seems to have emerged in new forms. Today initiation for men requires learning the correct use of power, intimacy, and relationship to the feminine.

Individuation, or the development of the personality, requires a series of initiatory processes. Adolescents are archetypally moved to seek initiation, but our culture has few acceptable cultural outlets for some of them, in which case the pressure for initiation is acted out unconsciously—the psyche tries to initiate the person. If there are no suitable adults available to act as ritual elders, adolescents may seek out initiation in dangerous forms, such as gang behavior, dangerous driving, or adventurous sports (see Corbett, 2007, pp. 70-70, for more discussion of this issue). Some people are initiated by alcoholism, divorces, severe illnesses, accidents, or major depressions at mid-life—the point is that the person is made to feel helpless or even broken by a life crisis, which often appears to be essential for psychological transformation. Our culture emphasizes performance, results, and accomplishments, but during the liminal period, the transition itself is the important focus, whether the end result of the liminal process is leading us to death, widowhood, a new experience of the body due to illness, and the like. The danger is that we may never emerge fully from the suffering produced by the liminal state, in which case we remain stuck in a kind of liminal limbo, a chronic transitional state. Often it is hard to get out of liminal space without help, which is when psychotherapy can be of value.

It may be therapeutically helpful to think of serious illness or suffering as a period of initiation, in which case the psychotherapist has a role analogous to that of the ritual elder in tribal cultures, helping to hold the space as sacred space. The psychotherapist may see images of initiation in dreams at critical periods of the life cycle such as puberty, marriage, or the approach of old age. If there is no social process of initiation, the Self may provide an initiatory experience by means of a dream such as the following:

> I am lying in bed stretched flat and tall on my back. My hands are folded together on my belly as if in prayer. I feel my eyes rolling back into a place of surrender and inner consciousness. Suddenly I hear a loud drilling sound and I feel a vibration at the third eye, as if a hole were being bored there. At the same time, I see a range of intense colors: reds with patterns, mostly lines and diamond shapes, shades of indigo followed by a vast view into the universe, green lines against black like a code language and the sense that other beings are trying to contact me, for which I give them permission, then a bright golden white light that becomes more intense and engulfs me. All the time I try to focus my eyes to see better, but that only makes the vision dim. It is only through the hole of my third eye that I can experience this glorious vision of color accompanied by a deep sense of peace and ecstasy. I awaken to the sense that I must be somehow changed now.

The opening of the third eye in the esoteric traditions is traditionally associated with the development of clairvoyant ability or the ability to intuitively sense subtle energy. These kinds of initiatory dreams may occur at a young age; Jung believed that his childhood dream of the underground phallus, described in his *Memories, Dreams, Reflections*, was an initiation into the realm of the unconscious that presaged his life's vocation. A psychotherapist, going through a period of doubt about his vocation for this work, had the following initiatory dream:

> I'm lying in the center of a city square which has an old, cobbled-stone surface, surrounded by several other people. We are all dying, and as we die our souls are emerging from our bodies. In the form of a soul, I realize that the souls around me are

uncertain what to do or which direction to take; I realize that I have to guide them or point the way to a door in a tunnel some distance away, and make sure they enter.

This dream, which depicts the therapist in the archetypal role of the *psychopomp* or guide of souls, had a profound effect on the dreamer, who felt that he had been given the authority to do the work for which he had trained. These examples illustrate the Jungian notion that the sacred or transpersonal dimension manifests itself by means of the unconscious, often in the form of dreams, and any contact with the sacred has an initiatory effect.

During life transitions, we sometimes look for liminal space in a search for regeneration—we are then looking for space that offers the possibility of renewal and re-orientation. Often we do not know exactly what we are looking for, and there may not be an obvious place in our culture to find it. Much behavior that looks incomprehensible is unconsciously motivated by this search, which is not always triggered by a crisis; sometimes we simply sense an inner voice saying that change is needed.

We may need help with these transitions, but there is a shortage of initiatory processes in the culture designed to help with a transition or crisis. The archetype may then become active but there is no way to live it consciously, because of an absence of ritual leadership. Psychotherapy can often fill in this need by containing the suffering produced by liminality, although our professional literature does not often think of suffering in terms of liminality, and the ritual dimensions of psychotherapy have only been acknowledged to a limited extent.

Mythic Depictions of Suffering

Mythology is important to the depth psychotherapist because mythic stories depict archetypal situations and their psychological and spiritual truths. We resonate with these stories because their themes still happen—we have all felt like the mythic Sisyphus.

We can sometimes locate our own story in a myth, or locate mythic themes in our own life, and it may be helpful to link our own situation to a generally human experience so that we do not feel completely alone. The mythic theme of descent into the underworld is often used as a metaphor for entrance into a period of suffering or deep personal exploration.[55] These stories metaphorically depict the need of the conscious personality to go into unknown realms of the unconscious. When the process works well, the protagonist returns with some kind of treasure or knowledge, indicating that such descent, although dangerous, can result in a precious discovery. The descent can happen without warning; in the ancient Greek story, Persephone is an innocent young girl, suddenly seized and dragged down to the realm of Hades, the Lord of the Underworld, which happens to anyone who is raped, mugged, or unexpectedly violated in any way. Metaphorically, the underworld represents a layer of the psyche that contains much that is undeveloped or unknown to us, including deep veins of meaning. If one is not able to negotiate the journey, one may not be able to return. But those who do return are radically transformed.

A very early myth of descent is that of Inann, a story that was written on clay tablets about 3000 BCE. Inanna (also known as Ishtar, or the planet Venus) was the Sumerian Queen of Heaven and Earth, a goddess of the grain, of war, love, fertility, and sexuality. The story begins as she listens to a call from the "Great Below," presumably a deeper level of herself. Such a call appears as the sense that something in us needs attention. Sometimes people in mid-life who seem to be completely stable and successful hear this call when they realize that they are not living their true vocation. They then want to radically change things, go back to school or start a new career.

When Inanna hears the call, she announces that she will attend the funeral of her sister's husband. Ereshkigal, queen of the underworld, is Inanna's dark, shadow sister. Psychologically, Ereshkigal and Inanna could be thought of as two aspects of the same personality, one of which lives in the light and is a glorious queen, while the other is rejected and consigned to the dark. Ereshkigal has no relationships; she is lonely, unloving, unloved, abandoned, and full of rage, greed, and desperate loneliness. To compensate for this, she is sexually insatiable—one story tells of a male god entering the underworld with whom she has sex for six days and six nights. When he leaves on the seventh day, she has still not had enough. That is, Inanna's shadow contains compulsive sexuality that tries to compensate for her loneliness and abandonment fears. Apparently, Inanna senses the need to get to know this

---

55   Ulysses descended to the underworld to consult Tiresias, Dante was led down by Virgil, and Faust by Mephistopheles. Out of his grief for his dead wife, Orpheus descended to try to persuade Hades to release Eurydice. Osiris, Adonis, Dionysus, and many other gods of antiquity, long before Christ, made this descent.

part of herself. When we descend to the underworld, we discover aspects of ourselves that have been repressed or ignored, or that lie dormant.[56]

When Inanna arrives at the gates to the underworld, Ereshkigal is not happy to see her sister, who is described as "all-white." Ereshkigal is enraged at having been ignored, and she is envious of Inanna's glory and splendor while she has to live in a dark place, eating clay and drinking dirty water. As an internal object, Ereshkigal represents a figure in Inanna that is envious of her success. Inanna is the goddess of love, a bright star, and Ereshkigal wants her to know what it is like to be rejected. Accordingly, Ereshkigal insists that Inanna be treated according to the rules for anyone entering her domain, that she be bowed low.

There are seven gates to the underworld, a traditional number to express cyclical processes, the end of one period and the beginning of another. Therefore, the number 7 is often associated with a process of initiation into a new status. At each gate, Inanna has to pay a price to enter by sacrificing one of her royal garments. Each time she is shocked and indignant, and she asks "what is this?" but she is told not to question the ways of the underworld. So she removes in turn her magnificent headdress, her lapis necklace, her strands of beads, her breastplate, her ring, and her measuring rod. At the last gate, her robe is taken from her so that she is totally naked. In other words, all her symbols of power and prestige are removed. Psychologically, this reminds us of how suffering makes us give up our persona, our usual way of appearing to the world. Ereshkigal orders Inanna to be left to die, hanging on a hook until her corpse turns into a piece of rotting meat, a vivid metaphor for intense suffering. At this point in the story, to our surprise we discover that Ereshkigal is actually in labor, so one could think of her as a part of Inanna that wants to give birth to something new. This is a part of the pain that Inanna hears from above which induces her to descend.

Before Inanna descended, she had told her assistant, Ninshubur, to appeal to the father gods if she does not return in three days. The first of these gods, Enlil, is the director of rationality; he wants nothing to do with her in the underworld. The second father god, Nanna, also cannot understand why she made the journey; they are both angry with her and will not help. It is not uncommon for the patriarchal establishment, the guardians of what passes for common sense, to have little sympathy for the

---

56   It is interesting that another name for Hades/Pluto was Lord of Riches—the one who knew the location of hidden jewels.

need for radical change. But Enki, the god of wisdom and healing, values her journey and realizes its importance. From the dirt under his fingernails, he creates two asexual creatures who become professional mourners who empathically mirror Ereshkigal's pain. As she moans, they moan; they echo her pain and anguish, which touches her deeply, in a scene that is a profound testimony to the healing effect of empathy and witnessing. Ereshkigal offers them gifts, but they only ask for her to release Inanna, although usually no one is ever allowed to leave the underworld. However, Inanna had not just visited, she had died and been reborn there, and so new rules are made. She is allowed to leave the underworld if she will provide someone to take her place. Accordingly, the demons of the underworld return with her to the upper world to find someone to replace her. These demons are remorseless, willing to tear apart wives and husbands, children and parents. The demands of the unconscious are relentless.

On her return, Inanna found that her sons and her servants had mourned for her, but her husband Dumuzi hardly noticed that she was gone; he did not weep for her, nor did he greet her return. It is as if he ignored her spiritual journey, refused to help her and showed no compassion for her. Instead he made himself more powerful. Inanna cursed him and made the demons of the underworld seize him, thereby forcing him to meet her dark aspects. As a result of a dream, Dumuzi realized he would have to go down to the underworld, but his sister shared this fate so that they each had to be there half a year.

In the process of meeting the part of her that suffered, Inanna had to die to her old self, but she was eventually brought back to life and spiritually transformed in the process. She now knows the darkness, and she returns more powerful and assertive of her own rights, determined to survive. Inanna's story in some ways prefigures the story of Jesus, who is also humiliated, tortured, and hung to die before descending to the underworld; Inanna is therefore an early image of a dying and resurrected deity.

Ereshkigal, the queen of the underworld, is a metaphor for unconscious parts of ourselves that can only be approached with difficulty, and only by means of a descent. The myth says that she was angry and grieving at the same time as she was giving birth. There is often a good deal of grief in the unconscious that we can avoid until we suffer intolerably. We are then confronted with this grief in the form of regret and pain about missed opportunities, mistakes we have made, and necessary sacrifices. This story suggests that meeting all this may result in transformation. Innana's stay in the underworld transforms her, because now that she knows her shadow sister she can better integrate that aspect of herself.

The story of Inanna is a mythic representation of what happens to us when we suffer. Suffering may reduce our authority and personal power, and often produces a loss of dignity and persona as well. When our usual way of being in the world no longer works for us, we may be plunged into a depression, metaphorically represented as the mythological underworld. At that time, our favorite distractions such as alcohol, religion, work or entertainment, are no longer useful. But the underworld realm of the soul into which we descend is a part of us, an area that we have so far managed to avoid. Often, periods of intense suffering reveal other aspects of our lives that are not working, such as an unrewarding job or a marriage that needs attention. In the case of chronic illness, it may take years for the descent to the underworld to occur. The illness gradually changes our identity and appearance; think of the changes produced by radiation and chemotherapy.

Most folklore and mythologies of descent, such as the story of Innana, depict the radical change produced by an initiatory experience. At the end of her ordeal, Innana is empowered, she is conscious of her darkness, and she has discovered who really cares about her. The kind of descent that Inanna went through is an initiation into the deep mysteries of the soul. To reach these levels requires a sacrifice of our usual attitudes for the sake of retrieving certain values of which we were unaware. Suffering makes the ego face what it has been ignoring, strips the persona, and makes us pay attention to parts of ourselves that have never had a chance to live. During periods of suffering, the hegemony of the ego is reduced, so that it is common for suffering people to have numinous experiences of non-ordinary reality.

Reincorporation

The final stage of the initiatory process is the return to one's society in the new status. The timing of this return to the individual's new life is variable; for some people it is quick, for some it is gradual, while others oscillate back and forth between liminality and their new state for some time. Sometimes the new adjustment is made difficult by the lack of understanding from the individual's family and colleagues, especially if for their own reasons they need the individual to think and behave in the old way.

Psychotherapy and ritual process

Psychotherapy can be seen as a contemporary form of ritual process, which deals with people going through liminal periods. In the broad sense, a ritual is an action that symbolically expresses thoughts, feelings, ideologies such as religious beliefs, and social norms. Rituals focus our attention and allow us to concentrate on an important value. In the context of religion, ritual expresses a connection to the sacred and often re-tells a mythic story such as the exodus from Egypt told at the Passover Seder. The Eucharist re-enacts the Last Supper as recorded in the New Testament. Rituals particularly emphasize the body and gesture, so they affect the non-rational or unconscious levels of the mind. There are many types of ritual beside its religious variety, allowing us to give expression to experiences of change and marking critical moments of life; common types are rituals of transition, greeting, continuity, seasonal change, healing, birth, and death. A communal meal at an occasion like a wedding or a funeral wake is a ritual of aggregation and bonding, and these familiar social rituals sometimes have a therapeutic effect. We use private and public rituals to remember and commemorate a major event. After a tragedy such as 9/11 or a mass shooting we see flowers, candles, photographs, and other mementos at the site of the disaster. Many of us have daily routines which are simple personal rituals to help us release stress, such as making tea or having a glass of wine at a certain time of day.

The audience for a ritual is important; it is supportive and helpful to be surrounded by a communion of the faithful. For example, Alcoholics Anonymous has a ritual process; there is always an introduction, a story, a discussion, and the working of the 12 steps, which are a kind of sacred text. The alcoholic in AA ritually announces that he is powerless over alcohol, and this acceptance takes place within a helpful group who are important witnesses to this confession. In a way, being alcoholic is a life-long form of liminality because one is always recovering, never fully recovered.

Death produces one of the clearest indications of the human need to experience ritual, so that all cultures have funeral rites, which may be the most common form of ritual. Some religious traditions teach that the rituals around death facilitate the onward movement of the soul of the deceased, which is making a transition into a new dimension. Mourning rituals mark a liminal period for the survivors; the bereaved person's life is not as it was, but it is not yet what it will become. The bereaved person feels less sure of life ahead. He or she is emotionally vulnerable, with a mixture of emotions;

sadness, despair, perhaps freedom. The rituals of grief act as containers for these feelings. People are brought together, we recognize our shared humanity, our membership in a particular group, and our mortality.

Joseph Campbell (2008) describes the initiatory process in terms of the mythic theme of the hero's journey. This begins with a call to transformation, which may be accepted or refused. There follows an ordeal, and sometimes helpers appear giving guidance. If all goes well, one discovers the treasure, the pearl of great price. It is important to note that this kind of initiation may fail, and even when successful it is a cyclical or recurrent process. Joseph Henderson (1967/2005) points out that while the hero myth is about ego development, there are forms of initiation that transcend the ego. Developmentally, moving from the heroic position in which one has to struggle, to the sense that one is being initiated and must submit, is a movement from a need for personal power to a quest for meaning. Henderson believes that initiation is a process that must be endured if it is to be successful; only the necessary suffering will open the individual to what he or she would otherwise be unable to see. He suggests that historically the archetype of initiation suffers the fate of "continually being forgotten and having to be rediscovered" (p. 9).

In the early years of psychoanalysis, ritual was regarded ambivalently because most writers associated it with traditional religion, which, following Freud, was dismissed as superstitious. However, it is possible to see psychotherapy as a secular form of ritual process within our society, although ritual has a bad name in modernity, so this may not be a popular idea among scientifically-oriented therapists. Nevertheless, therapeutic rituals have been used during couples therapy, family therapy, and as part of grief work (Cole, 2003; Imber-Black, 1988, Kobak, 1984; Bewley, 1995; Moore, 2001). Psychotherapy has its ritual norms of behavior and takes place in a special place, at a special time—entering the consulting room is a kind of separation phase. The liminal period is the time of trying out new behavior, new ideas, new identities, new information, and psychological change. Some analytic training programs believe they provide rites of passage, and the gatekeepers at these institutes see themselves as initiating trainees. The shadow side of this approach to training is that the abuse of candidates may be rationalized as a form of initiation.

The ritual aspects of psychotherapy include the frame and the holding environment. When psychotherapy is seen as a process of initiation, the therapist is analogous to a ritual elder who is providing a kind of spiritual direction and ritual leadership in a time of crisis. The psychotherapist has specialized knowledge and she has been through the process herself. This is a priestly role which is affected by the transference and by personal material as well as the archetypal process of initiation.

Jung believed that the exploration of the unconscious by means of psychotherapy is a contemporary form of initiation (*Letters*, vol. 1 p. 141). For him, the analysis of the unconscious is the only initiation process which is still practiced today in the West (CW 11, p. 515). He wrote that although psychotherapy is a contemporary rite of initiation, it is not a collective rite because the symbols that arise from the unconscious in dreams and symptoms are individual, spontaneous, and not prescribed by tradition (CW 11, p. 523). Following Jung's lead, Henderson (1967/2005) describes three components of initiation which are repeated in the therapeutic process; submission, containment, and liberation, to which Moore (2001) adds enactment. We submit to a therapeutic process which has its own autonomy. We submit to a contract, a frame, and to a sacrifice of time and money. Containment allows us to face difficult truths in therapy and express painful feelings without fear of retaliation, with the hope that the therapist can hold what emerges. Enactment means trying on new ways of thinking and new behavior, developing new ideas about oneself, and trying on a new self-image. There may be a literal enactment such as psychodrama, sand tray work, behavior therapy or active imagination.

Psychotherapeutic rituals are often carried out to help with a transition such as a bereavement or divorce, or to release anger or to forgive. To develop a ritual, the therapist and patient begin by jointly deciding on a symbol that is a concrete manifestation of the situation and the goal. For example, it is not uncommon for a person in the midst of a divorce to collect material from the person's married life, such as photographs or letters, and ritually burn them. Such individual rituals do not have roots in tradition and history, but they can be emotionally significant for the individual.

Sometimes a therapeutic ritual includes a spiritual element such as prayer or meditation which draws on the person's religious tradition, or perhaps the person simply acknowledges the presence of transpersonal forces outside the ego, in which case the ritual requires faith that change will be supported by the transcendent powers. Working with the psychotherapist, the ritual is planned and designed based on the change that is needed. A candle may be lit, and a sacred circle delineated with salt and water. Particular clothes are worn, such as a ritual robe. An altar is prepared. If the person is so inclined, the transpersonal level is invoked. A letter or photograph is burned and the ashes dispersed. Seeds are planted to represent positive affirmations, while negative self-statements are written and burned. The person may draw a map of two different life paths with way-stations depicted; one map is the one she is on and one as she would like it to be. The person may add features such as forests, mountains, rivers, or cliffs. The symbols that are chosen may arise spontaneously through journaling, meditation, focusing or discussion. An archetypal or mythic figure such as a god or goddess can be used to represent the previous state or the new state—Cole's (2003) patient invoked St. Brigid, the namesake of Brigid of Celtic mythology, who was a goddess of healing and fertility. For this patient, Brigid embodied the power and creativity she wanted to cultivate in herself. The therapist is a guide or witness as the person enacts the ritual. Some kind of closure and thanks follows.

Examples of psychotherapeutic mourning rituals are given by Rando (1985). A woman and her therapist visit the grave of the patient's daughter; she places flowers on the grave, speaks of her loss, and talks of when she will be united with her child. She takes half the flowers home, leaving half on the grave. This simple ritual allows her to acknowledge her loss, promotes the grief process, and maintain her daughter's memory. A man whose brother committed suicide returns to the field in which it happened and plants a tree on the spot. Rando notes the ability of such rituals to concretize the intangible, to allow "acting out" in the sense of expressing emotions behaviorally, including emotions that may be poorly defined. Rituals not only mark transitions, they also help us make transitions.

10

RADICAL ACCEPTANCE OF SUFFERING: THE PROCESS OF SURRENDER

The need for acceptance

There are occasions in life when suffering leads one to a point at which one has completely exhausted the ability to cope. Everything possible has been tried, but to no avail; intense suffering persists. Radical acceptance of unavoidable suffering is then a viable option both for atheists and for people who believe that there is a spiritual dimension of reality. Radical acceptance of the situation, or surrender to it, may both foster the development of the personality and also deepen the spirituality of those open to that possibility. To insist on independence and mastery of one's situation at all times, even when relinquishing control is a more sensible course, suggests characterological rigidity and lack of trust in or connection to others. Emotional maturity demands that we discern whether an attempt at mastery or surrender is the appropriate course to take in any given situation.

Working with individuals who are in desperate straits, the psychotherapist might see a variety of responses. Non-religious individuals may simply believe that what has happened is nothing more than random misfortune—one of life's inexplicable tragedies. For these suffering individuals, when nothing further can be done, surrender to the situation may seem to be nothing more than a necessary adaptation. When people who are committed to a traditional religion undergo intense suffering, they may surrender to what they perceive as the divine will or transcendent reality, however they imagine this, in which case surrender is a spiritual practice. Surrender is then intended to establish or maintain a connection to the transpersonal realm, whether that is understood as the Judeo-Christian God, the Self, one's True Nature, or what William James referred to as a higher power. Whether or not one's motive for surrender is spiritually oriented, the process usually has beneficial psychological effects, often producing a feeling of relief from struggle. Wallace (2001) refers to this combination of spiritual and psychological processes as transformative surrender. If one is suffering, attention and opening to the suffering, accompanied by compassion for oneself, is an alternative to resistance and dread. This process provides a little space between the suffering itself and our reaction to it. Much spiritual teaching is about disconnecting suffering from our instinctive or conditioned resistance to it.

Surrender may allow mature dependence on others or a level of connection to others that the sufferer has never before experienced. In the face of unbearable suffering, surrender may also involve letting go of one's previous beliefs and opinions, or letting go of a life-long attempt to omnipotently control one's life or to control others. Serious suffering makes us realize that we are not necessarily master of our fate, and life may not conform to our own preferences. One may then surrender to one's limitations, vulnerabilities, and finitude. However, surrender is difficult for people who need to be constantly vigilant because they grew up exposed to dangerous caregivers, for people who lack basic trust, or for those who need to control their environment. Surrender is also difficult if one cannot contain painful affective states with a degree of equanimity. This process is especially difficult for people with narcissistic character structures for whom grandiosity, entitlement, domination, and control are defenses against painful emptiness and shame. The process of letting go of these life-long defensive operations may be very difficult, or may engender fragmentation anxiety if they have been used to buttress an enfeebled sense of self. Mature personality adaptations such as a sense of peace or harmony may arise to take the place of narcissistic defenses such as grandiosity, but if these defenses collapse with nothing to replace them, the person may become depressed or anxious.

Radical acceptance means total receptivity to the situation one is in. Having done everything one can, realizing that one has no control and further struggle is futile, one stops trying to control the situation and simply allows whatever unfolds to continue to do so, without resistance, even (according to some spiritual traditions) experiencing the way things are as necessary. However, the word "surrender" has cultural connotations of defeat and failure, so this process may be difficult to accept in a culture that values autonomy, mastery, and control. It is also unfortunate that the word surrender also has militaristic overtones. However, there are times when one simply has to accept a state of unhappiness before anything will change. Certain states of mind have to be suffered or consciously carried for some time until we understand their purpose and meaning. This attitude requires consent to the situation in which we find ourselves, which is by the way an antidote to self-pity.[57]

A good example of the need for radical acceptance is found among people with chronic pain, who may need to accept that they have to live with pain and perhaps learn from it, rather than constantly fighting it. This approach requires opening to the pain and letting go of resistance to it. To accept pain does not mean resignation to it; it means to pursue important activities without avoiding or controlling the pain. When possible, this approach is associated with positive pain-related outcomes (McCracken et al., 2007). If we are ill, the illness becomes a part of who we are; that does not mean that we have to be passive and not try to deal with it, but it can be accepted at the moment as unavoidable.

There is some debate about whether surrender can be brought about deliberately (volitional surrender) or whether it happens spontaneously, in which case surrender seems to be an act of grace. Those who adopt the latter opinion point out that if one tries to surrender in order to regain control of a situation, one is not really surrendering. Surrender certainly may happen spontaneously, sometimes as a result of spiritual practice such as prayer or meditation, and sometimes seems to happen as a result of extreme exhaustion during a life crisis. It then feels as if something gives way inside the person, sometimes gradually and sometimes instantaneously. Religious conversion experiences, for example, may occur during periods of despair and hopelessness when the sufferer gives up struggling. William James (1958, p. 121) says that the process of surrender is "frequently sudden and automatic, and leaves on the subject an impression that he has been wrought by an external power."

Those who see surrender as a state of mind that can be achieved by effort typically stress preparatory spiritual practices combined with the desire to surrender. These factors are thought to be conducive to surrender. In this camp of those who believe that one may deliberately try to induce surrender, Rosequist and her collaborators (2010) describe the process of "active surrender," a deliberate practice of receptivity and surrender to the sacred. She describes some ways in which patients suffering from cancer are encouraged to actively accept the physical, emotional, and psychological

---

57   It is useful to recall the etymology of the word "suffer," which originates in the Latin verb *ferre*, meaning to carry, and the prefix *"sub,"* or under. That is, suffering means that we bear a weight. In contrast, the word "depression" implies being pressed down. That is, one can suffer or carry a load consciously and meaningfully or one can feel oppressed in a meaningless way.

changes produced by the illness. Patients are taught various techniques of stress reduction and meditation, and they are encouraged to discover their life purpose and identify beliefs which may hinder its achievement. For this approach, spiritual surrender means recognizing the higher value of an apparently negative situation, the experience of seeing oneself in relation to a transcendent reality, or connecting with the sacred as a way of dealing with the existential challenges of the illness.

Surrender in religious traditions

Radical acceptance of suffering, or true surrender, is not dependent on any specific religious tradition or any particular theistic image of God. One is often forced to surrender during a period of liminality (discussed in chapter 9), at which time one has no idea of the outcome, so that surrender requires trust or faith in a larger process. Among religious people, surrender has been shown to reduce the individual's level of stress (Clements et al., 2012). Typically, theistic religious traditions recommend surrender in order to foster spiritual development; the process is often described as "letting go" (Cole et al., 1999). For adherents to these traditions, as William James (1958) pointed out, their religion "makes easy and felicitous what in any case is necessary" (p. 67). Surrender to God is central to Islam, Christianity, and Judaism. In the Hindu tradition, the *Bhagavad Gita* (7:14) teaches that only those who have surrendered to God can become enlightened, able to see beyond the illusion of *maya*, which prevents our realizing the nondual nature of reality—the wisdom to see that there is no distinction between oneself and the universe or oneself and the divine. Taoism teaches the practice of *wu-wei*, which is a kind of action through inaction, meaning that if we allow things to happen naturally, surrendering our need to control what happens, the universe will spontaneously unfold the way it should. Buddhism teaches that we have to let go of the sense that we have a self which is an entity or permanent identity, and let go of attachment to what is transitory. Meditation and mindfulness require surrender of the will to the ongoing flow of experience. Nondual traditions such as Buddhism, Advaita Vedanta, and Taoism teach the existence of a nondual level of reality, a unitary level at which everything and everybody is connected. This philosophy recommends radical acceptance of reality however it manifests itself, without complaining that it is somehow wrong when it is unpleasant. This philosophy assumes that reality is in perfect order the way it is, and whatever happens is part of the intelligent order of the universe, with no need for human judgments, or even the attempt to discover meaning in suffering. From a non-dual point of view, when we declare that something is evil because it will cause suffering, this judgment is a human projection onto the unity nature of reality, which simply is what it is. The nondual approach to suffering therefore suggests radical acceptance of what-is, or whatever is the present reality. I hasten to add that this does not mean passivity or inaction, since one will respond to the situation according to one's conditioning, and it does not mean grudging tolerance or resignation. Radical acceptance means that we embrace the situation because we recognize that there is a transcendent background of which we are a part, which we cannot avoid. Any necessary action will arise out of an attitude of acceptance and not out of resistance, bitterness or anger at the situation. "To the extent that we respond to suffering out of anger or fear, we are in danger of causing more suffering, whereas action that arises out of acceptance reduces friction and allows us to be peaceful internally" (Corbett, 2011, p. 256.) It is important not to use the notion of surrender in a defensive way, to avoid taking necessary action. (The nondual approach to psychotherapy is discussed in more detail in Corbett, 2011.)

Today, the psychotherapist sees many people who have a personal form of spirituality but do not feel a part of any religious tradition. When they suffer, one possible spiritual response for such individuals is to fall back onto trust in a transcendent level of reality which they do not conceptualize in any traditional theistic way—not necessarily in terms of a personal God. The Jungian approach to spirituality is useful for some of these individuals because attention to the manifestations of the transpersonal psyche in dreams, visions, and synchronistic events allows the development of a personal spirituality (Corbett, 2007).

Surrender in psychotherapy

Our western models of psychology and psychotherapy have focused on the development of a strong sense of self or a strong ego, with firm boundaries. This ego is considered to be the subject of experience who decides how to behave, how to defend against anxiety, how to relate to others, and how to order the world and make sense of it. Such an ego is free to make choices and control itself. With good mental health, the sense of self or the ego is fairly self-sufficient and self-aware, but may be fragile to varying degrees in the face of conflicts, relational or attachment failures, or developmental deficits. Traditionally both psychotherapist and patient relate to each other from their own unique ego positions, which seem to be two separate centers of subjectivity. Depending on the therapist's school of thought, the therapeutic goal is to strengthen the self, make the individual more self-aware, less conflicted, more tolerant of painful affective states, better related to others, and so on.

Some of the psychotherapeutic emphasis on the development of a firm ego is the result of our cultural bias towards mastery and control. This preference is partly a function of the historical dominance of a mechanistic, scientific worldview, combined with the rejection of qualities such as surrender which have been considered to be a sign of weakness. Among psychotherapists, some of the preference for mastery and a strong ego seems to have begun with Freud himself, who disliked any kind of surrender, either to his colleagues who suggested innovations or to the world at large. Perhaps because of his distaste for surrender, he insisted on the primacy of rational thought, devalued religion, and was unable to appreciate music. However, he believed that patients must surrender to the transference relationship and to the process of free association. In his 1922 *Group Psychology and the Analysis of the Ego*, he says that by merging with a powerful leader or group, people surrender their autonomy to relieve feelings of helplessness. Similarly, in his 1927 *The Future of an Illusion*, he sees religious surrender as a way of coping with helplessness. Subsequent ego psychology continued the emphasis on the ego's strength, meaning its ability to master internal impulses and cope with the external world.

Gradually, especially since the work of Kohut and more recent relational theorists, we have come to understand that the contents of our mind and the sense of self are derived from a relational, interactive field. The sense of self is not isolated; it is constructed by relationships and it is embedded in a matrix of relationships without which it cannot exist. Relational theorists now emphasize relative symmetry and mutuality in the therapeutic relationship, no longer giving the therapist a privileged position of superior knowledge. Both participants bring their own subjectivities into the therapeutic field and both are affected by it. Many psychoanalytic writers today feel that the primary mechanism for change in psychotherapy is the mutual emotional engagement which occurs between therapist and patient. Sometimes this involves the emotional surrender not just of the patient but also of the therapist (Knight, 2007).

The work of Emmanuel Levinas implies an approach to psychotherapy which is even more radical than these contemporary departures from the classical psychoanalytic approach. Levinas sees the self in a radical light. For him, the other person, or what he calls "the other," evades any possible theoretical category that we might try to impose—the other cannot be represented conceptually. Furthermore, the self has responsibilities that go far beyond itself; the self is not only constituted by the other but is also summoned to be totally responsible for the other—including people we do not know. These responsibilities are more important than the self's own being. As he puts it: "The word 'I' means to be answerable for everything and everyone" (Levinas, 1996, p. 90). The self is actually born out of its ethical responsibility to the other; our identity emerges as a hostage to this responsibility and not from our ability to be self-reflexive. Whereas traditionally the ego may be altruistic, caring for itself while also being kind to the other out of compassion, Levinas is more radical; he believes one is responsible for the other to the extent that one should substitute oneself for the other, if necessary sacrificing oneself (Bernasconi, 2002).

Sacrifice (discussed in more detail in chapter 3) is a form of surrender. The patient in psychotherapy is expected to make sacrifices in terms of time, money, effort, and emotional investment in the therapy, and must surrender to the transference. Less often mentioned are the sacrifices made by the therapist. It has long been understood that the psychotherapist must not gratify personal needs at the expense of the patient—these personal needs must be sacrificed. There are few other occupations in which one is daily subjected to the pain, frustration, anger, rejection, helplessness, and seduction of another person. The therapist must surrender to all this, just as the patient must surrender to the process of psychotherapy with its unknowable outcome. The psychoanalyst Emmanuel Ghent believes that therapeutic transformation emerges through this process of surrender, and "there is something like a universal need, wish or longing" (1999, p. 218) for surrender, which may assume many forms. Ghent is one of those theorists who, like Winnicott and Kohut, believe there is a unique core self which is distorted in early development; he believes this self desires a state of transcendence, in which it may surrender fully with no defensive armor. This true self yearns for freedom and exposure of itself, but its drive for surrender is corrupted in development when the caretaker is impinging or intrusive, whereupon submission happens instead of surrender. When we submit, we are simply resigned to the other, who has all the power and bullies the self; at best, submission is only an expedient adaptation. In true surrender, Ghent suggests, we discover the reality of the other, we respond with what is real about ourselves, and we discover a unity with other living beings. The direction of true surrender is the discovery of one's identity and wholeness. Surrender is a process of self-emptying which produces personal growth and transformation. He suggests that we have a deeply buried longing for something in the environment that will allow us to let go of our false self, in Winnicott's sense of this phrase. Ghent draws on Winnicott's belief that psychotherapy offers the hope of a new opportunity for an unfreezing of the true self, for its birth or re-birth.

As Alvin Dueck (2007) points out, both Levinas and Ghent share the goals of self-emptying and surrender, and the sacrifice of the traditional bounded Cartesian ego. Ghent however believes there is a real self, an ontologically real identity, and surrender is for the sake of this self, while Levinas opposes any ideology that proposes an ontological form of the self—he would therefore be unhappy with Jung's notion of the transpersonal Self. Furthermore, while Ghent views submission to the power of the other in a negative light, for Levinas, one only has a self when one loses oneself to the other. Levinas would say that as therapists we should sacrifice ourselves for the patient as expiation for the suffering to which he has been exposed, for which we are responsible even though we did not actually commit the abuse ourselves. Dueck points out that Ghent's focus on surrender and sacrifice makes an important contribution within psychotherapy, but Ghent remains within traditional western assumptions about the notion of the self as an ontological entity and the importance of a firm ego. The other as the source of ethical behavior is not stressed as it is in Levinas. However, Dueck believes that Levinas's position "undermines the entire concept of relationship as a tool and client as a project." This happens because the Levinasian therapist "is persecuted and accused. He/she cannot retreat to a safe inner sanctum removed from all others...the therapist stands accused without even knowing why" (2007, p. 613). The therapist is troubled by the other, made uncomfortable and speechless—; the walls of his ego are breached and his sense of identity is sacrificed, because the therapist assumes responsibility for the other. The therapist substitutes her own sense of identity for the sake of the other, and sacrifices a commitment to self-sufficiency on behalf of the other. This is a process of self-emptying, of carrying the guilt and sins of the other and the burden of responsibility for the oppression of the patient by others.

Particularly if one works relationally, there are moments in psychotherapy when both participants—not just the patient—must surrender some of their defenses and be exposed to each other. This is a humbling situation for both participants in which all kinds of fears may emerge: fear of vulnerability, fear of too much closeness, fears of being too much or not enough, and fears of rejection and other painful affective states. The therapeutic acknowledgment and exploration of this material is extremely helpful. This kind of healthy psychotherapeutic surrender contrasts with sadistic domination and masochistic submission that is mutually damaging. This latter situation may be the result of the relational pattern of either participant in psychotherapy, and it may lead to a therapeutic impasse (Ghent 1999).

Hidas (1981) points out that surrender many not produce instant transcendence, but could open the door to "various levels of darkness and purgation reflective of a spiritual journey" (p. 28). It is therefore important that the therapist have some awareness of the patient's spiritual path, and not insist on the strengthening of the sense of self in a person who is trying to let go of it, for example in a Buddhist context. In other words, surrender or letting go in the spiritual sense may conflict with some of the traditional goals of psychotherapy which stress the development of personal power and taking charge of one's life.

There are times in one's life when one simply has to withdraw or pull back for the sake of safety or in order to conserve one's energies for the future. During a difficult time, one might for example consult the *I Ching* and receive hexagram 33, which clearly advises seclusion or retreat in order to advance at a better time—what the French refer to as *reculer pour mieux sauter,* taking a step back in order to make a better jump. Or, hexagram 39 advises pulling back and not acting when facing an obstacle. Much depends here on the type of therapy to which one is committed; rather than trying to strengthen the ego, Jung is one example of many writers who stresses the need for the ego to surrender to the transpersonal Self or to the Inner Voice or to powers beyond the ego. Suffering cannot be transformed until it is accepted. One can tell that this has happened because the atmosphere around the person seems to lighten; there is a sense that the person is internally more free.

Surrender is a common practice among the world's mystical traditions, based on the idea that if we let go of or empty the individual ego, we will experience union with or a deeper relationship with the divine. For this purpose we have to abandon individual will and desire and be totally receptive. Our will and preferences, or a focus on ego-consciousness, are often seen as the limitations which prevent our connection to the transpersonal dimension.

We can only find the divine Self if we surrender the personal self. In the Zen tradition, the 7th century third Patriarch Seng-T'san says that: "The great Way is not difficult for those who have no preferences. Let go of wanting and avoiding, and everything will be perfectly clear." Of course the problem is that whether we are talking about faith in the theistic God or faith in the teachings of the Buddha, such an attitude of renunciation of one's own will requires complete trust in the Absolute, whose ultimate purpose—if there is one—is hidden.

For Jung, the process of individuation, or the full development of the personality, requires that the ego surrender to the transpersonal levels of the psyche, or the Self. We see this most clearly when intense suffering occurs, often produced by a life crisis, and the ego is rendered helpless, but even the day-to-day process of individuation invariably involves suffering, as the ego is forced to sacrifice aspects of itself in the service of psychological development. Jung believes that as we individuate, the ego gradually realizes that it is "the object of a supraordinate subject": that is, we realize that there is Something that is aware of us, whereupon the ego has to let go of its sense of centrality. It is as if we have to sacrifice our cherished illusions about ourselves to allow something deeper to emerge (Jung, CW 7, p. 265). For an addict, this might require the proverbial "hitting bottom." Facing this level of surrender allows the necessary development of consciousness or spiritual awakening, albeit after much suffering. Jung recognizes that not everyone is capable of the necessary surrender (CW 16, p. 82). In psychotherapeutic practice, this sacrifice of the ego is sometimes symbolized in dreams of dismemberment or death.

Surrender vs. submission

It is important to distinguish surrender from submission, which has the connotations of giving up power and authority to another who dominates the individual. Ghent (1990) suggests that submission leads to an atrophy of one's sense of self, so that one becomes a puppet under the control of another person. Submission therefore sounds forced, and it is damaging or destructive in relationships, whereas surrender in the sense I am using the word is a way of sacrificing one's own importance for the sake of something larger. But I must also acknowledge pathological forms of surrender, as we seen in the case of masochistic suffering.

Masochistic suffering

There is a danger that radical acceptance of suffering, rather than being an authentic spiritual practice or a process that is important for the development of the personality, will become confused with neurotic masochism. I should preface this section by noting that the term "masochism" has been controversial because of fears that it could be a misogynistic way of blaming women for societal failures. Partly for this reason it has been excluded from the DSM. Nevertheless, in spite of the historical gender bias in this area, it remains true that there are both men and women who are chronically self-defeating for unconscious reasons. In traditional psychoanalytic theory, masochism implies an unconscious need for punishment based on a sense of guilt, which leads to unconsciously self-inflicted suffering by means of recurrent accidents, financial losses, and destructive relationships. Intersubjective theorists believe that when early trauma has interfered with the development of the self, masochistic behavior attempts to hold together the sense of self when it seems to be crumbling (Stolorow et al. 1980). Whatever its etiology, the masochistic character is characterized by chronic suffering, complaining, self-depreciating attitudes, and sometimes the unconscious wish to torture others with one's pain. Importantly, the term "masochism" does not imply that the person enjoys pain and suffering. Freud noticed that sometimes masochism occurs in a non-sexual way, so he coined the term "moral masochism" to describe the idea of suffering in the service of a more important goal, some greater good, rather than in the service of sexuality. There is a purpose behind masochistic behavior because there is some other kind of relief which is being pursued (consciously or unconsciously) that makes the suffering worthwhile, such as the feeling that being hurt is the price one has to pay for a relationship. Behavior which looks like moral masochism is not necessarily pathological if it means that we risk our life or well-being in the service of a greater value—that is partly why it is not clear whether religious martyrs are masochists. Some moral masochists are a little grandiose or feel morally superior to their abusers, or they are contemptuous of people who cannot endure difficulty with grace—then, masochism is a way of enhancing self-esteem, as in "I can take it." Whereas depressive characters feel that they are bad, masochistic people project their own sense of badness in a way that makes the abuser seem morally inferior. Unlike depressive characters, masochists easily feel resentment about the way they are treated because they do not feel they deserve poor treatment.

Masochistic people are self-sacrificing; they project their own needs onto others and then take care of those others (a defense known as reversal). They tend to complain about being a victim of fate and of malevolent people. They are self-effacing and overly compliant when it comes to their own needs. The emotional relief that is thereby obtained is greater than the pain they suffer. Masochism is important in psychotherapy partly because it tends to be confused with depression and partly because the patient's unconscious reluctance to get better can produce resistance to improvement.

There are various developmental sources of masochistic behavior. The earliest attempt at explanation was Freud's; he had difficulty explaining why people would act in ways that hurt themselves, until he saw masochism as an expression of the death instinct, an idea which has met with limited success because it seems too metaphysical. Masochistic behavior may occur among children who learn that one way to get attention or care is to suffer. Or the child has to sacrifice his own well-being in order to stay connected to a parent—suffering is then the price of attachment and relationship. Accordingly, whereas depressive people feel there is no one there for them, the masochistic patient feels that if he constantly shows the therapist how much he is suffering, he will get what he needs.

Masochistic surrender is a problematic form of surrender. Ghent (1990) believes that surrender does play a part in some instances of masochism, but masochistic submission to the power of another person is a perversion of true surrender. In fact, submission and masochism are the antitheses of true surrender, which means to let go of defensive barriers or one's persona, and expressing one's true self. He suggests that masochism is testimony to the urgent need for some buried part of the personality to be exhumed.

Behind the masochistic behavior lies the deeper yearning to be reached rather than isolated, to see the other and be seen and known in a safe environment, which would allow the masochist to feel real. Unfortunately, the parents of the future masochist were critical of the child's true self and they suppressed the child's self-expression, so the masochist feels that to expose his true self will be unacceptable to others. One of the major problems for masochistic people is a fear of their own affective experience, especially feelings of vitality and joy, which have to be sacrificed because they would have challenged the patient's original tie to his or her parents. Suffering is then the only way to relate to others without risking loss. As a cautionary note, I should point out that acceptance of suffering for the sake of a greater good is not necessarily pathological. At times we may have to suffer for the sake of something more worthy than our own comfort, or risk our own life for another person. (I discuss the issue of whether altruism, or giving oneself to another person or a cause, is authentic or defensive in chapter 5). Rather than describe this behavior as masochistic, one may willingly accept suffering because one realizes that it is somehow necessary for one's development, or it has meaning in term of a larger process.

In this context, it has been recognized for some time that being a psychotherapist may have a masochistic aspect to it, part of the emotional price paid for being a therapist, and it is important to understand one's own tendencies in this area. The therapist's masochism can appear in the countertransference in the form of discouragement with the work of psychotherapy as a whole, with intense boredom, or with masochistic responses to the patient's hostility or excessive demands. The therapist is the object of intense feelings as he or she helps others to fulfill their destinies. Ghent therefore suggests that surrender is a deep underlying motive for some psychotherapists.

Finally, I would like to mention a possible link between masochism and religious observance. Rosemary Gordon (1991) sees masochism as the shadow side of the human need to worship and venerate something which transcends one's personal being. She believes that there is a thin line between masochism and surrendering oneself to something beyond oneself. By scrutinizing what a person worships, we may be able to discern what the person needs to struggle with. She feels that masochism underpins religious rituals, practices such as fasting, and other forms of deprivation and asceticism which deny physical and emotional needs. For her, the physical postures in religious rituals which communicate submission and humility, such as bowing, kneeling, and prostration, are all motivated by masochistic obedience. She suggests that when suffering, submission, and self-abasement are the primary objective, rather than only a means of connecting with the holy, we are dealing with masochism rather than authentic religious surrender.

An excursion into etymology

The word "suffer" comes from two Latin roots: *sub*, meaning under, and *ferre*, meaning to carry or bear. Hence our sense that suffering means to carry a burden. But interestingly, *ferre* is also the root of the word "fertile," which means to be bear fruit or to be prolific, suggesting that suffering can produce something. When Jesus says "suffer little children to come unto me" (Mark 10: 14) he means "allow them to come to me," because in its older usage the word "suffering" has the connotation not only of distress but also of allowing or experiencing something, and in early English this word implied enduring hardship patiently. But to allow suffering or to suffer patiently requires acceptance, which may be why the word "suffer" no longer carries the connotation of patience—it is no longer culturally fashionable because we want to eradicate suffering.

11

SUFFERING, FATE AND DESTINY

Does suffering have to happen?

When working psychotherapeutically with suffering people, the question of fate and destiny arises when people ask themselves or the therapist whether their suffering had to happen, or whether it could have been avoided. A great deal of philosophy and literature takes up this question. A famous 9th century Sufi teaching story known as "The Appointment in Samarra" is a good example (Shah, 1993). The student of a famous Sufi teacher in Baghdad was sitting in the corner of an inn one day when he heard two figures talking. He realized that one of them was the Angel of Death, who was telling his companion that he had several calls to make in Baghdad during the next three weeks. The student became terrified that he might be one of those the Angel would visit. He decided that if he kept away from Baghdad, he could not be touched by death, so he hired the fastest horse available and raced towards the distant town of Samarra. Meanwhile Death met the Sufi teacher and asked him the whereabouts of this student. The teacher replied that the student should be in Baghdad, in contemplation. The Angel of death was surprised, "because he is on my list...I have to collect him in four weeks' time at Samarra, of all places" (p. 191). Clearly, in the attempt to avoid his fate, the student has raced towards it. Could the student have avoided the Angel if he had not gone to Samarra? Paradoxically, the student's own volition participated in his fate. This is a good example of the notion that we meet our destiny on the road we take to avoid it. Our volition may make a difference to what happens to us. William James (1949) pointed out that faith in the outcome of a situation may be the only thing that makes it happen. He gives the example of a mountaineer who needs to leap across a gap; if he doubts himself he is less likely to succeed. He must believe in what he has to do.

At other times, events take a course over which we have no control at all, as in the case of the caterpillar who looked up and saw a butterfly flying by. The caterpillar thought to himself: "You'll never get me up in one of those things." However, becoming a butterfly is the inevitable destiny of the caterpillar. Nevertheless, most people in our culture would resist the idea that an inexorable fate is in charge of our lives. This idea would threaten our sense of autonomy, and the idea of fate as a transpersonal power behind the scenes of our lives seems too irrational or superstitious. Nevertheless, when suffering strikes, people often find themselves asking whether what has happened is their fate.

In general, for many writers, fate is about those aspects of our lives that we do not choose and cannot control, events which shape our lives, while destiny is about the future but requires effort and choices. In this area, we may feel two things at the same time; we are affected by forces outside our control (social, developmental, and biological) and at the same time we can control our own behavior based on reason and foresight. We are free to choose what we do, but we are also subject to the laws of nature; both these propositions may be true even if they seem to contradict each other.[58]

There are historical distinctions in the way the words fate and destiny have been used by philosophers and other writers. As a rule, when people talk about fate it has rather a negative connotation, meaning something unpleasant happens which we do not choose and cannot control, or which makes us feel powerless. Doob (1998) suggests that this may be because it reminds people of words like fatalism, fateful, and fatal—which all sound unpleasant.

Fate often appears as an unwelcome event that causes suffering, although unexpected pleasant events can also feel fated. It is true that much is determined before we have any possibility of choice, although at times people speak as if their fate is in their own hands. After all, if there is an inexorable fate, what use is good behavior and personal effort?

In Latin the word for fate is *fatum*, which means an oracle, or literally "that which is spoken," since it is the past participle of the Latin verb *fari*, meaning to speak. The English words fairy is also derived from the Latin *fatum*. The French word for fairy, *une fée*, has the same root. The word "destiny" sounds more pleasant than fate, although it too can be associated

---

58   In his *Critique of Pure Reason*, Kant called this the antinomy of freedom. Antinomies are apparently mutually incompatible statements neither of which can be rejected.

with irrevocable events that may be damaging. Destiny comes from the Latin *destinare,* meaning to secure or make firm, and also to intend, as in to have a purpose or design. This word is the root of the English word destination, suggesting a plan and a direction, or that destiny is about the individual's development. Some dictionaries find the etymology of the word destiny in Latin roots (*de-stare*) meaning to stand apart, so that destiny means what makes one unique from others.

Destiny is often used to mean that we have a future which we are trying to achieve. It is often thought that we can do something about our destiny by making the right choices, so compared to fate, destiny suggests a more active role in determining what happens to us (Bargdill, 2006). Some authors like to think we can transform blind fate into conscious destiny (Bollas 1991), because they think of fate as the presence of internal constraints which hamper the development of one's true self. Bollas believes that a person who feels fated is someone who experiences reality as not "conducive to the fulfillment of his inner idiom" (p. 33), here meaning the person's distinct character and style. To talk of one's destiny can also mean to consciously acknowledge what has happened, creating a coherent, meaningful story out of it. He suggests that while fate emerges from the word of the god, as in an oracle, destiny is the chain of events that the oracle announces. Destiny is therefore about action that we take, a preordained path that we may or may not be able to fulfill—it is more positive than fate, which he sees as "a feeling of despair to influence the course of one's life" (p. 41). He believes there is a kind of destiny drive that tries to express the true self in Winnicott's sense of one's inherited potentials and one's psychological and bodily reality—a notion quite similar to the idea of individuation in Jung. The Jungian writer John Sanford (1995) also sees fate as inevitable, while we may or may not fulfill our destiny.

The idea of fate is found in many mythological systems. Here it is important to say that we cannot dismiss mythological imagery as nothing but the products of archaic cultures. From a Jungian point of view, mythopoetic imagery is an expression of a deep level of the psyche, and although this dimension is covered over by modern thinking it is still active. The language of myth is not literally true but it speaks psychological and spiritual truth; it is a language of the soul. In ancient Greece, fate and destiny were not distinguished; they were expressed by the same word: *moira.* The Greeks believed the gods were in charge, but one's character also plays a part in one's destiny—there is an interaction between character and destiny, as if character affects how we live out our destiny. There were two ways one could learn about one's fate: from the three Fates or through an oracle. The Fates were three mythological goddesses called the *Moirai*, (or sometimes the Erinyes) who determine what kind of life the person will have. (*Moros* means a portion or allotment.) The Fates also punished people who had escaped human justice, or one who slighted a god. Even the gods could not change what the *Moirai* decree. They sometimes appeared to a baby's parents at birth and announce its fate. Clotho the spinner spins the thread of one's life and its important aspects; Lachesis determines its length; Atropos cuts the thread of life at its end, choosing the manner of death. In Freud's (1913) discussion of the 3 fates, he suggests that Clotho represents one's innate constitution, which cannot be changed. Lachesis he believes represents accidental or chance events which either allow us to fulfill our destiny or prevent us from doing so, while Atropos represents the inevitability of death. In Norse mythology the Norns are female creatures who rule the destiny of gods and humans. The Norns arrive when a child is born in order to determine his or her future; some of them are good and protective, some malevolent.

In other words, the mythic intuition is that there is something besides heredity at work—some archetypal background, an innate natural law which is represented mythologically as one's allotment in life. As well as the Moirai, for the Greeks, the mythological goddess *Ananke* or Necessity personified a kind of inevitability, limitation, or even servitude to a power that one could not escape; Necessity was like a yoke around one's neck. The Moirai were the children of Necessity, so that Fate and necessity are bound together.

The Greeks thought that fate was a kind of universal moral order; the Moirai deal justice when we behave badly or transgress the limits of necessity. Much Greek tragedy was concerned with the problem of hubris, or lack of humility before the gods, which leads to a tragic retribution by the fates. Hubris means one is overstepping the boundaries that the fates have set for one. Another child of Ananke was one's *daimon*, a kind of determining force which shapes one's life or drives one to do something. The Romans also believed strongly in fate—in the *Aeneid* the gods are running everything in the background, and the only thing that humans can do is try to respond.

In Greek mythology, the fates are female. Liz Greene' (1984) suggests there is an association between the feminine and fate because the world begins with mother, who is the initial arbiter of life and death. Mythology always connects the feminine with life, death, the earth, and the body, and fate is experienced in the body. So our instincts such as sexuality and aggression are all part of our fate.

Christianity preferred the notion of divine providence to the idea of the three fates in the ancient Greek sense, since they seem to be associated with doom, but God's providence has the connotation of benevolence. Free will became important in Christianity because if one is fated, the Church and its moral teachings are irrelevant. Judaism has a sense of fate as a divine decree; the lot of each person is inscribed in a book at the beginning of the new year. In the East, the nearest equivalent to the western idea of fate is the idea of karma. The Sanskrit word "karma" means an act or deed. The idea is often misunderstood to imply moral retribution for one's actions, although it is actually morally neutral, and simply refers to a process of action and reaction; what we have sown, we will reap in this life or another. It is therefore not entirely fatalistic, because our actions in the present create what happens to us in the future. Most Hindus believe that karma occurs for the purpose of the evolution and growth of the soul, which reincarnates again and again, so that one brings the soul's karmic history into each lifetime. From this perspective, if we look at events in isolation, the idea of fate makes no sense, because we all start life with different advantages and disadvantages. The idea of fate makes more sense if we accept the idea of reincarnation, which was abolished from Christianity in the 6th century CE.

Both in the East and in the West, the idea of fate has been connected to the development of astrology, the idea that the movement of planetary bodies corresponds to events on earth, a mythology which suggests that human lives are not the product of chance but of an ordered cosmos. (Incidentally, if we really did not believe in fate we would not be interested in methods of divination such as the *I Ching* or the Tarot or astrology, but these are popular. Some of the attacks on astrology may be due to an unconscious resistance to the idea of fate, or to fear of fate.) Belief in fate may have arisen with the development of agriculture, because fate seemed to determine the success or failure of crops. Perhaps the mythology of fate in the hands of transpersonal powers developed because it was preferable to seeing the world as entirely random and chaotic.

In antiquity, if one wanted to know one's fate, one could consult an oracle, which mediated between gods and humans. Typically however the oracle gave ambiguous answers to questions, and seekers often misinterpreted them. The story of King Croesus of Lydia describes his asking the Delphic oracle to tell him if he should attack the Persian army led by King Cyrus; the oracle told him that a great empire would be destroyed if he did so. Croesus assumed that would be the Persian Empire, but it turned out to be his. Typically the seeker interprets an oracle in a way that reveals a flaw in the seeker, such as arrogance. Apparently, human beings are not equipped to handle knowledge about the future: to know one's fate may lead to over-confidence or poor planning, or it causes too much anxiety about the future.

Psychological contributions to the question of fate

Freud discusses the feeling that one is fated to behave in a certain way in his 1920 *Beyond the Pleasure Principle,* where he introduces the issue of a "fate neurosis." He writes that some people give the impression of being pursued by a malignant fate, as if they were possessed by a demonic power, but for psychoanalysis this "fate" is actually the result of early infantile experiences which unconsciously drive behavior. Fate neurosis means that one attributes every misfortune to an unavoidable fate, which the individual has in fact unconsciously instigated because of guilt and an unconscious need for punishment. Even when the subject appears to be a passive victim of fate, the painful events that befall him are due to a repetition compulsion which makes him constantly repeat a painful experience from childhood, in an attempt to master the trauma. The person has an unconscious wish for difficulties (Freud called it "unpleasure") which seem to come at him from the surroundings but which in fact he has unconsciously arranged. (See also a discussion of Helene Deutsche's work on the "hysterical fate neurosis," in Kaplan, 1984.) If the therapist can discover the unconscious organizing principle that is driving the behavior, the individual might be able to stop it. In a sense then, the purpose of psychotherapy is to allow conscious choice instead of unconscious fate—to the extent that one believes that one's fate is in one's own hands.

The psychoanalyst Carlo Strenger (1998) believes that some people feel that the circumstances of their lives prevent them from living a worthwhile life; they are denied choices because of a pathological sense of fatedness, as if their lives are governed by necessity outside their control. Their lives feel unbearably limited by fate, and they seek a sense of authorship, the wish to live according to their own nature and desires, the wish to re-create themselves. He points out the enormous suffering of those who protest against fate, who cannot accept the limitations of their life. He suggests that no therapeutic approach may be able to soften such pain and rage, which is at least in part an effort to protect the true or core self. This work begs the question of whether the unfolding of the true self would invariably produce a life of happiness in the face of fate. As a rule, most psychoanalytic work on fate suggests that the belief that one's life is fated indicates psychopathology. Unlike Jungian authors, traditional psychoanalysts do not admit the possibility that the individual has a destiny that is transpersonally determined.

Jungian approaches to fate

Jung believed that the personality has a *telos* or goal that is given by the transpersonal Self. Thus, what happens to us as fate is not random or accidental; fate is the action of transpersonal forces. As he puts it, fate may "contrive some annoying incident for the sole purpose of bullying our Simple Simon of an ego-consciousness into the way he should go." (CW 9, i, p. 227). Or, when fate is opposed to the ego, "it is difficult not to feel a certain 'power' in it, whether divine or infernal. The man who submits to his fate calls it the will of God; the man who puts up a hopeless and exhausting fight is more apt to see the devil in it" (CW 12, p. 30, note 17).

In terms of his own life, Jung writes that from early on he had a sense of destiny, "as if my life was assigned to me by fate and had to be fulfilled" (1965, p. 48).

Overall however, Jung's attitude to fate seems to have been mixed. On one hand he writes that the creativity and will of the ego is responsible for its fate, because if we do not believe we are the makers of our fate we will not put our whole strength into life (1936/1988). However, he always acknowledges a transpersonal force behind the scenes which may conflict with the ego, and no matter how rational we are, "it is a fundamental error to subject our own fate at all costs to our will," because it cannot be shown that life and fate are in accord with reason (CW 7, pp. 48-49). Accordingly he also writes of fate as an impersonal process, consisting of events which happen to the ego that seem to be the effects of the transpersonal Self. It is as if we are moved about like a figure on a chessboard by an invisible player who decides the game of fate (CW7, p. 161). His attitude to fate seems to have been influenced by the idea of karma, a kind of memory trace or disposition in the soul that results from actions in previous lives (CW14, pp. 293-301). In his 1932 lectures on Kundalini Yoga, he suggests that archetypal images might be the psychological equivalent of these memory traces or *samskaras*. Jung (CW 7, p. 77, n. 1) says that the theory of karma is essential to an understanding of the concept of the archetype.

We see Jung's respect for the power of fate in his dream seminar of 1930, where, talking about relationships, he notes that "when one treats those cases one learns an extraordinary tolerance for the manifold ways of fate. People who have to live a certain fate get neurotic if you hinder them from living it...these things have a certain purpose" (Jung 1938/1984, p. 450). He notes that even behind a neurosis is the individual's destiny; in fact, "It is the man without *amor fati* [59] who is neurotic" (CW 17, para. 313). That is, he believes one has to recognize and love one's fate, and to deny it is to be neurotic. Here, Jung was influenced by Nietzsche's frequent use of this Latin phrase in order to unequivocally affirm life. For Nietzsche, fate means a combination of necessity and freedom. Jung's attitude contrasts vividly with Freud's suggestion that to feel fated is neurotic. Jung believed that "when an inner situation is not made conscious, it happens outside, as fate" (9,ii, p. 71). This means that the unconscious can be experienced in the form of an outer event that corresponds (synchronistically) to one's internal psychological structures. He believed that if we are not conscious, the unconscious directs our life and we call it fate—this idea is reminiscent of Freud's notion, except that for Jung the unconscious is much more than repressed childhood material.

In his essay titled "Psychotherapists or the Clergy", Jung (CW 11) asks what would have happened if Saul (St. Paul of the Christian tradition) had allowed himself to be talked out of his trip to Damascus, since on this journey Saul had a powerful conversion experience when Christ spoke to him (Acts 9: 4). The development of Christianity and perhaps western civilization would have taken a different turn. Jung implies here that Saul had to take the road to Damascus, because it was his destiny to do so. We sometimes hear some kind of adventure proposed in psychotherapy, when the therapist might have misgivings about what may turn out to be a misadventure.

For classical Jungians, the Self arranges what happens to us so that it is in accord with our destiny. However, Jung's notion that the Self gives the personality a specific *telos* or goal is controversial. If the idea is correct, it means that our suffering is somehow necessary to achieve this end, and we

---

59   Amor fati is a Latin phrase meaning the love of one's fate, or an embrace and affirmation of the situations in one's life.

should be careful to try to understand the intention of our suffering even as we try to alleviate it. In this view, life provides just the experiences we need for our individuation process, even though these may be painful. The implication is that the unfolding of the personality has a definite purpose, which may be that the Self is trying to realize a particular expression of itself within the individual personality, and arranges the circumstances of the individual's life accordingly. This is the position of classical Jungians such as Whitmont, (2007) who believe that the cooperation of the ego is necessary for the realization of one's destiny, within the limits of the ego's capacity, while realizing that we do not control the outcome. He uses the analogy of the way we use the wind while sailing. The wind, like the pressure of the archetype, is impersonal; it moves the boat, but the sailor must use it properly to maintain a course. The wind is analogous to the spirit; the ego is trying to adjust the sails. Using this metaphor, one way the therapist can assist in the discovery of meaning is to ask where a particular situation is leading the person, how it is changing the course of his or her life.

An important consequence of the Jungian approach to symptoms is that it allows the therapist to ask the patient: "Where is this problem taking you?" If it is true that the personality has a *telos*, we must embrace what happens to us because it is part of our archetypal purpose. Painful events that produce suffering are manifestations of that destiny. In other words, suffering steers us in a particular direction that we would otherwise not have taken. The classical example of this is the wounded healer; typically the future shaman suffers a prolonged, mysterious illness which eventually resolves, and in the meantime the shaman develops spiritually and is able to help others out of his own wound. He or she did not know that was his or her destiny.

Existentialist approaches

Psychotherapists with an existentialist orientation take the position that we are free and responsible for working towards our true potential, even though there is much we have not chosen and that cannot be changed. We must acknowledge the givens and make choices that allow us to live life as well as possible. Some existentialists believe we can choose to rebel against the dominant social forces, and we always have the ability to choose our attitude towards a situation. Rollo May defines destiny as "the pattern of limits and talents that constitutes the 'givens' in life...we can choose how we shall respond" (1981, p. 89). The givens of life are things like the times of birth and death, our genes, race, etc., and our culture, family, language, and so on. For him, fate means events over which we have no control, which cannot be changed; destiny is what is created out of what was given, so it can be affected by choice.

It seems that there are times when fate just cannot be avoided, as we see in the story of Oedipus. He tries to avoid what the oracle tells him—that he will kill his father and marry his mother. He leaves home because he assumes the oracle is referring to his adoptive parents, Polybus and Merope; he does not realize that the prediction refers to his biological parents, Laius and Jocasta. Trying to avoid his fate, he leaves the home of his adoptive parents and unknowingly meets his fate in the process. Fate makes him meet and kill Laius at a crossroad, without realizing he has killed his biological father, and he marries Jocasta without realizing she is his mother. This theme of inevitability also occurs in fairy tales such as Sleeping Beauty. A King invites 12 fairies to the christening celebration of his daughter, but a 13th fairy is not invited, and in a rage she curses the new-born baby, saying she will prick her finger on a spindle and die. Another fairy changes the curse from death to sleep. To ward off fate, the King orders that all spindles be removed from the kingdom. Exploring the palace as a teenager, the girl finds an old woman spinning flax, and the girl pricks her finger when she tries to spin. (In this context it is worth remembering Dieckmann's [1971] idea that there is often an uncanny resemblance between the theme of a child's favorite fairy tale and the subsequent course of the individual's life, as if the fairy tale announced his or her fate.)

For the spiritually inclined, the idea of fate as a transpersonal power that moves us in a particular direction has important implications. It implies that we suffer when there is a discrepancy between our true path in life (our vocation—*vide infra*) and what we are doing at the moment. Ideally we consciously conform to our fate, which means the ego has to give up the need for power and control. True power has to be held but rarely deployed.[60]

The notion that suffering is necessary to move the personality towards a particular goal is challenging, for many reasons. To see child abuse as "necessary" for the development of the personality in a particular direction raises difficult ethical – not to mention metaphysical – questions. The idea

---

60   That is why Jesus refused the devil's offer to prove his power (Luke 4, 1-13). Unless used with great discretion, the use of power leads to resistance and conflict. The will to power is an enemy of spiritual development. Only humility and love can deal with the ego's power drive.

that the personality has a specific destiny or goal implies that not only are we pushed from the past by developmental factors, we are also pulled towards a future which has not yet happened in time and space but which exists as a potential, perhaps at some other level of reality. This would mean that ordinary cause-and-effect is not the only process at work in our lives. Whitmont (2007) points to the way time works at the quantum level to justify this argument, because there is a debate among quantum physicists about the possibility of backwards causation, and it is possible that at the non-local level events in the past, present, and future are correlated with each other. However, it may be a conceptual mistake to assume that such quantum phenomena operate at the macro level. In summary, the notion that the individual has an essential destiny can only operate as a belief that we hold, a kind of personal myth that helps us deal with suffering by assuming that it must be the way it is. There are times when a situation demands action and other times when contemplation is more appropriate, but there are still others when one simply has to accept a certain fate as one's task in life. One's unique opportunity then lies in the way one bears the burden, as Frankl believed (1959).

Vocation

Some people suffer a great deal because they cannot find their true vocation in life, and this may become an issue in psychotherapy. Jung suggests that "[t]rue personality always has vocation, which acts like the law of God from which there is no escape." He refers to the importance of "fidelity to the law of one's own being," (CW 17, p. 174-175) which is preferable to a collective mode of life. In his words: "Personality is Tao"; that is, there is an "undiscovered vein within us" that is like "a flow of water that moves irresistibly to its goal" (p. 186). Our vocation should be a way in which we express our essential nature in the outer world. The important point for Jung is that we are *given* a vocation; it is a calling from the Self in the literal sense of the word. The biblical story of Jonah illustrates what happens if the call of the Self is rejected. Jonah is called by God to go to Nineveh to call the people to repentance, but he tries to escape his destiny by running away to sea. A great storm arises, and his shipmates discover that he is avoiding the will of God, so they throw him overboard, where he is swallowed by a whale. He finally ends up in Nineveh anyway. In other words, if we refuse the call we get there the hard way.

An important function of psychotherapy is to assist in the discovery of the individual's true vocation, which if Jung is correct, is part of the destiny of the individual. A well-known component of the mid-life period is sadness as a result of life-long attention to a useful career rather than the discovery of a true calling. At first this sounds as if it were a purely secular problem. But although they may overlap, a calling is not the same as a useful career, which one may train for without much passion. A true vocation can be seen as divinely given, as part of the spiritual destiny of the individual. This inner voice is often muffled and hard to hear, because of layers of social and family insistence on following a conventional path in life. However, "the law of one's own being" can be thought of as a spiritual blueprint for the development of the personality, and not merely a result of the chance interaction of genes and the environment.

In the discovery and mirroring of the individual's vocation, the therapist has to be conscious of the possibility of inflation; a powerful sense of vocation is found in characters like Hitler as well as in Gandhi, and it is a common feature of paranoid delusional states. However, it is possible to distinguish between a pseudo-calling based on a self-important need to be dominant, and an authentic following of the prompting of the Self. The need to be important is a defense, an attempt at supporting an enfeebled sense of self driven by feelings of vulnerability, shame, and inadequacy, and does not take into account the needs of others. An authentic calling feels more like an internal conviction, a task to which one is devoted, an unexpected, internal source of creativity, and sometimes a need to serve others, but it does not lead to messianic feelings of special election and privilege.

Fate and synchronicity

Synchronicity is Jung's (1969) term for the meaningful coincidence of an event in the physical world which coincides with the subject's psychological state. The inner and outer events do not cause each other, but they are related by a common meaning. For example, a person dreams of an event such as a death which happens in physical reality at the same time. Synchronistic events blur our usual boundaries between the physical world and the psyche, as if the inner and outer worlds are part of a unitary continuum, suggesting an acausal, transpersonal level of order that expresses itself both physically and psychologically. A common example is the "chance meeting"; a person looking for a job synchronistically meets someone looking for his exact skills.

Synchronistic events of this kind may be life altering. They often seem to have a quality that suggests they are "meant to be," as if something both incomprehensible and fateful is at work behind the scenes. Perhaps this is why synchronistic events seem to occur more frequently on occasions such as births, deaths, and other major life events. Needless to say, the skeptic will assume that we are in a heightened emotional state at such times, and the need to assign meaning to what is no more than a coincidence may simply reflect our anxiety and need for order. But for many people such "chance" events are evidence of a deeper reality that affects the course of our lives.

Some of our emphasis on developmental theory seems to be an attempt to make life predictable, but life is unpredictable. Accidents, chance events, and unexpected encounters are a part of life, so the past does not entirely determine what happens to us. Sometimes the present context of our life, rather than any developmental factor, determines our behavior.

In psychotherapy, we develop a story about what happened to us in childhood; some of this is accurate, but some is reconstructed memory that makes sense of what is going on now—we read the past in terms of the present. Some of the way psychotherapists describe what happened to their patients is based on current psychological and sociological theories of child development. Our history is therefore a story we construct, not something that was objectively recorded. The history we have is very much affected by ideology, interpretation, the need to avoid shame and blame, and so on. Psychological theories of development are attempts to explain what is happening now, but they cannot take into account unexpected, fated events. There is a great deal of discontinuity in life, and if we are too deterministic in terms of the past, we don't take into account the effects of consciousness, which can make choices in a way that differs from what one might expect from past behavior.

Free will

The issue of fate and destiny is intimately tied to the question of the degree to which we have free will, or self-determination. This means that when we consider doing something, at the same moment we can either perform the act or chose to refrain from doing so. Often this involves a moral choice. The question of free will occasionally arises in psychotherapy when the therapist works with someone on the horns of a moral dilemma which is causing considerable suffering, such as whether to leave a marriage. The question is then whether we can freely choose our response, or to what extent our choice is conditioned by factors of which we are unaware. One definition of addiction, for instance, is the loss of the ability to choose whether to use a substance or not. The therapist might be faced with a person suffering from a psychosis, who feels he is acting freely but who is actually under the influence of a delusion. Forensic psychologists are often faced with the question of the extent to which a person is acting freely and not affected by mental illness. The psychotherapist's view of the age-old problem of free will may well affect his understanding of the origin of an emotional problem and his interventions—the therapist has to balance biological, psychological, and social factors in deciding whether free will is operating. The main question is whether apparently voluntary action is free, an illusion (Wegner, 2002), or a useful delusion (Lipit et al., 1996).

This question is an old one, going back at least to the Stoic philosophers of ancient Greece, in the early 3rd century BCE, who believed that everything in the universe is subject to the laws of fate. One might act in or out of harmony with nature, but the Stoics did not think human beings could do much to change the outcome. Since then, the issue of free will has never died down. The monotheistic traditions stress the importance of free will, which is essential to maintain a doctrine of sin and obedience to God. Non-dual religious traditions deny free will, on the grounds that there is no separate entity acting on a separate world; everything that happens is a function of the totality.

Some people respond to suffering with integrity, courage, and even equanimity, others with passivity or despair. Suffering may harden us or destroy us; some people fight adversity while others become depressed and suicidal. There is a range of responses to the question of how much we are free to choose one of these responses. The doctrine of determinism teaches that all behavior and choices are determined by previous events, by our genes, brains, previous learning, the laws of nature, and the environment. Determinism implies a sequence in which one event inexorably causes the next. For strict determinists, given these causes and conditions, when something happens nothing else could have happened, and no behavior is really free. Logically, in that case, our response to suffering is largely decided for us, by our genes, our developmental history, and our character structure. There can then be no moral responsibility and no blame or punishment for the way we behave. Some philosophers believe that free will and determinism are compatible.

For example, we might be motivated to act in a certain way and feel free to do so if circumstances allow, even if the original motive was determined. In such a case, we are morally responsible for what we do. Another compromise position suggests that our will is influenced but not fully determined by prior experience; we do not need to take an either-or position (Slife et al., 2000). Thus fatalism, the idea that we cannot change what has been determined for us, is not the same as determinism because fatalism excludes the effects of the will completely—fatalism may also imply a transpersonal factor such as karma operating in the background. If the teleological view of human behavior is correct, then our behavior cannot be reduced to purely cause-and-effect explanations. In this debate, there seems to be a tension between our emotional need for free will and logical arguments for determinism. If we have free will, we have a certain power to change, and guilt and shame are problems. If we are determinists, we can explain what has happened to the person in terms of past events, and thus alleviate guilt and shame, but we tend to feel we have no control over our behavior. Few psychotherapists believe that our will is totally independent of previous psychological conditions, even though our legal system tends to ignore them except in obvious cases of psychological disorder.

Some people are concerned that modern neuroscience is undermining the idea of free will. Francis Crick's *The Astonishing Hypothesis* (1994) suggests that consciousness and the mind can be explained in terms of a vast assembly of neurons, and our sense of free will is only an illusion produced by brain functioning. This argument of course assumes that the mind and the brain are the same, and it seems doubtful to many of us that we can reduce the complexity of human choice to the function of neurotransmitters. Even if mind eventually proves to be an emergent property of brain, we might not be able to predict what would emerge from such a complex system. Many people believe that complex psychological choices and motivation can only be described using the language of psychology, not brain mechanisms. At present we have to be agnostic about the bearing of neuroscience on the free will argument.

The free will issue is important because human dignity and our emphasis on personal responsibility are called into question if we are fully determined, mechanical objects. Our legal system and much of our social practices are based on the idea that people make conscious choices, which seems like common sense, but common sense and the majority opinion (think of witch trials) are not always a reliable guide to reality. However, it does make a difference to the way we behave if we believe in free will—this belief tends to make people more altruistic, behave more ethically, and be more positive about their life. It makes a difference to the therapist if she feels that the patient makes a free choice or is totally determined by genes, developmental, and environmental factors—these are different worldviews. Many therapists believe that one of the purposes of psychotherapy is to allow people to exercise greater freedom in their lives.

Freud was a champion of unrelenting determinism in his *Introductory Lectures* of 1916, although some of Freud's supporters insist that he wanted to give his patients the freedom to decide how to behave, uninhibited by neurotic difficulties (Wallace, 1986). For a long time, psychic determinism—the idea that everything in the mind has previous causes—was a central tenet of psychoanalysis, but many contemporary psychologists have pointed out the scientific limits of this view. For example, the uncertainty principle in quantum physics undermines determinism, because quantum theory describes events in terms of probability. It is possible that some kind of analogous indeterminism or quantum uncertainty applies to the brain or to the psyche, although quantum events within small areas of the brain may be insignificant compared to the brain acting as a whole. Chaos theory also makes determinism less likely; the brain may be a chaotic system because there are trillions of events going on, and unexpected events may emerge out of them, which may be why phenomena such as meaning or creativity cannot be quantitatively analyzed.

In contrast to a purely deterministic viewpoint, which imagines symptoms fully determined by the past, Jung had a teleological view of symptoms—they are pointing us in a certain direction that we might otherwise not take. The teleological viewpoint asks "what is the point of this, where is it taking me?" Psychologists other than Jung have used teleological arguments by suggesting that we chose to behave in a certain way for the sake of something in the future, towards some aim (Rychlak, 1983), although without Jung's stress on the telos of the personality. Teleological approaches are incompatible with strict psychic determinism, and psychologists who believe in teleology often believe in free will and choice. However, it is hard for depth psychologists to reconcile the issue of free will with our belief that the unconscious is influencing our choices, unless free will also operates in the unconscious. One possibility is that free will is a subjective experience, and even if it is determined by factors in the unconscious, we still make conscious choices which we can consider to be free. Much of dynamic psychotherapy is based on the idea that we become more free as we become conscious of what is driving our behavior.

Jung believed that free will means doing gladly what we must do anyway. He believed that the Self acts as a guiding spirit, a *spiritus rector* or a "central manager" in the personality (9, ii, 257; 3, 507). That is, there is an invisible presence that arranges the different aspects of the personality as if in the form of a drama in which each part plays a role. His idea is that the development of the personality, or the individuation process, has a blueprint or ground-plan that is given by the Self. In other words, for Jung, development is not only a matter of one's childhood environment, early relationships, and one's genes; development is also influenced by the *telos* of the individual, as if some future goal is pulling us towards it.

Jung believes that the Self is the archetypal basis of the ego, meaning that the Self provides a set of potentials for the development of the personality. It follows that if the Self is truly an *imago dei*, an image of the divine, then the empirical personality is spiritually determined. One's life story is then a spiritual biography, and work on one's own psychology is a spiritual practice. If Jung is correct that the archetypes, which are aspects of the Self, are truly tools of God or organs of God, and the archetypes are at the center of our complexes, then spiritual elements participate in the structure of the personality, or the personality is permeated with elements of the divine. This is a radically different notion of the development of the individual than we find in any personalistic psychology. The potential to develop complexes, or psychopathology, must also be given by the Self as part of this telos or destiny, so there is a spiritual basis to our suffering. In that case, when we work therapeutically with psychopathology we are working spiritually as well as psychologically, and with this sensibility psychotherapy becomes a spiritual practice. For example, mirroring becomes not only affect attunement but also a recognition of the divine child within the other person. Idealization is the result of the search for the Self, which is projected onto another person.

The psychology of luck

Sometimes our fate seems to emerge in the form of a lucky event. Many people believe that luck plays an important part in the outcome of important events in their lives, and luck has become a popular topic in the literature of both psychology and philosophy. However, we do not know exactly what luck is, and there is no easy definition; luck may be synonymous with chance, or accident, or events over which we have no control, or synchronicity. A large number of people believe in good and bad luck—as evidenced by wearing lucky charms or other objects that seem to have some power to influence events. Superstitious behavior such as touching wood is very common. Most psychologists would say that having a lucky charm that one believes in makes one feel more confident, and this allows better performance and persistence in the face of difficulties, which makes events turn out well. Wiseman (2003) believes that people make their own good and bad luck using four basic principles: they are good at noticing opportunities; they listen to their intuition; they create self-fulfilling prophecies via positive expectations; and their attitude is resilient. Wiseman thinks that extraverts tend to be luckier than introverts because they meet more people and keep in touch with more friends.

For philosophers, an important question is the extent to which luck affects our moral responsibility. In Nagel's (1979) example, two drunk drivers have car accidents but only one has the misfortune to kill someone. We disapprove much more strongly of the one who causes death, so luck seems to influence our moral judgments, but the only difference is the drivers' luck—and all events could be affected by luck.

Some of the psychological approaches to luck are based on determining the person's locus of control—whether the person believes that the outcome of an event is mainly determined by the individual's effort or by outside factors he or she cannot control, such as fate or luck. Some people simply regard themselves as generally lucky or unlucky based on how events have turned out for most of their lives, a difference that seems to be due to whether the person is generally optimistic or pessimistic. Optimists tend to recall events that worked out well for them, while pessimists tend to dwell on difficult events in their lives (Seidlitz et al., 1993). This difference could bias their view of how lucky they are, either because optimists view life more positively than pessimists, or because they feel more confident and are more persistent when they attempt a task. It may also be that people who see themselves as lucky are more likely to feel that they can control events, even if this belief is illusory. Or, lucky people may have unconscious skills that they attribute to luck. A controversial possibility involves a parapsychological or extrasensory (psi) effect; in this view, some people are able to use a parapsychological ability to increase their luck (Smith et al., 1996).

12

SUFFERING DUE TO ILLNESS

The experience of illness

Illness begins as an intrusion into one's life, and disrupts our assumption that life will take a particular course. We often unconsciously believe that our lives are predictable and orderly, and that the world is coherent and fair; when a serious illness strikes, these beliefs are violated, which adds to the shock of discovering that one is ill. After being given a diagnosis of a life-threatening illness, it may be very difficult to make sense of what has happened or find any meaning in it. Serious illness has profound effects on the sufferer, and our health care system does not always remember that the patient is much more than her or his illness.

Healing is more than technology applied to the body, just as illness is much more than physiological dysfunction. The mechanical or purely biological view of the body typical of the medical model of illness is not much use when we try to understand the subjective experience of illness. The ill patient's subjectivity, and the social and psychological changes which serious illness brings to the patient's life, tend to be ignored by physicians, but illness is not just a biological process; it is a new way of being in the world, a new form of existence. In previous generations, patients tended to assume that they should conform to the discourse of medicine and focus on symptoms and treatment, as if their existential situation, their own voice and story, was less important, but this is now beginning to change as more and more literature about the subjective effects of illness is appearing. Nevertheless, the experience of illness remains difficult to talk about and quite private. During a serious illness, we feel concerned about the future and our loss of function, but we are sometimes subtly pressured to be upbeat and positive. Apart from the biological effects of the illness, what matters is how we actually experience being ill, what it is like to have a disruption in the way we experience the body rather than seeing the body simply as biologically dysfunctional. The effects of illness are not localized to the body because illness changes the context of one's whole life, so that different people may experience the same disease differently. Illness modifies life plans, values, and existence in general. Everything is thrown into question, and we look at the world in a new way, so illness is an opportunity to examine life and choices we have made. This kind of reflection on life and the world is imposed by illness because we can no longer take for granted our usual approach to the world. Eventually, chronic illness can become a way of life or a way of being. It is misleading to see oneself, one's illness and one's body as somehow different things, as if there is a "me" fighting a cancer that is not a part of me. The reality is that illness means I have a different body than the one I used to have, so I have a different sense of self. Illness disrupts the unity of body and self, producing loss of faith in the body, or the body becomes a threat to the sense of self. When we become ill we have to develop a new relationship to the body and to the environment. This may mean giving up trying to live up to society's idea of an ideal body.

Chronic illness gradually changes our identity; think of the changes produced by radiation and chemotherapy in our appearance and vitality. These kinds of descents are potentially an initiation into deep mysteries of the soul, and they allow us to retrieve values of which we were unaware. We can access this realm by means of attention to the unconscious, using dreams, fantasies, or creative expressions. During periods of severe illness or injury, it is common for people to have experiences of non-ordinary reality, such as visions of deceased friends or relatives, or near death experiences. These experiences may occur spontaneously or they may be induced by the use of entheogens,[61] which can be very helpful especially during the dying process if administered under properly controlled circumstances.

Illness means we lose certainty and control, we lose our freedom to act, and we suffer from loss of our familiar world (Toombs, 1987). The world becomes unpredictable and the future is uncertain. The world is now full of obstacles; distances seem to increase and routines take more time; space is modified. Pain changes one's experience of time (Toombs, 1990). One might feel more useless than usual. One has to re-think priorities because there may

---

61   I use the term "entheogen" instead of the more common "psychedelic" because I believe these compounds allow access to spiritual dimensions of reality.

not be much time left, and one is very conscious of one's mortality. A sick body makes one feel fragile, dependent, and vulnerable. If the body does not function well, we have to learn to do ordinary things in new ways. Illness therefore deepens our understanding of what it means to live; ill people are forced to understand the fragility of life and appreciate it more than they did before they became ill. Illness is an opportunity to stop taking life for granted. Those close to the ill person are also affected in some of these ways.

For people who are spiritually inclined, a serious illness may lead to a crisis of faith, or the individual's spirituality may be helpful in allowing a certain amount of acceptance and peace. But spiritual explanations may also be unhelpful if they see illness as a punishment. It is worth noting that some people who have a lifetime commitment to a religious tradition become bitterly disappointed when their prayer seems to have no effect on their illness. Overall, however, it feels helpful to believe that a larger power is controlling the situation, even if one has no control oneself. Even people who do not consider themselves religious in any formal sense may nevertheless admit that they believe that what happens to them is the result of fate, which consciously or not implies some kind of transpersonal background to their lives. Rationalists consider explanations in terms of fate as superstitious, or merely the result of an intense need for closure.

Whether or not we look at illness through a traditional spiritual lens, life-threatening illness often challenges the global meaning we find in life, our fundamental goals, commitments and beliefs about whether life is worth living. The effects of illness on these large-scale attitudes may be more important than the situational meaning or the particular way we appraise the illness (Park 2010; Sherman, 2010). Nevertheless, finding meaning in illness can be of value.

Finding meaning in illness

The ability to find meaning in illness has a positive effect not only on psychological well-being but also on the course of chronic illness (Fjelland et al. 2008; Dezutter et al, 2013). Finding spiritual meaning tends to reduce anxiety, for example by seeing the illness as the will of God or as necessary karma. Atheists may discover meaning of a secular kind, on their own terms, or they may simply see illness as part of the tragic side of life with no particular meaning.

Culture helps to determine the meaning we discover in illness. Morris (1998) points out that we can look at AIDS as a biological disorder, but it also has important cultural meanings; it has a cultural backdrop of homophobia, the politics of giving life-extending medicines to third world countries, and the politics of advocacy groups. The use of alcohol and cigarettes and the effects of stress and obesity are lifestyles partially determined by culture.

One of the ways we can discover meaning is by telling stories about our illness; a story allows us to at least put the illness into the larger context of our life, in which case it may seem less chaotic. Arthur Kleinman (1989) shows that we can use narrative to create meaning from illness. He distinguishes between illness, which is the lived experience of the patient, and disease, the objective classification of a medical disorder. There is a difference between a myocardial infarction and the lived experience of a heart attack. Telling the story of the illness can allow us new understanding of it. Stories can restore a sense of coherence in a life whose continuity has been disrupted by illness. Stories help to form a new sense of self, and they are a way of helping others understand what is happening. Stories of illness express our distress to others and allow an empathic connection to them. Illness narratives sometimes reflect the dominant cultural values about being self-reliant or brave or taking responsibility for one's health, and so on. Telling stories brings this kind of material to consciousness and allows dialog with it. Our illness story expresses our unique experience of illness, and the official medical story is incomplete without this.

Arthur Frank proposes that narrative has a moral function; the ill person has the responsibility to tell the story; the listener is responsible to witness and be compassionate. Frank (1995) proposes a typology of narratives; a restitution narrative is about being healthy, becoming ill and recovering, which is the culturally preferred narrative and which reinforces what medicine expects of the ill person. The chaos narrative says that things will never get better; there is no end in sight and no control. The quest narrative confronts the illness and embarks on a journey of discovery in the mode of Campbell's hero's journey.

Many cultures have recognized that suffering may lead to wisdom and understanding that may otherwise be unattainable, and what is true for suffering in general is often true for illness. Like any form of suffering, illness may lead to new realizations about how one wants to live one's life and about what really matters to us. For example, when a serious illness occurs, people who have been driven and over-ambitious may realize that they must slow down and re-evaluate their lives, sometimes radically transforming them. They may re-evaluate jobs they hate, re-consider relationships which drain or abuse them, and they may wake up to what they really want out of life. I do not wish to naively imply that changing these factors will necessarily lead to recovery, or that the illness was simply the result of a lifestyle problem. But it is true that illness may make us aware of self-destructive behavior, and may makes us pay attention to what we have been neglecting, or to parts of ourselves that have not had a chance to live. Or we may contact levels of grief and rage about missed opportunities and mistakes, and this awareness has the potential to lead to profound transformation. This phenomenon is sometimes referred to as post-traumatic growth, leading to positive life changes such as improved relationships, increased self-confidence, and deepened spirituality.

The meaning of an illness may depend on the part of the body which is affected. Illnesses may have narcissistic significance, especially when they involve the face, hands or genitalia. Illness may affect one's sense of adequacy and may produce shame, anger or a feeling of being defective or ugly, but illness may also lead to compensatory efforts such as counterphobic behavior— for example the blind or one-legged skier. In World War 2, Douglas Bader lost both legs but became an ace fighter pilot.

It is possible to look at illness as the result of an individuation process, which has gone awry, so that one is not following one's true path in life, or one could see the illness as a necessary part of one's individuation, deepening one's sense of identity. In the former case, there can be a naive New Age tendency to blame the ill person for becoming ill, as if this were a simple matter of choice, ignoring the unconscious and all the social and developmental forces that have combined to move us into particular life situations. If we become ill as a result of a block to the individuation process, we need tools to discover what our real calling should be. Here, one useful idea is the notion that there are dominant archetypal motifs within any personality which influence the course of the individuation process. Some people are constitutionally destined to be teachers, healers, priests, warriors, merchants, scholars, and so on. We tend to be good at doing the work typified by these archetypal qualities. Kings and Queens are good at leading people, using power, and developing wealth. Warriors are interested in conquest and exploration, courage and strength, dying for a cause, submitting their will to the ruler, and protecting their people. Priests are interested in spiritual phenomena and in mediating between humans and the transcendent dimension. Scholars are good at intellectual pursuits, compiling information, and research. Sages seek wisdom for its own sake; they study the human condition and life itself, not simply for the sake of acquiring new knowledge, like the scholar. Monks are natural ascetics and solitaries, devoted to spiritual practice. Lovers see all levels of reality as linked by love. Teachers feel an urge to teach, mothers take care of anything and anyone that needs growing, shamans talk to the spirits, and so on. We have to live in accord with these innate dispositions in order to feel that life is meaningful. Otherwise, we are in a career that is not our true vocation, in which case illness may happen when there is a need for change that cannot be brought about in any other way.

How do we know what we are supposed to be doing in life? Some of this is a matter of intuition, or a kind of internal knowing or following our instincts, a sense of the rightness of some activities and not others. Some of it is a matter of discovering what activity fascinates us and for which we have an innate talent or facility. Another clue is that, when we are doing what is really authentic for us, we lose track of time, we are in a situation of flow or absorption, so that time seems to pass without our realizing it. The work seems to happen of its own accord, things click, and new ideas flow. By contrast, when we are doing work for which we are not suited, time seems to drag. Many people work for narcissistic reasons, to buttress self-esteem or to please the family. As the old joke has it, we struggle to get to the top of the ladder and then discover it has been leaning against the wrong wall. The tragedy is that some people do not realize the depth of their suffering while they are climbing a ladder that will lead them to a place that is wrong for them. Laurence LeShan (1994) found that his cancer patients were more likely to go into remission if they found a vocation that gave them a zest for living. This is not easy to do if, for example, we have been trained from childhood to put others' needs before our own, but it is a possible discovery.

If Jung is correct that every personality has its own telos, a goal towards which it is moving, then illness is not necessarily an accident; in accord with the notion that illness is a part of the individuation process, illness is an integral part of one's life and must be accepted as necessary. Illness can also be the liminal phase of a process of initiation, in which we die to the old way of life, and develop a new consciousness. Healing therefore may require a conscious sacrifice, which often means acceptance of change and loss, giving up the idea of returning to life as it was before and accepting the way one is now.

Illness in relation to character structure

In the face of suffering that renders the individual helpless, narcissistic character pathology characterized by arrogance makes it impossible to maintain the sense that the person can control everything. We sometimes see depression in such individuals when they suffer severe illness, because illness deals them a blow to their omnipotence and to their sense of personal worth. Such a person may be arrogant in order to cope with feelings of worthlessness and shame; these feelings surface when an attitude of superiority is no longer adaptive in coping with illness, especially if the ill person has to depend on others, which may feel humiliating to someone with a fragile sense of self which is being defended with grandiosity. The sense that one is invulnerable or special is diminished by illness, which often feels degrading. Very often, the grandiose character has never been empathic for the suffering of others, because to be empathic requires that we put aside our own self and its problems and concentrate on others. This is impossible if the sense of self is fragile and is being shored up by narcissistic defenses such as grandiosity. Some people are impermeable to other human beings until they are forced to be open because of the intense suffering produced by illness. Lifelong feelings of worthlessness and inadequacy are often reinforced by suffering that seems to confirm a devalued self-image. Illness is particularly difficult for obsessional characters who try to maintain rigid control of their lives and their bodies. They are unconsciously terrified of the unknown, of helplessness, powerlessness, and uncertainty. Control becomes a way of coping with these fears. When control is no longer possible because of illness, the underlying anxiety surfaces.

On the question of psychosomatic or psychogenic illness

The golden age of psychoanalytic interest in psychosomatics during the 1940's and 1950's petered out because of a failure to find good evidence to support theories that suggested that a specific physical illness was caused by a specific psychological conflict. It proved impossible to correlate particular mental states with corresponding organic illness, or to cure organic illness with psychotherapy, even though the research did find evidence that emotions affect physiological processes such as gastric secretion and blood pressure. Since then, new theories have arisen, such as the idea that psychosomatic illness is related to difficulty using symbols and language, so that the mental apparatus cannot bind extreme somatic excitation by putting it into words. It is as if a certain quantity of affect overflows into somatic symptoms, and the patient can be helped if he can put words to his feelings. Psychosomatic patients find it difficult to do this, just as they are said to be unable to move to abstract from concrete thinking. However, it is not at all clear that these issues really predispose to psychosomatic illness; they may be the result of being ill.

It is possible to see illness as an expression of the unconscious by means of the body, without thinking in terms of the unconscious as purely psychological. The unconscious is not exclusively psychological or physical, or it is both. The distinction between body and mind is only verbal; body and mind are a unity.[62] There is no "relationship" between mind and body, because that word implies they are two different things, when in fact they are two aspects of the same reality, or the same reality expressed in different modalities. Using Jung's (CW 8, p. 211) metaphor of the light spectrum, the body is at the red end and the mind at the blue end, but both red and blue are components of the same light. The same problem, or the same archetypal process, expresses itself both somatically and psychologically. We can only separate mind and body as a convenient way of talking. Every illness is psychosomatic in the sense that illness is a state of the unitary mind-body spectrum, although in practice it is important to remember that if we make too much of the psychological components of illness we may overburden the sick person. It is true that sometimes a person cannot express distress psychologically, so that the distress is expressed by the body, but that is the result of problematic mind-body splitting, which has developmental origins. Because mind and body are part of a unitary spectrum, when one pole of the mind-body totality is not allowed to become conscious, the unconscious reaches consciousness in any way it can, if necessary at the other pole.

It is a mistake to think of illness in terms of a hierarchy in which mind or body is given priority. There is no such thing as psychological distress which does not also involve the body—emotion begins as raw affect, which is mediated by the autonomic nervous system in the body. The opposite error would be to think of a problem as primarily physical while also having secondary psychological components. A somatic problem always has a psychological correlate, and the expression of genes which produce somatic illness can be affected by our emotional state. That is to say, it is preferable to

---

62   One only has to think of the complex indicators of Jung's word association test, some of which are somatic, even though the complex is a psychological structure.

avoid the idea that either the psychological problem comes first or the bodily symptom comes first; if they are two aspects of a unitary reality, each expresses the same situation simultaneously, synchronistically, in their different modes, as Meier (1963) suggested. By thinking in terms of synchronicity we do not need to think of mind and body causally. An unconscious archetypal pattern can express itself either psychologically or physically because the archetype has a somatic and a psychic pole, and these are not two separate things.

The body can express symbolic meaning. A complex can appear as a bodily symptom which is a mirror of the psychological situation. A middle-aged man came to psychotherapy complaining of depression and chronic pain following coronary artery bypass surgery. For months after the operation he had suffered constant pain in the area of the sternum (the breast bone). The pain was initially misdiagnosed until eventually it was discovered that his sternum, which has to be split to allow access to the heart, had never healed after the surgery—so called nonunion. However, surgical repair of the sternum did not alleviate his pain and the nonunion persisted. Eventually, a second repair of the sternum about nine months after the initial surgery did help, but a year later he was still suffering sternal pain. Each breath was painful. For many months he had been unable to work, and he began to despair that he would ever regain his health. This man's father had died when the boy was 10 years old. His mother was insensitive and made him feel responsible for her distress and her emotional well-being. He tried everything he could to make her feel better, including going to work at the age of 13 to help support her financially, but nothing he did made her any better. He was completely unable to protect himself from her emotional blackmail, and he felt guilty and vulnerable to any form of criticism by her that he was not doing enough. He went into a helping profession in which he was expected to be available to help others without regard for himself, thus continuing this pattern, with no capacity to protect himself against intrusion by the needs of other people. Looking at this situation symbolically, it became clear that the sternum represents the capacity to protect the heart, and he had never learned to protect his heart emotionally. His heart had always remained open to the intrusions of others' needs, and synchronistically at the time of the surgery he was in a relationship with a woman whose demands on him were similar to those his mother made. Needless to say, he could not protect himself from her constant intrusions. He noticed that every time she attacked him, his sternal pain worsened. He felt guilty whenever she was unhappy, and he felt he had to take care of her. He could not protect his heart physically or psychologically; the physical aspect of the problem and his psychology mirror each other. As a result of the therapeutic work, he was able to extricate himself from his current relationship and see its connections to his mother problem. As this happened, and he was learning to protect his feelings and defend himself, his sternum began to heal. It would be a mistake to think of this correlation in terms of causality; it was synchronistic. The psychological situation was expressing itself symbolically in the body. The meaning of this chronic pain was a call to do this work.

In spite of such examples, in today's medicine there is resistance to the idea that there can be any relationship between illness and meaning, because the medical profession in general still adheres to mind-body dualism and does not take into account the patient's subjectivity. There is a long but controversial tradition which sees illness in the body in terms of its symbolic meaning, but medicine knows no mechanism by which the body can express symbolic meaning in the form of illness, which is one source of resistance to the idea.

Conditions that are medically unexplainable at present, such as chronic fatigue syndrome, are the limit cases for the traditional medical approach; here is where it stops working well. Chronic fatigue causes a great deal of controversy and a range of opinions. Some people believe this is a primary psychological problem expressed physically, while others suggest there is an unknown biological cause producing both psychological and physical symptoms. However, as in any illness, chronic fatigue produces a network of physical symptoms, feelings, behavior, and so on. There is no need to think in terms of any of these having causal priority, just as there is no point in looking for one of them as the root cause. The situation might be closer to what is called a strange loop or a tangled hierarchy, which is a system in which by moving in any direction we find ourselves back where we started, as in Escher's drawing of hands drawing each other. There is no higher or lower level; we always return to the starting point.

Medically unexplained symptoms are very common in primary care medicine. Because of their academic training, many physicians believe that only what is physical is real. This is the model which characterizes most traditional western approaches to illness, which is partly why we have separate hospitals for mental and physical illness. In contrast, Jung for example insists that the psyche is a domain in its own right, just as real as material reality. We cannot experience the world without at the same time giving it some kind of meaning, so there are no sharp distinctions between subject and object, or self and world, or physical and mental, or psyche and matter; they are inextricably linked. The psyche gives us our experience of the world, and the world and language have a major effect on the brain and psyche.

Meaning is not the only important factor when suffering a serious illness. The attitude of the sufferer also makes an important difference. Bernie Siegel (1998) describes a group of patients who did exceptionally well; they can express feelings and act on their own behalf, and they are the (approximately 20% of) patients whom physicians consider most difficult because they ask many questions and learn about their illness. They want to know every detail of the situation; X ray results, laboratory reports, treatment options, side effects, etc. They go for second opinions, support groups, lifestyle changes, psychotherapy, and dietary changes; anything that can make a difference. Apparently it does not always pay to be too compliant with one's physician. Siegel also found that about 20% of patients actually want to die, consciously or unconsciously, because their illness was a way out of an impossible situation; they show no signs of distress, and do not resist the illness. The survival rates for cancer patients who are docile and helpless is much worse than among those who fight.

The work of Laurence LeShan (1994) suggested that those cancer patients who not only found meaning in life but also found a vocation they were enthusiastic about, and an authentic way of life that they really enjoyed, did much better than patients who could not do so. The problem for most people is that such fulfillment is difficult to attain when we have been trained to put others first, or if our self-esteem has to be maintained by the pursuit of status, income, and power, even if these pursuits mean that we have to ignore our real vocation. LeShan also found that his therapy had to focus on what is right with the person, not just on what went wrong in childhood. He focused on the patient's special abilities, on his potential, on his creativity, and on finding whatever would make the patient enthusiastic about living; having a reason to live seems to mobilize healing. This is true because health is a much larger concept than simply not having an overt disease. Healing is very complex; belief, hope, meaning, conscious attitude and the unconscious make a difference in ways that we don't fully understand.

There is a common misunderstanding about the issue of meaning and the psychological aspects of illness, exemplified by some of Susan Sontag's writing (1990). What is useful about her work is that she points out the negative associations around cancer, reinforced by the use of military metaphors such as "battling" cancer, which demonize the disease and indirectly stigmatize the

337

patient, as if it were his fault. However, she does not like the idea of taking any responsibility for one's illness; she thinks that psychological interpretation of illness and metaphorical thinking about illness are moralistic, so she wants to get rid of this approach, ignoring the fact that illness can have symbolic meaning which is not necessarily moralistic or negative. But Sontag argued forcefully that illness is not a metaphor and that illness is resistant to metaphoric thinking. She complains about psychological explanations for disease, suggesting that psychological approaches undermine the reality of disease and seem to blame the victim. She prefers a focus purely on the physical aspects of illness. However, like the New Age approach that she critiques, and indeed like much "psychosomatic medicine," Sontag has misunderstood the relationship between physical illness and the psychology of the sufferer. As discussed above, it is misleading to say that the mind "causes" the disease in the body, as if body and mind were different entities. The psychological situation and the physical situation express the same problem in different ways, as we saw in the case example. The psychological problem does not "cause" the physical problem; they correlate with each other synchronistically. Furthermore, we need metaphor to describe our illnesses, to tell stories about them, and to express our feelings about them. It is true that if we make too much of the idea of psychological components of illness we overburden the sick person. But Sontag takes the extreme position that illness has no meaning; it is just a biological process with no psychological background causing it—implying a radical mind-body split. However, one can at least make a good case for the idea that the ill person is responsible for his response to the illness, if not for getting ill, and a psychological and symbolic approach to illness helps us deepen this response.

AFTERWORD

Having now read *The Soul in Anguish* for oneself, I am sure that the reader will agree with me that encountering the mind, the experience, the professional perspective, and, much more, the soul of Lionel Corbett, is an enlarging experience. One of the many things I admire about Dr. Corbett is that is he not afraid to take on the largest, most difficult, most mine-laden subjects and wrestle with them. Surely by now, most readers will have soured on the tripe that is for sale in most 'Self-Help' sections of bookstores, those which promise great marriages, weight lost, addiction management, and spiritual fulfillment in thirty days, or five easy steps. If these books worked, we would all know by now and there would be no need for any other books. But they don't and everybody knows it. Lionel Corbett is someone with the courage and the imagination to tackle issues for which there is no resolution, only the summons to repeated encounters: the religious nature of the human psyche, the intractability of so much suffering, and the inevitability that sooner or later we will all be tested beyond our understanding and coping strategies. What will we do, or become, then? That is where this book begins.

Suffering is always a subjective experience, that is, an encounter with the world which seizes us, activates our fears, our historic adaptive measures, our various forms of denial, and evasive flight from any rendezvous with that which we fear. When we recall that the etymology of *anguish* derives from the Latin *angustia*, which means "narrowness, difficulty" and *angere* "to press together," we realize why we suffer so immensely—our very freedom itself is abridged by "another," another who refuses to negotiate. Corbett brings to our awareness how it becomes necessary, then, to negotiate with our own attitudes, since that "other" will not be summoned to the bargaining table.

As we remember that pain is physical, and suffering psychological, the issue then devolves around how that encounter with the radical "other" gets "storied" by our psyche. Life happen to each of us, in quite different ways, but all of us will sooner or later experience an encounter with the unwanted, the usurpation of will, the over-throw of whatever "contract" we think we have with life or with the recondite powers of the universe. Our most common exercise in "magical thinking" is the presumption of a "contract": "If I mean well, do the right thing, and behave properly, the universe will spare me suffering, perhaps aging and mortality as well." While the fantasy of that presumptive contract was dramatically challenged at least three millennia ago in *Gilgamesh, Ecclesiastes*, and directly in the *Book of Job*, we often share the phantasy with our ancestors that we can strike independent, individual deals with the universe.

Perhaps the deepest level of suffering, and therefore, anguish, arises from the narrowing, or constriction of that phantasy by the autonomous powers of the universe, and our own human unconscious, to submit us to suffering. That same etymological trail leads even further back to the Indo-Germanic *angh*, which means "to constrict," and from which we get, *anxiety, anger, Angst*, and *angina*. Accordingly, the deepest subjective affront to human consciousness is the incessant reminder that we are not in charge of our lives, or our destinies, and that we are always at the potential mercy of constricting forces outside of us, and inside of us. No wonder, then, the appeal of the self-help books; they delude us into thinking there is magic, such magic as a few possess, and for a fee, will share with the rest of us poor souls. If there if a place in Dante's world for this charlatanry, it will surely involve such practitioners sitting in that eternal place amid their remaindered, unsold copies, books which they themselves are obliged to read over and over.

Corbett reminds us of the subjective nature of our "anguish." Life is an on-going phenomenological event, a series of experiences, which, because our psyche is tasked with survival and continuance, is immediately "storied." That is, narrative threads begin to adhere around an event. When we touched a hot iron for the first time, the phenomenon of pain got "storied," and in a protective way. Often that "story," interpretation, narrative explanation is erroneous, however, or is tied to a particular time and place, and does not warrant application to subsequent chapters of life. Part of the task of psychotherapy is to examine the "stories" we accrued in life's passages, and to discern how they exercise a form of sovereignty in our lives up to the present. Making those stories conscious, noting what they have made us do, or kept us from doing, is central to recovering a measure of autonomy for ego consciousness. Thus, the real damage to a person is less what happened but how it gets storied, what role these fractal narratives play in the psychic economy of our histories, and what they make us do, or keep us from doing.

Corbett's book explores how these "stories," epiphenomenal interpretations of phenomenological experiences, extend into the many tangential areas of our lives, what "collateral damage" they provoke in us, and thus in those who share our lives. Baseball manager Leo Durocher once observed, "Some days we win; some days we lose; some days it rains." And Koheleth, the unknown "Preacher" of *Ecclesiastes*, noted that the rain falleth on the just and the unjust *alike*. Strangely, then, the final democracy is not only aging and death, but that time and chance "happeneth to them all."

Part of the richness of this book is that we are led to survey the various forms of suffering. How can envy, for example, compete with the pain of metastatic bone cancer? But both are suffered as wounds to the soul; each eats away at the spirit. And, anguish is always a torment of the spirit. The 'spirit' is that energy which animates our corporeal presence, and engages in life. Suffering can eat away, erode, deplete the spirit. We have all seen that happen, or experienced it directly ourselves. Yet, as Jung noted, without that quickening of the spirit, we would all fall back into the torpor which is so tempting to all of us as well. The summons to show up in life is perhaps nowhere more tested than in the precincts of pain and suffering.

Somewhere in our cultural development we all were inoculated with the phantasy that the goal of life is happiness. For sure, happiness is a desirable experience, but one of considerable transience. And the more we pursue it, the more elusive it seems. The more we seek to own happiness the more it will slip from our fingers, and the more threatening the powers of the universe which may intrude upon our project. But what abides in our brief transit on this spinning globe, is the task of meaning.

Inevitably, our choices, with their unintended consequences, the choices of others, or the unfathomable acts of the dark gods, will bring us to swampland places of the soul. In such swamplands, we experience the loss of autonomy, the constriction of freedoms, and the imposition of agendas which we would evade. Yet, in every swampland encounter there is a summons to a task of some kind, the addressing of which moves one from victimage to an active engagement with mystery of life. I think often of the clerical opponent of Hitler, Pastor Dietrich Bonhoeffer, who, imprisoned and subsequently executed in a concentration camp for his acts of conscience, asked himself: "Is this place and my being here the will of God?" No, he concluded, but my task is to work my way through this suffering to find the will of God for me in this terrible place. We are told that even his captors came to respect his steady spirit, and the courage with which he faced his murder at the hands of a criminal empire.

While few of us may find the courage of a Bonhoeffer, we all have our appointments with suffering, with the anguish of the soul. How then do we respond? Is it possible that we, too, may ask, "what is my task here, in this situation over which I have so little freedom?" And even there, we are blessed with the terrible freedom of the power to choose an attitude, a practice, a humility, a growth, an enlargement whereby our small journey is reframed and our soul's anguish dignified by the glimpse of meaning.

The most radical form of meaning is perhaps found in a radical acceptance of life, as it is—not on our terms, nor with guarantees of anything other than the dignity of a good fight. What I admire about the work of Lionel Corbett is that he is utterly realistic, psychologically informed, full of fellow-feeling for our common condition, and fully engaged in the good fight which brings dignity—even to the most tormented hours of our brief moment here amid all the mysteries.

James Hollis, Ph. D.
Jungian Analyst
Washington, D. C.

CODA

In our culture, there tends to be an automatic assumption that suffering is necessarily a bad thing, but I hope this book has shown that there are times when enduring and even embracing necessary suffering may lead to important personality developments. Suffering which is severe enough to radically shake up one's sense of self may lead to the reconstruction of a more authentic sense of self. One's suffering is a part of one's identity and one's life story, so that even as one struggles to deal with it, suffering can be claimed and not rejected. Looked at retrospectively, events that seemed very negative at the time may eventually be seen as critically important for the individuation process.

The development of wisdom and maturity requires us to develop an attitude to suffering, since suffering is inevitable. Wisdom and maturity may at times be born of suffering, and wisdom may offer solace for suffering. Wisdom means that we accept our transience and vulnerability as part of being human, and as Kohut (1978, p. 855) put it, we can then contemplate our strengths and weaknesses "with tolerance and composure." Psychotherapy can be a source of such wisdom; the therapist's attitude of exploration, acceptance, understanding, and empathy combined with the provision of a new perspective, are conducive to its development. The psychotherapeutic exploration of painful states of mind and painful life situations leads to unexpected discoveries and unexpected attitudes to suffering. In the end, the psychotherapist's very effort to ameliorate suffering is itself a balm to those who suffer.

REFERENCES

Abraham, K. (1927) A particular form of neurotic resistance against the psychoanalytical method. In *Selected Papers of Karl Abraham*. London: Hogarth Press and the Institute of Psycho-Analysis.

Adorno, T., Frenkel-Brunswick, E., Levinson, D., & Sanford, N. (1950). *The authoritarian personality*. NY: Harper.

Akhtar, S. (2000). Mental Pain and the Cultural Ointment of Poetry. *International Journal of Psycho-Analysis, 81*(2), 229-.

Adams, R. (2000). Loving Mimesis and Girard's 'Scapegoat of the Text': A Creative Reassessment of Mimetic Desire. In W. M. Swartley (Ed.), *Violence Renounced: Rene Girard, Biblical Studies and Peacemaking*. Telford PA: Pandora Press (pp. 277-).

Adams, C. J. (1994). Bringing peace home: A feminist philosophical perspective on the abuse of women, children, and pet animals. *Hypatia, 9,* 63-84.

Adorno, T.W. (1962). Commitment. In Eagleton, T. & Milne, D. (Eds.), *Marxist literary theory: A reader*. NY: Oxford University Press, pp. 11-30.

Agosta, L. (2010). *Empathy in the context of philosophy*. NY: Palgrave Macmillan.

Ahn, D., Jin, S., & Ritterfeld, U. (2012). "Sad movies don't always make me cry": The cognitive and affective processes underpinning enjoyment of tragedy. *Journal Of Media Psychology: Theories, Methods, And Applications, 24*(1), 9-18.

Akhtar S (1995). Some reflections on the nature of hatred and its emergence in the treatment process: Discussion of Kernberg's chapter 'Hatred as a core affect of aggression'. In S. Akhtar, S. Kramer & H. Parens (Eds.), *The birth of hatred: Developmental, clinical, and technical aspects of intense aggression*. New Jersey: Jason Aronson.

Altemeyer, B. (1996.) *The authoritarian specter*. Cambridge, MA: Harvard University Press.

Akhtar, S., & Varma, A. (2012). Sacrifice: Psychodynamic, Cultural and Clinical Aspects. *The American Journal of Psychoanalysis, 72,* 95-117.

Albright, M. (2002). The Stigmata: The Psychological and Ethical Message of the Posttraumatic Sufferer. *Psychoanalysis & Contemporary Thought, 25*(3), 329-358.

Alford, C.F. (2005). Hate is the imitation of love. In R. Sternberg, (Ed.), *The psychology of hate*. Washington, D.C.: American Psychological Association.

Alfredsson, E., Wiren, B., & Lutzen, A. (1995). Comfort, a flow of best wishes and well-being. *Nordic Journal of Nursing Research and Clinical Studies, 15*(1), 34-39.

Almond, G., Appleby, R., & Sivan, E. (2003). *Strong religion: The rise of fundamentalism around the world*. Chicago: University of Chicago Press.

Altemeyer, B., & Hunsberger , B. (1992). Authoritarianism, religious fundamentalism, quest, and prejudice. *International Journal of the Psychology of Religion, 2,* 113-134.

Amsel, A. (1976). *Rational Irrational Man*: Torah psychology. NY: Feldheim Publishers.

Anderson, R.W., (1997). The envious will to power. *The Journal of Analytical Psychology, 42*(3), 363-383.

Andrykowski, M.A., Brady, M.J., Hunt, J.W. Positive psychosocial adjustment in potential bone marrow transplant recipients: cancer as a psychosocial transition. *Psychooncology, 2,* 261-276.

Ansbacher, H. & Ansbacher, R.R. (Eds.). (1956). *Individual psychology of Alfred Adler: A systematic presentation in selections from his writings.* NY: Basic Books.

Armstrong, K. (2001). *The battle for God*. NY: Ballantine Books.

Anderson, D.J., & Hines, R.H. (1994). Attachment and pain. In R.C. Grzesiak & D.S. Ciccone (Eds.), *Psychological vulnerability to chronic pain*. New York: Springer.

Appio, L., Chambers, D., & Mao, S. (2013). Listening to the Voices of the Poor and Disrupting the Silence About Class Issues in Psychotherapy. *Journal Of Clinical Psychology, 69*(2), 152-161.

Arendt, H. (2006). *Eichmann in Jerusalem: A report on the banality of evil*. NY: Penguin Books.

Arluke, A., Levin, J., Luke, C., & Ascione, F. (1999). The relationship of animal abuse to violence and other forms of antisocial behavior. *Journal of Interpersonal Violence 14,* 963-975.

Asay, T. P. , & Lambert, M. J. (1999). The empirical case for the common factors in therapy: Quantitative findings. In M. A. Hubble, B. L. Duncan, & S. D. Miller (Eds.), *The heart and soul of change* (pp. 23-57). Washington, DC: American Psychological Association.

Ascione, F. R. (1993). Children who are cruel to animals: A review of research and implications for developmental psychology. *Anthrozoös, 6* (4), 226-247.

Attig, T. (2000). *The heart of grief: Death and the search for meaning.* NY: Oxford University Press.

Balint, M. (1952). On love and hate. *The International Journal of Psychoanalysis, 33,* 355-362.

Baumeister, R. F. (1991). *Meanings in life.* NY: Guilford.

Baumeister, R. F., Twenge, J.M., & Nuss, C.K. (2002). Effects of social exclusion on cognitive processes: Anticipated aloneness reduces intelligent thought. *Journal of Personality and Social Psychology, 83,* 817-827.

Badcock , C. R. (1986), *The Problem of Altruism: Freudian-Darwinian Solutions,* NY: Oxford University Press.

Bargdill, R.W. (2006). Fate and destiny: Some historical distinctions between the concepts. *Journal of Theoretical and philosophical psychology, 26,* 205-220.

Barnhart, W.J., Makela, E.H., & Latocha, J. (2004). Selective serotonin reuptake inhibitor induced apathy syndrome: A clinical review. *Journal of Psychiatric Practice, 10*(3), 196-199.

Barnstone, (1984). *The other Bible.* San Francisco: Harper Collins.

Baruchello, G. (2010). No pain, no gain. The understanding of cruelty in western philosophy and some reflections on personhood. *Filozfia, 65*(2), 170-183.

Basoglu, M., Jaranson, J. M., Mollica, R., & Kastrup, M. (2001). Torture and mental health: A research overview. In E. Gerrity, T. M. Keane, & F. Tuma (Eds.), *The mental health consequences of torture* (pp. 35–62). New York: Kluwer.

Bauer, J. (1993). *Impossible love—or why the heart must go wrong.* Dallas, Tx: Spring Publications.

Batson, C.D. (1991). *The altruism question: Toward a social-psychological answer.* NJ: Lawrence Erlbaum Associates.

Batson, C.D. (2010). *Empathy-induced altruistic motivation.* In M. Mikulincer & P. R. Shaver, (Eds.), In *Prosocial motives, emotions, and behavior: The better angels of our nature* (pp. 15-34). Washington, DC: American Psychological Association, 2010.

Beach, S. R., Schulz, R., Yee, J. L., & Jackson, S. (2000). Negative and positive health effects of caring for a disabled spouse: Longitudinal findings from the Caregiver Health Effects Study. *Psychology and Aging, 15,* 259– 271.

Beck, R. (2004). The function of religious belief: Defensive versus existential religion. *Journal of Psychology and Christianity, 23,* 208-218.

Beirne, P. (1999). For a nonspeciesist criminology: Animal abuse as an object of study. *Criminology, 37,* 117-147.

Ben-Ze'ev, A. (2000). *The subtlety of emotions.* Cambridge, MA: MIT Press.

Bennett, M, Dennett, D., Hacker, P., & Searle, J. (2007). *Neuroscience and philosophy.* NY: Columbia University Press.

Berenbaum, M., & Firestone R. (2004). The Theology of Martyrdom. In R.M. Fields (Ed.), *Martyrdom: The psychology, theology, and politics of self-sacrifice* (pp. 117-145). Westport, CT: Praeger.

Berger, A.S. (2012). The evil eye—an ancient superstition. *Journal of Religion and Health, 51*(4), 1098-1103.

Berger, P.L. (Ed.) (1999). *The desecularization of the world: Resurgent religion and world politics.* Washington, D.C.: Ethics and Public Policy Center & Grand Rapids, MI.: William B. Eerdman Publishing.

Bergner, R. M. (2007). Therapeutic Storytelling Revisited. *American Journal Of Psychotherapy, 61*(2), 149-162.

Berke, J. (1986). Shame and envy. *British Journal of Psychotherapy 2*(4), 262–70.

Bernasconi, R. (2002). What is the question to which 'substitution' is the answer? In S. Critchley & R. Bernasconi (Eds.), *The Cambridge companion to Levinas* (pp. 234–251). NY: Cambridge University Press.

Bernstein, R. J. (1991). *Beyond Objectivism and Relativism: Science, Hermeneutics, and Praxis.* Philadelphia; University of Pennsylvania Press.

Bewley, A.R. (1995) Re-membering spirituality: Use of sacred ritual in psychotherapy. *Women & Therapy, 16,* 201-213.

Bierhoff, H.M., & Rohmann, E. (2004). Altruistic Personality in the Context of the Empathy-Altruism Hypothesis. *European Journal of Personality,* 18(4), 351–365.

Binswanger , L. (1994). The Case of Ilse. In R. May, E. Angel, & H.F. Ellenberger (Eds.), *Existence*. New York: Jason Aronson. (Original work published in 1958).

Bion, W. (1963). *Elements of Psycho-Analysis*. London: Heinemann.

Bion, W. (1970). *Attention and interpretation*. London: Maresfield Library.

Black, W. A. (1991) An existential approach to self-control in the addictive behaviours. In Heather, N., Miller, W.R., & Greeley, J. (Eds.) *Self-control and the Addictive Behaviours*, pp. 262-279. Sydney, Australia: Maxwell-MacMillan Publishing.

Black, D. M. (2004). Sympathy reconfigured: Some reflections on sympathy, empathy and the discovery of values. *International Journal Of Psycho-Analysis, 85*(3), 579-595.

Blackburn, S. (2003). *Being Good*, New York: Oxford University Press.

Bluhm, R. (2005) From hierarchy to network: a richer view of evidence for evidence-based medicine. *Perspectives in Biology and Medicine, 48* (4), 535–547.

Bollas, C. (1989). *Forces of destiny: Psychoanalysis and human idiom*. Northvale, NJ: Jason Aronson.

Boleyn-Fitzgerald, P. (2003). Care and the Problem of Pity. *Bioethics, 17*, (1), 1-20.

Bower J.E., Kemeny M.E., Taylor S.E. & Fahey J.L. (1998) Cognitive processing, discovery of meaning, CD4 decline, and AIDS-related mortality among bereaved HIV-sero-positive men. Journal of Consulting and Clinical Psychology 66(6), 979–986.

Bowker, J.W. (1970). *Problems of suffering in religions of the world*. NY: Cambridge University Press.

Bradford, D. T. (1990). Early Christian martyrdom and the psychology of depression, suicide, and bodily mutilation. *Psychotherapy: Theory, Research, Practice, Training, 27*(1), 30-41.

Brady, M.J., Peterman, A.H., Fitchett, G., Mo, M., Cella, D. A case for including spirituality in quality of life measurements in oncology. *Psychooncology, 8*, 417-428.

Brandchaft, B. (1993). To free the spirit from its cell. In A. Goldberg (Ed.), *Progress in Self Psychology, vol. 9: The widening scope of Self Psychology*. Hillsdale, NJ: Analytic Press.

Breggin, P.R. (1991). *Toxic psychiatry*. NY: St. Martin's Press.

Breitbart, We., Heller, K.S. Reframing hope: meaning-centered care for patients near the end of life. *Journal of Palliative Medicine 6*, 979-988.

Brown, J.C. & Parker, R. (1989). For God so loved the world. In J.C. Brown & R.C. Bohn (Eds.). *Christianity, patriarchy, and abuse: A feminist critique*. NY: Pilgrim Press.

Buss, D. (2000). *The dangerous passion: Why jealousy is as necessary as love and sex*. New York: Free Press.

Bynum, C. W. (1991). *Fragmentation and Redemption: Essays on Gender and the Human Body in Medieval Religion*. New York: Zone Books.

Cacioppo, J. & William, P. (2008). *Loneliness: Human nature and the need for social connection*. N.Y.: WW Norton.

Campbell, J. (2008). *The hero with a thousand faces*. Novato, CA: New World Library.

Camus, A. (1969). *The Myth of Sisyphus and Other Essays*. Trans. Justin O'Brien, New York: Knopf.

Carlat, D. (2010). *Unhinged: The trouble with psychiatry—A doctor's revelations about a profession in crisis*. New York, NY: The Free Press.

Carver, C.S., & Connor-Smith, J. (2010). Personality and Coping. *Annual Review of Psychology, 61(1)*, 679-704.

Carveth, D. (1992). Dead end kids: Projective identification and sacrifice in 'Orphans.' *International Review of Psychoanalysis, 19(2)*, 217–227.

Cassell, E.J. (2004). *The nature of suffering and the goals of medicine* (2nd ed.). NY: Oxford University Press.

Gila, C. (2006). Social Support, Spiritual Program, and Addiction Recovery. *International Journal Of Offender Therapy & Comparative Criminology, 50(3)*, 306-323.

Chismar, D. (1988). Empathy and Sympathy: The Important Difference. *The Journal of Value Inquiry, 22*, 257-266.

Clements, A. D., & Ermakova, A. V. (2012). Surrender to God and stress: A possible link between religiosity and health. *Psychology Of Religion And Spirituality, 4(2)*, 93-107.

Cohen, A. (1981). *The Tremendum: A theological interpretation of the Holocaust*. NY: Crossroads.

Cohen, M., & Gereboff, J. (2004). Orthodox Judaism and psychoanalysis: Towards dialogue and reconciliation. *Journal of the American Academy of Psychoanalysis, 32*, (2), 267-286.

Cole, B.S., & Pargament, K.I. (1999). Spiritual surrender: A paradoxical path to control. In W.R. Miller (Ed.), *Integrating spirituality into treatment* (pp. 179-189). Washington, D.C.: American Psychological Association Press.

Cole, D. (2012). Torture and just war. *Journal of Religious Ethics,40*(1), 26-51.

Cole, V.L. (2003). Healing principles: A model for the use of ritual in psychotherapy. *Counseling and values (47)* 3, 184-195.

Cook, D. (2007). *Martyrdom in Islam.* NY: Cambridge University Press.

Corbett, L. (2007). *Psyche and the sacred.* New Orleans: Spring Publications.

Corbett, L. (2011). *The sacred cauldron: Psychotherapy as a spiritual practice.* Wilmette, Il: Chiron.

Corbett, L. (2013). Jung's approach to spirituality and religion. In E. Shafransky & K. Pargament (Eds.), *APA Handbook of psychology and religion.* Washington, D.C.: APA publications, pp. 147-167.

Corbett, L. (2013). Silence, presence, and witness in psychotherapy. In U. Wirtz, S., Wirth, D. Eggar & K. Remark (Eds.), *Echoes of silence: Listening to soul, self, other.* New Orleans, LA: Spring publications.

Coyle, N. (1996). Suffering in the first person: Glimpses of suffering through patient and family narratives. In B. R.Ferrell (Ed.), *Suffering.* Sudbury, MA: Jones & Bartlett. pp. 29– 64

Crelinsten, R. (1993). In Their Own Words: The World of the Torturer. In Ronald D. Crelinsten and Alex P. Schmid, (Eds.), *The Politics of Pain: Torturers and Their Masters.* Boulder, Co.: Westview Press.

Crick, F. (2004). *The astonishing hypothesis.* NY: Touchstone.

Cwik, A. J. (1995). Active Imagination: Synthesis in Analysis. In M. Stein (Ed.), *Jungian analysis* (pp. 137-169) Chicago, Il: Open Court. (2nd. Edition.)

Cushman, P., & Gilford, P. (2000). Will managed care change our way of being? *American Psychologist 55*:985–996.

Dallman, M.F. (2006) Make love, not war. *Behavioral and Brain Sciences, 29*:227–228

Damasio, A. R. (1994). *Descartes' Error: Emotion, Reason, and the Human Brain.* N.Y: Putnam.

Dare, C. (1993). The family scapegoat: An origin for hating. In V. Varma, (Ed.), *How and why children hate.* London: Jessica Kingsley Publishers. pp. 31-45.

Darley, J., & Bateson , C. (1973). From Jerusalem to Jericho: A study of situational and dispositional variables in helping behaviour. *Journal of Personality and Social Psychology, 27,*100-108.

Daud, A., Skoglund, E.,& Rydelius, P. (2005). Children in families of torture victims: Transgenerational transmission of parents' traumatic experiences to their children. *International Journal of Social Welfare, 14,* 22–32.

Davis, S.T. (2001). *Encountering evil: Live options in theodicy.* Louisville, KY: Westminster John Knox Press.

Deflem, M. (1991). Ritual, anti-structure, and religion : a discussion of Victor Turner's processual symbolic analysis. *Journal For The Scientific Study Of Religion, 30*(1), 1-25.

DeNavas-Walt, C., Proctor, B. D., & Smith, J. C. (2011). U.S. Census Bureau, Population Reports. Income, Poverty, and Health Insurance Coverage in the United States. Washington, DC.

DeViney, E., Dickert, J., & Lockwood, R. (1983). The care of pets within child abusing families. *International Journal for the Study of Animal Problems, 4* (4), 321-329.

Dezutter, J., Casalin, S., Wachholtz, A., Luyckx, K., Hekking, J., & Vandewiele, W. (2013). Meaning in life: An important factor for the psychological well-being of chronically ill patients? Rehabilitation Psychology, 58(4), 334-341.

Diekmann, H. (1971). The Favorite Fairy-Tale of Childhood. *Journal of Analytical Psychology, 16* (1), 18-13.

Doctors, S. (1981). The symptom of delicate self-cutting in adolescent females: A developmental view. *Adolescent Psychiatry, 9,* 443-460.

Doob, L.W. (1988). *Inevitability: Determinism, fatalism and destiny.* NY: Greenwood Press.

Dovidio, J. F., Piuavin, J. A., Schroeder, D. A., & Penner, L. A. (2006). *The social psychology of prosocial behavior.* Hillsdale, NJ: Erlbaum.

Dreifuss, G. G. (1977). Sacrifice in Analysis. *Journal Of Analytical Psychology, 22*(3), 258-267.

Duclow, D. (1979). Perspective and Therapy in Boethius' *Consolation of Philosophy. Journal of Medicine and Philosophy, 4,* 334-43.

Dueck, A., & Goodman, D. (2007). Expiation, Substitution and Surrender: Levinasian Implications for Psychotherapy. *Pastoral Psychology, 55*(5), 601-617.

Durckheim, K.G. (1992). *Absolute living: The otherwordly in the world and the path to maturity.* London: Arkana Books.

Edgar, I. R. (2007). The inspirational night dream in the motivation and justification of jihad. *Nova Religio, 11,* 59– 76.

Edelson, M. (1984). *Hypothesis and evidence in Psychoanalysis.* Chicago, Il: University of Chicago Press.

Ehrman, B. (2008). *God's problem: How the Bible fails to answer our most important question: why we suffer.* NY: HarperCollins.

Eigen, M. (1981). The area of faith in Winnicott, Lacan and Bion. *International Journal of Psycho-Analysis, 62,* 413-433.

Eigen, M. (1986). *The psychotic core.* Northvale, NJ: Jason Aronson.

Eissler, K. R., Meyer, M., & Garcia, E. E. (2000). On Hatred: With Comments on the Revolutionary, the Saint, and the Terrorist. Psychoanalytic Study Of The Child, 55, 27-44.

El-Mallakh, R.S., Yonglin, G., & Roberts, R.J. (2011). Tardive dysphoria: The role of long term antidepressant use in inducing chronic depression. *Medical Hypotheses 76,* 769-773.

Eliade, M. (1965). *Rites and symbols of initiation: The mysteries of death and rebirth.* (W.R. Trask, Trans.) NY: Harper and Row.

Engel, G. (1959). "Psychogenic" pain and the pain–prone patient. *American Journal of Medicine,26,* 899–918.

Erikson, E. (1997). *The Life Cycle Completed.* New York: Norton.

Farber, B. A., Manevich, I., Metzger, J., & Saypol, E. (2005). Choosing psychotherapy as a career: Why did we cross that road? *Journal of Clinical Psychology(61),* 1009–1031.

Falk, R., Gendzier, I., & Lifton, R. J. (Eds.) (2006). *Crimes of war: Iraq.* New York: Avalon Publishing Group.

Farley, W. (2011). Duality and non-duality in Christian practice: reflections on the benefits of Buddhist-Christian dialogue for constructive theology. *Buddhist-Christian Studies, 31,* 135-146.

Favazza, A. R. (1996). *Bodies Under Siege: Self-Mutilation and Body Modification in Culture and Psychology.* Baltimore, MD: Johns Hopkins University Press.

Felix, A. (2001). *Silent soul: The miracles and mysteries of Audrey Santo.* NY: St. Martin's Press.

Ferenczi, S. (1933/1955). Confusion of tongues between adults and the child. In *Final Contributions to the Problems and Methods of Psycho-Analysis.* London: Hogarth Press, pp. 156-167.

Figley, C. R. (2002). Compassion fatigue: Psychotherapists' chronic lack of self care. *Journal Of Clinical Psychology, 58*(11), 1433-1441.

Fischer, P., Krueger, J. I., Greitemeyer, T., Vogrincic, C., Kastenmüller, A., Frey, D., & Kainbacher, M. (2011). The bystander-effect: A meta-analytic review on bystander intervention in dangerous and non-dangerous emergencies. *Psychological Bulletin, 137*(4), 517-537.

Fjelland J. E., Barron, C. R., & Foxall, M. (2008). A review of instruments measuring two aspects of meaning: search for meaning and meaning in illness. *Journal Of Advanced Nursing, 62*(4), 394-406.

Fleming, M. (2005). Towards a Model of Mental Pain and Psychic Suffering. *Canadian Journal Of Psychoanalysis, 13*(2), 255-272.

Fleming, M. (2006). Distinction Between Mental Pain and Psychic Suffering as Separate Entities in the Patient's Experience. *International Forum Of Psychoanalysis, 15*(4), 195-200.

Flynn, C. P. (2000b). Woman's best friend: Pet abuse and the role of companion animals in the lives of battered women. *Violence Against Women, 6,* 162-177.

Fonagy, P. Gerber, A., Kächele, H., Krause, R., Jones, E., Perron, R., & Allison, E. (2002). *An Open Door Review of Outcome Studies in Psychoanalysis.* 2nd rev. ed. London: International Psychoanalytical Association.

Fonagy, P., Gergeley, G., Jurist, E., & Target, M. (2005). *Affect regulation, mentalization, and the development of the self.* London: Karnac Books.

Frank, A. W. (2001). Can We Research Suffering? *Qualitative Health Research, 11*(3), 353-363.

Frankl, V. (1959). *Man's search for meaning.* Boston, MA: Beacon Press.

Frankl, V. (1967). *Psychotherapy and existentialism: Selected papers on logotherapy.* NY: Simon and Shuster.

Frankl, V. (1969). *The will to meaning: Foundations and Applications of Logotherapy.* NY: World Publishing.

Frasure-Smith, N., Lespérance, F., & Talajic, M. (1995). The impact of negative emotions on prognosis following myocardial infarction: Is it more than depression? *Health Psychology, 14*(5), 388-398.

Freud, S. (1900). The interpretation of dreams. *Standard Edition,* vol. 4. London: Hogarth Press.

Freud, S. (1901/1955). *The psychopathology of everyday life.* SE vol. 6. London: Hogarth Press.

Freud, A. (1946). *The Ego and the Mechanisms of Defense.* New York: International Universities Press.

Freud, S. (1907). Obsessive actions and religious practices, *Standard Edition* vol. 9, pp. 115-128.

Freud, S. (1912). Recommendations to physicians practicing psycho-analysis. *Standard Edition,* vol.12, 111-120.

Freud, S. (1913). *The theme of the three caskets.* London: Penguin Freud Library, vol. 14.

Freud, S. (1915). Instincts and their vicissitudes. *Standard Edition,* vol. 14, 117-140.

Fromm-Reichmann, F. (1990). Loneliness. *Contemporary Psychoanalysis, (26)* 305-329.

Fromm, E. (1941). *Escape from freedom.* New York: Farrar & Rinehart.

Furnham, A., & Brown, L. B. (1992). Theodicy: A neglected aspect of the psychology of religion. *International Journal for the Psychology of Religion, 2,* 37–45.

Gallagher, L. (1997). "The Place of the Stigmata in Christological Poetics." In: *Religion and Culture in Renaissance England.* Claire McEachern and Debora Shuger. (Eds.). NY: Cambridge University Press.

Gamsa, A. (1994), The role of psychological factors in chronic pain. *Pain,* 57: 5-29.

Gantt, E.E. (2000). Levinas, Psychotherapy, and the Ethics of Suffering. *Journal of Humanistic Psychology,* 40, 9-28.

Garrison, J. (1983). *The darkness of God: Theology after Hiroshima.* Grand Rapids, MI: Eerdmans Publishing.

Gelhous, P. (2012). The desired moral attitude of the physician: (II) compassion. *Medical Health Care and Philosophy, 15,* 397-410.

Geller, S.M. & Greenberg, L.S. (2002). Therapeutic presence: Therapists' experience of presence in the psychotherapeutic encounter. *Person-Centered and Experiential Psychotherapies, 1,* 71-86.

Geller, S.M. & Greenberg, L.S (2012). *Therapeutic presence.* Washington, D.C.: APA press.

Geller, J.D. (2006). Pity, suffering, and psychotherapy. *American Journal of Psychotherapy, 60,* (2): 187-205.

Gelles, R. J. (1997). *Intimate violence in families.* Thousand Oaks, CA: Sage.

Gergen, K. J. (2001). Psychological science in a postmodern context. *American Psychologist, 56,* 803-813.

Ghent, E. (1999). Masochism, submission, surrender: Masochism as a perversion of surrender. In L. Aron & S. A. Mitchell (Eds.), *Relational psychoanalysis: The emergence of tradition,* Vol. 14 (pp. 211–242). Relational Perspectives Book Series. Hillsdale, NJ: Analytic Press. Original work published in 1990.

Gilligan, J. (2000) *Violence: Reflections on our Deadliest Epidemic.* London, UK: Jessica Kingsley.

Girard, R. (1987). *Things Hidden since the Foundation of the World.* Stanford: Stanford University Press.

Girard, R. (1977). *Violence and the Sacred.* Baltimore: Johns Hopkins University Press.

Girard, R. (1986). *The scapegoat.* Baltimore, MD: Johns Hopkins University Press.

Girard, R. (2008). *Evolution and conversion: Dialogues on the origin of culture.* NY: Continuum International Publishing Group.

Glasberg, A.L., Eriksson S. & Norberg A. (2007). Burnout and 'stress of conscience' among health personnel. *Journal of Advanced Nursing 57,* 392–403.

Glenn, J.D. (1984). Marcel and Sartre: the philosophy of communion and the philosophy of alienation. In Shilpp P.A., Hahn L.E. (eds.). *The philosophy of Gabriel Marcel.* La Salle, IL: Open Court Publishers. pp. 525–50.

Glucklich, A. (2003). *Sacred Pain: Hurting the body for the sake of the soul.* NY: Oxford University Press.

Goetzmann, L. (2004). "Is it me, or isn't it?"—Transplanted organs and their donors as transitional objects. *The American Journal of Psychoanalysis, 64,* (3), 279-289.

Goldberg, J.S. (1993). *The dark side of love: The positive role of our negative feelings—anger, jealousy and hate.* NY: Putnams.

Gottlieb, R. M. (2004). Refusing the cure: Sophocles's Philoctetes and the clinical problems of self- injurious spite, shame and forgiveness. *International Journal Of Psycho-Analysis, 85*(3), 669-689.

Greene, M., & Kaplan, B. (1978). Aspects of loneliness in the therapeutic situation. *International Review of Psychoanalysis, (5),* 321-330.

Greene, L. (1984). *The astrology of fate.* Boston, MA: Red Wheel/Weiser.

Greenberg, J., Pyszczynski, T., & Solomon, S. (1986). The causes and consequences of a   need for self-esteem: A terror management theory. In R. F. Baumeister (Ed.), *Public self and private self* (pp. 189 –212). New York: Springer-Verlag.

Greenberg, L. S. (2012). Emotions, the great captains of our lives: Their role in the process of change in psychotherapy. *American Psychologist, 67*(8), 697-707.

Greenspan, M. (2004). *Healing through the dark emotions: The wisdom of grief, fear, and despair.* Boston, MA: Shambhala.

Greenstein, M., Breitbart, W. (1999). Cancer and the experience of meaning: a group psychotherapy program for people with cancer. *American Journal of Psychotherapy, 54*(4): 486-500.

Groenhout, R. (2006). Kenosis and feminist theory. In C. S. Evans (Ed.), *Exploring kenotic Christology,* pp. 291-312.

Grote, N. K., Zuckoff, A., Swartz, H., Bledsoe, S. E., & Geibel, S. (2007). Engaging women who are depressed and economically disadvantaged in mental health treatment. *Social Work, 52,* 295–308.

Grunbaum, A. (1984). *The foundations of Psychoanalysis: A philosophical critique.* Berkeley, CA: University of California Press.

Guntrip, H. (1969). *Schizoid Phenomena, Object Relations, and the Self.* New York: International Universities Press.

Gushee, D. P. (2006). Against Torture: An Evangelical Perspective. *Theology Today* 63: 349–64.

Gut, E. (1989). *Productive and unproductive depression*. London: Routledge.

Hall, M. E., & Johnson, E. L. (2001). Theodicy and therapy: Philosophical/ theological contributions to the problem of suffering. *Journal of Psychology and Christianity, 20*, 5–17.

Harding, E. (1981). The value and meaning of depression. *Psychological perspectives 12(2)*, 113-135.

Hardy, A. (1979). *The spiritual nature of man*. NY: Oxford University Press.

Harrington, E.R. (2004). *The social psychology of hatred. Journal of Hate Studies, 3*(1), 49-82.

Hartmann, H., & Milch, W. E. (2000). The Need for Efficacy in the Treatment of Suicidal Patients: Transference and Countertransference Issues. *Progress In Self Psychology, 16*, 87-101.

Heisel, M.J. & Flett, G.L. (2004). Purpose in life, satisfaction with life, and suicidal ideation in a clinical sample. *Journal of Psychopathology and Behavioral Assessment, 26*, 127-135.

Helin K. & Lindström U.Å., (2003) Sacrifice: an ethical dimension of caring that makes suffering meaningful. *Nursing Ethics 10*, 414–427.

Helsel, P. (2009). Simone Weil's passion mysticism: The paradox of chronic pain and the transformation of the cross. *Pastoral Psychology, 58*(1), 55-63.

Henderson, J.L. (2005). *Thresholds of initiation*. Wilmette, Il: Chiron publishers.

Hersch, E.L. (2000). Making Our Philosophical Unconscious More Conscious: A Method of Exploring the Philosophical Basis of Psychological Theory. *Canadian Journal Of Psychoanalysis, 9*(2), 165-186.

Herzog, H, & Arluke A. (2006) Human–animal connections: recent findings on the anthrozoology of cruelty. *Behavioral and Brain Sciences, 29*, 230–231

Hidas, A. M. (1981). Psychotherapy and surrender: A psychospiritual perspective. *The journal of transpersonal psychology, 131*, (1), 27-32.

Hillman, J. (1995). Pink madness, or why does Aphrodite drive men crazy with pornography? *Spring, 57*, 39-71.

Hillman, J. (1997). *Re-Visioning psychology*. San Francisco: Harper and Row.

Hoffman, M.L. (1978). Psychological and Biological Perspectives on Altruism. *International Journal of Behavioral Development, 1*(4), 323–339.

Hoffer, E. (2002). *The true believer: Thoughts on the nature of mass movements.* NY: Harper Collins.

Hoffman, M. (2000). Empathy *and Moral* Development: *Implications for Caring and Justice.* Cambridge: Cambridge University Press.

Horney, K. (1937). *The neurotic personality of our time.* New York: W.W. Norton.

Horney, K. (1950). *Neurosis and Human Growth.* New York: Norton.

Horwitz, A. V. (2002). *Creating mental illness.* Chicago, IL: The University of Chicago Press.

Howarth, R. (2011). Concepts and Controversies in Grief and Loss. *Journal Of Mental Health Counseling, 33*(1), 4-10.

Huebner, B., & Hauser, M. D. (2011). Moral judgments about altruistic self-sacrifice: Whenphilosophical and folk intuitions clash. *Philosophical Psychology, 24*(1), 73-94.

Huett, S. D., & Goodman, D. M. (2012). Levinas on managed care: The (a) proximal, faceless third-party and the psychotherapeutic dyad. *Journal Of Theoretical And Philosophical Psychology, 32*(2), 86-102.

Hutchens, B. C. (2007). *Psychoanalytic Review 94* (4), 595-616.

Hyde, G.E. (1961). *Spotted Tail's folk: A history of the Brule Sioux.* Norman, OK: University of Oklahoma Press.

Imber-Black, E., Roberts, J., & Whiting, R.A. (1988). *Rituals in families and family therapy.* NY: Norton.

Jackson, P., Meltzoff, A., & Decety, J. (2005). How do we perceive the pain of others?: a window into the neural processes involved in empathy. *NeuroImage, 24*(3), 771–779.

Jacoby, M. (2006). *Longing for paradise: Psychological perspectives on an archetype.* Toronto: Inner City Books.

James, W. (1949). *Essays on faith and morals.* London: Longmans Publishers.

James, W. (1902/1958). *The varieties of religious experience.* New York: Penguin Books.

James, E.O. (2003). *Origins of sacrifice.* Whitefish, MT: Kessinger Publishing. (Original work published in 1933).

Jamison K.R. (1997). *An Unquiet Mind: A Memoir of Moods and Madness.* NY: Vintage Books.

Janoff-Bulman, R. (1992). *Shattered assumptions: Towards a new psychology of trauma*. New York: Free Press.

Jay, N. (1992). *Throughout your generations forever: Sacrifice, religion and paternity*. Chicago: University of Chicago.

Jecker, N. & Self, D. (1993). Separating care and cure. An analysis of historical and contemporary images of nursing and medicine. *Journal of Medicine and Philosophy, 16,* 285-285.

Jobst, K., Shostak, D., & Whitehouse, P. (1999). Diseases of meaning, manifestations of health, and metaphor. *The Journal of Alternative and Complementary Medicine, 5*(6), 495-502.

Jonas, W.B. & Crawford, CC. (2004). *Journal of Alternative and Complementary Medicine,(10)* 5, 751-756.

Jopling, D. A. (1998). First do no harm: Over-philosophizing and pseudo-philosophizing in philosophical counseling. *Inquiry: Critical Thinking Across Disciplines, 17,* 100– 112.

Jung, C.G. (1965). *Memories, dreams, reflections*. NY: Vintage Books.

Jung, C. G. (1969). Synchronicity: An acausal connecting principle. In *The collected works of C. G. Jung* (Vol. 8). Princeton, NJ: Princeton University Press (Bollingen Series). (Original work published in 1931).

Jung, C. G. (1961/1975) Letter to William G. Wilson, 30 January, 1961, in: Adler, G. (Ed.) *Letters of Carl G. Jung*, vol. 2, pp. 623-625 (London, Routledge & Kegan Paul).

Jung, C.G. (1936/1988). *Nietzsche's Zarathustra: Notes of the seminar given 1934-1939*. (W. McGuire, Ed.). Princeton, NJ: Princeton University Press.

Jung, C.G. (1938/1984). *Dream analysis: Notes of the seminar given in 1928-1930*. (W. McGuire, Ed.). Princeton, NJ: Princeton University Press.

Jung, C.G. (1939). *Modern man in search of a soul*. NY: Harcourt Brace.

Jung, C.G. (1956/1967). *Symbols of transformation*. CW 5. Princeton, NJ: Princeton University Press.

Khalil, E.L. (2004). What is altruism? *Journal of Economic Psychology, 25,* 97-123.

Khan, M. R. (2001). From masochism to psychic pain. *Contemporary Psychoanalysis, 17,* 413-421.

Kaplan, D.M. (1984). Reflections on the idea of personal fate and its psychopathology: Helene Deutsch's 'Hysterical Fate Neurosis Revisited." *Psychoanalytic Quarterly, 53,* 240-266.

Kasher, M.M. (1956). *Torah Shelemah.* Jerusalem: American Biblical Encyclopedia Society.

Kaslow, N. J., & Aronson, S. G. (2004). Recommendations for Family Interventions Following a Suicide. *Professional Psychology: Research And Practice, 35*(3), 240-247.

Kernberg, O.F. (1992). *Aggression in personality disorders and perversions.* New Haven, CT: Yale University Press.

Kernberg, O. F. (1995). Hatred as a core affect of aggression. In Akhtar, S., Kramer, S., & Parens, H. (Eds.), *The birth of hatred.* Northvale, NJ: Jason Aronson. pp. 55-82.

Khema, A. (1987). *Being Nobody Going Nowhere: Meditations on the Buddhist Path.* Boston, MA:Wisdom Publications.

Kilner, J. M. & Lemon, R. N. (2013). What We Know Currently about Mirror Neurons *Current Biology, 23,*(23), 1057-1062.

van Kleef, G. A., Oveis, C., van der Löwe, I., LuoKogan, A., Goetz, J., & Keltner, D. (2008). Power, distress, and compassion: Turning a blind eye to the suffering of others. *Psychological Science, 19*(12), 1315-1322.

Klein, M. (1957/1975). Envy and Gratitude. In *The Writings of Melanie Klein,* vol. 3, *Envy and Gratitude and Other Works.* London: Hogarth Press.

Klein, S.B. (2015). A defense of experiential realism: The need to take phenomenal reality on its own terms in the study of the mind. *Psychology of Consciousness: Theory, Research, and Practice, 2*(1), 41-56.

Klugman, C. M. (2007). Narrative Phenomenology: Exploring stories of grief and dying. In N.E. Johnston & A. Scholler-Jaquish (Eds.), *Meaning in Suffering: Caring practices in the health professions.* Madison, WI: University of Wisconsin Press. pp. 144-185.

Knox, J. (2004). Developmental aspects of analytical psychology: New perspectives from cognitive neuroscience and attachment theory. In J. Cambry & L. Carter (Eds.), *Analytical psychology: Contemporary perspectives in Jungian analysis.* NY: Brunner-Routledge. pp. 56-82.

Koltko-Rivera, M. E. (2004). The Psychology of Worldviews. *Review Of General Psychology, 8*(1), 3-58.

Krishnamurti, J. (1954). *First and last freedom*. San Francisco: Harper and Row.

Krishnamurti, J. (1983). *The flame of attention*. San Francisco: Harper and Row.

Krishnamurti, J. (1981). *The wholeness of life*. San Francisco: Harper & Row.

Klein, J. (1979). *Psychology encounters Judaism*. NY: Philosophical Library.

Klein, M. (1937/1975). Love, guilt and reparation. In *Love, Guilt and Reparation and Other Works* 1921-1945. New York: Delacorte press/Seymour Lawrence, pp. 306-343.

Klein, M. (1959/1975). On the sense of loneliness. In *Envy and Gratitude and Other Works 1946-1963*. New York: The Free Press. pp. 300-313.

Kleinman, A. (1989). *The illness narratives: Suffering, healing, and the human condition*. NY: Basic books.

Knight, Z. G. (2007). The analyst's emotional surrender. *Psychoanalytic Review*, 94(2), 277-289.

Kobak, R. R. & Waters D.B. (1984). Family therapy as a rite of passage. *Family Process 23*, 1, 89-100.

Kohut, H. (1997). *The restoration of the self*. Chicago, Il: University of Chicago Press.

Kohut, H. (1984). *How does analysis cure?* Ed. A. Goldberg. Chicago, Il: University of Chicago Press.

Kosloff, S, Greenberg, J., & Solomon, S. (2006). Considering the roles of affect and culture in the enactment and enjoyment of cruelty. *Behavioral and brain sciences*, 29, 3, 231-232.

Kray, L.J., Hershfield, H.E., George, L.G., & Galinsky, A.D. (2013). Twists of fate: Moments in time and what might have been in the emergence of meaning. In Markman, K.D., Prouix, T., & Lindberg, M.J. (2013). *The psychology of meaning*. Washington, D.C: American Psychological Association, pp. 317-337.

Kriegman , D. (1988), Self psychology from the perspective of evolutionary biology: Toward a biological foundation for self psychology. In: *Frontiers in Self Psychology: Progress in Self Psychology*, In A. Goldberg (Ed.), Hillsdale, NJ: The Analytic Press, pp. 253-274.

Laato, A. & de Moor, J. (2003). *Theodicy in the world of the Bible*. Brill Academic Publishing.

Lakhan SE, Schofield KL (2013) Mindfulness-Based Therapies in the Treatment of Somatization Disorders: A Systematic Review and Meta-Analysis. *Public Library of Science 8*(8), p. 1-13.

Lambert M. J. (1992). Implications of outcome research for psychotherapy integration. In Norcross J.C. & Goldstein M.R., (Eds.), *Handbook of psychotherapy integration*. New York: Basic Books, pp. 94-129.

Lamers, S., Bolier, L, Westerhof, G., Smit, F. & Bholmeijer, E. (2012). The impact of emotional well-being on long-term recovery and survival in physical illness: a meta-analysis. *Journal of Behavioral Medicine, 35*(5), 538-547.

Langegard, U., & Ahlberg, K. (2009). Consolation in Conjunction With Incurable Cancer. *Oncology Nursing Forum, 36*(2), E 99-E106.

Lansky, M. R. (2003). Modification of the Ego Ideal and the Problem of Forgiveness in Sophocles' Philoctetes. *Psychoanalysis & Contemporary Thought, 26*(4), 463-491.

Larson, D. B., Sherrill, K.A., & Lyons, J.S. (1992). Associations between dimensions of religious commitment and mental health reported in the American Journal of Psychiatry and Archives of General Psychiatry: 1978-1989. *American Journal of Psychiatry, 149*, 557-559.

Larson, D.B., Swyers, J.P., & McCullough, M.E. (Eds.) (1998) *Scientific Research on Spirituality and Health: a consensus report.* Rockville, MD: National Institute for Healthcare Research.

Lazarus R.S. & Folkman S. (1984). *Stress, Appraisal, and Coping.* New York: Springer.

LeShan, L. (1994). *Cancer as turning point: A handbook for people with cancer, their families, and heath professionals.* NY: Penguin Books.

Lester, D. (2004). Suicide Bombers: Are Psychological Profiles Possible? *Studies In Conflict & Terrorism, 27*(4), 283-295.

Levine, S. (1982). *Who Dies? An Investigation of Conscious Living and Conscious Dying.* NY: Anchor Books.

Levinas, E. (1969). *Totality and infinity* (A. Lingis, trans.). Pittsburgh, PA: Duquesne University Press.

Lévinas E (1985) *Ethics and Infinity.* Pittsburgh, PA: Duquesne University Press.

Levinas, E. (1996). Substitution. In A. T. Peperzak, S. Critchley, & R. Bernasconi (Eds.), *Emmanuel Levinas:Basic philosophical writings* (pp. 80–95). Indianapolis, IN: Indiana University Press. (Original work published in 1968).

Levinas, E. (1998a). *Entre nous: On thinking-of-the-other.* NY: Columbia University Press.

Levinas , E. (1998b). *Otherwise than being or beyond essence* (A. Lingis, trans.). Pittsburgh, PA: Duquesne University Press.

Levinas, E. (2001). *Is it righteous to be? Interviews with Emmanuel Levinas* (J. Robbins, Ed.). Stanford, CA: Stanford University Press.

Lakatos, A. (2010). War, Martyrdom and Suicide Bombers: Essay on Suicide Terrorism. *Cultura: International Journal Of Philosophy Of Culture & Axiology, 7*(2), 171-180.

Latané, B. & Nida, S. (1981). Ten years of research on group size and helping. *Psychological Bulletin, 89,* 2, 308-324.

Latané, B. & Darley, J. (1970). *The unresponsive bystander: Why doesn't he help?* NY: Appleton-Century Crofts.

Lee, B. Y., & Newberg, A. B. (2005). Religion and health: A review and critical analysis. *Zygon, 40,* 443–468.

Leichsenring, F., Klein, S., & Salzer, S. (2014). The Efficacy of Psychodynamic Psychotherapy in Specific Mental Disorders: A 2013 Update of Empirical Evidence. *Contemporary Psychoanalysis, 50*(1-2), 89-130.

Lerman, H. (1992) The limits of phenomenology: A feminist critique of humanistic personality theories. In Ballou, M., & Brown, L. (Eds.) *Theories of Personality and Psychopathology.* New York: Guilford.

Lewis, C.S. (1952). *Mere Christianity.* NY: Harper Collins.

Libet, B. (1985). Unconscious cerebral initiative and the role of conscious will in voluntary action. *Behavioral and Brain Sciences,* (8), 529-566.

Lifton, R. J. (1986). *The Nazi doctors. Medical killing and the psychology of genocide.* New York: Basic Books.

Lincoln, B. (1991). *Emerging from the chrysalis: Rituals of women's initiation.* NY: Oxford University Press.

Lipet, B. (1996). Free will in the light of neuropsychiatry. *Philosophy, Psychiatry and Psychology, 3,*95–96.

Lippitt, J. (2009). *International Journal of the Philosophy of Religion,* 66:125–138.

Litman , R. E. (1980), The dream in the suicidal situation. In J. M. Natterson (Ed.), *The Dream in Clinical Practice.* New York: Jason Aronsen.

Longino, Helen E. (1990). *Science as Social Knowledge: Values and Objectivity in Scientific Inquiry*. Princeton, NJ: Princeton University Press.

Luborsky L., Diguer L., Seligman DA., Rosenthal R., Krause ED., Johnson S., Halperin G., Bishop, M., Berman JS., Schweizer E. (1999). The researcher's own therapy allegiances: A 'wild card' in comparisons of treatment efficacy. *Clinical Psychology: Science and Practice 6*, 95-106.

Lucas, E. (1986). *Meaning in suffering: Comfort in crisis through logotherapy*. Berkely, CA: Institute of Logotherapy Press.

Luyten, P., Blatt, S. J., & Corveleyn, J. (2006). Minding the Gap Between Positivism and Hermeneutics in Psychoanalytic Research. *Journal Of The American Psychoanalytic Association, 54*(2), 571-610.

Mahoney, M.J. (2005). Suffering, Philosophy, and Psychotherapy. *Journal of psychotherapy integration, 15*, (3), 337-352.

Maltsberger, J. T. (1997). Ecstatic Suicide. *Archives Of Suicide Research, 3*(4), 283-301.

Maltsberger, J. T. (2004). The descent into suicide. *International Journal Of Psycho-Analysis, 85*(3), 653-667.

Mannack, P. L. (2003). The question of cognitive therapy in a postmodern world. *Ethical Human Sciences and Services: An International Journal of Critical Inquiry 5*(3), 209-224.

Manning, R. J. S. (1993). *Interpreting otherwise than Heidegger: Emmanuel Levinas's ethics as first philosophy*. Pittsburgh, PA: Duquesne University Press.

Marcus, P. (2006). Religion Without Promises: The Philosophy of Emmanuel Levinas and Psychoanalysis. *Psychoanalytic Review, 93*(6), 923-951.

Margolese, H.C. (1998). Engaging in psychotherapy with Orthodox Jews: A critical review. *American Journal of Psychotherapy, 52*, (1), 37-

Marinoff, L. (1999). *Plato not Prozac! Applying philosophy to everyday problems*. NY: HarperCollins.

Markman, K.D., Prouix, T., & Lindberg, M.J. (2013). *The psychology of meaning*. Washington, D.C: American Psychological Association.

Marvin, C. & Ingle, D.W. (1999). *Blood sacrifice and the nation: Totem rituals and the American flag*. NY: Cambridge University Press.

May, R. (1969). *Love and will*. NY: W.W. Norton Company.

May, R. (1981). *Freedom and destiny*. NY: Norton.

McAdams, D.P., & Bowman, P.J. (2001). Narrating life's turning points: Redemption and contamination. In D.P. McAdams, R. Josselson, & A. Lieblich (Eds.),*Turns in the road: Narrative studies of lives in transition* (p. 3-34). Washington, DC: American Psychological Association.

McCaffery M. (1972) *Nursing Management of the Patient with Pain*. JB Lippincott, Philadelphia, PA.

McCoy, A. W. (2006). *A Question of Torture: CIA Interrogation, from the Cold War to the War on Terror*. New York: Henry Hold and Company.

McCracken, L. M., Vowles, K. E., & Gauntlett-Gilbert, J. (2007). A prospective stigation of acceptance and control-oriented coping with chronic pain. *Journal of Behavioral Medicine, 30*, 339–349.

McWilliams, N. (1984). The Psychology of the Altruist. *Psychoanalytic Psychology, 1*(3), 193-213.

Meier, C. A. (1963). Psychosomatic Medicine from the Jungian Point of View. Journal Of Analytical Psychology, 8(2), 103-121.

Mendelson, M. D. (1990). Reflections on Loneliness. *Contemporary Psychoanalysis, (26)*, 330-355.

Merton, T. (2007). *New seeds of contemplation*. NY: New Directions Books.

Mijuskovic, B.L. (1979). *Loneliness in philosophy, psychology, and literature*. Assen, Netherlands: Van Gorcum.

Mikulincer,M., & Shaver, P.R. (2005). Attachment, Security, Compassion, and Altruism. *Current Directions in Psychological Science, 14*, 34–38.

Milgram , S. (1974). *Obedience to authority*. New York: Harper & Row.

Miller, A. (1985). *For your own good: Hidden cruelty in child-rearing and the roots of violence*. NY: Farrar, Straus and Giroux.

Miller, R.B. (2004). *Facing human suffering*. Washington, D.C.: American Psychological Association.

Mill, A.E. & Spencer, E. M. (2003). Evidence-based medicine: Why clinical ethicists should be concerned. *HEC Forum 15*(3), 231-244.

Minuchin, S, Rosman, B., & Baker, L. (1978) *Psychosomatic Families*. Cambridge, MA: Harvard University Press.

Michener, W. (2012). The individual psychology of group hate. *Journal of Hate Studies, 10*(1), 15-48.

Monin, J.K., & Schulz, R. (2009). Interpersonal effects of suffering in older adult caregiving relationships. *Psychology and Aging, 24*(3), 681-695.

Monroe, K.R. (1996). *The Heart of Altruism.* Englewood Cliffs, NJ: Princeton Press.

Moore, R. (2001). *The archetype of initiation.* Xlibris Corp.

Moos R.H., & Holahan, C.J. (2003). Dispositional and contextual perspectives on coping: toward an integrative framework. *Journal of Clinical Psychology, 59,* 1387–403.

Morris, D. B. (1998). *Illness and culture in the postmodern age.* Berkeley: University of California Press.

Morse, J.M., Botorff, J.L., & Hutchinson, S. (1995). The paradox of comfort. *Nursing Research, 44*(1), 14–19.

Moseley, G.L. (2007) Reconceptualising pain according to modern pain science. Physical Therapy Reviews, *12,* pp. 169–178.

Nakao, H., & Itakura, S. (2009). An Integrated View of Empathy: Psychology, Philosophy, and Neuroscience. *Integrative Psychological & Behavioral Science, 43*(1), 42-52.

Nagel, T. (1979). *Mortal questions.* NY: Cambridge University Press.

Nagel, T. (1986). *The View from Nowhere.* New York: Oxford University Press.

Nelson, C.J., Rosenfeld, B., Breitbart, W., Galietta, M. (2002). Spirituality, religion, and depression in the terminally ill. *Psychosomatics, 43,* 213-220.

Nell, V. (2006.) Cruelty's rewards: the gratifications of perpetrators and spectators. *Behavioral and Brain Sciences, 29,* 211–57.

Ness, D.E. & Pfeffer, C.R. (1990). Sequelae of bereavement resulting from suicide. *American Journal of Psychiatry, 147,* (3), 279-285.

Neimeyer, R.A. (2001). *Meaning reconstruction and the experience of loss.* Washington, D.C.: American Psychological Association.

Newshan, G. (1998). *Journal of Advanced Nursing 28*(6), 1236-1241.

Nilsson, T., Svensson, M., Sandell, R., & Clinton, D. (2007). Patients' experience of change in cognitive-behavioral therapy and psychodynamic therapy: a qualitative comparative study. *Psychotherapy Research, 17,* 533-566.

Norberg, A. A., Bergsten, M. M., & Lundman, B. B. (2001). A Model of Consolation. *Nursing Ethics, 8*(6), 544-553.

Odegaard, C.E. (1986). *Dear Doctor.* Menlo Park, CA: The Henry J. Kaiser Foundation.

Ogden, T. (1979). On projective identification. *International Journal of Psychoanalysis, 60,* 357-74.

Ogden, T. (2000). Borges and the art of mourning. *Psychoanalytic dialogues,* 10: 65-88.

Oliner, S., & Oliner, P.M. (1988). *The Altruistic Personality: Rescuers of Jews in Nazi Europe.* NY: The Free Press.

Orange, D.M. (2011). *The suffering stranger: Hermeneutics for everyday clinical practice.* NY: Routledge.

Ortiz, D. Sr. (2001). The survivors' perspective: Voices from the center. In E. Gerrity, T. M. Keane, & F. Tuma (Eds.), *The mental health consequences of torture* (pp. 13–34). New York: Kluwer.

Ostow, M. (1959). Religion and psychoanalysis: The area of common concern. *Pastoral Psychology, 10,* 33-38.

Ostow, M. (1995). Ultimate intimacy: *The psychodynamics of Jewish mysticism.* London: Karnac Books.

Panskepp, J. (1998). *Affective neuroscience: The foundations of human and animal emotions.* NY: Oxford University Press.

Parens, H. (2012). Attachment, aggression, and the prevention of malignant prejudice. *Psychoanalytic Inquiry, 32*(2), 171-185.

Parfit, D. (1984). *Reasons and persons.* NY: Oxford University Press.

Park, C.L. (2010). Making sense of the meaning literature: An integrative review of meaning making and its effects on adjustment to stressful life events. *Psychological Bulletin, 136,* (2), 257-301.

Paris, G. (2011). *Heartbreak.* Minneapolis, MN: Mill City Press.

Pawelski, J. O. (2003). William James, Positive Psychology, and Healthy-Mindedness. *Journal Of Speculative Philosophy, 17*(1), 53-67.

Pearlman, L. A., & MacIan, P. S. (1995a). Vicarious traumatization: An empirical study of the effects of trauma work on trauma practitioners. *Professional Psychology: Research and Practice, 26,* 558–565.

Pearlman, L. A., & Saakvitne, K. W. (1995b). *Trauma and the practitioner: Countertransference and vicarious traumatization in psychotherapy with incest survivors.* New York: W.W. Norton & Company.

Phillips, R.E., Pargament, K.L., Lyn, Q.K., & Crossly, C.D. (2004). Self-directing religious coping: A deistic God, abandoning God, or no God at all? *Journal for the Scientific Study of Religion, 43,* 409-418.

Piaget, J. (2007). *The child's conception of the world.* NY: Rowman and Littlefield. (2nd. Edition.)

Pigman, G. W. (1995). Freud And The History Of Empathy. *International Journal Of Psycho-Analysis, 76,* 237-256.

Pilgrim, D. (2009) Abnormal psychology: Unresolved ontological and epistemological contestation. *History and Philosophy of Psychology* 10(2):11–21.

Pillari, V. (1991). *Scapegoating in families: Intergenerational patterns of physical and emotional abuse.* NY: Brunner-Mazel.

Pincus, D., & Sheikh, A. A. (2009) *Imagery for pain relief.* New York: Routledge.

Polanyi M. (1964). *The tacit dimension* New York: Doubleday.

Popper, K. R. (1963), *Conjectures and Refutations: The Growth of Scientific Knowledge.* New York: Harper.

Prendergast, J., & Bradford, K. (2007). (Eds.). *Listening from the heart of silence: Nondual wisdom and psychotherapy.* St. Paul, MN: Paragon House.

Price, J., Cole, V., & Goodwin, G.M. (2009). Emotional side-effects of selective serotonin reuptake inhibitors: A qualitative study. *British Journal of Psychiatry,* 195: 211-217.

Proner, B. (1986). Defenses of the self and envy of oneself. *Journal of Analytical Psychology, 31:* 275-279.

Pytell, T. (2006). Transcending the Angel Beast: Viktor Frankl and Humanistic Psychology. *Psychoanalytic Psychology* 23(3): 490–503.

Pytell, T. (2007). Extreme Experience, Psychological Insight, and Holocaust Perception: Reflections on Bettelheim and Frankl. *Psychoanalytic Psychology* 24 (4): 641–657.

Rando, T. A. (1985). Creating therapeutic rituals in the psychotherapy of the bereaved. *Psychotherapy: Theory, Research, Practice, Training, 22*(2), 236-240.

Rescher, N. (1990). *Human Interests: Reflections on Philosophical Anthropology.* Stanford, CA:Stanford University Press.

Ricoeur, P. (1977). The question of proof in Freud's psychoanalytic writings. *Journal of the American Psychoanalytic Association, 25,* 835-871.

Richardson, F.C., Fowers, B. J., & Guignon, C.B. (1999). *Re-envisioning psychology: Moral dimensions of theory and practice.* San Francisco, CA: Jossey-Bass.

Ritsher, J. B. & Phelan, J. C. (2004). Internalized stigma predicts erosion of morale among psychiatric outpatients. *Psychiatry Research (129),* 257-265.

Rizzuto, A-M. (1999). "I always hurt the one I love—and like it.": Sadism and a revised theory of aggression. *Canadian Journal of Psychoanalysis, 7(2),* 219-245.

Roesler, Christian. (2013). Evidence for the Effectiveness of Jungian Psychotherapy: A Review of Empirical Studies. *Behavioral Sciences (4),* 562-575.

Ross L,. & Nisbett R.E. (1991) *The person and the situation: perspectives of social psychology.* Boston, MA: McGraw-Hill.

Rosen, D.H. (1976). Suicide survivors: Psychotherapeutic implications of egocide. *Suicide and Life-Threatening Behavior, 6,* 4, 209-215.

Rosequist, L., Wall, K., Corwin, D., Achterberg, J., & Koopman, C. (2012). Surrender as a form of active acceptance among breast cancer survivors receiving Psycho-Spiritual IntegrativeTherapy. *Support Care Cancer 20,* 2821-2827.

Rossides, D. W. (1998). *Social theory: Its origins, history, and contemporary relevance.* Dix Hills, NY: General Hall, Inc.

Roth, A. & Fonagy, P. (2005). *What works for whom: A critical review of psychotherapy research* (2nd ed.). London: Guilford Press.

Routledge, C., & Arndt, J. (2008). Self-sacrifice as self-defence: Mortality salience increases efforts to affirm a symbolic immortal self at the expense of the physical self. *European Journal Of Social Psychology, 38*(3), 531-541.

Roxberg, Å., Eriksson, K., Rehnsfeldt, A., & Fridlund, B. (2008). The meaning of consolation as experienced by nurses in a home-care setting. *Journal Of Clinical Nursing, 17*(8), 1079-1087.

Royzman, E.B., McCauley, C., & Rozin, P. (2005). From Plato to Putnam: Four ways to think about hate. In Sternberg, R. (Ed.), *The psychology of hate.* Washington, D.C.: American Psychological Association, pp. 3-35.

Rubenstein, R.L. (1968). *The religious imagination: A study in psychoanalysis and Jewish theology.* Indianapolis, IN: Bobbs-Merrill Company.

Russ, M.J. (1992). Self-injurious Behavior in Patients with Borderline Personality Disorder: Biological Perspectives. *Journal of Personality Disorders, 6*, 64-81.

Rychlak, J. F., (1983), Can psychology be objective about free will? *New Ideas in Psychology, 1,* 213-229.

Saklofske, D., Yackulic, R., & Kelly, I. (1986). Personality and loneliness. *Personality and Individual Differences, 7* (6), 899-901.

Sanford, J.A. (1995). Fate, love, and ecstasy: *Wisdom from the lesser-known goddesses of the Greeks.* Wilmette, Il: Chiron publications.

Santiago, C., Kaltman, S., & Miranda, J. (2013). Poverty and Mental Health: How Do Low-Income Adults and Children Fare in Psychotherapy? *Journal Of Clinical Psychology, 69*(2), 115-126.

Scarry, E. (1985). *The body in pain: The making and unmaking of the world.* NY: Oxford University Press.

Schafer, R. (1976). A new language for psychoanalysis. New Haven, CT: Yale University Press.

Schafer, R.(1982). The relevance of the 'here and now' interpretation for reconstructions. *International Journal of Psycho-Analyis, 63,* 77-82.

Schulz, R., McGinnis, K. A., Zhang, S., Martire, L. M., Hebert, R. S., Beach, S. R., (2008). Dementia patient suffering and caregiver depression. *Alzheimer's Disease & Associated Disorders, 22*(2), 170– 176.

Searles, H. (1975/1981). The patient as therapist to his analyst. In R. Langs (Ed.), *Classics in Psychoanalytic Technique.* New York: Jason Aronson. pp. 103-135.

Seidlitz, L. & Diener, E. (1993). Memory for positive and negative life events. *Journal of Personality and Social Psychology, 64,* 654-664.

Shedler, J. (2010). The efficacy of psychodynamic psychotherapy. *American Psychologist, 65*(2), 98-109.

Siegel, B. (1998). *Love, medicine and miracles: Lessons learned about self-healing from a surgeon's experience with exceptional patients.* NY: HarperCollins.

Silfe, B. D. & Fisher, A.M. (2000). Modern and postmodern approaches to the free will/determinism dilemma in psychotherapy. *Journal of Humanistic Psychology, 40,* 80–107.

Sherman, A., Simonton, S., Latif, U., & Bracy, L. (2010). Effects of global meaning and illness-specific meaning on health outcomes among breast cancer patients. *Journal Of Behavioral Medicine, 33*(5), 364-377

Sivil, R. (2009). Understanding Philosophical Counseling. *South African Journal Of Philosophy, 28*(2), 199-209.

Smith, B.K. (2000). Capital punishment and human sacrifice. *Journal of the American Academy of Religion, 68*, 1,

Smith, D.L. (2011). *Less than human: Why we demean, enslave, and exterminate others.* NY: St. Martin's Press.

Smith, M.D., Harris, P., & Joiner, R. (1996). On being lucky: The psychology and parapsychology of luck. *European Journal of Parapsychology, 12*, 35-43.

Steinbock, A. J. (2007). The Phenomenology of Despair. *International Journal Of Philosophical Studies, 15*(3), 435-451.

Stern, D. (2004). *The present moment in psychotherapy and everyday life.* NY: W.W. Norton.

Shah, I. (1993). *Tales of the Dervishes.* NY: Penguin Books.

Schaufeli, W. B., & Buunk, B. P. (1996). Professional burnout. In M. J. Schabracq, J. A. M. Winnubst, & C.L. Cooper (Eds.), *Handbook of work and health psychology* (pp. 311–346). New York: Wiley.

Schertz, M. (2007). Avoiding 'passive empathy' with Philosophy for Children. *Journal of Moral Education, 36*, 2, 185-198.

Schimmel, S. (1982). Free-will, guilt, and self-control in rabbinic Judaism and contemporary psychology. In R.P. Bulka & M.H. Spero (Eds.) *A psychology-Judaism reader.* Springfield, Il: Charles C. Thomas.

Schindler, F., Berren, M.R., Hannah, M.T., Beifel, A., & Santiago, J.M. How the public perceives psychiatrists, psychologists, nonpsychiatric physicians, and members of the clergy. (1987). *Professsional Psychology: Research and Practice, 18*, 371-376.

Schoeck, H. (1966). *Envy: A theory of social behavior.* NY: Harcourt, Brace & World.

Schoenewolf, G. (1991). *The art of hating.* Northvale, NJ: Jason Aronson.

Shaw, G. B. (1930). *Man and Superman.* London: Constable.

Sigmund, K. & Hauert, C. (2000). Altruism. *Current Biology, 12*, (8), R270-R272.

Slife, B. D., & Williams, R. N. (1995). *What's behind the research? Discovering hidden assumptions in the behavioral sciences.* Thousand Oaks, CA: Sage Publications.

Slife, B. D., Reber, J. S., & Richardson, F. C. (2005). *Critical thinking about psychology: Hidden assumptions and plausible alternatives.* Washington, D. C.: American Psychological Association.

Slife, B. D., Wiggins, B. J., & Graham, J. T. (2005). Avoiding an EST monopoly: Toward a pluralism of philosophies and methods. *Journal of Contemporary Psychotherapy, 35*, 83–97.

Slote, M. (2010). *Moral sentimentalism.* NY: Oxford University Press.

Smith, R. H., Parrott, W. G., Diener, E., Hoyle, R. H., & Kim, S. H. (1999). Dispositional envy. Personality and Social Psychology Bulletin, 25: 1007–1020.

Snow, N. (2000). Empathy. *American Philosophical Quarterly, 37*(1), 65-78.

Solomon, R.C. (1993). The passions: Emotions and the meaning of life. Indianapolis, IN: Hackett Publishing Co.

Sontag, S. (1990). *Illness as metaphor and AIDS and its metaphors.* New York: Farrar, Straus and Giroux.

Spero, M.H. (1992). *Religious objects as psychological structures: A critical integration of object relations theory, psychotherapy, and Judaism.* Chicago, Il: University of Chicago Press.

Speer, R.P., & Reinert, D.F. (1998). Surrender and recovery. *Alcoholism Treatment Quarterly, 16*(4), 21-29.

Spillius , E. B. (1993). Varieties of envious experience. *International Journal of Psycho-Analysis, 74*, 1199-212.

Staub, E. (2000). Genocide and mass killing: origins, prevention, healing and reconciliation. *Political Psychology, 21*, 367-382.

Strean, H. (1994). *Psychotherapy of the Orthodox Jew.* Northvale, NJ: Jason Aronson.

Steger, M. F., Frazier, P., Oishi, S., & Kaler, M. (2006). The Meaning in Life Questionnaire: Assessing the presence of and search for meaning in life. *Journal of Counseling Psychology, 53*, 80–93.

Steger, M. F., Kashdan, T. B., Sullivan, B. A., & Lorentz, D. (2008). Understanding the search for meaning in life: Personality, cognitive Style, and the dynamic between seeking and experiencing meaning. *Journal of Personality, 76,* 199–228.

Steger, M.F. (2012). Experiencing meaning in life: Optimal functioning at the nexus of well-being, psychopathology, and spirituality. In P.T.P. Wong (Ed.), *The human quest for meaning: Theories, research, and applications* (2nd ed., pp. 165-184). New York: Routledge.

Stein, M. (1990). Sibling Rivalry and the Problem of Envy. *Journal of Analytical Psychology, 35*(2), 161-175.

Stivers, R. (2004). *Shades of Loneliness: Pathologies of a Technological Society.* Lanham, MD: Rowan & Littlefield.

Stöber, J. (2003). Self-Pity: Exploring the Links to Personality, Control Beliefs, and Anger. *Journal of Personality, 71,* (2), 183-220.

Stolorow, R. D., & Lachmann , F. M. (1980). *Psychoanalysis of developmental arrests: Theory and treatment.* New York: International Universities Press.

Sturgeon A & Zautra A (2010) Resilience: a new paradigm for adaptation to chronic pain. *Current Pain and Headache Reports 14,* 105–112.

Styron, W. (1992). *Darkness visible: A memoir of madness.* NY: Vintage books.

Stueber, K. "Empathy" *Stanford Encyclopedia of Philosophy* at http://plato. stanford.edu/archives/sum2008/entries/empathy/.

Sugar, M. (2002). Commonalities Between the Isaac and Oedipus Myths: A Speculation. *Journal Of The American Academy Of Psychoanalysis, 30*(4), 691-706.

Summers, F. (2006). Fundamentalism, Psychoanalysis, and Psychoanalytic Theories. *Psychoanalytic Review,* 93, 2, 329-352.

Suyemoto, K. (1998). The functions of self-mutilation. *Clinical Psychology Review, 18*(5), 531-554.

Szasz, T. (1963). The concept of transference as a defense for the analyst. *International Journal of Psychoanalysis, 44,* 435-444.

Rubenstein, R.L. (1982). The Meaning of Anxiety in Rabbinic Judaism. In Mortimer Ostrow, (Ed.)*Judaism and psychoanalysis.* Jersey City, NJ: Ktav publishing.

Tallis, R. (2012). *Aping mankind: Neuromania, Darwinitis and the misrepresentation of humanity*. Durham, UK: Acumen.

Taylor, R. (1970). *Good and evil*. London: Macmillan Publishing Company.

Taylor, G.J. (2002). Mind–body–environment: George Engel's psychoanalytic approach to psychosomatic medicine. *Australian and New Zealand Journal of Psychiatry, 36,*449–457.

Theriault, B. (2012). Radical Acceptance: A Nondual Psychology Approach to Grief and Loss. *International Journal Of Mental Health & Addiction, 10*(3), 354-367.

Thoreau, H.D. (*2004*). *Walden*. New Haven, CT: Yale University Press.

Thurston, N. S. (2000). Psychotherapy with Evangelical and Fundamentalist Protestants. In P. Richards, A.E. Bergin, (Eds.), *Handbook of psychotherapy and religious diversity*. Washington, D.C.: American Psychological Association, pp. 131-153.

Tiebout, H.M. (1949). The act of surrender in the therapeutic process. With special reference to alcoholism. *Quarterly Journal Studies on Alcohol, 10*: 48-58.

Tillman, J. G. (2006). When a Patient Commits Suicide: An Empirical Study of Psychoanalytic Clinicians. *International Journal Of Psycho-Analysis, 87*(1), 159-177.

Tilley, T. W. (2000). *The evils of theodicy*. Eugene, OR: Wipf & Stock.

Tilvis, R. S., Kähönen-Väre, M. H., Jolkkonen, J., Pitkala, K. H., & Strandberg, T. E. (2004). Predictors of cognitive decline and mortality of aged people over a 10-year period. *Journal of Gerontology, 59A,* 268– 274.

Titmuss, R. (1970). *The Gift Relationship: from Human Blood to Social Policy*. London: Allen & Unwin.

Toombs, S. K. (1987). The meaning of illness: A phenomenological approach to the patient-physician relationship. The Journal of Medicine and Philosophy 12:219–240.

Toombs, S.K. (1990). The temporality of illness: Four levels of experience. Theoretical Medicine,11, 227-241.

Trendler, G. (2009). Measurement theory, psychology and the revolution that cannot happen. *Theory & Psychology, 19,* 579–599.

Tresan, D. (1996). Jungian metapsychology and neurobiological theory. *Journal of Analytical Psychology, 41*(3), 399-436.

Trivers, R. L. (1971). The Evolution of Reciprocal Altruism. *Quarterly Review of Biology*, 46 (1): 35-57.

Trungpa, C. (1973). *Cutting through spiritual materialism*. Boston, MA: Shambhala Publications.

Turner JA, Holtzman S, & Mancl L., (2007) Mediators, moderators, and predictors of therapeutic change in cognitive-behavioral therapy for chronic pain. *Pain* 127: 276–286.

Turner, V. (1967). *The forest of symbols: Aspects of Ndembo ritual*. Ithaca, NY: Cornell University Press.

Turner, V. (1987). The Liminal Period in Rites of Passage. In Louise Mahdi, (Ed.), Betwixt and Between, La Salle, Il: Open Court Press.

Turner, V. (1995). *The ritual process; Structure and anti-structure*. Piscataway, NJ: Aldine Transaction.

Ulanov, A. & Ulanov, B. (1983). *Cinderella & her sisters: The envied and the envying*. Philadelphia, PA: Westminster Press.

Vaillant, G. (1977). *Adaptation to Life*. Boston: Little, Brown.

van de Ven, N., Zeelenberg, M., & Pieters, R. (2009). Leveling up and down: The experiences of benign and malicious envy. *Emotion*, 9: 419–429.

van de Ven, N., Zeelenberg, M., & Pieters, R. (2010). Warding Off the Evil Eye: When the Fear of Being Envied Increases Prosocial Behavior. *Psychological Science*, 21(11), 1671-1677.

van Gennep (2010). *The rites of passage*. NY: Routledge. (Original work published in 1908).

van Lange, P. A. M., Rusbult, C. E., Drigotas, S. M.,Arriaga, X. B., Witcher, B. S., & Cox, C. L. (1997). Willingness to sacrifice in close relationships. *Journal of Personality and Social Psychology*, 72, 1373-1395.

Vogel, E. F., & Bell, N. W. (1960). *A Modern Introduction to the Family*, New York: The Free Press.

von Witzleben, H. D. (1958). On loneliness. *Psychiatry* (21), 37-43.

Wallace, E. R. (1986), Determinism, possibility, and ethics. *Journal of the American Psychoanalytic Association*, 34, 935-976.

Wallace, G. (2001). *Dying to be born: A meditation on transformative surrender within spiritual and depth psychological experiences*.

(Unpublished doctoral dissertation). Pacifica Graduate Institute, Santa Barbara, CA.

Waller, J. (2002). *Becoming evil: How ordinary people commit* genocide *and mass killing.* New York: Oxford University Press.

Wamser, R., Vandenberg, B., & Hibberd, R. (2011). Religious Fundamentalism, Religious Coping, and Preference   for Psychological and Religious Treatment. *International Journal for the Psychology of Religion, 21,* 3, 228-236.

Wegner, D. M., & Wheatley, T. (1999). Apparent mental causation: Sources of the experience of will. *American Psychologist, 54,* 480–492.

Weil, S. (1951). *Waiting for God.* NY: G.P. Putnam's Sons.

Weil, S., (1968). *On science, necessity, and the love of God.* NY: Oxford University Press.

Weil, S. (1976). *Notebooks, volume 2.* London: Routledge & Kegan Paul.

Weil, S. (2002). *Gravity and grace.* NY: Routledge.

Welsh, J. (1990). *When gods die: An introduction to John of the Cross.* Mahweh, NJ: Paulist Press.

Whitman, R.M. (1990). Therapist envy. *Bulletin of the Menninger Clinic, 54*(4), 478-487.

Whitmont, E.C. (2007). The Destiny Concept in Psychotherapy. Journal of Jungian Theory and Practice, (9)1, 25-37.

Wilkinson, M. A. (2003). Undoing trauma. Contemporary neuroscience: a clinical perspective. *Journal of Analytical Psychology, 48*(2), 235-53.

Williams, J. G. (Ed.), (1996), *The Girard Reader.* NY: Crossroad Publishing.

Willock, B., Bohm, L.C., & Curtis, R.C. (2011) (Eds.). *Loneliness and longing; Conscious and unconscious   aspects.* NY: Routledge.

Wilson, Timothy D. (2002). *Strangers to Ourselves: Discovering the Adaptive Unconscious.* Cambridge, MA: Harvard University Press.

Winnicott, D. W. (1949), Hate in the countertransference. *International Journal of Psycho-Analysis, 30,*69-74.

Winnicott, D. W. (1958). The capacity to be alone. *International Journal of Psycho-Analysis* (39), 416-420.

Winnicott, D.W. (1960). Ego distortion in terms of true and false self. In *Maturational processes and the facilitating environment* (pp. 140–152). New York: International Universities Press.

Winnicott, D. W. (1963). The development of the capacity for concern. *Bulletin of the Menninger Clinic, 27,* 167-176.

Winnicott, D.W. (1969). The use of an object. *International Journal of Psycho-Analysis, 50,* 711-716.

Winnicott, D. W. (1974) *Playing and Reality.* London: Penguin Books.

Wilson, S. L. (1985). The Self-Pity Response: A Reconsideration. *Progress In Self Psychology, 1,* 178-190.

Wiseman, R. (2003). *Skeptical Inquirer: The Magazine For Science And Reason. 27,* 3, 1-5.

Witonsky, A., & Whitman, S.M. (2005). Puzzling pain conditions: How philosophy can help us understand them. *Pain Medicine, 6*(4), 315-322.

Wolf, S. (1997). Happiness and meaning: Two aspects of the good life. *Social Philosophy and Policy 14*(1), 207-225.

Wolf, S. (2010). *Meaning in life and why it matters.* Princeton, NJ: Princeton University Press.

Wong, P.T.P. (Ed.) (2012), *The human quest for meaning: Theories, research, and applications.* New York: Routledge.

Wright, D.P. (1987). *The disposal of impurity.* Williston, VT: Society of Biblical Literature.

Wright, L. M. (2005). *Spirituality, suffering, and illness.* Philadelphia, PA: F.A. Davis.

Yalom, I. (1980). *Existential psychotherapy.* NY: Basic Books.

Yao, (1987). *Addiction and the fundamentalist experience.* NY: Fundamentalists Anonymous.

Ybema, J. F., Kuijer, R. G., Hagedoorn, M., & Buunk, B. P. (2002). Caregiver burnout among intimate partners of patients with a severe illness: An equity perspective. *Personal Relationships, 9*(1), 73-92.

Young-Eisendrath, P. (1996). *The gifts of suffering: Finding insight, compassion, and renewal.* NY: Addison-Wesley.

Yucel, B. (2000). Dissociative Identity Disorder Presenting with Psychogenic Purpura. *Psychomatics 41,* 279-281.

Zahn-Waxler C., Radke-Yarrow, M., Wagner, E., & Chapman, M. (1992). Development of Concern for Others. *Developmental Psychology, 28*(1), 126–136.

Zimbardo, P. (1996). *Psychology and life.* New York: Harper Collins College Publishers.

Zoya, L. (1989). *Drugs, addiction and initiation: The modern search for ritual.* (M. E. Romano & R.Mercurio, Trans.). Boston, MA: Sigo Press.

Zweig, C. (2008). *The holy longing: Spiritual yearning and its shadow side.* NY: Jeremy Tarcher/Putnam.

CPSIA information can be obtained
at www.ICGtesting.com
Printed in the USA
FFOW02n1647021115
18227FF